The Cambridge Introduction to
Francophone Literature

The literature of French-speaking countries forms a distinct body of
work quite separate from literature written in France itself, offering a
passionate, creative engagement with their postcolonial cultures. This
book provides an introduction to the literatures that have emerged in
the French-speaking countries and regions of the world in recent
decades, illustrating their astonishing breadth and diversity, and
exploring their constant state of tension with the literature of France.
The study opens with a wide-ranging discussion of the idea of
francophonie. Each chapter then provides readers with historical
background to a particular region and identifies the key issues that have
influenced the emergence of a literature in French, before going on to
examine in detail a selection of the major writers. These case studies
tackle many of the key authors of the francophone world, as well as new,
up-and-coming authors writing today.

Patrick Corcoran is Assistant Dean in the School of Arts at Roehampton
University.

Cambridge Introductions to Literature

This series is designed to introduce students to key topics and authors. Accessible and lively, these introductions will also appeal to readers who want to broaden their understanding of the books and authors they enjoy.

- Ideal for students, teachers, and lecturers
- Concise, yet packed with essential information
- Key suggestions for further reading

The Cambridge Introduction to
Francophone Literature

PATRICK CORCORAN

CAMBRIDGE
UNIVERSITY PRESS

CAMBRIDGE UNIVERSITY PRESS
Cambridge, New York, Melbourne, Madrid, Cape Town, Singapore, São Paulo, Delhi

Cambridge University Press
The Edinburgh Building, Cambridge CB2 8RU, UK

Published in the United States of America by Cambridge University Press, New York

www.cambridge.org
Information on this title: www.cambridge.org/9780521614931

First published 2007

Printed in the United Kingdom at the University Press, Cambridge

A catalogue record for this publication is available from the British Library

ISBN 978-0-521-84971-5 hardback
ISBN 978-0-521-61493-1 paperback

Contents

Acknowledgements

This book has been several years in the preparation and consequently the influences upon it have been as diverse as they have been diffuse. Friends and colleagues in the Society for Francophone Postcolonial Studies have helped increase my knowledge of, and shaped my views on, the francophone literatures examined here. I offer them my sincere thanks.

In more practical terms my thanks are also due to colleagues in the School of Arts at Roehampton University, particularly, but not exclusively, to those working in the developing area of Modern Languages. Jacqueline Page deserves a special mention for shouldering many additional burdens while I worked on this project. A period of research leave in 2005–6, supported by funding from Roehampton University and matched funding from the Arts and Humanities Research Council, ultimately made it possible for this book to be written. Thanks are also due to helpful staff in a number of University libraries, particularly those of the School of Oriental and African Studies, University College London and Kings College London.

Above all I feel I owe a deep debt of gratitude to Professor Charles Forsdick of Liverpool University and to Dr Nicholas Harrison of Kings College London. Without their support this book would never have progressed beyond the planning stages.

Finally my thanks to Céline, Camille and Mathilde, my 'three noisy girls', for their love and patience.

All translations into English of French quotations are my own.

Blan napa capav travay san nwar?
– Plim bizwin lank.

Note on the text: references to primary sources are given as page numbers in the text; full details of the works cited are provided in the bibliography.

Introduction

Some of the most exciting and stimulating literature to appear during the last few decades has been written by men and women living in, or originating from, former colonies of the various European powers. This is certainly true in the case of France and francophone literature. While not quite matching the regularity with which non-metropolitan 'English' authors have carried off the Mann Booker prize in recent years, winners of the most prestigious French literary prizes have included a significant number of 'francophone' writers: the Moroccan Tahar Ben Jelloun, the Martinican Patrick Chamoiseau, the Lebanese Amin Maalouf (Prix Goncourt), Ivory Coast's Ahmadou Kourouma (Prix Renaudot) and a string of writers such as Jonathan Littell (Goncourt), Dai Sijie, François Cheng (Prix Femina) and Andreï Makine (Goncourt/Médicis) who are at best French by 'adoption'. Moreover, one of the latest additions to the group of forty 'immortels' who make up the Académie française is the celebrated Algerian novelist Assia Djebar. The tenuousness of the link between the French national space and an increasingly dynamic domain of literary output is one of the key, perhaps defining, characteristics of the field this book sets out to investigate: francophone literature. Yet it is highly questionable whether the term 'francophone literature' can be applied with any degree of accuracy to an easily identifiable and unchallenged corpus of texts. Part of the reason for this is that the word 'francophone' itself has become something of a label of convenience that often masks as much as it reveals. So any attempt at providing even a working notion of what 'francophone literature' is must begin by examining the terms francophone and *francophonie* in some detail.

The francophone world

Undoubtedly the most graphic way of representing the notion of *francophonie* is through maps. Just as vast tracts of the globe were formerly coloured pink to represent the territories ruled by the British Empire, so it is still possible today to map the world in ways that demonstrate how considerable areas of

1

its surface remain within the economic and cultural sphere of influence of metropolitan France. As this analogy with the history of Empire suggests, it is virtually impossible to discuss *francophonie* without connecting it to the history of European expansion, the imperial aspirations of individual nations and colonisation. The exact nature of this French influence today, how it operates, to what purposes and to whose benefit, are questions that will preoccupy us when we move on to discuss the concept of *francophonie* below. In this attempt to 'map' the field, however, it is probably sufficient to note that representations of the francophone world generally prefer to focus not on such politically sensitive ideas as 'influence' but on apparently more concrete and less controversial notions such as 'language use'. This is all well and good if we are content to view the map of the francophone world as a static snapshot. It is rather less satisfactory if we want to understand something of how and why French came to travel into so many foreign parts of the world. That sort of understanding comes at the price of acknowledging the fact that the French language was spread through the actions of individuals and groups and that it currently serves other individuals and groups in a variety of different ways. French did not travel abroad as a disembodied language and the history of its journey cannot easily be dissociated from its current state of health or its current pretensions to having status as a world language.

The journey of the French language to overseas territories can be seen as having occurred in two distinct waves that happened at two different periods of history. From the outset, however, political and economic considerations seem to have been paramount. These were certainly the motivations driving François Ier when, in 1533, with papal assent secured, he actively encouraged French ship-builders and navigators to challenge the supremacy of Spain and Portugal in trade across the Atlantic. Thus began what might be considered the first wave, a period of exploration and largely mercantilist activity that lasted almost two and a half centuries until the Treaty of Paris of 1763. It saw French vessels, explorers and traders active not only in the North and mid Atlantic but in the Indian Ocean and beyond. Nor did the discovery of a territory necessarily imply any commitment to an enduring presence or to occupation. Canada, discovered in 1534, did not begin to attract settlers as such until concerted efforts were set in train by Richelieu when he became 'superintendent of navigation and commerce' in 1626. Only slowly through the course of the seventeenth century did the settlement in *Nouvelle-France* take hold but it gradually expanded to cover the valley of the St Lawrence river, the Great Lakes region, Newfoundland and Acadia, while to the south the French had travelled along the course of the Mississippi to establish a colony in Louisiana and gain access to the Gulf of Mexico. By the early decades of the eighteenth century the French presence in North America covered significant expanses of territory. This expansion led to conflict with the British colonial presence on the east coast that would eventually see the defeat of the French forces in 1759 and the handing over of the whole of Canada and its dependencies through the treaty of 1763. Part of Louisiana was ceded in the same treaty while the second part was sold to Britain by Napoleon in 1803. Within a short space of a few decades a whole American world seemed to have slipped between the fingers of a French monarchy keen to reap the benefits of its trade monopolies but oblivious to any wider implications that might attach to the possession of overseas territories. As for the populations that remained in the various francophone enclaves of North America, their fate was to play itself out into modern times as a struggle for cultural survival and ongoing interrogations about identity that continue to the present day.

Elsewhere, this period of mercantilist activity lasting almost three centuries saw the establishment of trading posts, forts, storage depots and embryonic colonial settlements as circumstances and necessity dictated. Much of it was regulated through state monopolies operating through companies created for the purpose and endowed with a royal charter. The transatlantic trade also involved the trade in slaves that provided the workforce on the Caribbean plantations, repopulating islands whose indigenous populations had effectively been exterminated by the Europeans. European historiography prefers to present this tale in terms of beginnings, providing dates for the 'discovery' or 'settlement' of various locations: Martinique, 1625; Guadeloupe, 1635; Cayenne, 1637; Louisiana, 1682; Saint-Domingue (later Haiti), 1697. For the indigenous populations, of course, it was experienced not as the beginning of history but as its end. The fact that French expansion in the Caribbean relied on the slave trade led traders to follow in the footsteps of those Portuguese traders who, as early as the sixteenth century, had established forts along the West African coast as holding posts for their human merchandise. Only the serious hazards of inland exploration in Africa (before the discovery of quinine in the mid nineteenth century) prevented more permanent forms of settlement being established at this time. Instead, trade centred on the major rivers flowing into the Atlantic and the Gulf of Guinea, although fortified posts at Saint-Louis on the Senegal river and Gorée would eventually provide France with a platform for later expansion into the African interior.

Such French presence as there was in West Africa at this time also served to provide supply points for traders heading for the Indian Ocean and eventually for the Far East and the Pacific. In the course of the seventeenth and early eighteenth centuries a number of trading posts or settlements were established, among them l'Ile Bourbon (later, Ile de la Réunion), 1638; Madagascar, 1643;

various *comptoirs* in India: Pondichéry, 1674, Chandernagor, 1676; and when the Dutch withdrew in 1715, l'Ile de France (later, Mauritius). Initial trading contacts were also made with Vietnam and Siam in the 1680s. The visit of a Siamese ambassador to the court of Louis XIV in 1684 would suggest that these early contacts were conducted on a relatively equal footing. As had been the case in North America, the growing rivalry between the French and the British on the Indian subcontinent hung in the balance throughout the first half of the eighteenth century. The Treaty of Paris considerably reduced French ambitions here too, however. By the mid century the Compagnie française des Indes had held sway over an area of Indian territory of more than a million square kilometres whereas a decade later, after 1763, the company withdrew to the five *comptoirs* that have maintained a vastly reduced French presence in India to the present day.

The bigger picture that is sketched out through these piecemeal ventures and adventures involving French traders, troops and missionaries is one of essentially Francocentric activity. Ultimately, the only justification for it was that it would provide immediate, material benefits for France. This explains the monarchy's relative readiness to concede Canada and other parts of North America to the British, to the great chagrin of the francophone populations there, or to throw in its hand in India. The Bourbons were committed to expansion for pragmatic reasons rather than as a matter of principle. For the French monarchy there was a dual attraction in the mercantilist activity: firstly, there was profit to be made, and secondly, overseas expansion allowed France to position and reposition itself in the power play of political inter-action between the European states, effectively the geopolitics of the day. But France under monarchical rule was never committed to overseas expansion as a strategic political doctrine, and was probably incapable of even conceiving it in such terms. Indeed, after the Treaty of Paris, in the decades leading up to the Revolution of 1789, the defence of France's overseas possessions was pursued as much as an extension of European rivalries as it was for its own sake.

In the wars that ranged the Napoleonic revolutionary armies against the successive coalitions and alliances headed by England, France's overseas terri-tories were both a theatre of combat and prizes to be seized. By 1810–11, the majority of French possessions had passed under British control and it was only with the restoration of the monarchy in 1815 that the tide gradually began to turn. The event that most clearly signalled more aggressively expansionist poli-cies on the part of France was the military expedition to Algiers of 1830. This proved to be the first of a series of expeditions and invasions that were increas-ingly invested with a nationalist and imperialist significance as the century progressed. The pattern that quickly became established as characteristic of this second wave of overseas expansion was the use of military force either of an expeditionary nature or mobilised in defence of endangered French missionaries or commercial interests. The military activity itself then paved the way for civilian settlement and colonisation. In the course of the century, following the invasion of 'Algeria', French forces began the colonisation of Senegal (1854), Indochina (1859), Nouvelle-Calédonie, French Polynesia and Tahiti (1860 onwards), Equatorial Africa (1880 onwards), Tunisia (1881) and Madagascar (1883), and tightened France's hold over the older colonies of the Caribbean and the Indian Ocean.

The infrastructure put in place to support the colonial presence and administer the territories concerned became increasingly regimented, centralised and formalised by the French state as the imperial mission took shape. An important element of France's efforts to theorise and justify its colonial practice, to its own people as well as to the wider world, was the notion that superior European cultures owed it to their less fortunate fellow men and women in the colonies to bring them the benefits of civilisation. Language, of course, was a key vector through which this *mission civilisatrice* [civilising mission] could be carried out and schools were the conduit through which the elite members of indigenous society could be assimilated to French language, customs and values. So throughout this second wave of French expansion overseas, it is increasingly difficult to envisage the journey of French as that of a disembodied language, accidentally transferred and transplanted into distant parts of the world. On the contrary, its journey was planned as a matter of policy: French was actively and consciously exported as part of a concerted drive to suppress indigenous cultures and languages and replace them with the culture and language of the French colonisers.

One measure of the success achieved by colonial France's promotion of the French language is the extent to which it was eventually employed by opponents of colonial rule when the decolonisation struggles began to gather a head of steam in the latter half of the twentieth century. Within the often artificial colonial boundaries that France had erected to bring order to the colonial world it administered, French was one of the few effective unifying forces. The tool that had been used to assimilate populations to a French way of viewing the world, and a French ordering of affairs in general, was also used by those who sought to reject that order and win independence from France. This is true both on the political level, wherever negotiations needed to be conducted, and on a cultural level, wherever alternative world views and alternative expressions of identity needed to be articulated and defended. France's disengagement from its long flirtation with the colonial adventure was a messy and violent affair.

Within a decade of the end of the Second World War the terrible repression in Madagascar (1947) and wars in Indochina (1946–54) and Algeria (1954–62) could bear testimony to the difficulty France had in coming to terms with the disintegration of its empire.

Yet these politically decisive and, in humanitarian terms, tragic events cannot in themselves be considered decisive in so far as the journey of the French language is concerned. For many of the territories and nations that gained independence or came into being in the early 1960s, particularly in Africa, French was the only viable choice as official language since it alone was not associated with specific ethnic or tribal groups. In contexts where national unity was (and still is) threatened by tribal affiliations, French offered a prestigious alternative to local languages and had the added benefit of providing access to the international political scene. Even in countries like Algeria where resentment against the French and the desire for cultural self-affirmation ran high, the policy of Arabisation of the machinery of state has proved a long and painful process. The language of the education system or the language in which affairs of state are conducted cannot be changed overnight. Nor is it insignificant that the year that saw the end of the Algerian War of Independence (1962) also saw the beginning of a series of initiatives to promote the concept of *francophonie* and to give it some form of concrete institutional presence in relations between states. The publication of a special issue of the review *Esprit* in November 1962 is often seen as the starting point of these attempts to redefine *francophonie*. The first president of Senegal, Léopold-Sédar Senghor, was a contributor to the publication and in the years that followed he was one of the most energetic promoters of a drive to extend bilateral agreements between France and various ex-colonies into a network of multilateral agreements that could collectively become the institutional framework of *francophonie*.

Conceptualising *francophonie*

This chequered history of often violent, always confrontational, expansionist activity, and the corresponding violence and confrontations of decolonisation, provide the historical context with which any contemporary use of the word 'francophone' must in the long run seek to be reconciled. Yet as a linguistic term the meaning of the word 'francophone' is quite straightforward. It is generally understood as a mere synonym for 'French-speaking' or 'using French as a medium of expression'. But it is precisely because French is spoken in so many different contexts and situations across the world (including of course mainland France), precisely because it occludes the dramatic historical context outlined above (that it nevertheless inevitably connotes), and precisely because the variety and range of francophone literature is so great, that the term 'francophone' can so frequently be seen as meaning different things to different people and consequently as serving no useful purpose other than as a mere label. Worse than that, the single term 'francophone' is the only expression available to us when we want to describe what can be very distinct and frequently antagonistic versions of *francophonie*.

The problem here is not one of semantics since the meaning of the word 'francophone' is relatively easily inferable from its etymology: the two elements of 'francophone' derive from the Latin word *Francus*, the name given to members of the Frankish tribe which 'invaded' Gaul in the fifth and sixth centuries AD and destined to lend its name to that of modern-day France, and the Greek word *phônê* providing the notion of 'sound' or 'voice'. Thus 'francophone' indicates 'French-speaking' in much the same way that cognate expressions such as 'anglophone', 'hispanophone' and so on, are used to designate English speakers, Spanish speakers or other such groups. But whereas these latter terms remain relatively neutral, each describing a community of language users, the term 'francophone' has been invested with a range of additional ideological and political meanings. Consequently, it must really be considered as a classic example of a *faux ami* [a linguistic 'false friend']. Whereas the English version of the word is a relatively unproblematic, objective linguistic term, its French equivalent carries with it a panoply of connotations and is applicable to a far broader set of contexts. So, rather than restricting ourselves to interpreting the word 'francophone' through its narrow *semantic* content we would do well to consider the pragmatics of actual usage.

Indeed if we look to 'usage' rather than semantics we find that the word 'francophone' is used in two quite distinct sets of contexts. Firstly, it can be taken as in some way serving to *extend* the scope of the words 'France' or 'French', almost as though what is involved is a redrawing of some hidden boundary, or rather the pushing back of some invisible frontier. Thus it is common to hear mention of 'France and the francophone world' or 'French and francophone studies' or even, 'French and francophone literature'. In such expressions the yoking together of 'French and francophone' is very largely pleonastic. It gives the impression that we are simply being served extra helpings of the same dish: any difference between the two terms is minimised since both are understood to express a sense of common roots and common identity. Indeed their coupling is a way of promoting rather than interrogating the shared common ground. Thus we are in the presence of a homogenising effect: 'francophone' has the function of *supplementing* the words 'France' or 'French' in an inclusive gesture suggestive of the fact that what is on offer is 'more of the same'.

This view of *francophonie* is not one that invites us to dig deeper and worry about the underlying meanings the word is conveying. It diverts attention away from questions of semantic quality to focus on geographical quantity. In an expression like 'France and the francophone world', 'France' functions as the key reference point. By and large it remains what it always was when the supplementary term 'francophone' is tacked on. So the addition of 'and francophone' is a way of recognising (perhaps proclaiming or celebrating too) that France overflows its borders and that those elements which give meaning to the words 'France' and 'French' (French language, French culture, French sociopolitical values) are applicable to other geographical contexts than that of the national, metropolitan space. The source of authority remains 'France' or 'French' while the term 'francophone' serves merely to extend the applicability of that authority into other spaces and other situations. The conceptual framework elaborated to deal with metropolitan realities (including a whole range of value-laden notions about linguistic, cultural, social and political behaviours) is not challenged or even called into question because these other contexts and situations are seen as mere extensions of the metropolis and are not envisaged as being fundamentally different.

There is quite a large and ever-growing body of literature on the institutional, administrative and political aspects of what we might term 'official *francophonie*' in which this type of usage is very much the norm. The history and politics of francophone institutions is not a subject of central interest to us here but it is certainly an influential field since it is within this context that the official discourse on *francophonie* is to be most readily found, perpetuating a world view that not only confounds more questioning forms of analysis but actively counters their emergence. Much of the discourse celebrating the 'official', state-sponsored version of *francophonie* has a hagiographic, spiritualistic tone. Indeed, as one commentator has suggested in a recent article: 'one could be easily forgiven for mistaking *la Francophonie* for a new form of religion, such is the zeal it inspires in some of its most fervent supporters'.[1] It is characterised by a tendency to homogenise French/francophone interests and to conflate them, if only by locating them on one side of a binary, the other pole of which is the anglophone world. This is only natural since *francophonie* in its current guise is essentially a branch of the Fifth Republic's foreign policy. Although it is more generally understood as part of France's belated response to the loss of its empire and the unavoidable process of decolonisation, its origins are not unrelated to earlier efforts by President de Gaulle, in the immediate aftermath of the Second World War, to promote French geopolitical interests and simultaneously to resist the spread of American influence throughout the world. Just as French and British imperial ambitions had been fuelled by competition that led to the creation of their respective empires, so the processes of decolonisation coincide with parallel rearguard actions to preserve power and influence: Britain moved shortly after the Second World War to create the Commonwealth while France, perhaps partly in denial and no doubt distracted by the Algerian War, took considerably longer to realise the importance of creating *francophonie* as its own network of former colonial territories. What seems absolutely clear from these adversarial origins, and perhaps more importantly from the ongoing sense that 'Anglo-Saxon' (including American) interests remain in direct competition with francophone interests, is that *francophonie* is an important element of French statecraft, embroiled in geopolitical realities that go far beyond the linguistic and the cultural.

If the cement that really binds *francophonie* together is political and economic rather than cultural there is a case for re-examining the assumption that it is the ties of language that bind together the disparate members of the francophone community. It may well be the case that the desire to maintain mutually beneficial, good relations with France is a sufficient motivation for partners in the francophone 'contract' to align themselves with France and French interests, but this is a case of *post hoc non propter hoc*. If it is true that what brought the partners together was the (imposed) common thread of language it is probably equally true that the asymmetrical nature of power relations between centre and periphery, the overwhelming dominance of France over the vast majority of its weaker partners, is the real reason why the marriage endures. But these harsh, largely economic, realities rarely take centre stage. The homogenising discourse of official *francophonie* is, of course, part of the process of creating and sustaining a myth that serves to mask such realities. Indeed, the French *Académicien* Maurice Druon's recent claim that there is 'a spiritual and mystical dimension' [un sens spirituel et mystique] to the word *francophonie* is an example of such myth-making in action.[2] Benedict Anderson's much-quoted claim that nations are largely 'imagined communities' applies equally well to *francophonie*, but the effort to 'imagine' it through the prism of language alone at times seems inordinately artificial and counter-intuitive.

This first context of usage identified here could be caricatured as 'France looking outwards', embracing the francophone world within a unifying vision and a homogenising discourse that says more about itself than it does about the world it thus embraces. It has clear affinities with what Marie Louise Pratt has dubbed the 'imperial gaze' which both proceeds from and helps to construct the seer's position as 'Master-of-all-I-survey'.[3] By way of direct contrast, the second major context of usage assumes the word 'francophone' to serve precisely as a marker of difference and diversity. It is tempting to suggest that the direction of the gaze is simply reversed and to cast the francophone periphery as 'looking inwards' towards France, but this would be an oversimplification and the image is inaccurate. The periphery cannot be constituted as a unified, coherent subject position and, in any event, there is no reason why the multiple paths along which such a gaze (or gazes) might travel should have a real or imagined France as their final objective.

Although dictionaries tend to be rather coy about foregrounding this particular function of the word 'francophone' it is commonly used as a term of 'opposition' and as a way of marking a contrast between metropolitan France/French and 'other' speakers of French. In blunt terms, being able to state that one is 'French' is to claim a particular identity whereas the fact of being 'francophone' merely indicates a relationship to an 'identity' that belongs to someone else or, at best, to locate oneself in terms of a culture that is not one's own. The word 'francophone' *alludes* to identity without ever quite conferring it. Inevitably, this is a context of incompletion, marked by difference, an inescapable sense of lower status and ultimately, possibly, exclusion rather than inclusion. These are emotive issues and deserve to be treated with some circumspection. It is not the case that the homogenising discourse of official *francophonie* works against inclusiveness. On the contrary, the rhetorical thrust of such discourse is unashamedly inclusive but it is invariably an inclusiveness that proceeds by way of assimilation. The celebration of difference and diversity is a fundamentally unrepublican sentiment and it can only be allotted a space within official discourse and official thinking to the extent that its real implications remain unexamined. In a republican context what the unexamined future holds for such diversity is its eventual assimilation and transformation into a republican uniformity. The contention here then is not that the French/francophone distinction repeats colonialist or racist distinctions, or reinforces particularist views, but that it is constructed on the same type of binary opposition that characterises such distinctions.

Ultimately, of course, any attempt to assign meaning involves establishing differences and making distinctions: identity and 'otherness' are, after all, mutually dependent (mutually constitutive) concepts. But what is most striking in the case of the word 'francophone' is its radical ambivalence. The homogenising discourse of official *francophonie* appears to co-exist alongside a conception of the 'francophone' individual as irreducibly Other. Clearly these two notions are incompatible and allow scope for interpreting the systematic tension between the centre (metropolitan France) and the periphery (the francophone world) as an archetypal binary opposition separating 'us' from 'them'. Once again it is worth considering the fact that the words 'anglophone' and 'francophone' display a remarkable degree of dissymmetry in this respect. 'Anglophone' is used to designate 'a person who speaks English' and although it may be used to refer especially to native speakers of the language it is also used of other English speakers. It is thus a neutral, linguistic term, with connotations of inclusiveness and without connotations of hierarchy. There is none of the over-determination of the word that we find in the way 'francophone' is commonly used to refer to a particular category of French-speaker, occupying a particular, frequently inferior, position with regard to metropolitan France / French speakers.

Clearly both these contrasting usages of the word 'francophone' relate to two quite different ways of conceptualising *francophonie*: in hierarchical terms, the first might be seen as a top–down version that emphasises the unified vision radiating outwards from the French centre; the second is a bottom–up version which intrinsically values and celebrates diversity for its own sake and consequently challenges the (republican) authority of the centre. Arguably, the first usage has never ceased to dominate the institutionalised, political discourse of *francophonie*. The will to maintain influence, power and control, as well as to defend and promote French interests has underpinned this conception of *francophonie* from the outset. The second usage is the one that has come to dominate *francophonie* in the domain of cultural practice and cultural production and is therefore directly relevant to our investigation of the francophone literary scene. For one thing, the implicitly subaltern status it confers on the 'francophone' reflects not only the historical reality of the ways French–francophone relationships largely came into being and evolved, it squares more accurately with what we know about the contemporary world and contemporary international relations. Moreover, the emphasis on 'difference' reflects the wider heterogeneity of the various types of francophone identity and through a process of retroaction it helps call into question the stability and homogeneity of the notion of Frenchness itself, particularly when portrayed as a characteristic of the metropolis alone. If we pursue this line of thinking, we find not only that 'meanings' need to be interrogated more closely but that conceptual frameworks need to be adapted and recast to reflect the decentring of France and French from the position of authority these words continue to occupy in the first type of usage. Indeed, the two types of usage could themselves be caricatured as, on the one hand, an imperial (or post-imperial) usage which seeks to extend the sway of Frenchness over other spaces while assimilating the 'francophone' into a single homogenised totality, and on the other a counter-hegemonic usage which insists on respecting the individuated identity of the francophone 'other' and its capacity for autonomous agency.

So what tends to be the problem at the heart of these two contrasting types of usage is not so much what is *meant* by the word 'francophone' in each case, as how each serves to highlight (or to mask) the situation of the speaker in relation to the word's meaning. In other words, the expression 'francophone' inevitably evokes a relationship or a set of relationships. To argue for a view of *francophonie* as foregrounding *relationships*, spoken or unspoken, is both to echo and to advocate an essentially pragmatics-based approach to understanding the word. In practical terms this means paying careful attention to subject positions (who is speaking? where from? and for what purpose?), delving into historical and cultural contexts so that we avoid imposing our own values and hierarchies on others, and laying bare conceptual and ideological affiliations that otherwise might easily be left unexamined. These type of concerns are all consistent with a view of francophone literatures as postcolonial literatures, rather than as exotic offshoots of the national literature of France.

The importance of the 'positioning' of the subject can be easily illustrated. On a relatively abstract level it can be demonstrated once again by contrasting the way the words 'French' and 'francophone' are used. Unlike the adjective 'French', which is relatively unidimensional and homogeneous (the nation talking to itself or to its own kind), the word 'francophone' is multidimensional and always connotes the presence of 'otherness' somewhere within the chain of communication. Whether this 'otherness', this difference, is seen as a threat or as a resource, as desirable or undesirable, as something to be preserved or something that should be allowed (or encouraged) to be gradually assimilated and reduced, will depend on the perspective of the parties involved. These perspectives themselves will have deep and complex motivations with psychological, political, economic, cultural, social and gender dimensions. The term 'francophone' tells us nothing substantive about such attitudes and motivations. In this respect it is a very blunt instrument indeed. Its job is merely to remind us that such issues vaguely form part of the context in which the word is used and that they possibly deserve our attention.

On a more concrete level the importance of the subject position can be exemplified by applying the epithet 'francophone' to two contrasting individuals: it can used with equal accuracy to describe both the Congolese writer Sony Labou Tansi, the 'colonised subject' who claimed 'J'écris en français parce que c'est dans cette langue-là que le peuple dont je témoigne a été violé, c'est dans cette langue-là que moi-même j'ai été violé' [I write in French because it is in that language that the people to whom I bear testimony was raped, it is in that language that I myself was raped], and Leopold II of Belgium (the colonising European ruler responsible for the 'rape' in question).[4] This example is all the more pertinent in that it clearly serves to conflate as many distinctions as it can be called upon to elucidate. Moreover, it actually locates both of these very different uses of the word 'francophone' outside metropolitan France. But whereas Leopold's claim to francophone status is grounded in contiguity (France and Belgium share a common border) and overarching solidarity of purpose (France and Belgium were both metropolitan colonial powers), Sony Labou Tansi's francophone identity can be seen as foregrounding conflictual relations and resistance to 'Western' domination. There is something scandalous about the fact that a single term can be used to describe two such different men. But what we should not lose sight of is the lesson this juxtaposition teaches us about the limits of the word's usefulness, indeed its power to occlude vital historical and political distinctions.

The shortcomings of the term 'francophone' identified here are bound up with the fact that it is inevitably used in contexts where power relations are crucial and yet it purports, by and large, to remain silent about such questions. To understand the full extent of this silent complicity with power structures it is worth looking a little more closely at the way the word emerged as a particular way of encoding French nationalism as this was mutating into fully fledged imperialism.

Historicism and historiography

As is well known, the first recorded use of the word 'francophone' is attributed to the geographer Onésime Reclus who published a number of works in the latter third of the nineteenth century in which he militates in favour of colonial expansion. His originality lay precisely in the importance he accorded to language as a key element of the imperialist project. In his view, the prestige of France and the cultural values France held dear were inextricably linked to the French language: so much so that imperialist expansion itself could be envisioned primarily in linguistic terms. In the early 1880s far more influential figures than him, such as Jules Ferry, then minister of foreign affairs, were also arguing that France must pursue expansionist policies and were 'justifying' their stance by appealing to notions of racial superiority, commercial self-interest and the internal power play of European political influence. Reclus argued from a more abstract and far narrower position. He believed that ensuring the spread of the French language to other regions of the globe and to other populations was sufficient as an end in itself. What both men shared was a large dose of nationalistic pride and a conviction that expansionist policies were right for France. For Reclus these could be figured metaphorically in terms of 'mapping' the globe but more tellingly through the synecdoche by which the nation and its civilisation were figured through language. The aspiration to export the French language to far-flung corners of the world was in effect the way that nationalism could be translated into imperialism.

Both Reclus's expansionist views and his nationalistic pride were of his time, of course, and the date of the neologism's creation more or less coincides with the date of the Berlin conference of 1884–5, generally accepted as marking the beginning of the so-called colonial 'Scramble for Africa'. The Berlin conference marked the centenary of another less frequently cited, but in the context of this discussion not insignificant, event: the publication in 1784 of the *Discours sur l'universalité de la langue française* by the émigré count Rivarol. In this remarkable eulogy of the French language Rivarol not only professes a blind faith in the intrinsic merits and importance of French, he makes a leap from the particular to the general that allows him to claim a universal value for the cultural achievements which have found expression through French. 'It is French books that make up the library of human kind', he claimed. Like Reclus, Rivarol based his views partly on the notion of geographical spread. It was because French could claim to be the *lingua franca* of intellectual debate and international diplomacy across eighteenth-century Europe that he felt empowered to argue its status as a language of universal significance, capable of speaking to the whole of humanity about the full range of concerns humanity may have. It would, of course, be anachronistic to use terms such as 'nationalism' or 'imperialism' when discussing the pre-revolutionary writings of Rivarol, yet his essay provides as clear an example as one could wish to find of the phenomenon of cultural imperialism.

This view of French as a universal language, somehow sacralised by the role it had assumed as a conveyor of 'civilisation' and enlightened values, was one major part of the legacy which Reclus inherited. But the century which separated Rivarol and Reclus had been marked by an event which had also had a major impact on the French language and the myths generated around it: the French Revolution. This would provide another important part of the legacy. To the pre-revolutionary association of French with universal, humanist values could now be added an association between French and republican ideals, ideals which were constitutive of the nation itself. The egalitarianism of the revolutionary period brought a normalising, homogenising and standardising force to bear on linguistic matters as it did in every other area of public life. The celebrated speech by Barère (a notorious member of the Committee of Public Safety) to the Convention in January 1794, railing against the use of the various *patois* and regional languages then current in France, exemplifies the intolerance of heterogeneity that was so characteristic of this 'nation-building' phase of French history. It was echoed in a more moderate form by l'Abbé Grégoire, another major figure of the revolutionary period: 'Pour extirper tous les préjugés, développer toutes les vérités, tous les talents . . . fondre tous les citoyens dans la masse nationale . . . il faut identité de langage.'[5] [To eradicate all prejudices, nurture all truths and develop all talents . . . to meld all the citizens into the mass of the nation . . . we need to speak a single language.] Conceived in this way, language becomes a vital, political tool for building the nation.

In reality the two strands of Reclus's legacy highlighted here – the discourse of universal values and the discourse of nation-building egalitarianism – sustain and nourish each other. French was the language in which the first ever Declaration of the Rights of Man was drafted, but it was promulgated only a handful of years before the Convention passed the decree insisting that government agents should use French alone in the course of their official duties or risk imprisonment. The contention that French was, and in the opinion of many French people today perhaps still is, in some ill-defined way, inherently suited to expressing universal human values must somehow accommodate itself to the reality that, from the Revolution onwards, political leaders in France have never shied away from using the French language as an instrument for the implementation of unarguably nationalist policies

From its earliest uses then, the word 'francophone' is linked to (one might almost say complicit with) a way of thinking about 'Frenchness' that has deep historical roots in Enlightenment thought and the revolutionary politics of nation-building. Both strands provided arguments that weighed heavily in the balance as France expanded its colonial presence across the world during the latter half of the nineteenth century. The notion of the superiority of the French language, which could only with great difficulty (and possibly disingenuousness) be dissociated from the notion of the superiority of French culture and of French social and political institutions, was one of the cornerstones of attempts to rationalise and justify this colonial expansion. Since the step from nation-building to empire-building is one of degree rather than category, the different views and arguments about language that had been articulated by Rivarol and revolutionary leaders were equally influential and relevant to the context of imperialist expansion. And in the context of colonisation, as in that of revolutionary France, events on the ground were often decisive while the *post hoc* justifications and rationalisations of them struggled to keep pace. As we know, by the end of the decade following the conference of Berlin the area claimed as French territory would increase almost tenfold. As Raoul Girardet points out in *L'Idée coloniale en France*, the vaguely theorised imperialist impulse was largely generated by 'pressure groups', among which he specifically includes 'geographers' and therefore, by implication, Reclus. These groups made no claim to be representative or accountable and bore no responsibility to anyone but themselves, yet the pressure they exerted was transformed into a practice of colonial expansion which took centre stage in the politics of the day.

It is around this time that the rather abstract argument about the status and value of the French language, so valuable when enlisted to help articulate the imperialist 'credo' in the 1870s and 1880s, would be subsumed under the more general set of arguments about the need (or the duty) of the more advanced nations to participate in the *mission civilisatrice*. The shift may be seen as slight but it marked a generalisation of the argument. When the focus had been placed on the French language it had perhaps been understood that language was being seen both as the repository of cultural values and as the vehicle by which these values could be transmitted. In its more generalised form, the appeal to the notion of the *mission civilisatrice* allowed the argument to become focused on the cultural values themselves. It was thus divested of some of its nationalistic overtones. It could more easily be presented as a pan-European argument which each individual nation could adapt to its own ends. Implicit within this version of the argument was the notion of the superiority of European culture, European languages, European institutions, in short a Eurocentric view of the world. The irony is of course that many of the individual nations of Europe (France, Great Britain, Germany, Italy, Portugal, Russia) who deployed the argument of the *mission civilisatrice* as a 'one-size-fits-all', homogenising justification for expansionist policies would, within a few decades, be at each other's throats in the Great War of 1914–18.

These historical considerations are of course historicist considerations since they seek to explain how events were linked to ideas and beliefs prevalent at the time. The notion of *francophonie* was one of the significant strands of thinking which fed into the imperialist discourse that began to emerge from 1880 onwards. The defeat in the Franco-Prussian war of 1870 had been followed by a period of *recueillement* [retreat into oneself] that can easily be likened to the 'calm before the storm'. But the storm that was unleashed a decade later was, in a sense, displaced and its effects were felt not in Europe but in other parts of the world: the decade 1880–90 would see decisive French military action in Tunis in 1881, Annam in 1883, Madagascar in 1884, Tonkin in 1885 as well as expeditions in Congo and the Sudan.

The constitution and consolidation of this second empire, its history and its geography, its 'story' in its various ramifications, have tended to provide the raw material for the numerous accounts of *francophonie* that have appeared in recent years. But it is only if we adopt the Eurocentric bias that we have identified as underpinning the imperialist project that we can blithely assume that 'French' history provides the key to a master narrative on *francophonie*. Even the term 'Second Empire' belongs to a specifically French narrativisation of its own history. It is an inward-looking term used to refer to the régime in power in France between 1852 and 1870 and which intentionally evokes resonances with a Bonapartist 'tradition' harking back to the creation of the first empire in 1800. These choices of names for the régimes in power in France may seem natural and unproblematic, yet they can also be seen as involving a commodification of history designed, first and foremost, for internal consumption by the French. Hence these uses of the terms 'empire' and 'Second Empire' are self-absorbingly introspective; they have been 'used up' within a discourse that gives precedence to the glorious connotations of imperial power associated with Napoleon Bonaparte and his grandnephew, Napoleon III. Yet this leaves the field of French colonial history rather bereft, particularly when historians need to refer to pre-nineteenth century colonial adventures. French historians therefore tend to use the expression 'le premier empire colonial' [first colonial empire] when alluding to those territories brought under French rule prior to the Treaty of Paris in 1763. This treaty saw the effective dismantling of this first colonial empire. In what ways it was either colonial or an empire at all is, of course, highly debatable, but tacking the adjective 'colonial' on to the end at least allows the distinction to be made between France's overseas territories of the eighteenth century and Napoleon Bonaparte's later imperial ambitions focused on Europe. Similarly, the second French 'empire', the late nineteenth-century version, was alluded to by another name. It was generally referred to by the French as 'nos colonies'. Unlike the British, the French seem to have been remarkably reluctant to refer to their colonial possessions as an empire at all, possibly because the vocabulary which would have allowed them to do so was not available for use in this context.

Such questions of vocabulary are quite literally historiographical since they have a direct bearing on how the narrative of French 'imperial' history is conceived, structured and deployed. In this instance, an interrogation of the word 'empire' as used by the French points up the tension between an internally facing and an externally facing usage. Not that one is less Eurocentric than the other. On the contrary, both enable a French perspective on events to be articulated and allow no space for unfolding alternative histories, envisaged from the point of view of those on the 'receiving end' of the forces of history. Yet *francophonie*, seen as a generalising term for the plurality of voices and histories engaged in the relationship with France but contesting France's ownership of History, is precisely the framework within which such 'alternative histories' have begun to emerge. This is the 'postcolonial' version of *francophonie* that functions as a counter-discourse, challenging and interrogating 'official' *francophonie*, often from within. It is for this reason that the word 'francophone' can also so frequently be associated with a certain recalcitrance and scepticism with regard to French views about the legitimacy, authority and proprietorship of the French language itself. This is simply one illustration of the fact that the French–francophone relationship can be envisaged in a variety of ways but rarely as an unproblematic partnership between equals.

It is true that in historical terms 'French' is the marker of the originary language, culture and nationhood from which versions of *francophonie* have derived. The process by which the French language emerged as a national language from the Strasbourg oaths through the *Ordonnance de Villers-Cotterêts* to the founding of the Académie française and beyond, is punctuated by political and institutional efforts to create and consolidate firstly the state, and subsequently, in post-revolutionary France, the concept of the nation. The full force of this argument can only be felt when one accepts the organic links that bind together language, culture, literary representation and nationhood. But if narratives have helped to constitute nations they can also be deployed in ways that allow other groups to be 'imagined' and in ways that challenge the master narratives of nations and empires.

In fact, two overlapping foundational arguments need to be proposed here. The first is that the history of the French language is inextricably bound up with the emergence of the 'idea' of France as a state and later as a nation. The 'invention' of France depended on, and was enabled by, the emergence of French, firstly as a vernacular idiom challenging the use of Latin, later as the increasingly prestigious international language of the French state, French diplomacy and French culture, and ultimately, since the medium is the message, as the very material that France was exporting in fulfilment of its self-imposed *mission civilisatrice*. This defence (and illustration/promotion) of the French language was conducted with ever-increasing self-consciousness and ever-increasing awareness of the issues at stake. Nowhere is this more evident than in the late nineteenth century as French nationalism mutates into French imperialism and articulates an ideology of imperialism conceived in fundamentally linguistic terms. The second foundational argument is that which links the emerging sense of nationhood to literature. The consolidation of the idea of the nation-state relied on a set of supporting discursive practices that operated in the literary domain as much as in other areas of political and social life. To national literatures fell the task of codifying and exemplifying what was distinctive about the 'national community'.

To the extent that 'postcolonial' *francophonie* offers itself as an alternative to 'French' (by offering different variants of the language, different accounts of events, originating from different cultural contexts underpinned by different political relationships, expressed through different forms of representation) it constitutes a challenge to the hegemony of French language, and, by extension, to the narratives and discourses by which French political and cultural life legitimates itself as an originary authority. Once again, of course, the term 'francophone' has nothing substantive to say about these challenges to the authority of 'French', in the sense that it does not name or describe the processes by which the challenges are mounted, nor how they operate. It merely signals the location, literal or metaphorical, in which the co-presence of a plurality of voices inevitably generates the need for some sort of account to be given.

On the one hand, then, we have a state-sanctioned version of *francophonie* that operates under the sign of continuity and on the other, a postcolonial version which can best be envisaged as a counter-discourse in which difference, fragmentation and discontinuity are allowed free play. Each version involves a corresponding historiography. 'Official' *francophonie* emerges after decolonisation as a continuation and an extension of the very tradition that had provided the rhetorical resources and the ideological framework for the whole colonial adventure in the first place. As has been argued above, the notion of nationhood and the associated faith in the universal, eternal value of French culture, itself the founding argument of the *mission civilisatrice*, were the central building blocks of the justificatory apparatus of the colonial project. These remain central too to the official version of contemporary *francophonie* which combines a rhetoric of cultural diversity with a *de facto* conviction that France is ever the touchstone, ever the apex in the hierarchy of civilisational contacts which the movement orchestrates. Writing in 1971 in the epilogue to his book on the colonial idea in France, Girardet expressed a similar view about the underlying affiliations between colonialism and what was in the process of becoming *francophonie*:

> l'idéal officiellement présenté par l'actuelle politique d' 'aide' et de 'cooperation' ne se montre pas, à tout prendre, très sensiblement différent de celui qu'exprimaient en leur temps les grands doctrinaires de l'action coloniale essentiellement définie comme une 'mission de solidarité' ou 'une œuvre collective de charité'. Sa formulation recouvre les mêmes élans désintéressés et la même sincérité dans la générosité; elle recouvre également, maintenus dans un semblable et très discret arrière-plan, les mêmes calculs, les mêmes arrières-pensées, les mêmes présomptions et les mêmes vanités. A travers elle se retrouvent, d'autre part, à peine inchangées, la même conception des rapports de civilisation, la même assurance dans la bonne conscience, la même certitude dans la supériorité des modèles occidentaux de progrès humain qui avaient si longtemps donné aux vieux impérialismes européens leur légitimation morale.[6]

> [the ideal that is officially presented in current 'aid' and 'co-operation' policies is not, when all is said and done, so very different from the ideal that the great defenders of colonial intervention expressed in their own

day, when they defined it as essentially a 'humanitarian mission' or 'a collective work of charity'. Any account of it must include reference to the same disinterested enthusiasm, the same sincerity and the same generosity, it must also include, but as before hidden discreetly in the background, the same calculating self-interest, the same ulterior motives, the same presumptuousness, the same conceited attitudes. In the current formulation of the ideal we also find, scarcely altered with the passage of time, the same way of thinking about relationships between cultures, the same conviction about being in the right, the same sense of certainty that western models of human progress are superior, all the views that for so long had provided the old European imperial powers with a sense of their own moral legitimacy.]

Girardet is even-handed in the way he simultaneously ascribes both generous impulses and self-interested motives to the colonisers and by extension to those working today in a range of quasi-governmental, semi-official, international organisations in the developing world. No doubt this is wise; any attempt to talk at all about such collective sites of agency ('colonisers' or 'coopérants') requires that we remain open-minded about the range of mixed motives behind any course of action.

Over and above these considerations, however, it is clear that 'official' *francophonie* is directly related to a certain conception of French nationalism, largely imbued with republican values and which actively promotes a view of the world in which French interests and prestige are protected and advanced. The historiographical approach in this instance is in the style of the grand narrative of national destiny as it continues to unfold through time, despite the vicissitudes of war and decolonisation. It involves an implicit or explicit appeal to France's 'role in the world' and an appeal to some version or other of a historical teleology of human progress. Naturally both these appeals are predicated on universalising value systems that are all the more powerfully active in that they are largely unexamined.

Some may find such a version of *francophonie* perfectly understandable and perfectly defensible. Others of course may not, and, given the neocolonial spirit that can be associated with it, they would no doubt argue that such a version of *francophonie* is itself in urgent need of decolonisation. It is perhaps not surprising therefore that we have to look outside mainland France in order to gain some insight into what the alternative, 'postcolonial' version of *francophonie* might involve. With one or two notable exceptions, French academic circles remain highly suspicious of any kind of commentary or analysis that claims to examine 'postcolonial' perspectives. The adversarial politics that fuelled the

Scramble for Africa in the 1880s seems to be alive and well in contemporary academic life, fuelling French distrust of a 'postcolonial theory' that it tends to see as part of some perfidious Anglo-Saxon plot, and this despite the fact that many of the thinkers whose work has contributed to its elaboration as a theory were themselves French or francophone: Jean-Paul Sartre, Frantz Fanon, Albert Memmi, Michel Foucault and Jacques Derrida, to name but a few. Whatever one's views as to the respective merits of 'official' *francophonie* and 'postcolonial' *francophonie*, it is clear that they involve radically different historiographic traditions.

As far as critics are concerned, we have to wonder whether it is possible for them to question elements of 'official' *francophonie* while retaining the overarching framework of cultural assumptions on which it relies. That would seem like an attempt to translate into a matter of *degree* what is really a matter of *category*. This is the point that Robert J. C. Young is making when he points out that the shift we need to make when we take on board the point of view of the Other has very profound consequences:

> colonial discourse analysis is not merely a marginal adjunct to more mainstream studies, a specialised activity only for minorities or for historians of imperialism and colonialism, but itself forms the point of questioning of Western knowledge's categories and assumptions.[7]

For Young, postcolonial critique obliges us to question the whole structure of Western knowledge and the interests it more or less consciously serves. Once we have recognised the Eurocentric perspective for what it is: merely one possible outlook on the world among many, we have to be prepared to see that the former certainties and the universalising presumptions of the Western tradition are really contingent, relative, provisional, and culturally determined phenomena. If we bring this argument back to the francophone context it means that a postcolonial approach to francophone issues is basically incompatible with a view that francophone realities are merely the detail in a grand design that remains predominantly French.

Postcolonial theory and francophone literature

What then are the consequences of adopting a postcolonial approach to *francophonie* when embarking on a study of francophone literature? There are clearly a number of implications for the way this study has been organised, including decisions about what exactly to cover and how to cover it. But there are also implications in terms of the way individual authors and texts have been approached. Whereas most surveys and overviews of the field to date have implicitly tended to accept that francophone literature is an adjunct of French national literature, the approach adopted here implicitly rejects that view. Hopefully, it does so discreetly. The aim of this book is not to demonise 'official' *francophonie* but to contend that the key preoccupations of francophone literature are diametrically at odds with the aims and purposes of *francophonie* as an institution. Tangentially the various elements that make up each chapter will illustrate the fact that 'official' *francophonie* sustains itself by recuperating francophone texts and authors into a discourse which is largely incompatible with any contextualised reading of the literature itself. One of the underlying premises of this book, therefore, is that francophone literature, in so far as it exists as a single body of work at all, is first and foremost a *postcolonial* literature. The aim has not been to construct the argument through a presentation of the literature but rather to take this argument as a given and to present the literature accordingly. The principal aim has been to focus on the richness and diversity of francophone literature from around the world and only incidentally, as occasion warrants, to contextualise it within a specifically postcolonial framework. Yet the underlying and conscious assumption has been that francophone literature is indeed necessarily and unavoidably postcolonial.

Where this underlying assumption becomes, perhaps controversially, apparent is in the decision to exclude from this study the francophone literatures of European nations and regions other than France: those of Belgium, French Switzerland and Luxembourg for example. These literatures, like metropolitan French literature itself, are of course francophone, but they are most easily approached as examples of 'national' literatures. They may, as Belgian literature frequently has, devote considerable time and effort to expressing a distinctive cultural identity and refusing assimilation to French norms, yet they can hardly be considered postcolonial for all that. This is not to belittle the anxieties that minority cultures feel when they live in the cultural shadow of a powerful neighbour. It is rather a question of being clear about categories. For long periods of its history French-Canadian literature existed in a state of dependency with regard to France and French standards in respect of language and culture. It is no surprise that prior to the Second World War, this literature was so frequently discussed in terms of a regional literature and alongside the regionalist writers of mainland France. Only with the dramatic social and cultural changes that occurred in the 1960s was the dependency on France broken and a truly distinctive literature emerged. This has not happened in Belgium where increasingly writers like Marguerite Yourcenar, Jean-Philippe Toussaint or Amélie Nothomb, for example, have merged seamlessly into the French literary scene.

The exclusion of metropolitan French literature from this study, along with the literatures of the francophone European nations and enclaves, flows logically from the decision to explore francophone literature through its postcolonial affiliations and dimensions. But this decision renders attempts to organise the study as a unified narrative all the more difficult. It is far easier to provide a coherent narrative about the emergence of francophone literatures if one sees no objection to placing France and French history (particularly colonial history) at the heart of a giant web of interconnected elements. The refusal to assign such a privileged position to France and French history, insisting instead on acknowledging alternative historiographies and the intrinsic value of different cultural systems, is quite literally a process of decentring. It implies that each region examined should be approached in relative isolation and on its own terms as far as this is possible. Conceived of as a space from which 'other voices', other histories and other claims to legitimacy can emerge, 'postcolonial' *francophonie* is part and parcel of a decentring process that had its roots in decolonisation. As such it confirms its links with postmodernism, poststructuralist methods and the disparate body of approaches to cultural analysis that have come to be grouped under the misleadingly compact term, 'postcolonial theory'. Whatever else postcolonial criticism and theory may be, they are not, nor do they claim to be, a unified body of knowledge. At best they would appear to involve a set of 'reading practices', that is a way of looking at texts rather than a way of looking at the world.[8]

The preoccupations that are typically addressed by postcolonial critics tend to be focused on a relatively restricted number of themes. Probably chief among these has been an interrogation of identity that has been pursued alongside a theoretical reflection on how identity is best conceived. This is of paramount importance because colonialism assumed the superiority of metropolitan culture and tended to deny any value to indigenous cultures. When the struggle to counter such assumptions began there was a strategic advantage to be gained in portraying indigenous cultures in terms of an innate essence that characterised cultural, or indeed personal, identity. Postcolonial theory has rejected approaches based on such simplistic binary oppositions between 'them' and 'us', mainly because they perpetuate the same stereotypical assumptions upon which colonialism itself drew, albeit reversing them. A more nuanced approach to identity would argue that it be conceived in terms of negotiation and exchange. Identity is multilayered, as the Lebanese writer Amin

Maalouf has argued so convincingly in *Les Identités meurtrières*, and it is always under construction.[9] This more fluid approach to questions of identity allows scope for examining how forces, such as the asymmetrical power relations that structured colonial society, have impacted upon the ways individuals, groups and communities construct their own sense of selfhood. Representations of these processes are the very lifeblood of postcolonial francophone literature.

A second major preoccupation of postcolonialism concerns various forms of hybridity. The refusal to think of identity, cultural or otherwise, in terms of essential characteristics implies that notions such as cultural purity or cultural authenticity are always dubious. Cultures change and mutate as they interact but the change is always a two-way process, however much one culture may effectively dominate another in political or economic terms. The postcolonial emphasis on cultural, linguistic or simply racial hybridity serves as a reminder of this fact and postcolonial criticism usually involves demonstrating the myriad ways that cultural survival depends on recycling: the redeployment of slightly modified objects or practices for slightly different purposes or to slightly different effects, or the appeal to signs, symbols and languages in ways that are recognisable and familiar but nevertheless slightly unsettling in that they gesture towards new ways of accounting for reality, new forms of knowledge or new ways of understanding the world. In this respect creole cultures exemplify a canonical form of hybridity just as theories of creolisation are eminently postcolonial, decentring as they do the symbols and discourses through which we construct and articulate myths of cultural identity. In the chapters that follow, we will see how the literature from locations as different as Quebec, the Caribbean Islands and sub-Saharan Africa all evolve in very similar fashion, confirming that processes of creolisation are the fundamental dynamic of all cultural activity.

It is relatively easy to see how such preoccupations can inform the study of a single text, or even a single author's work. It is less easy to see how they can be taken out of context and applied to the entirety of a world literature without important distinctions becoming blurred in the process. Postcolonial criticism's distaste for grand, homogenising narratives and its declared respect for cultural differences and specificities sit ill with any attempt to provide an overarching survey of a world literature. These are tensions that this book makes no claim to have reconciled and the approach adopted in the following pages leaves such questions in abeyance. The need to provide a general context for study has been addressed by beginning each chapter with an overview of the region concerned. Each major region of the francophone world has therefore been presented in ways that may illustrate the connections with a narrative about France but that makes every effort to give due emphasis to the region's gradual disengagement from the various types of control metropolitan France has historically exerted. It would seem that one of the key conditions of emergence of the various francophone literatures from around the world has been the progress they have individually made towards self-sufficiency, with authors demanding the right to set their own aesthetic, cultural and political agendas. This can be understood as a rejection of some of the types of mediation that domination sets in place and jealously guards, the fact, for example, that speaking to the world can only happen through highly mediated channels, usually passing by way of Paris. Almost invariably this process of disengagement has involved dynamic and innovative uses of French language too, as writers have seized on opportunities to manhandle it, creolise it and make it a more fitting tool for their own purposes.

The second part of each chapter is devoted to more detailed studies of selected writers from the region concerned. Taken together, these presentations are intended to show the breadth and diversity of francophone writing. They provide readings of some of the most influential works (and authors) from across the francophone world while allowing the possibility of examining how local contexts, local conditions and personal preoccupations inform the output of specific individuals. In each case the selections make no claim to be providing representative samples of the region's output or to be illustrating the various stages through which that particular region's literature may be deemed to have passed. If anything the decision to provide selected studies was motivated by a belief that a critical engagement with texts, even texts that are untypical or unrepresentative, is nevertheless more useful to newcomers to these literatures than any amount of 'literary history' could ever be. It goes without saying that no claim to exhaustivity is implied at any level. The 'author studies', like the chapters, like the book as a whole, barely scratch the surface of a world that has tremendous depth and variety.

Some absences may shock, particularly the absence of work from the Pacific Ocean and the Far East. Despite the interesting work being produced by writers such as Flora Devatine in French Polynesia or Déwé Gorodé in Nouvelle-Calédonie, it has not been possible to discuss their output here. Inclusion would have no doubt added breadth but not necessarily sharpness to a study as general as this. The absence that may prove most controversial, however, as *francophonie* evolves in the decades to come, is the non-inclusion of texts by second- and third-generation 'immigrant' authors with connections to one or other of the minority communities in France. If francophone literature is a postcolonial literature, the work of Azouz Begag, Marie Ndiaye or Jean-Marie Le Clézio, for example, can make an equally strong claim to be so. Such literature is growing in importance because it exemplifies the reciprocal, transcultural nature of all cultural contact and problematises major categories, such as 'francophone' and 'literature', but from such a different angle that it deserves to be dealt with in a detailed independent study. The principle of selection that has been applied in this study is that of birthplace: the authors considered here were all born in a francophone country or region other than metropolitan France, whatever their subsequent country of residence happened to be.

Chapter 1

The Maghreb

Overview

Francophone literature from the Maghreb (Morocco, Algeria and Tunisia) is quite distinctive in both its tone and its preoccupations. It emerged as a literature of decolonisation in the post-1945 period when, for the first time, indigenous Maghrebi writers began to publish their work in significant numbers. The texts written in French by writers such as Driss Chraïbi, Mohammed Dib, Mouloud Feraoun, Mouloud Mammeri, Kateb Yacine, and Albert Memmi that began to appear in the early 1950s marked themselves off from earlier writings in French by their preoccupation with a broadly postcolonial agenda. At first glance it might seem paradoxical to use the word 'postcolonial' here since Tunisia and Morocco did not gain independence until March 1956 while Algeria, in the early 1950s, was about to embark upon a traumatic war with France that would not end until 1962. The apparent anachronism disappears, however, if we accept the now widely held view that the hyphenated 'post-colonial' is a term referring to the historical period following a period of colonial rule, while the unhyphenated 'postcolonial' is used to refer to a critical interrogation of colonial relationships and their aftermath. So, naturally, the critique of colonial society and colonial relationships can begin and be expressed in works of literature before colonial rule has effectively come to an end. Elleke Boehmer has formulated this idea succinctly: 'Rather than simply being the writing which "came after" empire, *postcolonial* literature is that which critically scrutinises the colonial relationship. It is writing that sets out in one way or another to resist colonialist perspectives.' Boehmer goes on to add, 'As well as a change in power, decolonisation demanded symbolic overhaul, a reshaping of dominant meanings. Postcolonial literature formed part of that process of overhaul.'[1]

In the Maghreb, where French control had begun to be imposed with the conquest of Algiers as early as 1830, the years following the Second World War provided a particularly violent and traumatic example of the decolonisation process at work. The process was dominated, of course, by the Algerian War of Independence. However, it is worth remembering that forms of direct action to combat colonial rule, ranging from peaceful political opposition to armed conflict, did not take place in a discursive void. Direct action was necessarily accompanied by 'discursive' challenges to colonial authority, including those sometimes rather indirect challenges that are part and parcel of literary activity. In this sense then, francophone literature from the Maghreb was part and parcel of the struggle for independence. It can be seen as originating in and accompanying the political challenge to colonial authority and its legacy. But to focus solely on the colonial/postcolonial nexus of issues would be to run the risk of setting a very Western set of parameters for the analysis, rather like arguing that the Maghreb is constituted through, and defined by its relationship with the West. It is true that the first generation of Maghrebi authors scrutinised the colonial relationship and its aftermath but they did so by scrutinising and interrogating Maghrebi social structures, patriarchy, family relations, group and individual identity issues, as well as a mosaic of diverse indigenous cultural traditions. So if it is true to say that this literature emerges as a literature of decolonisation, what this meant in reality was the gradual emergence of a literature that expressed a Maghrebi view of the world and which implicitly or explicitly challenged the dominant Francocentric view.

To understand how this came about it is helpful to examine the historical context. The Second World War marked a turning point in the collective consciousness of the peoples of the Maghreb where their relationship to France was concerned. In a settler colony like Algeria where an indigenous 'Arab' population of some eight million people co-habited with an estimated one and half million 'Europeans' the vicissitudes of daily life for the colonised majority, their institutionalised 'inferior status' and the inequalities of treatment and living conditions they experienced, could all easily be imputed to the ill-will and the shortcomings of the 'French' colonisers on the ground ('les grands colons' who had settled in Algeria over many generations since 1830), rather than to the failings of the metropolitan French who ran affairs from Paris, albeit through representatives often posted to the colony for relatively short periods of time. This rift between the 'Algerian French' and the 'Français de France' (the 'francaouis') was not entirely imaginary, however. In 1927, for example, the governor-general, Maurice Viollette, was actually recalled to France for upsetting the *colons* by daring to suggest that some sections of the Muslim population should be granted the right to vote. By and large, local opinion was far more reactionary and resistant to change than that of officialdom and policy-makers with close ties to Paris. Nevertheless, distance offered a ready-made excuse for inertia and dilatoriness; the remoteness of the colony from the metropolis could be exploited strategically, used as a justification for the lethargic way the centre dealt with the affairs of the periphery. Thus France was able to claim that it was pursuing a colonial policy of 'assimilation' that promised, in the course of time, to deliver French citizenship (and a significant change in status) to the Arabs while taking no practical steps whatsoever to implement it in the short to medium term.

The constant deferral by successive French governments of any practical steps to modify the inequalities of the colonial relationship had led to a deep sense of disillusionment across the Maghreb in the immediate aftermath of the Second World War. Algerian disillusion with the policy of assimilation was particularly profound. Albert Camus, the Algerian-born novelist who would go on to win the Nobel Prize, was working as a journalist in Algiers at the time. He was well placed to recognise this problem, as the series of articles he wrote for *Combat* in 1945 illustrates. On 18 May that year Camus wrote:

> J'ai lu dans un journal du matin que 80% des Arabes désiraient devenir des citoyens français. Je résumerai au contraire l'état actuel de la politique algérienne en disant qu'ils le désiraient effectivement, mais qu'ils ne le désirent plus. Quand on a longtemps vécu d'une espérance et que cette espérance a été démentie, on s'en détourne et l'on perd jusqu'au désir.[2]

> [I read in the morning paper that 80% of Arabs want to become French citizens. I shall sum up the present state of Algerian politics by saying that, on the contrary, that is what they did in fact want but that they no longer want it. When you have lived in hope for a long time and see that your hope has not been realised, you turn away from it and lose any desire to see it fulfilled.]

Camus went on, in this and other articles he wrote for the underground news-paper *Combat* at the time as part of a series entitled 'Crise en Algérie', to provide convincing evidence that a number of factors were coming together to bring about a radical change of outlook in Algeria. Firstly, there was the fact that French defeat in 1940 had represented a significant blow to the coun-try's prestige, a blow that the subsequent years of German occupation and Franco-German collaboration did little to soften. Secondly, Arab demands for a relaxation of the colonial régime and for a move to equal rights and duties with the colonisers had been voiced in Algeria and Tunisia from the early 1900s onwards. The French government had responded to these demands by a pro-posal to grant voting rights and limited citizenship to a small section of the Muslim elite (some 60,000 people). This was the celebrated Blum-Viollette project of 1936. It was the first concrete proposal ever made by France to insti-gate modest reforms that would allow elements of the local population a modest degree of political involvement. The proposals were never implemented. The objections raised by vested colonial interests in Algeria were strong enough to ensure that the project was left to gather dust on the ministerial shelves in Paris. Thirdly, a factor that should not be underestimated had been the mobilisation of significant numbers of Maghrebi soldiers to fight for the liberation of France. This experience had not only created opportunities for increased political awareness through the sharing of experiences with other colonised brothers-in-arms in the fight against totalitarianism, it had also created expectations that France would be disposed after the war to recognise in principle an equality that had been granted *de facto* to those who had taken part in the armed struggle against Nazism. So when de Gaulle decided in March 1944 to revive the Blum-Viollette project (which itself had been a very belated French response to demands made after the First World War) it was clear that this was offering the Arabs too little too late. In May 1945, Arab anger expressed itself in a series of demonstrations, notably in Sétif and Guelma where the brutal repression measures taken by French forces saw the massacre of thousands of peaceful demonstrators. It has been estimated that as many as 45,000 demonstrators were killed in the demonstrations themselves and in the 'mopping-up' exercises that followed. These atrocities certainly brought a sense of concrete reality to the view that the French colonial régime had entered the post-war era intending to rely on tactics of repression rather than reform. Further evidence was hardly needed that the ostensible policy of assimilation France had preached for decades was nothing more than a rhetorical exercise.

This potted history of the political landscape of the Maghreb at the end of the Second World War is not intended as a way of *explaining* developments in the literature of the region at the time. But it is clearly significant as a description of a climate in which artists as well as politicians were working. The passage from a time of hope to a time of disillusionment that Camus so clearly paints can be seen as corresponding to a shift in the way the function of literature was conceived and the type of practice of literature that could be envisaged. In the inter-war years, the period generally seen as the apogee of colonial rule, the prevailing mood across the Maghreb (and this in spite of a history of ongoing, albeit spasmodic, armed resistance to the French occupation) had been one of compliance. Since the latter decades of the previous century the development of an education system based on the French model had been deployed across the Maghreb and it was particularly well embedded in Algeria. As we have seen, *francophonie* had originally been conceived of as a tool for the spread of French culture, itself a synonym in the minds of many French people for the highest expression of (universally accepted) civilised values. Education was the key instrument for disseminating French cultural values and norms of course, and since culture, social progress and power in all its manifold manifestations were located within, and inextricably linked to, the life and language of the French colonisers, it was all the more understandable that many Maghrebis felt inclined to comply with them. But there is a sense in which this thumbnail sketch of the prevailing social mood in the inter-war years is relevant only to a particular section of society. It probably makes little sense to claim that the vast majority of the population in North Africa were compliant with a régime that ignored them, that took cognisance of them only as a population to be organised, administered and controlled. In reality the colonial administration was largely blind to the very existence of the great mass of the colony's inhabitants. It certainly did not consider them in any serious way as being capable of political agency or worthy of enfranchisement.

This political blindness is mirrored in the realm of literature. How could it be otherwise? Prior to the explosion of literary activity in French by educated indigenous North Africans in the early 1950s, agency, the capacity for action (in literature as in politics), had been located firmly within the hands of the 'French' minority. What that term covered exactly varied almost from generation to generation, as Peter Dunwoodie's book *Writing French Algeria* (1998) clearly demonstrates.[3] The Orientalists (the 'Tourist-writers', to use Albert Memmi's disparaging term), writers from the metropolis who travelled to the Maghreb and used the experience as a source of exotic material for their work, were one avatar. Thereafter, from Louis Bertrand with his focus on the Latin Mediterranean to the Algerianist novels of Robert Randau, and even beyond to the so-called 'Ecole d'Alger' of Gabriel Audisio, Albert Camus and Emmanuel Roblès, the trajectory can be mapped out in more or less distinct ideological stages.

The blatantly imperialist assumptions of Bertrand are attenuated and relocated as they acquire a more Maghrebi-centred focus in the writings of Randau. But in the work of both early and later exponents of the colonial novel (*le roman colonial*) the 'rightness' of the colonial enterprise is never questioned. The differences between Bertrand and Randau can be likened to a family quarrel in which the younger generation marks its distance from its elders and simultaneously affirms its own personality. Writers like Randau and the Tharaud brothers proclaimed the existence of a specifically Algerian colonial culture by emphasising local conditions, local knowledge and specific cultural information to which they, as insiders, had privileged access. Bernard Mouralis, albeit writing about sub-Saharan Africa rather than the Maghreb, makes a point that has a general relevance when he identifies such intermediary positions as hybrid forms of culture, unlike both metropolitan culture and the indigenous cultures existing in the colonies: 'La colonisation se caractérise . . . par la volonté du colonisateur d'imposer non sa propre culture mais une culture spécifique qu'on peut appeler la culture coloniale et qui n'avait pas d'équivalent dans les métropoles.'[4] [Colonisation can be characterised . . . as the will of the coloniser to impose not his own culture but a specific culture that can be called colonial culture and which had no equivalent in the mother-countries concerned.] Even with the next generation, the 'Ecole d'Alger' group of writers, there was a deep-rooted conviction that assimilation was the enlightened option for the indigenous population. What makes colonialism so unpalatable to modern-day observers (its racialist foundations and the economic exploitation it systematised) is occluded or filtered out so that a socially enlightened, politically committed and culturally tolerant version of assimilation theory is all that remains of the colonial enterprise in the works of a Camus or a Roblès. The racialist aspects of colonial ideology have been silenced as attention is firmly focused instead on the gulf between social classes and degrees of privilege rather than on cultural difference or on racial 'othering', both of which tend to remain unproblematised in their writing.

It is something of a truism to point out that writing by 'the French' and writing in French are two very different things. In the context of the Maghreb the distinction could hardly be starker. It is underscored by the historical rift that had taken place in the decade between the Brazzaville conference (1944), at which General de Gaulle had promised far-reaching reforms to the colonies, and the outbreak of the Algerian 'revolution' in 1954. As we have seen, the decade in question sees an awakening of political consciousness, the crystallising of the debate for equal rights around the twin notions of nationalism and independence and simultaneously, in the literary domain, the first concerted efforts to express these new ideas through fiction written by indigenous Maghrebi writers. Ten years later, in 1964, the Tunisian writer, Albert Memmi, published his *Anthologie des écrivains maghrébins d'expression française*, the first volume of an intended trilogy of anthologies. In seeking to characterise what he described as 'the 1952 generation' of Maghrebi writers, Memmi begins by explaining what the previous generations of writers had had in common. They had, he argued, been either writers from France who had treated Africa as a mere accessory, or, if born in North Africa, writers who had in their hearts considered it only as a second homeland, 'une seconde patrie'. (The second volume of the trilogy, published in 1969 under the title *Anthologie des écrivains français du Maghreb*, dealt with this group of French writers from North Africa, many of whom Memmi genuinely admired.) He went on to sum up the key distinguishing feature of their work as follows: 'Il est remarquable que dans toutes ces œuvres, les hommes de ce pays sont ou absents ou conventionnels: les petits garçons délices du touriste, la bédouine-sauvage-poupée-d'amour, le farouche-Arabe-du-désert.'[5] [It is worth noting that in all these works, local people are either non-existent or stereotypes: the small children who delight the tourists, the untamed-erotic-Bedouin-woman, the haughty-Arab-from-the-desert.] The emergence of Maghrebi writers, both commenting on and fuelling the historical process of decolonisation with literary works interwoven with its practical and theoretical preoccupations, marked a reversal of the cultural ventriloquism that had characterised the literature of previous generations. It naturally presented, implicitly or explicitly, a perspective on the Maghreb that was quite distinct from anything that a Franco-centric perspective, however sympathetic to indigenous concerns, could offer. It understood the past differently and envisaged the future in very different ways.

Before considering in greater detail some of the major literary figures and texts from the region, some cautionary points need to be made. The first is that the Maghreb is a region encompassing considerable cultural, ethnic and linguistic diversity. In the analytical presentations that follow there has been no attempt to emphasise what is specifically Moroccan, Algerian or Tunisian in each of them. Although each of the countries concerned has a distinct history and a distinct contemporary identity, lack of space has made it impossible to focus on such national specificities as a priority. It could be claimed that any use of the umbrella terms 'Maghreb' or 'Maghrebi' involves homogenising entities that deserve to be distinguished more carefully. This is true, but nevertheless the term also serves a useful purpose as a geographical descriptor. The decision not to pursue in detail and systematically the traces of cultural, ethnic and linguistic differences should not be taken to mean that they do not exist or indeed are not worth pursuing.

A second cautionary points needs to be made which is, in a sense, the obverse of the previous point about the dangers of homogenisation. It is probably the case that a far greater degree of cultural homogeneity existed in pre-colonial Maghreb than exists today, even if only in the sense that its diverse cultures were all 'pre-modern'. (From a wider historical perspective both colonialism and decolonisation can be seen as conduits through which the cultures of the Maghreb came into contact with modernity.) It is difficult to imagine how the process of decolonisation could have been undertaken at all without some mechanism for creating and maintaining a strong sense of common purpose. In Algeria, the harnessing of popular support for the armed struggle was not simply a matter of channelling emotional energy, it required political organisation and planning. Where no nation had previously existed, the Front de Libération Nationale (FLN), the main revolutionary group co-ordinating the fight for independence, set about creating the political infrastructure and the ideological concept of an Algerian nation. Camus's comments on Algerian nationhood, written in 1958, give an insight into the complexities that the FLN's efforts were intent on homogenising:

> Si bien disposé qu'on soit envers la revendication arabe, on doit cependant reconnaître qu'en ce qui concerne l'Algérie, l'indépendance nationale est une formule purement passionnelle. Il n'y a jamais eu encore de nation algérienne. Les Juifs, les Turcs, les Grecs, les Italiens, les Berbères, auraient autant de droit à réclamer la direction de cette nation virtuelle. Actuellement, les Arabes ne forment pas à eux seuls toute l'Algérie.[6]

> [However well disposed one may feel towards Arab demands, one nevertheless has to recognise that, as far as Algeria is concerned, national independence is an entirely emotive notion. An Algerian nation as such has never to date existed. Jews, Turks, Italians, Berbers would all have as much right as each other to aspire to the leadership of this virtual nation. At the present time, Arabs alone do not constitute Algeria.]

Camus's analysis distinguishes the Arab component from the other culturally specific components for two obvious reasons. Demographically the Arab population was far and away the most significant element in terms of numbers, and the association of 'Arab' with 'Muslim' gave it even greater weight. For example, although the Berbers were culturally, ethnically and linguistically distinct, they had nevertheless largely been converted to Islam. The Berbers could thus be subsumed under the heading 'Arab' as participating in a wider, spiritual grouping. Hence spiritual unity became (and has remained) a rallying cry for the notion of a political unity that had never previously existed, because it was never necessary, in pre-colonial Maghreb. Indeed, after denying the existence of an Algerian nation Camus went on to concede the existence of 'une sorte d'empire musulman' [a kind of Muslim empire] while insisting on the existence, alongside it, of 'un empire chrétien, au moins aussi important' [a Christian empire, at least of equal importance].[7] Unfortunately, this analysis, undoubtedly accurate in its day, merely draws up the battle lines not only for the Algerian war itself but for the way Algerian 'independence' was subsequently, and understandably, conceptualised in largely antagonistic terms.

Algeria has served here as the prime example of the way the struggle for independence was dialectically linked to the rise of nationalism, and of the way the homogenisation of underlying diversity has been both an end and a means to consolidating the nation. In different ways the same processes were at work in Morocco and Tunisia. Nowhere can this be more clearly glimpsed than in the paradoxes of the language policies that each of the states has pursued since independence. Across the region, political independence from France led to policies of Arabisation designed to replace French by Arabic as the language of the state and of public life. There can be no denying the symbolic importance of such an ambition: the rejection of the French language reinforced the rejection of French culture and French economic and political domination that is the defining feature of decolonisation. Yet the promotion of Arabic as a way of asserting national identity cannot be seen as a correspondingly straightforward measure for the simple reason that the spoken language(s) across the region are principally dialectal forms of Arabic. These often exist only (or mainly) in oral forms and are generally considered as popular varieties of language. They lack prestige, are subject to regional variation, and are generally ill-adapted to the range of usages that an official national language might reasonably be called upon to fulfil. Classical Arabic, on the other hand, is a formal, standardised, literary language that has the great prestige it derives from being the language of the Qur'an. But effectively it is a foreign language for many speakers of dialectal Arabic, who are only familiar with it as the language of religious observance. To date, with varying degrees of success, the countries of the Maghreb are still actively developing median forms of Arabic capable of serving as the official national languages that never actually existed when the policies of Arabisation were originally introduced.

This already complex situation is further complicated by the existence of significant numbers of Tamazight (Berber) speakers, especially in Morocco and Algeria, who are increasingly vocal in their demands for linguistic (and cultural) recognition. Within this evolving landscape, French has continued to be a widely used language enjoying considerable prestige. The symbolic power of Arabic as a marker of cultural independence is not incompatible with the continuing widespread use of French. It remains a vehicle for practical communication for the huge numbers of the Maghrebi population who have family members, across the generations, living and working in France. In many sections of the population and in many areas of public life, it provides easy access to international audiences. These various factors account for the many contradictions of linguistic policy-making in the Maghreb where practical realities are frequently ignored because of a desire to celebrate a rather abstract and often spurious notion of unity that flies in the face of the region's underlying complexity and diversity. Without exception, the writers and texts considered below recognise and celebrate that diversity.

As we have seen, francophone literature from the Maghreb arrived on the international scene in the 1950s as a literature of introspection. The earliest texts explored that classic postcolonial *topos* of the 'identity crisis' occasioned by, and inscribed in, colonial relationships and their aftermath. In different ways two of the three categories identified by Abdelkébir Khatibi in his important book on the Maghrebi novel, the 'ethnographic novel' and the novel of 'acculturation', can be subsumed under this heading, as examples of introspection.[8] It remained a literature of introspection once the Algerian war had wrested political independence from France, but as the inward-looking gaze focused on Maghrebi society and took stock of the cultural inertia that seemed the most salient feature of daily life in North Africa, it quickly transmuted into an iconoclastic literature, obsessed with transgression, interdictions and taboos of one sort or another. More often than not the sense of revolt was channelled in such a way as to target the family and repressive social structures; it invariably included the plight of women, doubly colonised in so far as the constraints, interdictions and taboos most directly affect(ed) them, under political conditions already determined by the oppressive structures of colonial rule.

There is, of course, a political dimension to the revolt expressed by writers such as Driss Chraïbi, Kateb Yacine, Rachid Boudjedra or Assia Djebar, but it largely operates through the metaphorical association of patriarchal sociocultural structures, on the one hand, with political authority, on the other. The importance accorded to the idea of unity in the emerging nation of Algeria operated almost immediately, in the aftermath of the war, as a force for repression: the FLN brooked little opposition and acted as a force for cultural homogenisation in ways that directly stifled the diverse range of aspirations that had been unleashed by the war itself. Consequently victory in the war and political independence from France brought no resolution to the social and cultural problems that bedevilled Algerian (and wider Maghrebi) society. If anything, in Algeria at least, the monolithic political culture installed by the FLN made the situation, in many ways, worse than before. The perceived need for unity was the reason for policies of Arabisation and for promoting the dominance of Arab/Muslim values over other sections of the diverse cultural landscape of Algeria. Officialdom in the fragile state emerging from war had neither the confidence nor the stability to engage in dialogue about greater freedoms, to interrogate its own diverse traditional and cultural make-up, or to set about modernising archaic attitudes, for example with regard to the role of women. For this reason, the writers of the post-independence period have no reason to see the acquistion of independence as marking a natural break with the past. As Tahar Bekri remarks:

> La littérature de cette génération est marquée par le refus d'une image officielle du Maghreb. C'est une littérature de la désillusion et de la déception. Aussi, fait-elle de son champ celui de la contestation de la suffisance et de ce que l'essayiste tunisienne Hélé Béji appelle le nationalitarisme . . . un véritable travail de critiques adressées aux pouvoirs, par œuvres littéraires interposées, s'installe . . .[9]

[The literature of this generation is marked by the refusal of an official image of the Maghreb. It is a literature of disillusionment and disappointment. Moreover it makes it its business to mount a challenge against self-satisfied complacency and against what the Tunisian essayist Hélé Béji calls nationalitarism . . . the real work of criticising the powers-that-be through the vicarious critiques contained in literary works, is beginning . . .]

No doubt the dissatisfaction is at its strongest among Algerian writers like Rachid Mimouni who attacks the indifference and inhumanity of the Algerian state that makes itself felt through its bureaucratic systems. This is the case in both *Le Fleuve détourné* (1982) and *L'Honneur de la tribu* (1989) in which liberation from colonialism does little to improve the lives of those who had fought to change a dehumanising system that has merely been perpetuated by agents of the state.

The Algerian war was first and foremost a war of decolonisation. As such it involved a struggle for freedom which, for the progressively minded, could be equated with a search for a new beginning. For many, colonialism had been the immediate target but an opening-up to modernity was the long-term prize. And yet in many respects the successful prosecution of the war resulted in sociocultural regression for the mass of people. Patriarchal, repressive tendencies were reinforced, while fear of change was so strong that it consolidated a certain conception, (not to say reinvention) of tradition as some sort of immutable, inviolable model for social interaction. Decades after the publication of Driss Chraïbi's *Le Passé simple* (1954) and Rachid Boudjedra's *La Répudiation* (1969), the very issues that had fuelled the revolt they expressed remained unresolved. A political authority that made use of community leaders espousing repressive religious and cultural attitudes in order to entrench its own power-base found itself increasingly outflanked in the early 1990s, as extremist views became more and more virulent with the rise of the fundamentalist Islamic organisation, the Front Islamique du Salut (FIS).

The civil war that resulted in the assassination of writers like Tahar Djaout and Abdelkader Alloula, who were among many hundreds of intellectuals, journalists and creative artists killed in the 1990s, provides a tragic backdrop to any discussion of contemporary literary activity in the region as a whole. The effects of the violence are still being felt. Yet the very fact that the extremists chose to target writers and intellectuals makes it all the more clear that the civil war, for all its barbarity and violence, was primarily a cultural rather than a political conflict. Expressed in these terms, it is perhaps easier to see that this particular struggle continues today, even though the violence may have largely abated. Moreover, the focus on culture and the elision of politics confirms it as a postcolonial conflict, rather than the opposite. It highlights the fact that the cultural dimension of power relations and the political dimension of cultural activity are inextricably interlinked, and that jointly this nexus of issues and concerns that were at the very heart of colonial domination sadly continue to mutate in postcolonial contexts.

Mouloud Feraoun (Algeria, 1913–1962)

Mouloud Feraoun was very consciously a writer of Memmi's '1952 generation' in that he was acutely aware that his vocation involved giving a voice to the hitherto silent 'Arab' population. Several years before Memmi was to take up this same point, Feraoun had noted, and commented on the significance of, the failure of writers from the 'Ecole d'Alger' group to portray 'Arab' characters in their work. In an article on Algerian literature published in 1957 (republished in *L'Anniversaire*), he remarks on the absence of indigenous characters in novels by the likes of Audisio, Moussy, Roblès and Camus in the following way:

> ce milieu familier où nous ne discernons ni parti pris, ni outrance, demeure malgré tout étranger au nôtre: voisin, si l'on veut, juxtaposé, bien distinct. On peut y rencontrer une chaude sympathie pour l'autochtone, parfois même de l'amitié mais en général l'autochtone en est absent . . . il ne s'agit pas d'une regrettable lacune littéraire, c'est tout bonnement une des tristes réalités algériennes.[10]

> [this familiar setting in which we can detect no bias, no extreme behaviour, remains in spite of everything foreign to the world we live in, if you like it is juxtaposed to it but it remains quite distinct. In these portrayals we can come across real warmth towards the natives, even friendship, but in general the native is not present . . . this is no regrettable literary lacuna, it is quite simply one of the sad realities of Algerian life.]

Feraoun's perspicacity and the mixture of approval and regret that he displays towards the writers concerned are a testament to his objectivity when writing about influential people with whom he enjoyed personal relationships. He goes on to write: 'si nous sommes absents dans l'œuvre d'un Camus . . . si les Algériens de Moussy . . . nous coudoient continuellement sans nous voir, c'est que ni Moussy ni Camus ni presque tous les autres n'ont pu venir jusqu'à nous pour suffisamment nous connaître.'[11] [if we are absent from the works of Camus . . . if Moussy's Algerians . . . continually rub shoulders with us without ever actually seeing us, it's because neither Moussy nor Camus nor practically any of the others have ever managed to come close enough to get to know us sufficiently well.] For Feraoun, the literary occlusion of 'Arab' characters was symptomatic of a failed connection in the Franco-'Arab' relationship that went to the very heart of the Algerian crisis that was gathering momentum in the last decade of his life. In an open letter to Camus written in 1958 (also republished in *L'Anniversaire*) he sums up this failed relationship thus:

> deux communautés vivaient côte à côte depuis un siècle, se tournant délibérément le dos, totalement dépourvues de curiosité et, de ce fait, aussi peu susceptibles de se comprendre l'une que l'autre, n'ayant de commun que leur mutuelle indifférence, leur entêtement à se mépriser et cet inhumain commerce qui lie le faible au fort, le petit au grand, le serviteur au maître.[12]

> [two communities had lived side by side for a century, deliberately turning their backs on each other, totally lacking in any curiosity and, as a result, equally unlikely to understand each other, sharing only their mutual indifference, their determination to consider each other with contempt and that inhuman relationship that binds the weak to the strong, the small to the big, the servant to the master.]

In many respects, Feraoun bridged the communities that the War of Independence was to pit against each other. The son of a poor peasant family from the Kabyle region, his childhood had given him first-hand knowledge of the misery that Camus exposed to the world in the series of celebrated articles he published in *Alger républicain* in 1939, later republished as *Chroniques Algériennes*. Despite his humble origins, Feraoun followed a formal education and eventually trained as a teacher at the Ecole normale de Bouzaréa in Algiers where he met and befriended Emmanuel Roblès. Roblès encouraged Feraoun's literary ambitions and was instrumental in publishing many of his texts, notably in the series he founded at Editions du Seuil, 'Méditerranée'. The self-imposed parameters of Feraoun's mission as a writer were relatively limited. They are adequately summed up in a phrase from the autobiographical first novel, *Le Fils du pauvre* (1950), when the young protagonist, Menrad, explains that his forays into literature have left him with a desire to tell his own story: 'la sotte idée de se peindre' (p. 10) [the silly idea of portraying oneself]. The self to be depicted in the self-portrait that his writings would construct was both the internal subjective world of his autobiographical fiction and the *Journal* (1962), and the self-conscious presentation of Kabyle culture, the culture from which he originated and with which he maintained strong emotional links.

These two poles of writing about the self are never kept neatly distinct. They merge the one into the other in a single continuum. Since presenting Kabyle life and culture is at the heart of Feraoun's project as a writer, he himself becomes as much a part of his 'material' as the mountain villages of his novels. There is a sense too in which the material is constantly recycled, appearing in different forms in different texts. An article like 'L'Entraide dans la société kabyle' is, for example, an ostensibly objective description of the social organisation to be found in a typical Kabyle village.[13] Feraoun assumes the role of 'native informant' to provide ethnographic insights into the various roles and functions assumed by individuals and groups within Kabyle society. But just as this particular essay closes with a lyrical narrativised celebration of the tradition of *Thiouizi* (a feast involving collective 'self-help'), thus slipping from one genre (scholarly exposition) to another (poetic), so his fictional works, particularly *La Terre et le sang* (1953), create a contrapuntal effect as passages of dramatic narrative are punctuated with passages of objectifying 'ethnographic' explanation.

La Terre et le sang is something of a hybrid text. The ostensible storyline relates the life of Amer-ou-Kaci following his return to his native village after many years of absence in Europe, spent first as a migrant worker in the mines of northern France and subsequently in a German labour camp during the years of the Great War. The novel opens with Amer's arrival at Ighil-Nezman accompanied by his white French wife, Marie. Through a series of flashbacks the narration gradually fills in the life story of the protagonist and his wife as well as providing their wider family histories although the focus of the novel as a whole is the history of the complex relationships that bind together the village clans. The cultural distancing that separates Marie from the other characters could potentially have been exploited as a means of foregrounding cultural differences and specificities, but this would have required a central role for Marie in any unfolding drama. In fact, her position in the novel is marginal and symbolic rather than a motor for dramatic action. (Her 'absence' from the novel is perhaps a reverse mirror image of the absence of North African characters in the Algerianist novel.) Similarly the theme of the traveller's return to his native land could have been used as a pretext for highlighting contrasts in perceptions and outlooks, yet Amer slots back into the life of the village with surprising ease. Despite this, the exposition of cultural differences and specificities is nevertheless a constant element of the text, either as objectified narration:

> Le lieu de réunion le plus spectaculaire est la fontaine. Là, les femmes ne connaissent ni Dieu ni maître. Les jeunes sont chez elles et en prennent à leur aise: libres propos, plaisanteries osées, chants . . . Souvent la cruche d'eau n'est qu'un prétexte pour sortir, se montrer, exciter des jalousies ou parler d'un 'parti'. (p. 29)

[The most spectacular meeting place is the fountain. There, the women recognise neither God nor master. The young women are entirely at home there and relax completely: they say what they like, make *risqué* jokes, sing . . . Often the water jug is no more than an excuse for getting out of the house, for showing oneself in public, for getting a neighbour's back up, or for discussing a possible husband.]

or incorporated into dramatised sequences of action, as in the following account of a quarrel among the womenfolk:

Quelques femmes raisonnables s'interposèrent, entourèrent Chabha qui souriait, toute pâle, pendant que de plus jeunes prenaient furtivement un caillou, crachaient dessus et le déposaient, le côté mouillé contre terre, ainsi qu'il est d'usage lorsqu'on désire qu'une dispute s'envenime.

(p. 208)

[Some reasonable women intervened, surrounded Chabha who was smiling, pale-faced, while some younger women furtively picked up a pebble, spat on it and placed it back on the ground wet side down, as is the custom when you want an argument to get worse.]

In these, as in countless other examples, the *assumed reader* is the narrative's cultural 'other' rather than Marie or the 'returning native', Amer. Cultural information along with detailed descriptions of the scenery and topography of the Kabyle region are a commonplace feature of the novel, as though Feraoun's intention is as much to provide a presentation of his own native land to the wider world as it is to narrate a story.

The drama that is simultaneously interwoven with this 'documentary' is a complex tale of family honour and fluctuating family fortunes that involves inter-clan and inter-generational rivalries. These extend geographically to the networks of migrant workers from Ighil-Nezman who travelled to the mine-fields of northern France, some to return, some not. At a variety of levels then, personal, family, clan, village and tribe, the customs and rituals of daily life and the spiritual and ethical beliefs that underpin relationships between men and women, rich and poor, young and old, are all explored and subjected to detailed portrayal if not critique. The land and blood of the novel's title here find their full significance: 'land' in the acute sense that Kabyle culture is ultimately rooted in and sustained by a relationship with the land, and 'blood' in the sense that the social and anthropological behaviours that are catalogued in the novel find their origins in the complex patterns through which family and inter-family relationships are encoded. The family blood that Amer accidentally spills in the French mine early on in the novel ruptures the cultural order in a way that distance from home, the harshness of migrancy, the politics of exploitative labour relations (in France or North Africa) and so on, can never equal. Only through the spilling of Amer's own blood at the hands of his uncle at the close of the novel can a sense of equilibrium be recovered. And so Marie's absence from the novel seems to confirm the fact that the relationships that are of central interest to Feraoun are between Kabyles and not 'Franco-Arab' relations. (In any event, 'Arab' is clearly a misnomer here since the culture in question is Berber not 'Arab').

Other texts, such as those assembled and published posthumously in *Jours de Kabylie* (1968), often draw on the same or similar 'ethnographic' material to that examined in many passages of *La Terre et le sang*: the social function of the *djema*, for men (a gathering where menfolk could talk among themselves), or of the fountain, for women; a dramatised presentation of a purification rite: the *timchret*, and so on. Undoubtedly, the intention is to present them in a celebratory manner to a French readership. Social roles that are culturally opaque to a Western readership, particularly when traversed by a gendered aspect (such as the expectation that women rather than men carry loads, fetch water, frequently remain cloistered in the home, and so on) are given psychological depth and dramatised so as to simultaneously 'humanise' and humorise them. Social improvement is not high on Feraoun's list of priorities: 'Il est souhaitable, certes, que s'améliore un jour le sort de nos ménagères . . . L'avenir sans nul doute, leur réserve toutes ces améliorations.'[14] [Without doubt it is desirable that the lot of our womenfolk should one day improve . . . There can be no question that the future holds all these improvements in store for them.] His work has a certain conservative edge to it but the lyricism that frequently dominates is not sentimental or nostalgic in tone. It is, however, unashamedly retrospective both in terms of the material conditions he describes and in terms of the value systems he often invokes as an integral part of the portrait he is painting: 'Les hommes ne vont pas à la fontaine. La règle le veut ainsi. Une règle tacite qui se transmet de génération en génération. Une indiscutable question de décence, de respect humain, si on préfère.'[15] [Men do not go to fetch water. That is the convention. A tacit convention that has been transmitted from generation to generation. It is a matter of what is proper, of human respect, if you like, and it can't be questioned.] But it would be wide of the mark to suggest that Feraoun is looking back to a 'culturally authentic', idealised past as a strategic response in the face of the dehumanising machinery of colonialism. It was rather the case that Feraoun would have preferred to continue to believe in the promise of assimilation and the pace of change it implied. As it became increasingly clear that this was impossible he opted for private and personal responses to the Algerian crisis rather than go in for public performances of political allegiance to the Revolution. Like many of his generation he had chosen to remain sympathetic to all that French culture offered (while refusing to accept the obvious corollary: the loss of his indigenous Kabyle culture) and, having profited from that initial choice, honesty demanded that he assume it to the full.

Feraoun's biculturalism, his assimilation to French culture and his links with the intellectual circles of French Algeria (including a significant correspondence with Camus) on the one hand, and his roots in Kabyle culture, on the other, proved to be the two poles of his existence. Jean Déjeux quite accurately described him as 'véritablement un 'homme-frontière' . . . Le romancier, enraciné dans sa société, se tient à cette place pour faire passer les valeurs de son peuple et les expliquer aux autres.'[16] [truly a man at the frontier of cultures . . . The novelist, rooted in his own society, occupies this frontier position in order to pass on the values of his own people and to explain them to others.] His attempts to give a voice to the Kabyle people were tragically and prematurely silenced in March 1962 when Feraoun was assassinated by gunmen fighting a rearguard action to maintain France's hold on Algeria.

Mohammed Dib (Algeria, 1920–2003)

According to a periodisation of the Maghrebi novel proposed by Abdelkébir Khatibi in *Le Roman maghrébin*, Feraoun is classified as an exponent of the 'ethnographic' novel alongside such writers as Ahmed Sefraoui, Mouloud Mammeri and the Mohammed Dib of the 'première manière'.[17] Khatibi is quite right to see Dib's Algerian trilogy (*La Grande Maison* (1952), *L'Incendie* (1954) and *Le Métier à tisser* (1957)) as having sufficient stylistic and thematic coherence to constitute a 'manner'. To an extent he is also right to claim that Dib went on to develop a 'second manner' with *Qui se souvient de la mer* (1962), a novel which Khatibi classifies as exemplifying 'la littérature militante centrée sur la guerre d'Algérie' [militant literature focusing on the Algerian War of Independence].[18] But Khatibi's essay was published too early (1968) to be able to take account of the fact that Dib was possibly less a writer with two 'manners' than an artist who would reinvent himself constantly throughout his long career until his death in 2003. The longer view of his output that is now possible, particularly the identifying of filiations and connections between early and later writings that can now be undertaken, has yet to be fully explored. The tendency to identify 'manners' (however defined and however many) is an unfortunate habit among literary historians and yet in critiques of Dib's work it is a recurring theme among commentators, not least, no doubt, because his prolific output over so many years (1947–2003) invites attempts to identify a succession of preoccupations and to demonstrate a technical evolution over time. Even Peter Hallward's recent, perceptive analysis of Dib's writings begins by dividing them into three moments:

> a first, relatively 'specified' beginning (c.1950- c.1960), where the dominant tone is shaped by a critique of colonialism and the movement towards a collective militancy; a second, longer, minimally 'specific' moment (c.1960–c.1990), characterised by the disruption of specifiable categories, the dissolution of historical continuity and the fragmentation of relations stretched to the very limits of madness and amnesia; a third moment, (c.1990–1996) that verges on the intuition of an absolutely singular space and experience . . . balanced precariously on the limits of the ineffable.'[19]

Such efforts at periodisation might more correctly be seen as ways of structuring and facilitating critical commentary rather than as a way of accurately reflecting aspects of the writer's work.

Part of the problem here is that such divisions are plausible and, to a degree, defensible. It is true that the emergence of francophone Maghrebi literature required the creation of a reading public for the texts, but the expectations of the readers also helped fashion the sort of texts that were produced. On the one hand, in the 1950s the political left in France was disposed to listen to the Maghreb as never before, but that is not to say that the forces of commodification were not at work in facilitating the transmission of certain kinds of message by writers who rose to prominence as authentic 'representatives' worth heeding. In his essay on the Maghrebi novel Khatibi frequently argues that this was a period in which Maghrebi writers were 'used' by France as temporary 'interlocutors' about events in Algeria, only to be subsequently rejected and forgotten.[20] We should note in passing that this is entirely consonant with the view widely held at the time, and succinctly voiced by Albert Memmi, that Maghrebi literature in French would quickly wither and die.[21] Dib, of course has proved that particular prediction to be unfounded, yet it is worth pondering why the Algerian trilogy should occupy such a preponderant position in the critical reception of his work. One of the reasons is that the three novels in question can be so readily linked to contemporary events: the struggle for Algerian independence. In this respect they have an immediate functional appeal for that other powerful segment of a readership that helped to 'create' Maghrebi literature: the political activists within nationalist circles in Algeria and anticolonial opinion across the Maghreb. However much Mouloud Mammeri, Driss Chraïbi, Assia Djebar, Kateb Yacine and others might (choose to) invoke the freedom of the artist as an overarching principle, in reality their writings were subjected to pointed political critique from the moment they were published. Early reviews of Mammeri's *La Colline oubliée* (1952), to cite just one example, accused the novel of serving the colonial cause through its failure to portray Algeria as a society in transition. The pressure on writers to visibly commit themselves and their work to furthering the cause of independence was palpable and not insignificant.

Unlike many of the writers of the 1952 generation, whom it is possible to accuse of modifying the ideological direction of their writings under such pressures, Dib's commitment to the cause is not generally questioned. Two years after his expulsion from Algeria in 1959, from exile in France, he declared: 'Il se trouve qu'étant écrivain, c'est sur le terrain de la littérature que j'ai choisi de combattre en faisant connaître les réalités algériennes.'[22] [It so happens that being a writer I have decided to pursue the struggle on the battlefield of literature, by acquainting people with the realities of Algeria.] Such statements give the impression that Dib was somehow prepared to write to order and indeed, in a 1958 interview, he evoked the idea of a contract between the writer and the public even suggesting that the writer is at the service of the people.[23] Yet a reading of any of Dib's fiction or poetry provides little evidence to support the view that Dib ever risked compromising himself artistically. He is considered to have been 'Africain quand il fallait l'être' [African when that was what was needed] yet in the immediate aftermath of the war he showed no hesitation about marking his distance from politics and reasserting his artistic freedom: 'Le temps de l'engagement est terminé . . . ou il n'est plus indispensable.'[24] [The time for commitment is over . . . or it is no longer indispensable.]

The novels of the supposedly 'realist' Algerian trilogy recount the experiences of a young boy, Omar, in the late 1930s and early 1940s, firstly at school in Tlemcen, then during a season spent in the surrounding countryside among the local peasants as they begin to develop a certain political awareness, and finally among the urban artisan class as Omar begins his apprenticeship as a weaver. Hunger is omnipresent in the first novel of the series, *La Grande Maison*, and Omar's childhood is haunted by the daily struggle of the families in the Dar-Sbitar as they try to feed themselves. This battle for survival (like the daily grind of the fellahs in *L'Incendie* and the weavers in *Le Métier à tisser*) clearly has a political dimension but it is nevertheless largely portrayed in physical rather than ideological terms. The accumulation of details building into a portrait of everyday life, the favoured technique of the 'ethnographic' novel, assumes a particular resonance in Dib's writing, possibly because it is not pressed into the service of a recognisable ethnographic discourse. The details of the constant misery and hardship of daily life reflect the fundamentally alienated condition of the urban and rural poor among whom Omar lives. The focus on everyday details stands in lieu of political commentary except on those rare occasions when the frustration boils over and the emerging political consciousness begins to find a voice. On one such occasion the elderly Ben Sari vents his frustration at the police's frequent intrusions into Dar-Sbitar searching for Hamid Saraj, the political activist:

> Je ne veux pas me soumettre à la Justice . . . Ce qu'ils appellent la justice n'est que leur justice. Elle est faite uniquement pour les protéger, pour garantir leur pouvoir sur nous, pour nous réduire et nous mater. Aux yeux d'une telle justice, je suis toujours coupable. Elle m'a condamné avant même que je sois né.   (p. 49)

> [I don't want to co-operate with the Law . . . What they call justice is only their justice, it is designed only to protect them, to ensure their power over us, to bring us to heel and make us submit. In the eyes of that sort of justice I am always guilty. It found me guilty even before I was born.]

But by and large, throughout the trilogy, Omar and the mass of characters surrounding him are almost pre-articulate, they function below the threshold of politically enlightened self-expression. So much so that the political meeting addressed by Hamid is presented not as an example of political oratory, impressive because of its rhetorical sophistication, but as a 'speech act' which is intrinsically revolutionary as an act. Hamid's strength lies less in the quality of what he has to say than in the simple fact of speaking the world as it is and daring to demand the right to speak at all. Omar reflects:

> Ces paroles qui expliquent ce qui est, ce que le monde connaît et voit, c'est étrange, à la vérité, qu'il se soit trouvé quelqu'un des nôtres pour les dire . . . Notre malheur est si grand qu'on le prend pour la condition naturelle de notre peuple. Il n'y avait personne pour en témoigner, personne pour s'élever contre . . . Nous, si nous essayons d'ouvrir la bouche pour en dire quelque chose, nous restons bouche bée. Nous n'avons pas encore appris à parler.   (p. 117)

> [These words that explain how things are, what the world knows and sees, in truth it's a strange thing, that there should be one of our own people to say them . . . Our misfortune is so great that it is taken to be the natural condition of our people. There was no one to bear witness to it, no one to rise up against it . . . If we, for our part, try to open our mouths to say something about it, we remain gaping open-mouthed. We have not yet learned how to speak.]

In the face of such inarticulateness the facts are called upon to speak for themselves and assume the force of symbols. The awakening political consciousness of the fellahs in *L'Incendie* may translate itself into strike action but without any accompanying rhetoric. It is left to the the the symbolic power of the conflagration that ravages the countryside around 'la ferme Villard' to convey a sense that the thirst for freedom and justice has been ignited in the hearts of the ordinary men and women whom Dib portrays:

> Un incendie avait été allumé, et jamais plus il ne s'éteindrait. Il continuerait à ramper à l'aveuglette, secret, souterrain; ses flammes sanglantes n'auraient de cesse qu'elles n'aient jeté sur tout le pays leur sinistre éclat . . . là-dessous, en profondeur . . . une volonté de révolte incommensurable, débordante, s'apprête à secouer le système tout entier.   (pp. 131–2)

> [A fire had been lit, and it would never again be extinguished. It would continue to spread blindly, secretly, beneath the surface, its bloody flames would burn on until they had cast their sinister glow over the whole country . . . deep down below . . . an immeasurable, overflowing desire for revolt was preparing to shake the whole system.]

The problem with describing Dib's journey as a writer as one of a progression from a realism bordering on the ethnographic towards increasingly abstract, deterritorialised, introspective and poetic forms of output is that these supposedly later characteristics were already in evidence in his poetic writings in the late 1940s, some time before he embarked on writing *La Grande Maison*. Moreover, the much acclaimed *Qui se souvient de la mer*, often cited as the point at which Dib breaks with the techniques of realist representation, is the work in which he most directly tackles the portrayal of the Algerian war. (The fact that he chooses to do so while eschewing realistic techniques of representation and opting for an impressionistic, poetic style of writing is perhaps confirmation of the fact that Dib was always driven by aesthetic rather than political priorities.) In fact there are grounds for grouping this supposedly watershed novel with the earlier *Un Eté africain* (1959) and the later *Cours sur la rive sauvage* (1964) and treating all three novels as introspective and highly personalised explorations of the affective universe of characters caught up in the different stages of the armed conflict and its aftermath. That the novels display varying degrees of groundedness in realistic settings (the atmosphere from novel to novel becomes increasingly surrealist and dreamlike and is increasingly associated with the fantastic) or that the novels deal with increasingly private and symbolically charged universes does not detract from the argument that Dib is perhaps exploring different facets of a single experience.

These texts were followed by what is more clearly a coherent series of novels (*La Danse du roi* (1968), *Dieu en Barbarie* (1970) and *Le Maître de chasse* (1973) in which he examines aspects of life in post-independence Algeria. In later work, however, the recognisable social and political dimensions tend to recede before a poetic, highly introspective treatment of material which often has an autobiographical bias. Memory, amnesia, exile, cultural difference (*Les Terrasses d'Orsol* (1985), *Le Sommeil d'Eve* (1989) and *Neiges de marbre* (1990)) and a concern to test the limits of decipherability (*Habel* (1977) and *Le Désert sans détour* (1992) seem to dominate as his writing becomes a laboratory for personal research in which an esoteric quest for forms of derritorialisation, both geographical and ethical, are carried out. In a relatively early interview, in 1961, Dib claimed that he was first and foremost a poet: 'Je suis essentiellement poète et c'est de la poésie que je suis venu au roman, non l'inverse.'[25] [I am essentially a poet and it is by way of poetry that I came to the novel, not the other way round.] If the first Algerian trilogy allows glimpses of this fact, despite the 'realist' pigeon-hole into which it is generally slotted, his later works leave little room for doubt about the matter.

Kateb Yacine (Algeria, 1929–1989)

As we have seen, Mohammed Dib's prolific output has provoked debate about how it might be classified into types of text and 'manners' of writing. Kateb Yacine, by contrast, could well be described as the poet of a single 'text' but a text that he constantly reworked and refashioned. In an interview in 1967 Kateb commented:

> Je crois bien, en effet, que je suis l'homme d'un seul livre. A l'origine c'était un poème, qui s'est transformé en romans et en pièces de théâtre, mais c'est toujours la même œuvre que je laisserai certainement comme je l'ai commencée, c'est-à-dire à la fois une ruine et un chantier.[26]

> [I really believe that I am indeed the man of a single book. In the beginning it was a poem that transformed itself into novels and plays, but it's always the same work that I shall certainly leave behind as I found it, that is to say at one and the same time a construction site and a ruin.]

The literary space evoked here is at one and the same time a 'ruin' and a 'construction site', a telling image that conveys the notion that Kateb's writing is indeed built on constructive tensions between the past (whether this be understood in terms of a tribal heritage and communal traditions or in terms of personal memories) and the present/future (the perhaps vain hope that the revolutionary nature of poetic creation can serve to reconstitute forms of community and individuality and thereby reimpose order on chaos). Kateb's brief comment is also suggestive of a complete disregard for the concept of literary genre. Indeed his writings are almost systematically fragmentary and both *Nedjma* (1956) and *Le Polygone étoilé* (1966) (particularly the latter) proceed as a form of textual collage, combining passages of poetry, historical narrative, personal diaries, dramatised sequences and more conventional narrative sequences. This confusion of genres is compounded by dislocations of space, time and narrative point of view to create a highly complex textuality which contains within it the seeds of its own destruction. This aspect of Kateb's work has been assessed by Khatibi in the following terms:

> Kateb peut être considéré comme principalement un poète qui n'emploie les formes romanesques et théâtrales que pour les détruire.
>   Cette confusion des genres littéraires est bien sûr chez lui une technique terroriste qui brise la structure propre au roman et qui crée un langage éblouissant fusant de toutes parts . . .[27]

> [Kateb can be considered principally as a poet who only uses novelistic and dramatic forms in order to destroy them.
>   This confusion of literary genres is naturally, in his case, a terrorist technique that smashes the characteristic structure of the novel and which creates a dazzling language that blazes out in all directions . . .]

The image of destruction and 'brisure' outlined here in a poetic context provides a bridge across to the more politically orientated view of the poet's role that Kateb frequently expressed through the image of the earthenware pot juxtaposed to the iron pot: if the two come into contact the earthenware pot will inevitably come off worse and be shattered. So poetry and politics exist in an antagonistic relationship. The fragility and vulnerability of poetry may condemn it to destruction but its revolutionary power is such that the destructive process itself can be constantly performed and re-enacted as a staging of poetry's challenge to the political. The circularity involved here is another figure which obsessed and fascinated Kateb, providing the fundamental structure of *Nedjma* as well as acting as a privileged figure in *Le Cercle des représailles*, the collection of largely dramatic texts published in 1959.

Kateb's experience as a 16-year-old participant in the demonstrations at Sétif on 8 May 1945, and his witnessing of the repression and the massacres that ensued, go some way to providing a context for understanding the complexity of his views on these links between poetry and politics. If Khatibi is correct to describe his subsequent work as translating 'l'engagement profond de l'auteur dans ses obsessions'[28] [the author's deep commitment to his own obsessions], it would seem reasonable to identify the traumatic events of 1945 (including his own imprisonment, his simulated execution by firing squad and his mother's descent into madness as a consequence of these events) as at least linked to those obsessions. On his release from prison Kateb's commitment to the concept of revolutionary activity originally found an outlet in political militancy, but he soon reverted to the more personal conduit of poetic activity as a way of expressing it. His nomadic existence from 1954 onwards gives form to a refusal of roots and rootedness that is belied by his writing, in which an obsessive search for origins (personal, collective and national) is an omnipresent preoccupation. Even on his return to Algeria in the early 1970s, his work with an itinerant theatre group in the remote south of the country fed (and fed on) this same tension between the fixed and the nomadic while maintaining the connection with popular forms of cultural expression: in his theatre work from 1971 onwards Kateb worked in dialectal Arabic, the mother tongue of the majority of Algerians.

While it could justifiably be argued that the theatre dominated Kateb's life as an individual, his reputation as a writer undoubtedly rests on the novel he published in the midst of the Algerian war in 1956, *Nedjma*. This complex novel marked a step change in perceptions as to how the Maghrebi literary scene should or could be perceived. Where the 'ethnographic' novel could be plodding and at times pedantic, *Nedjma* bordered on the incoherent. Instead of the easily digestible variety of regionalist literature that many of his Maghrebi contemporaries were providing, Kateb undertook to explore complex individual and collective psychological depths through writing techniques that were highly sophisticated. The enigmatic Nedjma is the focal point of the novel in that she functions as the centre around which all the events and characters gravitate. More a cluster of potential (symbolic) meanings than a portrait of a character with any psychological depth, Nedjma mesmerises the four friends, Mourad, Rachid, Lakhdar and Mustapha whose narratives form the bulk of the novel. Their attraction to her is tinged with suggestions of an illicit, incestuous desire, rendered all the more ambiguous in that there is no absolute certainty as to her own parentage. The complex web of family relationships and ties of consanguinity that is slowly revealed as the novel progresses is matched by an equally complex web of relationships linking the fathers of the four young men, who, a generation earlier, had fought, killed, kidnapped and supplanted each other as lovers of Nedjma's mother, a Frenchwoman.

Nedjma thus functions as a symbol on a number of levels but two particular readings would seem to demand a privileged status. Firstly, through the links that bind the male characters (as well as Nedjma) to the common ancestor, Keblout, the novel explores an interrupted and incomplete potential genealogy of Algerian nationhood. Nedjma ('star' in Arabic and symbol of Algeria) is positioned as a tributary of diverse elements from an occluded tribal past, a space and a point in time at which various ancestral components (including a French element) culminate and come together. She is also, as an object of desire for the four young men, a potential point of departure from which an unexplored future might emerge. But this unexplored potentiality is already bathed in an atmosphere of ambiguity, violence and transgression. Nedjma (the character), may also be read as symbolic of womanhood in a more general sense, and here links with Kateb's own youthful infatuation with an elder cousin become a significant source. The personal loss (the cousin in question married) doubles other losses: the symbolic loss of his Arabic-speaking mother at the point at which Kateb began his education through the medium of French, followed by the more concrete loss that occurred when her mental state required her removal to a clinic at Blida following the trauma of the 1945 massacre. These and other readings can never be mutually exclusive, however. On the contrary, they should be seen as mutually enriching. Just as *Nedjma* draws on characters who had figured in earlier writings (and earlier versions of the text) by Kateb, so *Le Polygone étoilé*, for example, draws on the same personal archive of obsessions, recycling them, extending them, re-enacting them and embroidering upon them. In much the same way, the essentially poetic nature of Kateb's writing invites speculative readings of his 'text' where the assignation of meaning is consciously and infinitely deferred.

Driss Chraïbi (Morocco, 1926–)

In 1954 when Driss Chraïbi's controversial first novel, *Le Passé simple*, was published it provoked a vociferous reaction in his native Morocco as well as in Paris. The storm was political rather than literary. In more settled times the novel's iconoclastic deconstruction of a middle-class Moroccan family might have been recognised as the fruit of the very individualised revolt it undoubtedly was. But 1954 was a critical moment in relations between France and the Maghreb: right-wing circles in Paris were able to claim the novel as evidence in support of their view that Morocco's status as a protectorate of France should remain unchanged. So within weeks of its publication the novel had became a significant weapon that could be used against those militants fighting for independence within Morocco. Fifty years on, in a very perspicacious analysis of this whole polemic, Nicholas Harrison, in his book *Postcolonial Criticism*, has used this incident as a way of raising a series of questions that straddle the political and the literary: in particular to elucidate what he describes as 'the way the individual may become embroiled in [the] varied dynamics of representation'. Harrison argues that in making Chraïbi a spokesperson and his text an act of testimony, his critics had oversimplified and misrepresented the relation between the author and his text and between the literary and the political . . . they had confused and conflated different orders of representation.[29]

This is of course true, and when Harrison develops the argument to demonstrate how 'particular aspects of the author's real or imagined biography . . . including notably "race" or national origins, are seen by the readers as pertinent to the text, and as providing a legitimate or even crucial means of making sense of it' he is implicitly suggesting that such reading practices, such wilful conflation of different orders of representation, should be resisted. This argument has to be interpreted as a plea that the *literarity* of texts should be allowed to take precedence over the political content they may convey, on the one hand, or the political uses their presence in the public arena may make possible, on the other. Part of Harrison's point is that the stereotyping that is involved in such (typically postcolonial) reading practices imprisons authors within a specific context and limits their freedom: their work is valued not for any intrinsic merit or interest but because it more or less meets the prior expectations of the audience and feeds certain prejudices. He writes:

> It is indeed members of minority groups who are most liable to be *read* as representative, that is, liable to stereotyping, and who find themselves unable to act as individuals to the extent that their every action may be taken as typical of the type to which they find themselves assigned.[30]

It is interesting to note that in the present discussion of Chraïbi's work thus far, we have felt obliged to focus on the 1954 polemic rather than on a (literary) analysis of the text of *Le Passé simple* itself. While Harrison's argument remains generally convincing, it is clear that the reception of a text like *Le Passé simple* has to be considered as part of its meaning; its 'literarity' cannot ultimately be dissociated from the surrounding 'noise' it provoked on publication. The yo-yo effect described by Chraïbi's recantation and disavowal of the book (something he later publicly admitted to regretting) demonstrates a certain amount of disarray. In a very real sense, then, the polemic itself 'determined' Chraïbi's career in quite a direct way. From the very outset of his career as a writer Chraïbi could never be anything but acutely conscious of the position from which he was writing, of the ambiguities inherent in that position and of the importance of the real or imagined persona of the author he was perceived to be. The issue is partly that a segment of his readership took him to be an 'authentic voice', a representative spokesperson for his country of origin, and his work was judged accordingly. But a far more complex issue for 'Chraïbi the writer' to resolve, in the aftermath of the polemic, was how to counter such stereotyping and work at developing 'the authentic voice' of Driss Chraïbi.

The most marked characteristic of the dominant voice in *Le Passé simple*, that of the young narrator Driss Ferdi, is one of revolt ('Ma religion était la révolte' [Revolt was my religion], he claims at one point. (p. 78)). The revolt is directed in the first instance against the authority of his father, 'le Seigneur', and through him against the entire social structure together with the ideological, economic and spiritual foundations on which that authority rests. Yet it is also a voice distinguished by self-loathing and with pronounced sado-masochistic overtones. The hatred of the father is partly directed back against the self in a form of schizophrenic doubling. The duality of Driss's education, for example, is not portrayed as an enrichment but as providing two sources for disgust, both directed against the self. He is particularly scathing about the Koranic school: 'ces écoles servent de cours tacites de pédérastie appliquée avec ou sans le concours de l'honorable maître d'école' (p. 39), [these schools provide tacit training in applied pederasty with or without the involvement of the honourable schoolmaster], while the French school he subsequently attends serves only to confuse and alienate him:

> Comme une chienne de vie, je poussais devant moi le poids d'une civilisation. Que je n'avais pas demandée. Dont j'étais fier. Et qui me faisait étranger dans cette ville d'où j'étais issu.   (p. 78)

> [Like a dog's life, I was pushing along in front of me the weight of a civilisation. That I had never asked for. That I was proud of. And that made me a foreigner in this town that I had been born in.]

The choppy, disjointed style of the text reflects the emotional turmoil of the narrator who displays all the symptoms of adolescent anguish as he lashes out at the repressive, stifling controls imposed by the family (symbol of the patri-archal nature of Moroccan society as a whole), the spiritual void that religious observance merely serves to mask, the scandalous treatment of women, the petrified structures of social interaction, and the supposed benefits offered by Western culture.

As Driss, the cultural hybrid, prepares to begin his French dissertation for the *baccalauréat* he realises that the proposed subject 'Liberté, Egalité, Fraternité' can only be treated as a form of symbiosis: 'symbiose de mon rejet de l'Orient et du scepticisme que fait naître en moi l'Occident' (p. 205) [symbiosis of my rejection of the East and of the scepticism that the West has nurtured in me]. Whether the anger is inwardly or outwardly directed, it is clear that Driss's revolt is a personal matter. However much it involves social critique and even a critique of power relations within the family (and society) it cannot easily be qualified as political. The real conflict that animates Driss is that between modernity and tradition. The title of the book alludes to the homogenised, monolithic nature of the 'Simple Past', the unassailable single tradition that blocks the horizon for Driss and, in his view, for the whole of Moroccan society. His revolt is a revolt against the dead hand of the past and the overarching dilemma he faces, couched here in a very individualised drama, is how to modernise and revitalise a moribund culture without falling under the sway of the false gods of Western civilisation and its soulless, technological, utilitarian, mechanistic values. In later works, the scepticism about Western civilisation's proposed way out of the impasse will grow and, in texts like *La Mère du printemps* (1982) and *Naissance à l'aube* (1986), Chraïbi looks to an earlier symbiotic moment for solutions: that of the clash between sedentary Berber tribes and proselytising Islam. Chraïbi's *œuvre* can thus be seen as centred on the human dilemma of a search for renewal located within quite specific social and cultural settings.

The tone that dominates *Le Monde à côté*, the autobiographical text Chraïbi published in 2001, is one of mild irony suffused with humour. In casting a retrospective eye over his life from the moment of his arrival in France in 1945 to the 'present' the critique he offers is satirical rather than impassioned. He is not reconciled to the injustices and suffering which the modern world continues to endorse and perpetuate, but the author/persona discernible behind the narrative is a much travelled, much experienced, rather disillusioned and worldly wise observer who is prepared to name the ills he denounces but never get overly excited about them. The contrast with the tone of *Le Passé simple* could hardly be starker. As he dreamily muses on the point of it all, Chraïbi is recalled to reality (and the riverbank where he is idly dreaming) by his wife who has noticed that he has a fish on the end of his line:

> Que valait la civilisation occidentale? Combien de mots et de morts avait-elle coûté dans d'autres pays qui avaient une autre civilisation? N'était-elle qu'une affirmation issue du doute et barricadée par les frontières de l'incompréhension? Pourquoi continuer d'écrire et dans quel but et vers quel monde? Là-bas, sur l'autre rive, les frontières étaient tout aussi imperméables à la circulation des idées . . .
> – Driss, Driss . . . Le bouchon! . . .   (pp. 156–8)

> [What was Western civilisation worth? How many words and how many deaths had it cost in other countries with other civilisations? Was it anything more than a statement made from a position of doubt and barricaded in on itself by the boundaries of incomprehension? Why carry on writing and to what purpose and in order to reach out to what sort of world? Over there on the other bank, the boundaries to the circulation of ideas were just as impermeable . . .
> – Driss, Driss . . . The float! . . .]

The description of trivial details of everyday life that had been deployed in the 1950s as a way of introducing (metropolitan) readers to the unfamiliar world of the Maghreb is used quite consciously here to create an effect of bathos. A type of reflection that could become intolerable (and which is still linked to the unresolved question of how to position oneself with regard to the reader) is defused by an appeal to humour and the brutal intrusion of everyday concerns.

This riverbank scene functions in much the same way as the whole series of relatively light-hearted novels that Chraïbi began to publish from 1981 onwards which have as their central character the Moroccan policeman, l'Inspecteur Ali. *Une Enquête au pays* (1981) was followed by *L'Inspecteur Ali* (1991), *L'Inspecteur Ali à Trinity College* (1996), *L'Inspecteur Ali et la C.I.A.* (1997) and *L'Homme qui venait du passé* (2004). On a number of levels Ali functions as Chraïbi's alibi. Within the texts, Ali can be read as a Moroccan man of the people: his appetites and zest for life are irrepressible; he is quick-witted, ironic and capable of great cunning. He displays a healthy contempt for authority and pomposity. He is painfully aware of his own weaknesses and failings but his humour and good spirits never allow him to take them (or those of his fellow men) too seriously. In short, Ali is a lucid observer of the world in which he evolves but he is above all a survivor. No truth is so important that Ali would not deny it in order to live to tell the tale. And yet along the way, as he pursues the various investigations Chraïbi invents for him, he also manages to give voice to an inordinate number of home truths about Moroccan society as well as about the Islamic and wider world in general. At one point in *L'Inspecteur Ali et la C.I.A.* Ali expatiates on Andalusian music:

> La vraie de vraie, telle qu'on la jouait à Cordoue ou à Grenade, dans l'Andalousie musulmane. Ah! ce que j'aurais voulu vivre à cette époque-là! C'était l'âge d'or. Tous faisaient partie intégrante de la communauté: arabes, juifs, berbères, chrétiens, païens. Et puis les Arabes se sont montrés ce qu'ils sont encore de nos jours: avides, voraces, antidémocratiques dans l'âme . . . Depuis lors, les Arabes n'ont eu d'autre avenir que leur passé. (p. 165)

> [The real thing, the way they used to play it in Cordoba or in Grenada, in Islamic Andalusia. Ah! how I would love to have lived at that time! It was the golden age. Everyone was an integral part of the community: Arabs, Jews, Berbers, Christians, pagans. And then the Arabs showed themselves to be what they still are today: greedy, voracious, undemocratic to the core of their being . . . Since then, Arabs have had no other future than their own past.]

The vision of a harmonious and tolerant Islamic community is evoked as a prelude to the criticism of the failings of modern Islam. Reprimanded by his superior for voicing such views, Ali replies: 'Mon enquête ne concerne pas seulement l'intrigue policière. Elle concerne aussi nous autres.' (p. 166) [My investigation is not just about the police inquiry. It's also about us too.] For Ali, his job as a policeman is synonymous with his 'job' as a human being: both involve being open to new ideas and self-enrichment.

Ali's investigations are a front for Chraïbi's own task of exposing the skeletons in the cupboard of modern (particularly Islamic) society. But the alibi Ali provides also functions on a macroscopic level: it allows Chraïbi to assume a position as author where issues to do with his own role as spokesman, or more accurately as critic, are deproblematised. The comic mode does not prevent Chraïbi from systematically deconstructing the weight of the past in Islamic culture or the myth of progress in Western culture. On the contrary, it allows him to pursue his own investigation into the nature of the values we claim as the basis of our civilisation.

Albert Memmi (Tunisia, 1920–)

It was the Tunisian born writer and academic Albert Memmi who first coined the expression 'generation of 1952' and he was himself one of the number of writers who first gave expression to an indigenous Maghrebi voice through the medium of French. Memmi has the distinction of being equally well known for his academic writings on various aspects of the sociology of oppression (notably, *Portrait du colonisé* précédé du *Portrait du colonisateur* (1995) [1957], *Portrait d'un Juif* (1962) and *L'Homme dominé* (1968) as he is for his 'literary' writings which include five novels, an autobiographical narrative entitled *Le Nomade immobile* (2000), and a collection of poetry. There is not a little irony in the fact that it was Memmi who predicted that Maghrebi literature in French was doomed to 'die young', while along with other writers of his generation, such as Dib and Chraïbi, he has continued to publish into the third millennium and thereby help to ensure its longevity. Perhaps the most striking feature of Memmi's output, seen as a body of work, is its remarkable coherence. The fictional narratives explore the same material that the sociological essays and portraits deal with in rather more abstract and analytical ways. It could be said that the latter grow out of the former and that by delving into the conflicting components of his own identity as a Jewish Tunisian (possibly of Berber, possibly of Roman origin) Memmi opened an archive that would provide a framework for later studies of relationships of domination, dependence and various categories of oppression. It is with some justification that he claimed 'La même idée . . . court à travers mon œuvre littéraire et mon travail de professeur.'[31] [The same idea . . . runs through both my literary work and my work as a teacher.]

The fictions he wrote at the beginning of his career, *La Statue de sel* (1953) and *Agar* (1955) in particular, are among the first writings in Maghrebi literature to explore the themes associated with 'acculturation': the psychological, social and cultural conflicts that arise when individuals affectively transfer from one cultural system to another. The name of the young protagonist/narrator of *La Statue de sel*, Mordekhaï Alexandre Benillouche, is itself indicative of a cultural heritage that can be split into at least three components (Jewish, European and Berber), each of which he sees as 'over-determining' his status and sense of identity. His attempts to imagine glorious antecedents through one or other of the three elements all founder on the contradictions that spring from their very juxtaposition, but also on the reality of his present status and condition:

> Toujours je me retrouverai Alexandre Mordekhaï, Alexandre
> Benillouche, indigène dans un pays de colonisation, juif dans un univers
> antisémite, Africain dans un monde où triomphe l'Europe . . . Comment
> faire une synthèse, polie comme un son de flûte, de tant de disparités?
>
> (p. 109)

> [I shall always remain Alexandre Mordekhaï, Alexandre Benillouche, a
> native in a colonised country, a Jew in an antisemitic universe, an African
> in a world dominated by Europe . . . How can you produce a synthesis,
> as polished as the sound of a flute, from so many disparate elements?]

Only in terms of history can the diversity be poeticised and seen as worthy of celebration, as on the occasion when he considers it as being inscribed in the very fabric of the town in which he was born: 'Phéniciens, Romains, Vandales, Byzantins, Berbères, Arabes, Espagnols, Turcs, Italiens, Français . . . Cinq cents pas de promenade et l'on change de civilisation.' (p. 110) [Phoenicians, Romans, Vandals, Byzantines, Berbers, Arabs, Spaniards, Turks, Italians, French . . . Walk five hundred yards and you change civilisation.] But in terms of the 'present' and his own developing personality, there is no single element of his make-up that does not feed the sense of alienation, referred to by Camus as 'l'impossibilité d'être quoi que ce soit de précis'[32] [the impossiblity of being anything at all with any precision].

La Statue de sel resembles all the later novels written by Memmi in that it is a fiction that can easily be associated with autobiographical material. But what is striking about this first novel is that the issue of identity is explored through the protagonist's own awakening consciousness of the world into which he has been born. It is at least as much a novel about childhood and the child's developing sense of identity as it is a postcolonial novel about cultural hybridity and cultural roots/routes. Alexandre opts (as Memmi himself had opted) for an active pursuit of acculturation: competence in French language and knowledge of French culture are both the means and the end of the process in which he is engaged and which will set him at odds with other aspects of his personality and his family context. His relationship with language is particularly important. Language and culture are embedded the one within the other in such complex ways that the individual's sense of being in the world is inextricably linked to the language through which the world is apprehended. He comments at one point, 'loin d'être un outil transparent, le langage participait directement des choses, en avait la densité' (p. 45) [far from being a transparent tool, language participated directly in the world of things and had their density]. Hence opting for French is ultimately, for Alexandre, equivalent to opting for a certain method of inhabiting the world. Committing to the language is synonymous with a commitment to the culture freighted by that language and Alexandre intuitively realises that certain aspects of his personality may only be fulfilled through acculturation to French: 'J'essayais de prononcer une langue qui n'était pas la mienne, qui peut-être ne le sera jamais complètement, et pourtant m'est indispensable à la conquête de toutes mes dimensions.' (p. 120) [I was trying to express myself in a language that wasn't my own, that perhaps will never completely be mine, and yet which is indispensable to me as I try to realise my full potential.] Herein lies the essence of his personal drama. The commitment to French language and culture is a choice with consciously existential dimensions. It makes his sense of his own identity a locus for cultural conflict, turning his life into a permanent paradox: 'Les deux parties de mon être parlaient chacune une langue différente et jamais ne se comprendraient.' (p. 247) [The two parts of my being each spoke a different language and would never understand each other.]

Alexandre's commitment to French sets him apart from his own family, the Jewish community and the mass of uneducated (colonised) Tunisian people. But by way of compensation for these 'losses' there is no guarantee of entry to any identifiable group. When war comes to Tunisia he altruistically volunteers to be shipped off to the prison camp only to be sidelined by his (mainly Arab) fellow prisoners on account of his middle-class, Jewish origins. When he finally escapes the camp and seeks to volunteer for military action with the Free French forces he is advised not to sign up under his own Jewish-sounding name but to sign as 'Mohamed' instead. Alexandre's rejection of his own cultural origins (African, colonised, Jewish) leaves him bereft and isolated at the novel's close. The harsh reality is that solidarity has been systematically refused by those to whom he himself has made a personal commitment. In miniature this is a dramatised version of the broken promise of French assimilationist colonial policy: Alexandre commits to French 'civilisation' only to discover that the sacrifices such a commitment entails (and indeed the commitment itself) are of no interest to anyone. He sums up his position thus:

> Moi je suis mal à l'aise dans mon pays natal et n'en connais pas d'autre, ma culture est d'emprunt et ma langue maternelle infirme, je n'ai plus de croyances, de religion, de traditions et j'ai honte de ce qui en eux résiste au fond de moi . . . je suis de culture française mais Tunisien . . . je suis Tunisien mais juif, c'est-à-dire politiquement, socialement exclu . . . juif mais ayant rompu avec la religion juive et le ghetto, ignorant de la culture juive . . . je suis pauvre enfin et j'ai ardemment désiré d'en finir avec la pauvreté . . .   (p. 364)

> [Personally I am ill at ease in my native land and yet I know no other, mine is a borrowed culture and my mother tongue is a sorry thing, I no longer hold any beliefs, have no religion, follow no traditions and I am ashamed of the residual pull these exert upon me . . . I am French by culture but a Tunisian . . . I am a Tunisian by birth but a Jew, that is, someone who is politically and socially marginalised . . . a Jew but because I have abandoned the Jewish religion and left the ghetto I am ignorant about Jewish culture . . . and last of all I am poor and I had passionately longed to have done with poverty . . .]

In *La Statue de sel* the character of Alexandre is, in a sense, the key *setting* of the novel since all the contradictions and conflicts are internalised and located within his person. Analysing and representing his fragmented identity and his nostalgia for an unproblematic sense of belonging involve an ongoing act of detailed introspection. Alexandre treats himself and his experiences as a spectacle. The protagonist's flight to Argentina at the end of the novel may be a mere device to bring a term to this introspection, but it is a flight in a forward direction, a 'fuite en avant'; looking backwards, as the novel's title suggests, is a sterile act.

Retrospection is nevertheless embedded within Memmi's second novel, *Agar*, which recounts the breakdown of a marriage between a couple of mixed race. The cultural conflicts and contradictions that were internalised in the person of Alexandre in the earlier novel are represented here through the difficulties experienced by the couple, a young Tunisian doctor who returns to set up practice in his native country with his French wife, Marie. As the hero learns to see (and re-evaluate) himself, his family and his native land through the increasingly critical gaze of his wife, Marie for her part finds it ever more impossible to overcome her own 'culture shock' and adapt to the varying demands made upon her. Like *La Statue de sel, Agar* is the chronicle of a failed attempt at integration and assimilation. Memmi's own claim that it somehow outlines the conditions in which a kind of liberation may be be achieved is more an indication of how the novel might potentially be used by some of its readers than an accurate description of the novel's subject.[33] The isolation that characterises the experience of both these protagonists is also a fundamental theme of the later novels, *Le Désert* (1977) and *Le Pharaon* (1988), where the quest for a sense of identity is associated with an ultimately existential project. However, before such a project could be embarked upon, Memmi first needed to deconstruct the very notion of identity. This would seem to be his purpose in the intervening novel, the far more complexly structured *Le Scorpion* (1969) in which the formal fragmentation of the text mirrors a destabilising absence of certainty about truth and falsehood in general. As the narrator of 'Le tapis' (one of the narratives embedded in the novel) remarks, 'demander à un écrivain d'écrire l'Histoire! Savent-ils seulement où est la vérité où est le mensonge?' (p. 309) [ask a writer to write History! Do they so much as know where truth and falsehood lie?]

Rachid Boudjedra (Algeria, 1941–)

The publication of Rachid Boudjedra's first novel *La Répudiation* (1969) was greeted with much the same sort of furore as that which had greeted Chraïbi's *Le Passé simple* almost a generation earlier. Like the earlier text it performs a virulent critique of the social and, by extension, political mores of the times, and it does so by attacking the patriarchal authority figure, the father, through a narrative that explores family relationships. In the case of *La Répudiation*, however, a consciously psychoanalytical purpose can be discerned both in the way Boudjedra structures the novel and in the hallucinatory quality of much of the writing. Here, as is frequently the case in subsequent novels, Boudjedra eschews realist techniques of narration preferring to nag away at key obsessions, a technique that provides the writing with its underlying energy and coherence. The narration itself is staged as a self-conscious act linking the narrator, Rachid, to the French woman, Céline, an ambiguous figure whose role and status are never absolutely clear. She appears to be cast at different times in the roles of lover, concubine, nurse or carer. The difficulty experienced by the reader in deciding whether she fills one or more of these roles (singly or concurrently) is compounded by Rachid's unreliable status as narrator/character. He himself is variously cast as psychiatric patient, lover and political prisoner, while the status of his narrative (why is he speaking and to whom?) can consequently be understood in many different ways. Is Rachid undergoing psychoanalysis? Is he being tortured? Is he dreaming aloud to his mistress? The delirious quality of much of his narrative is at different times compatible with any (and all) of these various reading hypotheses.

Rachid's narrative is fundamentally iconoclastic. The attack on the father is channelled through Rachid's childhood memories of the repudiation of his mother when Si Zoubir (the father) decides to take a younger wife. This despicable act of selfishness is sanctioned by Islamic religion and therefore by society as a whole. Rachid is appalled by this act and the uncritical acceptance of it by the family and the wider bourgeois milieu in which he lives. He sees the latter as a male conspiracy against women, yet a conspiracy in which the women are themselves largely complicit by virtue of their passive acceptance of the injustices they collectively suffer:

> Les salauds prolifèrent dans la ville mais personne ne s'occupe de ce mal qui ravage les femmes de la cité . . . Ma mère fait partie de ce lot des femmes sans hommes . . . Dans certains quartiers, il n'y a que des hommes en vadrouille qui crachent dans leur mouchoir quand ils veulent montrer qu'ils sont civilisés, prennent le tramway en marche, se saoulent dans les quartiers siciliens et, pour mieux jouir, donnent à leurs femmes des prénoms de putains . . . Les cafés sont pleins à craquer. Chaque tasse de café est une négation de la femme.   (p. 39)

> [These bastards are everywhere in the city but no one cares about the harm they wreak upon the women in the place . . . My mother is one of this group of women without men . . . In some neighbourhoods, all you see is men on the lookout, they spit into their handkerchieves to show how civilised they are, they jump onto moving trams, get drunk in the Sicilian bars and, for added excitement, address their wives by names whores use . . . The cafés are full to overflowing. Every single cup of coffee is a negation of women.]

Ideologically, then, the novel is openly hostile to a range of social practices. Key among these is the oppressive treatment of women, from which so many other unacceptable, often codified, types of behaviour follow: the hypocrisy and double standards of male behaviour, the widespread sexual repression, the misappropriation of religious doctrine to serve male interests, the general prevalence of superstition and charlatanism as popular 'coping' mechanisms. For Boudjedra, the evil that poisons all family and social interaction stems from the oppression of women. Women are controlled, guarded and used by men in dehumanising relationships that are justified by an appeal to the notion that male authority is inviolable and divinely sanctioned.

Yet to isolate the ideological dimension of the trauma that Rachid's child-hood represents would be to betray Boudjedra's far more complex and shocking treatment of the ills of Algerian society. In fact Boudjedra sees the political and sexual as interwoven and inseparable: the links across from a psychological to a political frame of reference are numerous and mutually enriching. Rachid's oedipal revolt against his father, his longing to kill him, his real or imagined sexual relationship with Si Zoubir's young wife, Zoubidar (herself a substitute figure for Rachid's repudiated mother), his incestuous rape of his half-sister Leila, all provide a catalogue of destructive erotic fantasies which simulta-neously serve to express Rachid's political revolt against a social order that conflates men, adults in general and all forms of politico-religious authority into a single target for his hatred. Indeed, the overtly political counterpart of the family is the 'Clan', the name given to the political party that, in the closing section of the novel, imprisons Rachid as surely as his family ever had. In this section there are frequent slippages between the narrative focused on family relations and the narrative to be read as an account of the political life of the nation.

While Rachid's narrativisation of the various horrors he has perpetrated or imagined suggests that he is undergoing a type of psychoanalytic therapy (or political interrogation), the novel as a whole may be seen as an attempt by Boudjedra to liberate the national psyche by openly articulating the collective 'heart of darkness': the generalised male 'repudiation' of women and all the psychological and sexual blockages and neuroses that flow from it. Looking back on *La Répudiation* some twenty five years after its publication, Boudjedra wrote: 'Dans mon premier roman publié en 1969, je disais déjà que le peuple algérien avait besoin d'une psychanalyse, d'une thérapie, pour que nous puis-sions enfin exprimer le non-dit, c'est-à-dire nous-mêmes.'[34] [In my first novel published in 1969, I was already saying that the Algerian people were in need of psychoanalysis, a form of therapy, so that we can finally express all the things we repress, that is to say, ourselves.] Boudjedra's own revolt is linked to this deeper purpose which he referred to in a recent debate as a quest to break down the taboos of Algerian society, in particular those of sex, religion and politics: 'j'ai seulement cherché à faire exploser les tabous, violenter le texte littéraire et introduire la sexualité et l'érotisme dans la littérature arabe contemporaine'[35] [all I have tried to do is explode taboos, do violence to the literary text and introduce sexuality and eroticism into contemporary Arab literature].

The complex staging of the narrative act to be found in *La Répudiation* is itself indicative of the importance that Boudjedra attaches to both structure and the free play of language. As a great admirer of the techniques explored by the French 'nouveau roman', Boudjedra would readily accept the view that the novel recounts the 'adventure of writing' rather than 'the writing of an adventure'.

The ostensible subject matter of the narrative, the story line, is for Boudjedra little more than a pretext for a formalist-inspired elaboration of the material it contains: 'Quand je lis un roman, l'histoire m'intéresse peu finalement, bien que j'aime beaucoup les histoires mais je préfère les écouter . . . dans les cafés, dans les bars, en ville, dans la rue. Mais pas sur le papier!'[36] [When I read a novel the storyline holds little interest for me in the long run, even though I like stories a lot, although I do prefer to listen to them . . . in cafés, in bars, in town, in the street. But not on paper!] Elsewhere, he refers to the notion of 'storyline' in terms of the novel's theme, which he sees as nothing more than a pretext for the real work of the writer: 'Dans le roman, la thématique n'est qu'un prétexte, seule compte la technique de l'écriture où la subjectivité joue un rôle central.'[37] [In the novel, the chosen theme is only an excuse, all that really matters are the technical aspects of the writing where subjectivity plays a central role.] This 'formalist' conception of the writer's role foregrounds the poetic potential of linguistic creativity and linguistic play as an end in itself. Boudjedra often quotes the thirteenth-century Soufi mystic Ibn Arabi's assertion that the physical act of writing is a sexual act, in support of his own view that writing is first and foremost a form of 'jouissance' [orgasm].

These formalist aspects of his technique are possibly more apparent in novels like *Topographie idéale pour une aggression caractérisée* (1975) and *L'Escargot entêté* (1977) than they are in *La Répudiation* or *L'Insolation* (1972). Both of the earlier novels display a preoccupation with psychotherapeutic narration and the play of language is embroiled with an exploratory journey through the internal labyrinthine structures of the human mind. In both of the later novels the city replaces the human mind as the locus for obsession-ridden journeys. In *Topographie* the metaphor of the labyrinth takes the very concrete form of the corridors and tunnels of the Paris metro in which a North African immigrant wanders back and forth until he meets his death at the hands of a gang of racist youths. In order to function in the obsessively repetitive universe of the metro a set of semiotic skills is required that the protagonist has not mastered. His failure to understand the way this alien system of signs and cultural references operates leads him ineluctably to his death. In *L'Escargot entêté*, the same obsessions with labyrinthine underground tunnels and systems of encoding information fascinate the narrator, a town planner who believes he is being followed by a snail. For both protagonists, violence and madness lurk on the confines of the worlds they are unsuccessfully intent on deciphering.

For all Boudjedra's professed interest in form, structure and the technical aspects of writing, his impact has always been highly significant in political terms. The various 'pretexts' for writing he has chosen to exploit thematically have invariably had a potential for subversion within them as he systematically works against the grain of political and religious conformity and accepted values. His early works did not exclude the nationalist political circles of post-independence Algeria from his sociopolitical critique: the 'Clan' of *La Répudiation* is a thinly disguised reference to the FLN and the stranglehold it exerted on Algerian political life in the years following the war. His translation of *L'Insolation* into Arabic in the early 1980s led to the issuing of a *fatwa* against him and later death threats were issued by the islamic fundamentalists of the Front Islamique du Salut (FIS) whom he subjected to an excoriating attack in *FIS de la Haine* (1992), an attack which has been echoed in some of his more recent non-fictional and fictional work, such as *Lettres Algériennes* (1995) and *Timimoun* (1994), where references to FIS-inspired atrocities punctuate the narrative. His decision to publish mainly in Arabic since the mid 1980s, to continue to live and work in Algeria despite the threats against his life and despite the assassination of many of his friends and fellow intellectuals throughout the 1990s, and his resolve to continue to argue against the particular forms taken by Islamic political correctness of whatever persuasion, make him something of an eternal dissident in political terms and a distinctive voice in contemporary Maghrebi literature.

Assia Djebar (Algeria, 1936–)

When Albert Memmi evoked his protagonist's triple cultural heritage in *La Statue de sel* it was in order to expatiate on the cultural impasse into which it had led Alexandre: the experience of simultaneously belonging to several cultures amounted, affectively and effectively, to a rejection by all three. His experience of acculturation was as a victim of a process marked by the inequalities of the colonial relationship and the lop-sided dynamics of power it presupposed. In October 2000, in an acceptance speech she made on the occasion of the award of the Prix de la Paix, Assia Djebar referred to her own triple linguistic inheritance: French, the language of the former colonisers in which she writes and thinks; Arabic, her mother tongue in which she loves, suffers and, on occasion, prays; and Berber, the ancestral tongue which she does not speak but which is present within her as the language of resistance and refusal:

> Langue, dirais-je, de l'irréductibilité . . . langue de la première origine [qui] se cabre, et vibre en vous, en des circonstances où le pouvoir trop lourd d'un Etat, d'une religion, ou d'une évidente oppression ont tout fait pour l'effacer, elle, cette première langue . . . c'est cette permanence du 'non' intérieur que j'entends en moi, dans une forme et un son berbères, et qui m'apparaît comme le socle même de ma personnalité ou de ma durée littéraire.[38]

[The language, I would say, of what is irreducible in me . . . the language of my first origins (that) rears up and resonates within me in circumstances when the excessive power of a state, of a religion, or of some obvious form of oppression have done their utmost to wipe it out, this first language . . . corresponds to the permanence of the internal 'No' I hear inside me, adopting the form and the sounds of Berber speech, and which seems to me to be the very foundation of my personality or of what is lasting in my writing.]

This comment on the composite elements of her 'linguistic identity' provides two quite different insights into Djebar's complexity. Firstly, the emphasis on the different functions performed by each language suggests a mobility and indeterminateness that contrasts sharply with the nostalgia for a unified personality and sense of belonging to be found in Memmi. Djebar has no such nostalgia for unity; her approach is to work at the layered, composite material that her individuality and her history amount to: interrogating her own subjectivity, as a woman, as an Algerian and as a member of a community that continues to be shaped and traversed by various historical forces and influences. Secondly, this comment says a great deal about the nature of her 'political' commitment, how the voice of resistance against oppression that 'vibrates' within her echoes and re-echoes a refusal to bow before certain forms of power. Her politics has no platform, no programme, no discernible ideological content as such; yet her work has always had political relevance and commitment.

As is well known, her early work, particularly *La Soif* (1957), met with uncomprehending criticism from a readership largely focused on the Algerian war and unreceptive to the novel's account of the sexual awakening of its protagonist. In the fullness of time, Abdelkébir Khatibi would point out that even this first novel had revolutionary elements: 'A-t-on vraiment compris que la découverte du corps pour le personnage de *La Soif* est aussi une révolution importante?'[39] [Has it really been understood that the discovery of her own body, for the protagonist of *La Soif,* is also an important revolution?] But at the time the criticism from nationalist quarters undoubtedly influenced the trajectory of her writing, as it did for others of that generation. It is against the background of a pressure to 'self-regulate' her work that she withdrew from the literary scene following *Les Alouettes naïves* (1967), and published nothing until *Femmes d'Alger dans leur appartement* appeared in 1980.

The Assia Djebar that emerged from the 'silent decade' had spent time on a cinema project which led her to travel widely, collecting the oral testimonies of Algerian peasant women, and to 'return' to her own roots in traditional Berber culture. The film that emerged from her travels, *La Nouba des femmes du mont Chenoua*, prefigures many of the preoccupations of later work, as Réda Bensmaïa's assessment, with its emphases on space and time, illustrates:

> avant d'être une exploration de la psychologie d'un ou de plusieurs personnages, *La Nouba* se présente d'abord comme un patient arpentage de *lieux féminins* (au sens géographique et rhétorique): la maison, le four, la chambre à coucher, la fenêtre, mais aussi la parole, la mémoire, le chant et le cri . . . il est d'abord question d'esquisser un tracé, une ligne de fuite, une carte . . . on est en train d'essayer d'explorer un nouveau rapport au temps, à la mémoire, aux différents lieux que les femmes ont habité ou investi [sic] de tout temps.[40]

> [rather than offering an exploration of the psychology of one or more characters, *La Nouba* comes across first and foremost as a patient surveying of *female spaces* (in both a geographical and rhetorical sense): the house, the baking-room, the bedroom, the window, but also words, memory and the cry . . . we are trying to explore a new relationship to time, to recollection, to the different spaces that women have inhabited or invested from time immemorial.]

These complex interconnections are not *themes* of Djebar's work but recurring preoccupations that have as much to do with method as they do 'content'. The film project can thus be seen as seminal for Djebar in that it activated a number of lines of investigation that resonate throughout her later literary works.

Foremost among these is the constant self-consciousness she displays with regard to the linguistic medium she is using. On one level this is expressed through her own sense of ambivalence with regard to the French language, the gift ('don d'amour') handed down by her father that she refers to at the end of *L'Amour, la fantasia* (1985) as the 'tunic of Nessus' (the poisoned garment inadvertently given to Hercules by his wife). In this text she considers French to be an arid tool, a 'langue marâtre' [step-motherly language] (by way of contrast with the 'langue-mère disparue' [vanished mother tongue]) and in writing her autobiography in the language of the 'other side' she is conscious of producing a mere fiction: 'L'autobiographie pratiquée dans la langue adverse se tisse comme fiction . . . Croyant "me parcourir", je ne fais que choisir un autre voile. Voulant, à chaque pas, parvenir à la transparence, je m'engloutis dans l'anonymat des aïeules!' (p. 302) [Autobiography written in the language of the other weaves itself into being as a fiction . . . Believing that I am 'running through my life', all I am really doing is cloaking myself in another veil. Wishing, with each step, to achieve transparency, I sink deeper and deeper into the anonymity of my female forebears!'] The oral roots of French derive the particular flavour they hold for Djebar from the one-sided relationship imposed by colonisation:

Langue installée dans l'opacité d'hier, dépouille prise à celui avec lequel
ne s'échangeait aucune parole d'amour . . . Le verbe français qui hier
était clamé, ne l'était trop souvent qu'en prétoire, par des juges et des
condamnés. Mots de revendication, de procédure, de violence, voici la
source orale de ce français des colonisés.   (p. 300)

[Language ensconced in the opaqueness of yesteryear, all that remains
of an affair with a partner with whom no word of love was ever
exchanged . . . The French tongue, that in former times was loudly
proclaimed, was all too often spoken only in courtrooms by judges and
those being judged. Words expressing demands, procedures, violence,
these are the oral roots of the French learned by those who were
colonised.]

By contrast, the oral roots that she can tap into when working through Arabic
and Berber voices allow her to reconnect with a history that has been doubly
silenced, firstly by the French colonisers and secondly by the panoply of constraints imposed upon women by patriarchal Algerian culture. The notion that
women have experienced a 'double colonisation' is undoubtedly one of Djebar's motivating convictions, yet the strategies she adopts in response to this
oppression are discursive rather than directly political. The form of resistance
that she relentlessly pursues through her writing involves immersing herself in
the discourses of the past, particularly those conveyed by female voices, often
speaking from beyond the grave, and which alone offer the possibility of nego-
tiating a way out of the impasse of petrified relationships that, in her view,
characterise modern-day Algeria.

   In 'Les morts parlent' (one of the texts in *Femmes d'Alger dans leur appartement*), for example, the voice of the aged Yemma Hadda lives on after her death
through those who have *listened* to her, notably Aïcha, the repudiated niece
whom she has taken into her household, and Saïd, the faithful retainer from
her native village who, from a distance, has continued to serve her into old
age. Hadda represents the 'authentic past', a harsh unromanticised version of
Algerian cultural traditions ('la tristesse, la noblesse aussi et son impitoyable
austérité', p. 122 [sadness, nobility too and its pitiless austerity]), while her
absent grandson, Hassan, who is away fighting with the resistance, belongs to
a forward-looking generation intent on building a new Algeria. Saïd is the link
in the chain of transmission through which Hadda seeks to communicate with
her absent grandson. Sensing that she will die before his return, she tells Saïd all
that she feels Hassan will need to know about a whole range of family matters:
'Tu lui diras . . . tu lui diras' (p. 121) [You'll tell him . . . you'll tell him], she
repeats. But the Hassan who returns from the war just in time to arrange his

grandmother's funeral is tuned to a different wavelength than that of Aïcha or Saïd. As a 'war hero' he is the incarnation of a type of direct political agency that preoccupies itself with those other dead, who have fallen in combat, rather than the homely death of an aged woman. At the story's close, while Hassan makes a speech to a political meeting of some two or three thousand people, Aïcha is alone in the cemetery overlooking the town, commemorating the seventh day after Hadda's funeral. The past fails to feed into the present and this is connected to the notion that the future that Hassan is preparing to usher in has the aridity of a desert.

> Un enterrement sans histoire certes, mais voilà que la mélancolie d'une cousine pauvre [Aïcha], la rêverie d'un métayer [Saïd] dans un cortège subsistent, tandis que sur le petit-fils seul les regards témoins se concentrent. En son cœur à lui, règne une étendue aride. Pire que l'oubli.
> Or les morts parlent. La voix de la vieille murmure près de Aïcha, elle frôle de fidélité la mémoire du métayer. Qu'en perçoit l'homme vers lequel les derniers espoirs de Hadda se sont tendus? Rien.   (p. 128)

> [A burial without incident, certainly, but the dejection of a poor cousin (Aïcha), the dreams of a peasant-farmer (Saïd) linger over the funeral procession, while the eyes of all the onlookers are concentrated on the grandson alone. Within his heart an arid expanse holds sway. Worse than forgetting.
> But the dead do speak. The voice of the old woman murmurs on close to Aïcha, with faithfulness it gently touches the peasant's memory. And the man on whom Hadda had pinned all her hopes, what does he notice of these things? Nothing.]

The preoccupation with language and the archive of voices that constitutes the oral history of Algeria may be seen as the bedrock of Djebar's work. As an accomplished film director as well as a writer, however, Djebar has two different and quite distinct outlets for this material. The literary treatment that concerns us here is nevertheless paralleled by a matching preoccupation with the rhetoric of the visual image and the politics of visual agency that this implies. So in an almost methodical way, *Femmes d'Alger dans leur appartement* juxtaposes and interweaves the visual (*le regard*) and the gendered voice. The gaze and the spoken word are male-controlled and are policed as tightly as the physical spaces which women are able to occupy. Such is the isolation and marginalisation of women, even of supposedly modern, middle-class, 'liberated' women of professional status, that the strategies of 'speaking/listening' and 'seeing' are proposed as mutually supporting, radically subversive strategies of resistance. Sarah in *Femmes d'Alger dans leur appartement* sums it up thus:

– Je ne vois pour nous aucune autre issue que par cette rencontre: une femme qui parle devant une autre qui regarde, celle qui parle raconte-t-elle l'autre aux yeux dévorants, à la mémoire noire ou décrit-elle sa propre nuit, avec des mots torches et des bougies dont la cire fond trop vite? Celle qui regarde, est-ce à force d'écouter, d'écouter et de se rappeler qu'elle finit par se voir elle-même, avec son propre regard, sans voile enfin . . .   (p. 57)

[– As for us, I can see no other way out than through this eventuality: a woman is speaking in front of another woman who is watching, is the woman speaking telling the story of the other woman with the hungry eyes, the black memory, or is she describing her own dark night, with words that shine like torches and like candles whose wax is melting away too quickly? Is it by dint of listening, of listening and remembering, that the woman who is watching ends up seeing herself through her own eyes, without a veil at last . . .]

and:

– Je ne vois pour les femmes arabes qu'un seul moyen de tout débloquer: parler, parler sans cesse d'hier et d'aujourd'hui, parler entre nous, dans tous les gynécées, les traditionnels et ceux des H.L.M. Parler entre nous et regarder. Regarder dehors, regarder hors des murs et des prisons! . . . La femme-regard et la femme-voix . . .   (pp. 60–1)

[– I can see only one way out of the impasse for Arab women: talking, talking endlessly about the past and the present, talking among ourselves, in the women's quarters, both in traditional homes and in apartment blocks. Talking among ourselves and looking. Looking outside, looking beyond the walls and the prisons! . . . Woman-as-watcher and woman-as-voice.]

Djebar's focus on the gaze and the female voice as crucial sites where questions of agency can be examined translates into a two-pronged attack: it contributes to a feminist critique at the same time as it opens up a space for a far more general debate about power relations in a postcolonial Algerian cultural setting. In this respect her critique is neither simplistically feminist nor simplistically postcolonial. It marshalls the dynamics of both feminist and postcolonial forms of resistance by constantly locating and relocating within an individual and collective, always specific, historical setting. Nowhere is this more in evidence perhaps than in the most autobiographical of her 'novels', *L'Amour, la fantasia*. If Djebar is invariably at pains to historicise her work, in this text she does so by alternating an autobiographical discourse with a 'historical' discourse that is itself made up of elements that 'official' historical accounts often disdain:

eye-witness accounts, personal memories, a whole series of voiced 'superim-positions' that give the novel, in Donadey's words, 'a palimpsestic structure'.[41] *L'Amour, la fantasia* dramatises a series of the key 'moments' in colonial history, from the 1830 invasion onwards, through the slow, often barbaric, conquest of Algeria to the War of Independence, bringing out the ambiguous mixture of desire and violence that Djebar identifies as characteristic of the whole process of colonial possession and domination. In simultaneously tracing her personal history she invites readings 'across' and readings 'over' her own relationship with the act of writing, with voices from her childhood, and with the French language as a medium of expression. The two series of narratives set up a lit-erary equivalent of musical counterpoint where themes are interwoven across both registers. Indeed, the third part of the text is divided into 'movements', interrupted by 'voices', 'mutterings', 'whispers' and other such interventions, described in a terminology that underscores both the musical and discursive themes.

The notion of the oral tradition (histories largely handed down through female chains of transmission) is the key historical archive to which she con-stantly returns and which she exploits in different ways in later texts such as *Loin de Médine* (1991), *Vaste est la prison* (1995) and *La Femme sans sépulture* (2002). Rather like the Martinican writer, Patrick Chamoiseau, who, in a dif-ferent context, literally recorded and transcribed the voices of market traders, using them as the material of his writing, Djebar produces narratives that tran-scribe and translate the female voices that alone are capable of telling the deep, unofficial history of Algeria. It is the weight and significance of this overarch-ing project that can sometimes leave 'Western' readers with the feeling that her feminist critique is insufficiently radical. If indeed it is softened and attenuated, it is because it is *cultural* critique rather than specifically feminist critique and yet it is through attending to the female voice and empowering the female gaze that Djebar believes a whole range of cultural and political issues can be best understood and tackled.

Hence, although elements of sociopolitical critique are omnipresent in her writings, the perspective from which such elements are approached (often in quite a literal, visual sense) and the space from which the voice enunciates its 'intervention' about them, are both foregrounded in such a way that they them-selves become implicated in the critique. The political urgency is matched by an urgency in terms of aesthetic methods and the shuttling between this twin set of demands opens up what Nicholas Harrison would no doubt consider as the space for new 'interpretation'. Indeed Harrison's reading of *Femmes d'Alger dans leur appartement* makes a crucial distinction between her frequently iron-ical treatment of patriarchy, social hypocrisy and political oppression on the one hand and, on the other, the far more subtle critique that Djebar opts to pursue, that of representing relationships 'as the fields of *interpretation* that they always are'.[42])

Tahar Ben Jelloun (Morocco, 1944–)

Like many Maghrebi writers Tahar Ben Jelloun began publishing poetry before turning to the novel. His early career was facilitated by the influential review, *Souffles*, founded by his compatriot Abdellatif Laâbi. A certain poetic lyricism and formal complexity are among the distinguishing features of many of his early writings, particularly works prior to and including *La Nuit sacrée* for which he won the Prix Goncourt in 1987. *La Réclusion solitaire* (1976), for example, draws substantially on Ben Jelloun's research in social psychiatry to present the sexually and socially dysfunctional lives of immigrant workers in France. Ben Jelloun approaches the plight of the immigrant worker from within, weaving together fragments of dreams, dialogues and more lucidly reflective insights about the nature of social exclusion and marginality. Such a subjective treatment of highly emotive issues does not so much depoliticise the text as poeticise material that is politically sensitive. The affective needs of the individual, cut off from family, friends and meaningful human contact, take centre stage, in preference to any sustained attempt to analyse the sociological or ideological dimensions of the immigrant's plight. *Moha le fou Moha le sage* (1978) is a similarly hybrid text that poeticises material with a significant sociopolitical content. The experience of exclusion and marginality is transposed from France to post-independence Morocco and embodied in the enigmatic persona of the protagonist, Moha. The space Moha occupies is primarily discursive although he does come into contact with 'realistic' characters and settings (the police, the cell of a prison/psychiatric hospital, a psychiatrist) which serve as a contrast to his own abstract and anarchic voicing of dissident views that deserve to be classified as more philosophical than overtly political. He also engages with other voices, those of the downtrodden and the oppressed, thus underscoring his own fundamentally marginal status.

The dual emphases on marginality and discursive spaces that are present in these two early examples of Ben Jelloun's work are of central importance to his most well-known novels *L'Enfant de sable* (1985) and its sequel *La Nuit sacrée*. The kernel of both novels is a narrative about a single, albeit protean, character, Ahmed/Zahra, destined by the circumstances of her birth to a life of sexual ambiguity. In *L'Enfant de sable*, Ahmed is born the eighth child in a family with no male children. The father, having decided that the baby will be a boy come what may, sets about deceiving his family and entourage as to the child's true gender. The girl grows up as a boy in a society that prefers men to women. This basic scenario provides multiple opportunities for a critique of patriarchal values, enshrined in social mores and Islamic jurisprudence. As the only 'male' child, Ahmed will inherit from the father and thereby disinherit his brothers. Since Ahmed is a female acting a male role in a male-dominated world the narrative is coloured by a permanent sense of transgression and illicit behaviour. The father's initial deception is taken up by Ahmed herself, who, despite her sexuality, assumes the gender roles and attitudes expected of young males: 'A l'école, il a appris à se battre; et il s'est battu souvent . . . Ensuite il a maltraité ses sœurs qui le craignaient. Normal! On le préparait à la succession. Il est devenu un homme.' (p. 42) [At school, he learned to fight; and he fought often . . . Then he bullied his sisters who were afraid of him. That's normal. He was being prepared to take control. He became a man.]

Ahmed's ambiguous sexual and social identity is largely presented through the words of a storyteller, at least, for the first part of the novel, until the story-teller disappears. His narrative is not, however, an authoritative unproblematic version of events. Like Ahmed's persona it is itself ambiguous, riddled with indeterminate features, subject to challenge and surmise by the audience and subject to different forms of supplement, notably from a journal containing letters Ahmed has addressed to an anonymous admirer. These latter fragments provide some of the more lucid and coherent commentaries on the complexities of Ahmed's situation and the insights it provides into everyday realities:

> La grande, l'immense épreuve que je vis n'a de sens qu'en dehors de ces petits schémas psychologiques qui prétendent savoir et expliquer pourquoi une femme est une femme et un homme est un homme. Sachez, ami, que la famille, telle qu'elle existe dans nos pays, avec le père tout-puissant et les femmes reléguées à la domesticité avec une parcelle d'autorité que leur laisse le mâle, la famille, je la répudie . . .   (p. 89)

> [The huge, the immense ordeal that I am living through, only has meaning outside those petty psychological formulations that claim to know and to explain why a woman is a woman and a man is a man. You should know, my friend, that the family, as it exists in our part of the world, with an all-powerful father and with the women relegated to domesticity and with the small scrap of authority that the male allows them, I repudiate that model of the family . . .]

and, 'Etre femme est une infirmité naturelle dont tout le monde s'accommode. Etre homme est une illusion et une violence que tout justifie et privilégie.' (p. 94) [Being a woman is a natural handicap that everyone comes to terms with. Being a man is an illusion and a form of violence that everything sanctions and condones.] The complex staging of the narrative's delivery is further complicated towards the novel's close, following the disappearance of the storyteller. Within the narrative itself Ahmed 'transmutes' into the female Zahra and begins a wandering life with a travelling circus in which her trans-sexuality becomes a staged performance. It is at this stage that the performance of the narration steals a march on the events narrated: after the disappearance of the storyteller three of the members of his audience meet to discuss the ending of the story. These three versions are complemented by an ever more labyrinthine conclusion, reminiscent of the fluid boundaries between different levels of fictionality to be found in the work of the South American writer Jorge Luis Borges.

La Nuit sacrée uses this first text as a springboard for yet another narrative that is constructed as a development from the same basic scenario of Ahmed's troubled sexual identity. In a first-person narration and from the vantage point of old age, Ahmed recounts her own life-story dedicated to attempts to forget the past rather than seeking to understand it. The staging of the narrative is far less complex than was the case in *L'Enfant de sable* but the hybrid intermingling of different levels of fictionality that was characteristic of the earlier novel is present here too. Banal details and objects of daily life are frequently evoked as the repositories of true significance, as when Ahmed opens her father's tomb and buries a jumble of possessions from her former life ('des chaussettes, des chaussures, un trousseau de clés, un ceinturon, une boîte de tabac à priser, un paquet de lettres, un livre de registres, une bague . . .', p. 56) [some socks, some shoes, a bunch of keys, a belt, a snuff box, a packet of letters, an accounts book, a ring . . .] in an effort at closure before beginning the wandering existence in which she hopes to find herself: 'Je me débarrassais de toute une vie, une époque de mensonges et de faux-semblants.' (p. 57) [I was discarding a whole life, a time of falsehoods and false pretences.] The bric-a-brac of daily life functions as the intrusive material from the 'real' world that she rejects and symbolically buries along with the dead father. By contrast, the life of wandering that she opts to pursue will take her into a universe dominated by dream, fantasy and the mystical realm of the imagination. The bulk of the ensuing narrative recounts her 'capture' and symbolic sequestration by the chivalrous figure of the blind 'Consul' and his jealous sister. 'Reality' (in a sense) intervenes once more, however, as characters from her earlier life track her down, inducing Ahmed to destroy the relative stasis of her life with the Consul by murdering the uncle who had been disinherited by her original subterfuge. This act of violence perhaps marks a refusal to be dragged back into a past life associated with all the hypocrisy and simulation demanded by a patriarchal social order. The quest for forgetfulness which Ahmed pursues in this novel is at one and the same time a world of inner fantasies, where rape, violence and sexual mutilation vie with evocations of mystical sanctity and harmony, and a world that conjures up the sociopolitical realities of post-independence Morocco.

The award of the Prix Goncourt to *La Nuit sacrée* has frequently been seen, not without a little condescension, as a form of public recognition of the fact that Maghrebi literature had come of age. Yet it did not mark a new beginning for either Maghrebi literature as a whole or for Ben Jelloun personally. Through the violence unleashed by the FIS, religious fundamentalism would soon rock the intellectual 'establishment' to its foundations in neighbouring Algeria, destabilising any notion of a collective dynamic among Maghrebi writers. Ben Jelloun's own activity as a writer seemed to lose something of its specifically literary edge as he diversified and 'professionalised' his output. Although, as we have seen, social issues had always been a key feature of his fictional work, his output throughout the 1990s and more recently has tended to involve a more documentary, less literary treatment of them. In *Les Raisins de la galère* (1996), for example, the social and political issues are not poeticised or filtered through a subjective, individualised perspective as they were in *La Réclusion solitaire.* Nadia's narrative is raw, unsophisticated and without literary pretensions. (This could, of course, be viewed as a 'literary' achievement in itself.) Yet it indicates a more general tendency in the evolution of Ben Jelloun's writing, as Charles Bonn has pointed out. Following the award of the Goncourt, Bonn claimed: 'Ben Jelloun saute d'un genre à l'autre, et parmi eux des genres sans prétention littéraire affichée comme le semi-reportage (*L'Ange aveugle*, 1992) ou l'essai (au sens large: *La Soudure fraternelle*, 1996, *Le Racisme expliqué à ma fille*, 1998) tiennent une grande place.'[43] [Ben Jelloun flits from one genre to another, and among these, genres with no declared literary pretensions such as the semi-journalistic report (*L'Ange aveugle*) or the essay (in the widest sense: *La Soudure fraternelle, Le Racisme expliqué à ma fille*) occupy an important place.] It is perhaps an over-simplification to argue that Ben Jelloun's prominence in the media, his regular articles in *Le Monde* and appearances on television, have fashioned him as a particularly acceptable 'specialist' voice on matters relating to the Maghreb, from literary to social issues, and that he has become side-tracked. It is certainly true however that much of his work is far more accessible than was the case in the early novels, and that a semi-autobiographical essay like *Eloge de l'amitié, ombre de la trahison* (2003) echoes many of the recurring themes of collections of stories like *Le Premier Amour est toujours le dernier* (1995) or *Amours sorcières* (2003), revealing the extent to which he has become content to explore general philosophical ideas in his fiction in a manner that is relatively undemanding.

Chapter 2

Sub-Saharan Africa

Overview

Francophone Africa south of the Sahara includes some seventeen different countries and stretches across almost a thousand miles of territory from the desert landscapes of Mauritania in the north-west to the equatorial forests of Congo in the south. Such diversity in climate, landscape, population and traditions argues against any attempt to present the region as a single unit when considering its literature. Even when approached as individual countries each with a supposedly 'national' literature, the question of diversity remains problematic. The countries granted independence by France or Belgium from the late 1950s onwards exist within boundaries that often reflect arbitrary colonial administrative habits and ignore pre-colonial patterns of tribal settlement. The border between francophone Togo and anglophone Ghana, for example, traverses the territories inhabited by Ewe-speaking tribes splitting communities down the middle. So in many cases the notion of nationhood began as an aspirational label rather than as an accurate description of any underlying political unity. Moreover, the linguistic, ethnic and tribal diversity that exists within national boundaries has proved to be one of the key reasons why French has continued to enjoy such a prominent role as the official language of government, the judicial system and education. In many countries no single African language is spoken by sufficient numbers of people to allow it to serve as the national language, but even where dominant African languages exist, promoting any one of these to the status of national language could be seen as politically divisive since it could appear to be a way of promoting the interests of a particular tribe to the detriment of others. These very practical considerations weigh as heavily in the balance as the more general advantages to be gained from the retention of French: its prestige as a world language and the access it provides to a variety of international forums, so crucial to developing countries.

When considering unity and diversity, then, it would seem that African realities invite us to consider the specificity of 'local' traditions and cultures

75

whereas the unifying, not to say homogenising, overview is associated with a metropolitan European vision. In the last four or five decades a wealth of fascinating francophone literature has been published by writers originating from the countries south of the Sahara, but they do not, by any stretch of the imagination, constitute a single body of literature. They can be granted a spurious unity by describing them as 'francophone' or 'African' but these are merely labels that allow them to be conveniently classified. They tell us nothing about the distinctive characteristics of the texts concerned. This tension between a unifying metropolitan vision and African diversity is present at all levels when we attempt to discuss francophone African literature. In a sense, it is present at the first stirrings of a distinctive literary production with the *Négritude* movement of the 1930s. Although focused on black cultural expression, the movement looked to African cultural roots for its spiritual inspiration as it mounted a challenge to a Western view of culture that projected itself as the universal norm. The Senegalese poet and statesman Léopold-Sédar Senghor and the Martinican Aimé Césaire, who were instrumental in launching *Négritude*, were both students in Paris in the late 1930s. It is one of the more obvious paradoxes of the African literary scene that from its very beginnings it has relied on Paris as a mediating centre of cultural exchange.

Senghor's own career illustrates a great many of the paradoxes and contradictions that characterise the francophone African literature of which he is considered by many to be one of the founding fathers. The first African to pass the prestigious French examination, the *agrégation*, Senghor was a brilliant student who assimilated French culture and language without supplanting the Wolof language and culture acquired during his childhood in Senegal. He would appear to be a perfect example of a biculturalism that could give credibility to France's ostensibly assimilationist colonial policy. He took full advantage of the opportunities that access to the French education system offered him. He fought in the French army in the Second World War and entered the Resistance from 1942 onwards. After the war he combined a career as a writer with a career in politics, first in the French *Assemblée nationale* and subsequently as the first president of Senegal (1960–80). He was elected to the Académie française in 1983. On the one hand, then, Senghor appears to embody complete complicity with metropolitan cultural values and the aspirations of benevolent colonialism as these eventually mutated into forms of neocolonial power and influence. By way of contrast, his poetics are marked by resistance rather than blind compliance. The emphasis on distinctive African cultural values and the dynamism of African civilisation underpin the many collections of poetry he published from *Chants d'ombre* (1945) onwards. This fundamental ambivalence as to Senghor's complicity with and resistance to French cultural domination echoes other contradictions. The affirmation of black cultural values is articulated through a European language and disseminated by way of Parisian publishing houses. Its belated endorsement by the leading French intellectual of the day, Jean-Paul Sartre, was a help in promulgating the fundamental theses of *Négritude* to a wider audience.[1] As many commentators have pointed out, the development of *Négritude* as a form of counter-discourse attacking Western cultural imperialism was formulated and made public in ways that drew heavily on the methods and practices of Western rather than African culture.

The figure of the poet-statesman so brilliantly embodied by Senghor is not an uncommon one in the early decades of francophone African literature. Authors among the many who have also held high political office include Cheikh Hamidou Kane of Senegal, Jean-Baptiste Tati-Loutard and Henri Lopes of the Congo and Ferdinand Oyono of Cameroon. There is something a little disconcerting about the marriage of literature and politics at this ministerial level but it is a direct consequence of the way colonial society formed its cadres. The small minority of young Africans who continued beyond primary schooling formed an elite trusted to work alongside white colonial administrators in a variety of rather limited functions. Others could aspire to becoming *instituteurs* [primary school teachers] themselves. Even fewer, were those who progressed to a secondary education and the possibility of pursuing further study in France. The French education system transplanted to Africa was egalitarian and rigorous, but it made no concessions to those from culturally different backgrounds and it was intransigent in its presumptions that French cultural achievements represented the acme of universal human culture. It is not surprising therefore that those, like Senghor, who had had the experience of studying at a French university formed a privileged group from which political as well as literary leaders emerged.

It is not surprising either that the literature that did begin to emerge either directly challenged or at least sought to problematise the dominant discourse of French cultural supremacy. Schools, schooling and education in general frequently figure within texts as a critical experience for young Africans since the 'French' school was often the location where they first encountered the alienating effects of assimilation to an alien culture. This is the case, for example, in Camara Laye's 1953 novel, *L'Enfant noir*, where the young Camara recounts a childhood divided between 'les deux voies' [the two paths] of traditional village life on the one hand, and the increasingly urbanised experience of French schooling on the other. His life naturally begins in the first setting and here he is gradually initiated into a tightly knit universe where his education is taken in hand by his father and extended family. Learning in this context consists of a series of initiations into mysteries that Camara feels he never fully penetrates since he leaves this world behind when he is still far too young. But such experiences as he has are sufficient to teach him that this is a world dominated by mystical and spiritual forces rather than rationality. It is also a world regulated by a distinctive ethos of mutual help and support. As he grows, circumstances lead the boy to grow away from the life that he realises would have been his had he been born in pre-colonial times. The novel thus brings Camara Laye's childhood to life not as a dramatic reconstruction of events but very self-consciously as a childhood *remembered* and in a mode that is heavily tinged with nostalgia for the loss of an idyllic rural past. Camara's experience, his sense of having lost a whole world in order to gain entry into a universe he still has to fathom out (the map of the Parisian metro bulges in his pocket as his plane leaves for France at the close of the novel), can clearly be interpreted as speaking to the general predicament facing Africans and African society under colonial rule. But the connections between the fate of the individual and that of the community are never explicitly drawn out, nor is there any direct allusion to the colonial régime responsible for the demise of traditional ways. The fact that the idyllic past Camara so regrets was more of an imagined construction than an accurate portrait has been one of the reasons the novel has attracted criticism. Another, more prescriptive response, now usually quoted whenever Camara Laye's novel is discussed, was that provided by the Cameroonian novelist, Mongo Beti, who railed at the fact that a novel set in colonial times could fail to include any reference to the political realities of life under colonial rule.[2]

The fundamental dichotomy outlined in *L'Enfant noir* is expressed in terms of a series of binary oppositions: past/present, village/town, mysticism/rationality, individual/community and so on, that are developed in the context of Camara's education. Education is central too in Cheikh Hamidou Kane's *L'Aventure ambiguë* (1961) where the protagonist, Samba Diallo, represents the collective quandary of his people, the Diallobé, as their traditional way of life comes into contact with French culture and customs. For Samba Diallo as for Camara, the conflict is also experienced in terms of schooling: he attends the traditional Koranic school until the decision is made to send him to the French school. This will lead him in due course to studies in Paris, geographically the capital of the foreign power that has colonised the lands of the Diallobé, but symbolically the repository of a post-Enlightenment, rationalist philosophy underpinning the materialist culture that has spawned colonialism. The novel wastes no time bemoaning the evils of colonialism or reflecting on the injustices of colonial rule. Rather, it accepts as a premise that the encounter between African and European cultures was an inevitable consequence of historical forces: an unavoidable encounter between the archaic and the modern.

The novel thus moves the debate away from any simplistic critique of colonial power doubled with a nostalgia for a lost pre-colonial innocence and demonstrates how the effects of French colonial rule had a devastating impact on the world view of the colonised. Samba Diallo as an individual does not survive the experience. The ambiguity surrounding his death (murder or suicide?) echoes the ambiguity of the educational adventure he has experienced and which allowed him to straddle, for a time, two incompatible cultural traditions. The implication of his death is that the way of life of the Diallobé too is doomed to extinction.

These two novels, in different ways, minimise the political by foregrounding the personal, in Camara's novel, or the philosophical, in Kane's. Other writers, such as Mongo Beti, Sembene Ousmane or Ferdinand Oyono, who were all publishing in the years leading up to the wave of accessions to independence that occurred in 1960, incorporated a more directly political critique into their work. Mongo Beti's early novels, from *Ville cruelle* (1954), published under the pseudonym of Eza Boto, to *Le Roi miraculé* (1958) illustrate his belief that literature should deal with the specific realities of life under colonial rule without adopting an attitude of resignation with regard to the ills of colonialism and without seeking solace in a projection of African traditional life as some sort of lost paradise.

Ville cruelle illustrates how Mongo Beti navigates a path between these two options. In the course of the novel the protagonist, a young cocoa planter by the name of Banda, journeys from his village to the town of Tanga and back again, in search of the dowry he needs to assemble that will allow him to marry. The journey serves to open his eyes to the cruelty and exploitation that is rife at every level in colonial society: in the spatial organisation of the town, in relations between employers and workers and even in the 'selling' of religious services by the missionaries who charge 100 francs to hear confession, 200 francs to baptise a baby, and so on. He turns an equally lucid, equally jaundiced eye on the extremely conservative, patriarchal structures that regulate African traditional life. Banda is one of several young protagonists invented by Mongo Beti to convey the frustration at the fact that colonial injustices are allowed to develop unchecked as the social inertia synonymous with traditional, patriarchal authority offers no effective resistance. These themes are picked up and developed in his two subsequent novels, *Le Pauvre Christ de Bomba* (1956), banned in Cameroon because the Catholic hierarchy was furious at the links of complicity it established between missionary activity and colonial conquest, and *Mission terminée* (1957) where the eyes of another young protagonist, Medza, are opened to the realities of his situation, ironically during a summer vacation following his failure at the *baccalauréat*.

In novels, pamphlets, essays and articles published after independence, Mongo Beti's writings tend to focus far more precisely on forms of political critique that are linked to recognisable political events and personalities in his native Cameroon. In a series of novels written throughout the 1970s and early 1980s he evoked the political activism that had preceded independence and denounced the complacency of Cameroon's leaders, Ahidjo and his successor, Paul Biya, whom he saw as the guardians of the neocolonialist interests of France. Beti was much criticised by some African-based intellectuals for the fact that he had preferred to live and work in self-imposed exile in France for the bulk of his working life, only returning to Cameroon to open a bookshop in Yaoundé in 1994. Yet there is no suggestion in anything he wrote that he ever wavered from a belief that literature, at least, should aspire to be anything other than revolutionary.

The career of Beti's fellow Cameroonian Ferdinand Oyono is not marked by the same single-mindedness. After publishing three novels in quick succession between 1956 and 1960 he turned his back on literature and opted for a career as a diplomat and eventually in politics, becoming a minister in Paul Biya's government in 1985. Despite the brevity of Oyono's flirtation with literature, two of his novels, *Une vie de boy* (1956) and *Le Vieux Nègre et la médaille* (1956), continue to be read as satirical masterpieces targeting colonialism as an institution and colonial rule as a set of practices. The protagonist of the first of these novels, Toundi, is a naive young boy whose admiration for his white masters (firstly a priest and subsequently a colonial administrator, thus emphasising the complicity between the spiritual and the material dimensions of colonial domination) is such that he longs for the assimilation that French colonial policy ostensibly advocated as the long-term aim of the whole colonial enterprise. Toundi is alone in failing to realise that the promise of eventual assimilation was merely a rhetorical device to justify colonial conquest rather than a practically realisable policy. Since the colonialists are not so naive as to believe their own lies, they come to see Toundi's attitude as an ironic game and a mocking criticism of their own behaviour. This seals Toundi's fate. The masks of benevolence generally worn by the colonial masters slip and reveal the violence that is ultimately always available to them to ensure their continuing power and dominance. Toundi dies fleeing from the prison where his masters have resorted to torturing him for his presumptious behaviour. The falsity and hypocrisy that underpins relationships between coloniser and colonised are in evidence again in *Le Vieux Nègre et la médaille* when the years of loyal service by the protagonist Meka receive recognition from the colonial authorities with the decision to award him a medal. The occasion is a source of great comic effect as Meka suffers the ordeal of preparing for the ceremony by squeezing his feet into shoes and then enduring the long wait for the award itself under a blazing sun. After the ceremony, Meka drinks too much, loses his medal and ends up spending the night in prison. Ironically, he is not recognised at all when he appears before the chief of police next day, thus exposing the sham of the whole ceremony. Like Toundi, Meka is punished for approaching too closely the world of the colonial masters and for taking their blandishments at face value.

Whereas Oyono's dissidence never extends beyond a critique of colonial rule, the political critique that underpins the work of Senegalese writer and film director Sembene Ousmane began in the years of struggle for independence from France and continued into the period of post-independence disillusionment with the first generations of African political leaders. Sembene's background makes him something of a rarity since he was a self-taught, former docker, who received little formal education. His personal experiences of life in France and as a trade-union activist fed into early works, in particular *Le Docker noir* (1956) and *Les Bouts de bois de Dieu* (1960). The latter novel is probably Sembene's most effective literary work and it combines an astute awareness of cultural politics with a Marxist approach to the problems of the African working man, whom Sembene identified beneath the figure of colonised victim of colonial oppression. The novel recounts a strike by workers on the Dakar–Niger railway and is loosely based on events that took place in 1947–8. Sembene's originality lies in his ability to think outside the categories that many of his contemporaries considered sacrosanct. In respect of traditional African values, for example, he systematically argues that they should be subjected to an ongoing critique and adapted to modern-day circumstances. While the usefulness of some traditional values and customs is clear, others need to be jettisoned as African societies confront the future. Always a critic of vested interests and male-dominated patriarchal authority, Sembene has consistently argued for greater parity between the sexes. When the strike by the railway workers enters a period of prolonged stalemate, it is collective action in the guise of a march organised by the workers's wives that eventually unblocks the deadlock.

After independence in 1960, Sembene simply changed target. Where he had formerly attacked the French colonial masters he now turned his attention to the new political class, headed by Senghor, denouncing their opportunistic alliance with the French state and French capital. In short stories (*Voltaïque* (1962) and *Le Mandat* (1966)) and novels (*Xala* (1973) and *L'Harmattan* (1980)), he continued to expose the shortcomings of the new political leaders and develop arguments favouring African interests and genuine autonomy in decision-making processes. A key theme of his latest novel, *Guelwaar* (1996), for example, is the idea that accepting foreign aid is little more than a form of modern enslavement that Africans should refuse point blank. Frustrated by the fact that literature can have only a relatively limited impact in Africa, where rates of illiteracy are high and reading written texts is not embedded as a popular cultural activity, Sembene turned his attention to the cinema in the early 1960s. His motives appear to have been both artistic and political. He was certainly aware of the power of the image as a vehicle for communicating ideas and has consciously harnessed film-making to the aim of raising the consciousness of his fellow Senegalese about a range of social, political and cultural issues.

The discussion thus far has presented emerging francophone African literature as though its horizons were limited by the politics of colonialism and its aftermath. The fact that the literature is written in French invites such a view. Any language carries with it, more or less implicitly, a world view and a system of values. So African authors using French as a vehicle for artistic expression necessarily found themselves involved in a tug-of-war between complicity and resistance, even if this only manifested itself at the level of linguistic processing rather than in terms of stark political outlook. Nor could the acquisition of competence in French occur in a vacuum; it implied an intensive level of socialisation either through schooling or some other form of prolonged contact. Yet all these reasons to suppose that the political dimension of francophone African literature is always of paramount importance deserve to be interrogated a little further, not least because they reinforce a fundamentally Eurocentric view. To pursue the argument that African literature must be viewed in terms of complicity and/or resistance to French, to French people or to colonialism in general, to the exclusion of all other approaches, is to imprison it in a postcolonial ghetto in which the African world only has any visibility, only comes into focus, when it is viewed from metropolitan perspectives.

With this word of warning in mind, it is worth reflecting on the efforts made by a range of authors, including some of those considered above, to include in their writings, or indeed to devote themselves more or less exclusively, to expressing aspects of African culture(s) through the medium of French. Pre-colonial African societies had thriving traditions of oral culture in which debate, storytelling, epic tales, genealogies, founding myths and popular proverbs all had a significant place. Oral traditions imply performance and performers as well as situations (births, initiation ceremonies, marriages, funerals, and so on) in which the rituals and the conventions of formal and informal social interaction could be marked by verbal productions of one sort or another. Although this was not always understood by the early colonisers, the absence of written literature did not mean an absence of culture. Quite the contrary, the repository of all the crucial 'texts' of West African culture was not a book but a human being: the *griot*, who combined the functions of praise-singer, genealogist, musician and poet. The work of ethnographers such as Leo Frobenius and Maurice Delafosse helped raise awareness about the depth of cultural richness of pre-colonial societies. But where 'literature' was centrally involved in this interaction between the archaic and the modern was in recuperating the ephemeral and the transient oral tradition and ensuring its transition into more permanent, fixed written forms.

This ethnographic dimension of francophone African literature can be traced from early collections of folk tales and proverbs, often organised on a regional basis and put together either by African or by French 'authors', through to fictional works, such as Ousmane Socé's *Karim* (1935) or Paul Hazoumé's *Doguicimi* (1938), which have considerable value as documentary texts for the detail they provide about the customs and traditions of specific African communties. In this respect, both the autobiographical and the 'fictional' writings of Ahmadou Hampaté Bâ, the 'sage of Bandiagara' in Mali, are highly significant. Although his literary reputation rests on books that portray the encounter between Africans and the colonisers, the two volumes of his own memoirs, *Amkoullel, l'enfant peul* (1991) and *Oui Mon Commandant!* (1994) or *L'Etrange Destin de Wangrin* (1973), the focus of his career was his work promoting a better knowledge and understanding of African civilisations. In the 1940s he left employment within the colonial administration to join the Institut Français (later Fondamental) d'Afrique Noire, IFAN, under the ethnographer Théodore Monod, where he was employed to work on oral traditions. He was responsible for collecting a wealth of material, particularly from the oral archive of the Peuls, many of which texts were subsequently published by the Nouvelles Editions Africaines in Abidjan. These include *Kaïdara* (1985), *Njeddo Dewal: Mère de la calamité* (1985), *Petit Bodiel* (1987) and *La Poignée de Poussière* (1987). It was Hampaté Bâ who is credited with having coined the expression, 'Chaque vieillard qui meurt c'est une bibliothèque qui brûle.' [The death of every elderly person is like a library going up in flames.]

To speak of the 'ethnographic' dimension of francophone African literature as though it were a phase of its development that has long been completed, or merely an historically exotic adjunct to a literature that is in the process of modernising, would be to misrepresent its importance. The centre of gravity of postcolonial African literature remains the encounter between African traditions (real or imagined) and a modernity that can stake less and less of a claim to be a Western phenomenon. The marriage customs of South Cameroon are an important element of Mongo Beti's *Ville cruelle*; Camara Laye spent two decades, following the publication of *L'Enfant noir*, travelling throughout West Africa interrogating *griots* and reconstituting the history of Soundiata and the ancient empire of Mali, publishing some of this material as *Le Maître de*

la parole (1978), Sembene, perhaps the most forward-looking of the francophone African authors of his generation, constantly conceives of Africa's future
as drawing on the traditions of the past in order to adapt and recycle those elements that still serve some useful purpose. The latest novel of Thierno Monenembo, *Peuls* (2004), is a vast historical fresco of consciously epic proportions,
recounting the history of this nomadic people from the late thirteenth century
to Samory's resistance to the incursions of French colonial forces at the end of
the nineteenth century. It is possibly because the history of Africa has been so
consistently and insistently denied and ignored that its literature has sought,
and continues to seek, to ensure that its voice now continues to be heard.

The constant appeal to African cultural reference points that has accompanied the evolution of francophone African literature since its origins also serves
the salutary purpose of decentring colonial history and relativising its intrinsic
importance. Following the spate of independences around 1960, a good many
authors rapidly began to consider colonialism less as an active force in African
affairs and more as an unfortunate legacy whose influence continued to be felt
in the economic sphere and in geopolitical terms through the self-serving and
unprincipled alignments of cold-war politics. In a little-known text, the Ivorian
novelist Ahmadou Kourouma describes how he sees the historical filiation from
colonialism to contemporary politics:

> Les guerres de libération furent dévoyées par la guerre froide. L'on ne se
> battait pas pour sa liberté mais pour son camp. Les dictatures africaines
> en profitèrent pour s'installer, profiter . . . Mais les dictatures africaines
> ont les dents plus longues. Elles s'accrochèrent à leur siège, à leur
> privilège. Le résultat fut que l'Afrique devient le pays des refugiés. Le
> continent de l'innommable, je veux dire le continent de l'Algérie, du
> Rwanda.[3]

> [The decolonisation struggles were side-tracked by the cold war. We
> were no longer fighting for freedom but for our own side. African
> dictators took advantage of the situation to take control, making the
> most of it . . . But African dictators are greedier than that. They clung on
> to power, to their privileges. The result was that Africa became the land
> of refugees. The continent of the unspeakable, I mean the continent of
> Algeria and Rwanda.]

Kourouma identifies African dictatorships as the root of Africa's current problems, but the ability of dictators to seize and maintain power was a consequence
of the rivalries that shaped international relations until the fall of the Berlin
Wall rather than of specifically colonial or neocolonial policies. An enormous
number of novels published in the last two or three decades attest to the
accuracy of Kourouma's analysis. Kourouma's own novels apart, dictatorships

are evoked as a vehicle for interrogating contemporary African realities in a plethora of novels from some of the continent's most respected francophone authors, including Williams Sassine's *Le Jeune Homme de sable* (1979), Labou Tansi's *La Vie et demie* (1979), Sembene's *Le Dernier de l'empire* (1981), Henri Lopes's *Le Pleurer-Rire* (1982), Aminata Sow Fall's *L'Ex-père de la nation* (1987), Cheikh Aliou Ndao's *Mbaam Dictateur* (1997) and Emmanuel Dongala's *Un fusil dans la main, un poème dans la poche* (2003).

This far from exhaustive list gives some idea how important the link between literature and politics remains in the context of African francophone literature. It is worth repeating, however, that the connection to politics is far more a matter of examining how the harsh social realities of life in Africa continue to be engineered by the politics of the developed world. The interest is less in politics *per se* than in the consequences of political action (or inaction) in, to take some examples from the last decade, Rwanda, Sierra Leone, Liberia or the Congo. The 1994 genocide in Rwanda was commemorated some three years later in a display of literary solidarity when Nocky Djedanoum, a writer from Chad, organised the project 'Rwanda: écrire par devoir de mémoire' [Rwanda: writing out of a duty to remember], that saw ten African writers undertake a journey to the killing fields of Kigali with a commitment to convey their impressions in writing. Among the outcomes were a number of moving texts, including Véronique Tadjo's *L'Ombre d'Imana* (2000), Abdourahman A. Waberi's *Moisson de crânes* (2000) and Thierno Monenembo's *L'Aîné des orphelins* (2000). Literary figures such as these seem increasingly to recognise that older, more partisan forms of political commitment in literature now need to be replaced by a more general ethical commitment to the plight of fellow human beings whose very survival is under threat. The need to speak out to an global audience about the devastating social consequences of international neglect of the African continent has motivated a spate of recent novels on the phenomenon of child soldiers, for example, including Kourouma's *Allah n'est pas obligé* (2000), Dongala's *Johnny Chien Méchant* (2002) and Waberi's *Transit* (2003).

Almost twenty years ago the Nigerian academic Chidi Amuta concluded a book on the theory of African literature with the following comment:

> It is not possible, even if it appears convenient, to practise literary theory and criticism as an abstract, value-free and politically sanitised undertaking in a continent which is the concentration of most of the world's afflictions and disasters . . . It is not possible to talk of literature and beauty or even to remain intelligent and credible in any area of academic discourse without taking our bearings from these unsettling realities.[4]

This statement echoes a response made by Kourouma when questioned about the role of African writers in an interview with Bernard Magnier:

> L'écrivain en Afrique n'a pas la même fonction que l'écrivain français . . . Comment écrire dans un pays où il n'existe pas de liberté sans faire allusion à cette situation? On passe pour un lâche, un amuseur de foire quand on parle de tout sauf de ce qui préoccupe nos lecteurs.[5]

> [Writers in Africa don't fulfil the same function as French writers . . . In a country where freedom is denied you, how can you write without mentioning that fact? One is looked upon as a coward or a fairground entertainer when one talks about everything under the sun except the things that preoccupy our readers.]

The ethical commitment that motivates Kourouma and which is so prevalent in much of the recent francophone literature from sub-Saharan Africa suggests that it has now outgrown its colonial and post-colonial preoccupations and is engaging with a more transnational postcolonial agenda.

Henri Lopes (Republic of Congo, 1937–)

A former prime minister of his country, a former high-ranking official at UNESCO, a recent candidate for the post as secretary general of the Organisation Internationale de la Francophonie (defeated in 2001 by Abdou Diouf, the former president of Senegal) and currently a serving ambassador, the novelist Henri Lopes has combined high political office with a successful career as a novelist. Since the death of Senghor he may justifiably be thought of as the present doyen of francophone literature. A retrospective glance over his output during the three decades separating *Tribaliques* (1971) from *Dossier classé* (2002) would seem to support the argument that his latest novels, possibly from *Le Pleurer-rire* (1982) but certainly from *Le Chercheur d'Afriques* (1990) onwards, differ quite dramatically from the earlier work on a variety of levels: they are technically more complex, they address a range of different themes and they are far more stylistically innovative.

What then are the chief characteristics of the earlier manner? Above all, *Tribaliques, La Nouvelle Romance* (1976) and *Sans tam-tam* (1977), are overtly concerned with issues of a sociopolitical nature but approached from a very concrete angle. Since they were written at a time when Lopes was a minister in the Congolese government it seems fair to suggest that he was using literature as another form of political activity. This accounts for the didactic and rather moralistic dimension to these narratives. Typically, Lopes starts with individuals in a situation of crisis and through his presentation of their case, implicitly or explicitly criticises the unsatisfactory social and political conditions which have given rise to their predicament. What is interesting, however, is that these scenarios largely exempt the former colonial masters from blame and it is Africans who are held responsible for any of the social ills identified. Indeed Gatsé, the protagonist of *Sans tam-tam*, is accused at one point of nostalgia for the colonial past because he consistently refuses to make blanket judgements. He prefers to tread the fine line between condemning the evils of colonialism and accepting that there are positive lessons to be learned from the experience. In the preface to *Tribaliques* Guy Tirolien alludes to the 'virus têtu' [stubborn virus] of colonialism not as an external phenomenon imported by metropolitan colonisers but as an African problem 'dont le nom va changeant au gré de nos intérêts: réalisme, traditionalisme, tribalisme, népotisme. Pour tout dire en un mot: arrivisme.'[6] [whose name keeps changing in line with our interests: realism, traditionalism, tribalism, nepotism. To put all these in a nutshell: self-seeking opportunism.] This seems entirely consonant with Lopes's project in these fictions. Over and over again he illustrates and exemplifies the implicit lesson that the post-independence construction of Africa depends on rigorous self-analysis by Africans themselves. He urges them to clear-sightedness about their own shortcomings and failings. Retrospective outrage at the misdeeds of the whites in the colonial period is, in Lopes's view, a way of fudging the issues, and it parallels that other form of mystification which is enshrined in the counter-ideology of *Négritude*. It is a reasonably well-documented fact that the Senghorian theses about *Négritude* found little favour in Congolese intellectual circles.

So the type of sociopolitical analysis which is discernible in these texts is not concerned with the promulgation of any programme, manifesto or ideology. In this respect, it can be seen as being empty of content while at the same time being rich in method and principle. Moreover, the criticism of African values and African patterns of behaviour seems at times to be conducted along moral lines. At very least, the sociopolitical dimension of the work is associated with a sense of moral vision. Hence characters in the early work tend to fall into two chief categories. On the one hand there are the opportunists who act out of self-interest and who are prepared to flout all sense of morality and all notion of the 'common good' in order to further their own ends. Contrasting with them are the altruists who base their actions on principles even when so doing may run counter to their own immediate comfort and well-being. For these latter, self-interest never takes precedence over the interests of the community. This simple opposition between the egoistic and the altruistic sets up categories that apply to both the sociopolitical and moral spheres. Gatsé in *Sans tam-tam*, for example, is worthy of respect because his decision to refuse the post of *conseiller culturel* in Paris is based on principle and not self-interest. He considers his work as a teacher in a remote town in the bush as of far greater value to his country than any role he could play in Paris. Characters in *Tribaliques* such as Dahounka in 'L'Honnête Homme' and Kalala in 'La Bouteille de Whisky' are of a similar ilk. Probably the best example of the obverse of this type of character is Delarumba, in *La Nouvelle Romance*. His career as footballer turned diplomat is a study in opportunism. Motivated by pure egoism and a desire to enjoy the good life, his indiscretions span marital infidelities, wife-beating, trafficking in drugs and the embezzlement of government funds. His punishment for the latter crime takes the form of a promotion as he is transferred from Brussels to a diplomatic post in Washington. In contrast to this his wife, Wali, is presented as a woman of principle and a victim not only of her personal and social circumstances but also of her gender. Her moral rectitude is demonstrated by her refusal to respond to attempts to seduce her by Kwala and Zikisso, despite her husband's own flighty behaviour and despite the example of the material benefits that accrue to her friend Elise as a consequence of her far laxer moral standards. Wali's irreproachable morals go hand in hand with a developing political awareness which will eventually lead her to break the mould and opt to free herself from the constraints which custom and tradition would seek to place upon her.

As if treating politics as a branch of moral philosophy were not enough, Lopes also seems guilty, in these early works, of proposing an essentially Manichean universe. This is supported not only by the characterisation but also by the tendency to rely on stark contrasts in situation and circumstances as a way of underscoring meaning. At times, in *Tribaliques*, the effect is quite blatant; for example, in the contrast between the lifestyles of Carmen, the maid, and that of her white employer in 'L'Avance', or the contrast between the public words and the private actions of the politician Ngouakou-Ngouakou in 'Monsieur le Député'. But it is present in far more subtle forms, for example, in the contrasting dress codes of whites and blacks in the presidential palace ('La Bouteille de Whisky') or in the demands made on the reader to reconstruct the contrasting interpretations which can be ascribed to the behaviour of Mobata in 'Le Complot': firstly, the paranoid view that he is a conspirator and secondly, the innocent/neutral view that he is a doctor performing his normal duties. These contrasts may be based on simple binary oppositions but they give rise to complex analyses of far from simple scenarios.

From *Le Pleurer-rire* onwards this simplicity of structure and narrative perspective ceases to be a characteristic of Lopes's work. Likewise, the portrayal of an essentially Manichean universe is replaced by types of representation which underline the multiplicity of points of view and give no precedence to any single system of values. The act of reading itself is foregrounded more and more as the act that constitutes the text. There is no longer a 'given' situation, lending itself to analysis. Instead, the reader is faced with different angles on events and a whole range of narrative points of view, the sum effect of which is to make the responsibility for assigning meaning a task that readers must assume for themselves.

Whereas the overtly political subject matter of *Le Pleurer-rire* would suggest its direct affiliation with the earlier work, its structural and stylistic inventiveness set it apart from those texts and herald the sort of changes which are common to the subsequent novels from *Le Chercheur d'Afriques* to *Dossier Classé*. None of these later works rely on linear or chronological narratives. They create their effects by the juxtaposition of a series of *tableaux*, which can be likened to a succession of cinematographic clips. In *Le Pleurer-rire*, the style, linguistic register and narrative point of view adopted in these *tableaux* display tremendous variety. But as the various subplots mesh together in an intricate web of relationships a sense of unity nevertheless emerges through the role of the central narrator, the *maître d'hôtel* who, through his control of the narrative process, is perhaps a mocking reflection of Bwakamabé himself, the despotic master of the fictional universe which the narrative ultimately portrays. The very possibility of making this comparison between a narrator who orchestrates the competing narrative voices and a tyrannical character who whimsically exercises absolute political power itself illustrates the distance that separates these sophisticated later texts from the earlier work.

A common feature of the later novels is that aspects of the act of narrating become events within the novel. Conversely, the events that are narrated can often be read as illustrations of the problems associated with the production and/or reception of works of art. In *Le Pleurer-rire* for example, very early on the narrative is identified as a narrative in the process of being written which the narrator submits to the critical judgement of a third party even as the narrative is taking shape. The feedback received, the critical opinion on the text so far, is itself incorporated into the text. Other types of discourse, usually vying with each other and proposing modified if not conflicting accounts of events are also a common device. There are editorials from the pen of Aziz Sonika, leaderwriter for the official newspaper of the Republic, *La Croix du Sud*, references to 'dépêches' from foreign radios and newspapers, including *Le Monde*, and above all the periodic intervention of the street-level rumour machine, *Radio-Trottoir*. The presence in the novel of these multiple voices and multiple perspectives means that the narrator's prime function is not to narrate events but to orchestrate the various competing discourses so that the 'reality' which is presented to the reader is not a sociopolitical portrait of Tonton Bwakamabé's Republic but a series of acts of language.

In *Le Chercheur d'Afriques* too, the act of reading takes on special significance: André's efforts to trace his lost father is an example of hermeneutic activity as he attempts to interpret childhood memories and evaluate the accuracy and the importance of the memories of his close family. His efforts at times become a matter of exegesis as he studies published texts which he believes to have been written by his father and later attends a conference at which the man he suspects of being his father is speaking. The search for the father does not take place only in fictional time and space but in fictional spoken and written texts. In Lopes's more recent novels, the sociopolitical content recedes almost entirely, to the extent that it seems possible to talk of some form of political disengagement. Instead, a different theme appears to dominate: the theme of identity. Lost, mistaken or simply threatened 'identity' has provided the basic subject matter for many classic African novels. With the series of novels including *Le Chercheur d'Afriques*, *Sur l'autre rive* (1992), *Le Lys et le flamboyant* (1997) and *Dossier classé*, however, Lopes deals with the theme in a way that widens its significance. By focusing the question of identity on issues of contested versions of personal origins it paradoxically acquires a universal significance.

Thematically, *Le Chercheur d'Afriques* is not, as has been suggested, primarily a novel about the anguish of racial and cultural 'métissage', although it deals with these matters too. It is essentially a novel about the masks, literal and metaphorical, which we use to conceal identity, protect identity or in an effort to create and project new versions of identity. By the same token, the novel describes various efforts to unmask and to reveal identity. André's search for his lost father is a dual quest. It is at one and the same time an attempt to unmask the father by substituting a single concrete version of that character for the multiplicity of personae which distant memory, dream, hearsay, a certain number of facts and a good deal of imagination have enabled André to create. But it is simultaneously an attempt by André to unmask himself. It is also a voyage of self-discovery through which he seeks to put an end to the ambivalences and ambiguities that dominate his own life and resolve the difficulty he has in creating a unified identity for himself. For André too is a character composed of numerous personae. His name changes according to his circumstances as does the way he is seen by others: he is not viewed in the same way by the children of his native village as he is by racist whites in Nantes or by his half-sister, Fleur, who is captivated by his physical beauty.

In terms of its structure, one might almost say architecture, *Le Chercheur d'Afriques* is far closer to the complexity of *Le Pleurer-rire* than it is to the earlier work. It is composed of some ninety-seven unnumbered narrative sequences that skip backwards and forwards in time, just as they also alternate between scenes set in Africa and scenes set in France. A close reading of the text is required in order to constitute the original chronology of events, particularly since the sections that take place in Nantes describe two separate visits to that town by the narrator. The fragmentation of the story allows Lopes to exploit an element of suspense as the drama surrounding André's search for his father unfolds. But it also reflects the fragmentation that is the chief characteristic of André's own psychological make-up.

Whereas *Le Chercheur d'Afriques* may be considered as a novel of quests for identity that conclude in various types of recognition, *Sur l'autre rive* is a novel about attempts to conceal identity. When the protagonist, Marie-Eve disappears from the Congo and creates a new life and a new persona for herself in the Caribbean, her action not only provides a practical way of dealing with the dissatisfaction she feels, it also has a symbolic significance. Her 'renaissance' in the Caribbean takes on the dimensions of an existential enterprise by which she seeks to gain and maintain control of her own identity. In many respects her 'crossing of the river/ocean' is the act by which she engenders herself and chooses that version of identity that she wishes to promulgate to the world. The dissatisfactions with her Congolese life imply that a sense of identity imposed on the individual by the expectations of others is effectively a straitjacket. The labels and definitions by which others categorise us (wife, childless, black artist; black female artist; black African female artist, and so on) are reductivist. They also ultimately serve to recuperate us into systems that can become alternative forms of slavery. Hence, at the outset of the novel, Marie-Eve feels under a dual threat. Firstly, she believes she has been recognised by a couple of African tourists and fears that she will be obliged to acknowledge her previous life and thus reactivate a past which she has chosen to suppress. Secondly, she is threatened by the Parisian art critic, Solange, whose overly intellectual responses to her paintings work to recuperate her in a different way.

With the possible exception of the pivotal work that is *Le Pleurer-rire*, the later works certainly display a preoccupation with philosophical rather than sociopolitical issues. They continue to anchor the narratives in the experience of individuals rather than in heavily theorised situations. Nor should Marie-Eve's refusal to intellectualise the processes of artistic creation, and her concern to develop a personal aesthetic free from social, political and ideological constraints be disparaged. The debate that such matters feeds into is a debate about artistic freedom, and beyond that a debate about human freedom. Marie-Eve's disappointment at the press reaction to her exhibition is perhaps an oblique reference to this. It is expressed thus:

> Après avoir décrit la cérémonie, ils parlent de moi en termes snobs,
> évoquent les tableaux en deux ou trois phrases stéréotypées pour leur
> valeur régionale selon les uns, nationaliste selon les autres, mais pas un
> mot sur mon style, mon travail et mon art.   (p. 50)

> [After having described the ceremony, they talk about me in snobbish
> terms, with two or three clichés from some of them about local colour,
> from others about nationalist politics, they dismiss the paintings
> without a word about my style, my work, my art.]

The confining of African literary or artistic production to some sort of region-alist or nationalist ghetto proceeds from the type of thinking which is founded on an appeal to racial and cultural stereotypes. It confirms that the spirit of colonialism is not dead. Lopes's second manner, despite its ostensible dis-engagement from overtly sociopolitical issues, refuses such classification and stakes a claim to a universal rather than an African or Afrophile readership. For all his involvement with official, state-sponsored instances of *francophonie*, Lopes's fiction deserves a closer reading than many postcolonial critics have afforded it to date.

Ahmadou Kourouma (Côte d'Ivoire, 1927–2003)

Ahmadou Kourouma came to the notice of the public by a roundabout route. His first novel, *Les Soleils des indépendances* (1968), having been refused by a number of Parisian publishing houses was published in Montreal after being selected as winner of a new prize organised by the Canadian journal *Etudes françaises*. As part of the publishing deal, Kourouma was invited to cut long sections of the third part of the novel which were considered overly 'political'. This shortened version of the novel was later republished by Editions du Seuil in 1970 and, in this form, has gone on to become one of the canonical texts of contemporary African literature. This history of the text's appearance, its *scénographie*, marks it out as a rather typical postcolonial text in terms of both space and time. Its journey into the mainstream required a detour by way of the Canada of the 'Quiet Revolution' and the fact that Kourouma was seeking publication at the precise moment when Quebec was redefining its own sense of identity, and looking to the francophone diaspora rather than to metropolitan France for inspiration, is one of those felicitous accidents of history without which Kourouma's career as a writer might never have taken off at all.

The editors of the Presses Universitaires de Montréal had, of course, been right to see the text as highly political. As is the case in all of Kourouma's writings, the links to historical personalities and events are quite direct: history and politics are subjected to only minimal transformation as they are fictionalised. *Les Soleils des indépendances* has its origins in Kourouma's personal experience, which was similar to that of many of his friends who were also caught up in Houphouët-Boigny's derailment of due political process shortly after becoming the first president of Côte d'Ivoire. In order to suppress at root any emerging political opposition, Houphouët-Boigny had publicly proclaimed the discovery of a far-reaching conspiracy to overthrow his government, allegations which he coolly retracted some years later. In the intervening years he had proceeded to imprison large numbers of the country's educated elite, including members of his own family, thus ensuring he was able to run the country's affairs as he saw fit. Kourouma has since explained that his own stay in prison in 1963 was undoubtedly shorter than that of many fellow prisoners simply because his wife happened to be French; Houphouët-Boigny was extremely sensitive to French opinion and feared the involvement of the French media. Kourouma's prime motivation for writing, then, was a desire to bear witness to the events that had marked this period of his life and that of his countrymen. He even considered writing a discursive essay as a way of exposing the conduct of the president to public scrutiny, but decided that a fictionalised account of events had far more prospect of publication.

The shortened version of *Les Soleils des indépendances* that appeared in 1968 no longer contains the long, surrealistic trial scenes that distinguish the original typescript of the novel. In this sense the editing process has weakened the link with contemporary events that Kourouma was keen to highlight. The editing also ensures that the novel focuses less on the national political scene and far more closely on the personal dilemma of the protagonist, Fama, as he struggles to survive in the post-independence world he no longer recognises and which no longer recognises him. The boundaries that had previously existed when traditional structures were in place have been demolished by encroaching modernity. On a personal level this translates into the collapse of Fama's social status, as the noble prince of Horodougou is reduced to the role of beggar. Horodougou itself has been superseded on the map, its territory dissected by the borders of two modern nation states, la République des Ebènes and la République de Nikinai. Since, in Fama's eyes, the physical person of the prince and the lands he rules are synonymous, this redrawing of the boundaries is an attack on his physical and metaphysical person. So, at every turn, Fama discovers that the post-colonial political dispensation in the newly independent République des Ebènes has effectively annihilated the power he had formerly enjoyed, and established a radically different basis for interpersonal relations. Even his relationship with his wife, Salimata, fails to survive the clash of cultures that colonisation and its aftermath have wrought upon the Malinké people. The novel closes with the death of Fama in his native town of Togobala in fulfilment of the ancient prophecy about his demise and the end of the line he represents, the Doumbouya. The novel thus conveys the message that, for good or ill, modernity cannot be resisted. Yet the manner of Fama's death suggests that the traditional Malinké world view he represents is, in a sense, authenticated even as it disappears from the scene. The natural world: animals, plants and the elements shudder at his passing, panic-stricken and stupefied by its significance:

> Les oiseaux: vautours, éperviers, tisserins, tourterelles, en poussant des cris sinistres s'échappèrent des feuillages . . . les crocodiles sortirent de l'eau et s'enfuirent dans la forêt . . . Les forêts multiplièrent les échos, déclenchèrent des vents pour transporter aux villages les plus reculés et aux tombes les plus profondes le cri que venait de pousser le dernier des Doumbouya.   (pp. 200–1)

> [Birds: vultures, sparrow hawks, weavers, turtle doves set up a lugubrious clamour as they fled the branches . . . crocodiles left the rivers and made for the forest. The trees multiplied these echos and raised winds to carry off to the remotest villages and into the deepest burial grounds the cry that had just escaped the lips of the last of the Doumbouya.]

If *Les Soleils des indépendances* has since become established as one of the classic texts of the francophone African literary canon, it is very largely because of the innovative style Kourouma employed to convey the specificity of Fama's world view. Having tried to write the novel in 'standard' French Kourouma found that the book didn't convey the atmosphere he sought to express: he was unable to enter Fama's mental universe through an idiom that was alien to Malinké speech patterns and ways of thinking. He therefore opted for a hybrid language which shared the rhythms, syntax and lexis of his mother tongue, and translated them quite crudely into a version of French that made no concessions to normative standards. Indeed his use of language in this and subsequent novels has always been distinctive and has provided a focus of attention for much of the critical interest that his work has enjoyed.

The taste for epic which is latent and implicit in *Les Soleils des indépendances* asserted itself more openly in the sweeping fresco of the life of the Malinké patriarch, Djigui, which is the subject of his second novel, *Monnè, outrages et défis* (1990). In scope and ambition, *Monnè* is a far more impressive work than the earlier novel but paradoxically it has never quite received the critical acclaim it deserves, despite the award of three separate prizes including the *Grand Prix du roman de l'Afrique noire*. The novel traces the life story of a Malinké prince, Djigui, from youth to old age. In the margins of this personal history there unfolds the history of his people, ranging from the time of colonial conquest to the period of colonial disengagement and independence. Hence the narrative simultaneously follows two tracks, but the history it recounts is not the history found in French history books. The perspective from which events are narrated is firmly that of Djigui, the Malinké prince, and the people of Soba preoccupied with their efforts to understand the traumatic events they are called upon to witness. The narrative thus constitutes a counter-discourse, not through its ideological content or any consistent critique of colonisation, but through adopting a narrative voice that presents the Malinké world view as the norm. As was the case with Fama, the portrait Kourouma offers is far from indulgent. There is little that is heroic about Djigui, for example. He is frequently arbitrary and his decisions lack consistency. He wavers between proud defiance and self-serving subservience in his relations with the colonial forces. But these human imperfections are merely accidental and have little real significance since Djigui is beyond judgement in the eyes of his people. His importance derives not from his individual worth or personal qualities but from the role and function he fulfils within traditional social structures. The complexity of this type of characterisation illustrates how Kourouma reverses the power structures inherent in the way narrative codes function. He is effectively reclaiming Malinké history for the Malinké people and in this act of narrative reappropriation, simultaneously recuperates some of the sense of dignity that the colonial enterprise as a whole had stifled and ultimately denied.

If it is reasonable to consider *Monnè* as instigating a form of counter-hegemonic history, then Kourouma's third novel, *En attendant le vote des bêtes sauvages* (1998), may be seen as a continuation of the same process but as it unfolds in a different period of African history, that of the dictatorships which endured in so many African states throughout the cold war period. In this novel too, the overtly political content, the critique of dictatorships, is not structured in accordance with any single coherent ideological position. There is no recognisable authorial voice behind the narrative but instead an extremely complex narrative framing device, modelled on the ritual *donsomana* of the Malinké hunting fraternity. (The *donsomona* was a purification rite involving a public recitation of the exploits of a master hunter.) By engaging with his subject through such complex techniques of the staging of the narrative, Kourouma effectively distributed shares in its 'ownership' among a range of actors, thus defusing any simplistic binary opposition that could be seen as setting one political opinion against another. A further consequence of this strategy is that the undeniably political content of the novel thus tends to recede into the background while the more broadly human dilemmas in which the various characters find themselves embroiled become the centre of attention. At one and the same time, the political dimension is trivialised and individualised while the horizons against which events are interpreted and judged are broadened and involve grander, perhaps more spiritual notions of a communal destiny working itself out over a longer time scale than the modernist concern for the immediate present.

The last novel Kourouma wrote, *Allah n'est pas obligé* (2000), continued his journey 'upstream' in terms of African history and brought him a step closer to contemporary events: its central character is Birahima, a child soldier involved in the civil war which raged in Liberia and Sierra Leone in the mid 1990s. Birahima's own Malinké origins allowed Kourouma to rely once again on Malinké cultural realities and language to provide a filter through which events and experiences are narrated. *Allah n'est pas obligé* is consistent with his earlier work in that it draws upon the tensions that exist between radically opposed world views, mindsets and cultural systems (and the role played by language in both constructing and articulating these). The novel sets out to interrogate an extraordinarily acute example of difference: by what mechanisms and processes do the child soldiers portrayed in the novel come to engage in such extreme forms of behaviour? It nevertheless goes beyond examining a specific kind of difference to raise broader questions about the nature of culture, society and what exactly constitutes shared humanity.

Whereas in earlier works radically different world views are portrayed as co-existing within a single narrative space, in this particular novel Kourouma set himself the task of bridging the gap between the horror of Birahima's world and the comparatively safe world outside the text that readers inhabit. Birahima inhabits a world of brutalising violence and general lawlessness that threatens to dehumanise all those caught up within its logic. Drug abuse, rape, gratuitous murder and wanton destruction are commonplace and the absence of any moral principles by which to judge actions and events is the defining feature of this universe. As he continues on his journey, and his narrative, Birahima has recourse to various dictionaries (a 'Larousse', a 'Petit Robert', the 'Inventaire des particularités lexicales du français en Afrique noire' and a Harrap's) ostensibly to translate relevant words for the benefit of the different audiences for which the narrative is intended. But ultimately, the constant punctuation of the text with frequently superfluous definitions serves to demonstrate the fact that the quest for meaning founders on the closed nature of the system within which Birahima is entrapped. The process is self-referential and doomed to repetition and circularity. There is no sense to be made of this apocalyptic world. Attempts to translate it simply re-inscribe its radical difference so that Birahima's glosses on words, like his narrative, amount to a gesture across an unbridgable divide. The challenge that Kourouma sets readers, positioned on the outside, is to recognise nevertheless the shared humanity of Birahima. In this respect, the novel retraces the journey from cultural specificity to questions of universal relevance that is ultimately emblematic of Kourouma's whole project as a novelist.

Given the importance of Malinké culture in Kourouma's work there is something of a grim circularity to the fact that his life ended in an exile that was directly related to his regional origins. In the early 1990s, following the death of President Houphouët-Boigny, the entourage of his successor, Henri Konan Bedié, began developing an extremely divisive ideological position by calling into question the right of certain sections of the population to consider themselves to be 'true' Ivorians. The purpose of this pernicious doctrine of *ivoirité* ('Ivorianness') was to secure the new president's political future by disenfranchising a whole swathe of people considered to be opponents to his régime. Because of his northern, Malinké origins, Kourouma's 'true' nationality was called into question by critics and he was obliged once again to flee into exile in France where he died shortly afterwards. This strange scenario from 'real-life' Ivorian politics has many of the features of the sort of storyline Kourouma frequently exploited in his fictions. Indeed, in several ways it echoes the fate of Fama, the Malinké prince, who had discovered he had no place in, indeed was no longer even recognised by, the new post-colonial political landscape and social order that had emerged in his native land. Even the issue of arbitrary national borders, that figures in the novel during Fama's final journey to Horodougou, resurfaces in the *ivoirité* dispute fomented by President Bedié's supporters. Kourouma would have been aware of these ironies. It was such abuses and misuses of power that not only provided the subject matter of his fiction but had inspired him to write in the first place, as the apt title of his posthumously published text, *Quand on refuse on dit non* (2004), reminds us.

Sony Labou Tansi (Democratic Republic of Congo, formerly Zaïre, 1947–1995)

The reputation enjoyed by Sony Labou Tansi as one of the leading figures of francophone literature is based on a reasonably substantial output for a writer who died at such a tragically young age. By the time he succumbed to the AIDS virus in 1995 he was in his late forties and had published some six novels and a similar number of plays as well as several poems and short stories. In the opinion of Labou Tansi's close friend, French critic Nicolas Martin-Grenel, the published output is only the tip of the iceberg and represents approximately 5 per cent of his writings. While some of these unpublished manuscripts appear to be early versions of works that now exist in published form, they also include substantial collections of unpublished poetry that may one day necessitate a complete re-evaluation of Labou Tansi's place in African literary history.

As things stand, it is probably true to say that his reputation rests as much on his achievements as a playwright as they do on his work as a novelist. Although he completed a first, unpublished novel, *Le Premier Pas*, in 1966 while still at school, it was by writing plays and regularly submitting them to the *Concours théâtral interafricain*, organised annually by Radio France Internationale, that he secured a breakthrough into publication. At the fifth attempt he won the competition with *Conscience de tracteur* (1973) and went on to win it twice more in fairly quick succession with *Je soussigné cardiaque* (1976) and *La Parenthèse de sang* (1978). Thematically these works draw on the same preoccupations as 'later' narrative writings, but given Labou Tansi's tendency to rework and rewrite his texts this is not surprising. Indeed, it is probably unwise to think of his novels and plays as 'finished' products at all. The original text of *La Vie et demie* (1979), for example, was lost on a train prior to submission for publication and Labou Tansi rapidly rewrote the novel from memory, while *L'Anté-peuple* (1983) is a reworked version of a much earlier text entitled *La Natte* written in the early 1970s. It is not surprising then that there are numerous points of overlap and common ground between the novels and the theatrical writings.

Je soussigné cardiaque centres on the struggle of Mallot, a village schoolteacher, to defend a very personal conception of individual freedom and agency in the face of an all-powerful establishment that combines commercial interests (represented by the colonialist Perono) and political power (represented by the minister Bela Ebara). Mallot makes a dramatic stand against Perono, refusing to accept his overbearing demands for obedience, not for any ideological reasons but in order to defend a rather abstract concept of what it means to be human:

> Quand je suis venu au monde, trois gros y étaient arrivés déjà: le Christ, Marx et Mao . . . Le premier avait semé la bonne histoire avec laquelle les papes ont tué, trompé et trahi pendant des siècles. Les deux autres, même malheur: ils ont monté . . . des édifices idéologiques dont les gens aujourd'hui se servent pour tuer et tromper . . . Eh bien, moi, je ne suis ni le Christ, ni Marx, ni Mao. Je suis L'IMPRENABLE. L'HOMME PREMIER!   (p. 101)

> [When I came into the world, three big guys had already arrived on the scene: Christ, Marx and Mao . . . The first had spread the good news that has allowed popes to cheat and to kill for centuries. Same unhappy story

for the other two: they built . . . ideological structures that people are using today to cheat and to kill . . . Well I am neither a Christ, nor a Marx nor a Mao. I am the one who CAN'T BE HAD. THE FIRST HUMAN!]

Despite his histrionic claims Mallot is himself caught up in the all-pervading corruption and deception: he browbeats his doctor cousin, Manissa, to provide a false sick note that will free him from teaching duties and allow him the time and space to investigate the machinations of the establishment against his person. Mallot is eventually crushed by the forces ranged against him and the play ends as he awaits his execution in a prison cell.

This extremely schematic play is perhaps most interesting because of the way it stages, in a rather embryonic form, some of the thematic proccupations that Labou Tansi would continue to address throughout his career. Such dramatic tension as the play manages to create derives from the conflict between the individual who exercises free will and those characters representing forces of tyrannical oppression. The latter are addicted to a biblical range of vices, including greed, lust and violence, and are inevitably supported by the faceless machinery of official power: the police and the military. Yet the basic conflict is never reduced to a simple binary between good and evil. Mallot is no paragon of integrity but is himself sullied as a result of his contact with Perono. It would seem that the positive value that Labou Tansi seeks to affirm here, as in many later works, is not some unachievable state of purity but simply an appetite for life, often associated with a thirst for freedom.

The nostalgia for life takes us to the heart of the bizarre problematic sketched out in *La Parenthèse de sang*. This play stages the confrontation between members of the family of Libertashio, a dead freedom fighter, and the soldiers whose orders are to capture him. The encounter dissolves into an exploration of various versions of 'life within death' and its obverse 'death within life', until the condemned family members are incapable of deciding whether they are awaiting execution or have already been executed. 'Life within death', because the fact that Libertashio is already dead is judged an irrelevancy by the soldiers who continue to seek him against all the evidence. Virtually the entire action of the play takes place in a space adjacent to his tomb. The soldiers' blind refusal to recognise that Libertashio is dead endows him with an enduring symbolic power. Their insistence on searching for a man who no longer exists gives a permanence to their mission (oppression never ends) and ensures that the struggle for freedom is also perpetuated. The soldiers' actions logically provoke the reaction of revolt and this is passed from generation to generation. Libertashio's daughter, Yavilla, confirms this. When the priest hears her confession she declares: 'Un seul péché: la liberté. J'ai passé ma vie à crier vive Libertashio.

Je ne suis que cette force de dire: à bas la dictature – celle des hommes, celle des choses, celle de Dieu si elle existe.' (pp. 48–9) [Only one sin: freedom. I've spent my whole life shouting Vive Libertashio. I am nothing more than this will to proclaim: down with dictatorship – the dictatorship of men, of things, of God, if it exists.] 'Death within life', because the civilians end up on the fourth evening of the play believing they are already dead although the soldiers have not yet executed them. This mistaken belief is merely a variant on a dominant figure exploited by the play which sees life and death constantly confused. Aleyo says at one point, 'La vraie mort se mêle à la vraie vie. Elles s'emboîtent parfaitement, l'une oubliant l'autre.' (p. 60) [True death mingles with true life. The one fits perfectly into the other, each forgetting about the other.] So the predicament of the family and other civilians who are threatened by the soldiers is not simply that of avoiding being condemned to death but of remaining 'human' (that is, 'alive' and hungry for life) in face of the threat posed by the military machine. In this system of moral economy it is the betrayal of what is human in each individual that is tantamount to the only meaningful form of death. Hence, the doctor is not worried about dying so much as the growing sense of his own inhumanity: 'Ce n'est plus tout à fait humain en moi' (p. 67) [It's no longer completely human in me], while the priest bemoans in general terms man's betrayal of his humanity: 'Les hommes ont disparu. Restent ces formes humaines, ces tombeaux humains, mais au-dedans, ce n'est plus humain.' (p. 52) [Men have disappeared. These human forms remain, these human tombs, but inside they're not human any more.]

There is a clear political content to these plays. As with later plays performed by the troupe Labou Tansi created in 1979, the Rocado Zulu Theatre, such as *Antoine m'a vendu son destin* (1986) or *Qui a mangé Madame d'Avoine Bergotha* (1989), they involve dictators and state apparatuses of repression that have a particularly postcolonial flavour to them. But it would be limiting to see them as merely political. They aspire to a universal significance and demand to be read as metaphysical dramas involving stakes that are as much spiritual as they are physical. Even 'life' is never simply 'human life' in Labou Tansi's vocabulary. It can usually be understood as encompassing the life of the planet. His dramas go beyond the moralising conundrums of postcolonial politics to ask questions that apply both to the ethics of interpersonal relations and to the ethics of consumption and pollution that face the planet as a whole with increasing consistency. Labou Tansi begins with the postcolonial but opens out on to the ecological as he details the unequal contest pitting forces that are blindly working to 'kill life' against individuals whose efforts are geared to preserving it. The connection between ecology and the idea of 'the human' is made quite explicitly in an essay written in 1986, in which he argues:

Nous avons gardé l'humanité intacte pendant deux millions d'années, alors que moins de trois cents ans de cannibalisme technologique ont suffi pour créer les monstruosités écologiques que vous connaissez ... L'Afrique c'est la preuve même que l'homme n'est pas encore humain, qu'il n'est pas encore au monde.[7]

[We have kept humanity intact for two million years whereas it's taken only three hundred years of technological cannibalism to create the ecological monstrosities that we all know about ... Africa is the very proof that mankind is not yet human, that he has not yet come into being.]

Labou Tansi's best-known novel, *La Vie et demie* (1979), echoes a good number of the themes already touched upon in the theatrical works of the 1970s. The title itself reflects the notion of exuberance for life that has been identified as a key reference in these writings. Libertashio's continuing influence from beyond the grave of the earlier play prefigures a similar device in this novel, where it is the dissident Martial who repeatedly refuses to die the deaths inflicted on him and who, once dead, refuses to remain so but continually reappears to haunt the dictator, the 'guide providentiel', who murdered him. Over and above the surrealistic tone of the novel and its well-documented Latin American influences, Labou Tansi infiltrates the zaniness and unpredictability of his narrative with a mood of underlying inevitability in respect of the violence and suffering he portrays. The roles and functions of oppressor and freedom fighter are almost ritualistically enacted and re-enacted through an accelerating process of repetition. The figure exists already in *La Parenthèse de sang* where each sergeant commanding the soldiers ends up being shot and replaced by another in a never-ending chain of indistinguishable sergeants, all equally wedded to their mission. In *La Vie et demie* this translates into the series of guides who eventually succeed the 'guide providentiel' as rulers of Katamalanasie and who remain in an eternal stand-off with 'les gens de Martial' [Martial's people]: 'C'étaient des Jean Coriace, Jean Calcaire, Jean Crocodile, Jean Carbone, Jean Cou, Jean Cobra, Jean Corollaire, Jean Criquet, Jean Carnassier. . .' (p. 148) The lists continue for almost a page.

The absurdity of this ludicrous enumeration of names, rather like the second article of the constitution that no one understands, 'Gronaniniata mésé botouété taou-taou, moro metani bamanasar karani meta yelo yelo-manikatana', is a circular, self-referential device that emphasises the opacity of language and ultimately language's inability to render this barbaric universe meaningful (p. 128). With his second novel, *L'Etat honteux* (1981), and indeed with subsequent works like *Les Sept Solitudes de Lorsa Lopez* (1985), the scandalous nature of dictatorships, and the social and political inequalities they maintain, are explored with a similar linguistic verve and a similar appeal to a humour born of despair rather than mirth. The preface to *L'Etat honteux* is explicit: 'J'estime que le monde dit moderne est un scandale et une honte' (p. 5) [I consider what we call the modern world to be a scandal and a cause for shame], but this does not prevent Labou Tansi from claiming to have written it while laughing, just as he believed that readers would laugh while reading it:

> *L'Etat honteux,* je l'ai écrit en riant et je suis sûr qu'il se lit en riant. Le rire grince parce que le sujet est sérieux: le pouvoir ou comment se servir de cette machine sans tête ni queue pour qu'elle puisse fonctionner au lieu de tuer et opprimer.[8]

> [I was laughing when I wrote *L'Etat honteux* and I'm sure that people laugh while reading it. The laughter jars because the subject is serious: power or how to make use of this topsy-turvy machine in such a way that it can actually work instead of killing and oppressing]

The ideas evoked here: scandal, shame, power, killing and oppression, are recurring themes in Labou Tansi's writing while linguistic playfulness, laughter and derision are key elements of his methodology as an artist. He shares with Henri Lopes, the Congolese novelist-diplomat who facilitated the early stages of his career, the view that laughing in the face of those who wield power is one of the few tactics available to the victims of despotic authority. Moreover, laughter, even laughter born of despair, is an assertion of something fundamental to the human condition. Although firmly rooted in a Congolese cultural context, Labou Tansi's writing cries out to be read in these general, universalising terms.

Ken Bugul (Senegal, 1948–)

In an article published in 1994 providing an overview of the work of African women writers, the Congolese critic Pius Ngandu Nkashama suggests that an inhibiting factor in the way African literature in general is 'received' is the tendency to see it simply as a means of accessing a different culture. So, just as African texts can be read for the information they provide about more or less exotic cultural systems, so 'autobiography', a genre particularly associated with women writers in the post-independence years, can be read for the information it provides about the lives of women. Ngandu rejects this narrow approach to autobiography and suggests that its prime function is to allow readers a better understanding of the personality of the writer:

L'autobiographie permet de cerner la personnalité même de son auteur, et c'est dans cette perspective qu'elle précède, complète ou accomplit le récit psychanalytique. Elle se veut une analyse introspective et une catharsis, et pas seulement un témoignage sur le temps vécu.[9]

[Autobiography enables a much closer contact with the personality of the author concerned, and in this respect it precedes, complements or gives full expression to the psychoanalytical narrative. Its aim is to provide an introspective analysis and a catharsis, not just an account of lived experience.]

Ngandu goes on to argue that the upsurge of feminism in the 1970s, fuelled in particular by attempts in the United States to define 'the female condition', encouraged African women writers to write precisely such informative accounts of their lives. He concludes that true autobiographical writing, in line with the narrower definition he provides, is far rarer than critics would have us believe. The one notable exception he cites is that of the Senegalese writer Ken Bugul.

The publication of Ken Bugul's three 'autobiographical' novels was staggered over a period of sixteen years and suggests a rather painful entry into her career as a writer. After *Le Baobab fou* (1983) more than a decade passed before the appearance of *Cendres et braises* (1994), with *Riwan ou le chemin de sable* closing the series in 1999. Since then, however, she has published four more novels in relatively rapid succession. It is tempting to portray this slow start followed by an accelerating rhythm of production in terms of a need to 'write through' certain personal problems before finding the freedom to write without inhibitions. In a recent interview, Ken Bugul invites just such an interpretation:

Pour moi, l'écriture du *Baobab fou*, de *Cendres et braises* et de *Riwan* est une écriture *thérapeutique*. Il y a dans ces trois livres une volonté de revenir sur soi. Ça m'a permis de libérer des choses enfouies en moi, que j'occultais en craignant le jugement de la société.[10]

[For me, the writing in *Le Baobab fou*, *Cendres et braises* and *Riwan* is *therapeutic* writing. In these three books there is a desire to go back over my life. It allowed me to give vent to certain things deep inside myself that I was hiding away for fear of being judged by the outside world.]

Yet this way of presenting her work to date is possibly a little too neat and itself smacks of a fictionalisation of reality. While it is true that her early writings clearly relate to her own lived experiences (although exactly how close the relationship is remains an open question) it is also true that her later 'fictional' works naturally continue to draw on such experience, often exploring what for Ken Bugul herself were deeply personal issues, such as the mother–daughter relationship that is central in *De l'autre côté du regard* (2003). Inversely, much of the interest of the three 'autobiographical' works derives from the fact that they include a direct engagement with, and critique of, wider sociopolitical themes.

In this respect *Le Baobab fou* is typical. The primary narrative recounts the experience of the narrator, Ken Bugul, who leaves her native village in Senegal to study in Belgium, but this account of an individual's life, 'Histoire de Ken' [Ken's story], is presented as having its roots in a wider, historic African narrative that is fleetingly sketched out in the opening pages of the novel, 'Pré-histoire de Ken' [Ken's pre-history]. In these pages, the dominant presence is the baobab tree that is accidentally seeded by one of Ken's female forebears on the site where the family have decided to found their village. The symbolic power of the baobab as a tutelary presence is clear. The baobab survives against all the odds, rooted in the landscape, providing a physical point of reference and bearing witness to the life of the village. Beneath its foliage occur such unexplained and inexplicable events as the departure of Ken's mother at a time when Ken herself is too young to understand its reasons. This abandonment of the child by the mother generates a sense of loss and loneliness that reverberates throughout the novel, echoed by and compounding, firstly, the loss of Ken's African cultural roots that resulted from her decision to attend French school and seek a future in Europe and, secondly, the experience of alienation and solitude that marks her stay in Belgium. (Ken Bugul, the pen name of Mariétou Mbaye, is itself an allusion to her early abandonment since it is a Wolof expression meaning 'personne n'en veut' [wanted by no one].) At the close of the novel, when Ken returns to the village after her disastrous encounter with European modernity, it is to discover that the baobab had grown 'mad' and died. The unspoken 'rendez-vous' between Ken and the tree (between Ken and her cultural roots) has been missed and the consequence readers are invited to draw is that the culture itself, like the baobab that remains visible in the village, still standing but dead, is no longer alive to receive her. Like her lost childhood it cannot be recuperated.

The various themes outlined here: abandonment, solitude, alienation, loss and the ongoing search for a meaningful sense of selfhood are recycled through-out the novel in different locations and contexts. In the main body of the novel where Ken recounts her experiences in Belgium, the alienation is represented as threefold: she is black, a woman and a colonised person, that is, someone 'cut off', at home neither in Europe nor in her culturally tarnished homeland. Each of these aspects of her being intersects with the others and deepens her sense that she belongs nowhere. Ken quickly comes to seek solace in sex, drugs and alcohol. As the novel progresses, her efforts to find her true self become increasingly frenetic and her despair increasingly apparent as she experimentally plays out a range of personae. She does this through adopting a variety of sexual and social roles or by swallowing, smoking or injecting a variety of substances. The fundamental alienation she feels cannot, however, simply be ascribed to a sense that she has been rejected by society in the former colonial metropolis where she finds herself. On the contrary, her difference opens as many doors as it closes and in many respects Ken seems to integrate remarkably well, even enjoying a certain celebrity in highly fashionable circles for a time. So the obstacles to integration are largely internal. It is Ken who cannot accept the constraints that life in the West imposes upon her. In Belgium her radical physical and cultural difference, as well as her gender, are all aspects of her personality that cannot be fully assumed in the ways she would wish. More often than not, when friends and acquaintances appear to accept her on her own terms, they are merely seeking to assuage their own sense of guilt for the wrongs of colonialism. More often than not too, she feels she is being accepted into certain circles as the representative token black, or indeed, token black woman, and hence is being used as a proof of tolerant, liberal attitudes among whites. At best these are highly artificial, synthetic forms of acceptance. At worst, they are a neocolonialist repetition of the exploitative nature of the original colonial relationships. In any event they push Ken deeper and deeper into isolation and make her more acutely aware that she has lost her bearings.

Frequently Ken's account of her life in Belgium leads her to make comparisons with her former life in Africa: the expression 'là-bas' [back there] echoes throughout the novel, introducing comments on African types of behaviour or forms of social organisation that contrast sharply with Western norms. The majority of such interjections focus on gender issues and castigate the individualism and isolation of Western women that are a direct consequence of the way they conceive of relationships between the sexes in terms of competitiveness and rivalry. Ken's awareness that all women share the same fate begins to dawn on her in the doctor's waiting room where she along with other women awaits a consultation for an abortion. The need for women to close ranks, co-operate and provide mutual support for each other is the essence of what she thinks of as her 'feminist consciousness'. It harks back to the quality of relationships women enjoy in her native Senegal, where despite the apparent rivalries inherent in polygamy, she claims that relationships are conducted with greater transparency and respect for individual dignity. This is in stark contrast to the behaviour of women in the West:

> Les femmes se haïssent, se jalousent, s'envient, se fuient. Elles ignorent qu'il n'y a pas 'des femmes', il y a seulement la femme. Elles devraient se retrouver, se connaître . . . Là-bas, dans le village, les femmes se donnaient des conseils, se confessaient, vivaient ensemble.   (p. 100)

> [Women hate each other, are jealous of each other, envy each other, avoid each other. They don't realise that 'women' don't exist, there's only womankind. They ought to meet up, get to know each other . . . Back there, in the village, women would offer each other advice, would listen to each other, live together.]

Such passages seem to sketch out a motif that has become a commonplace in postcolonial literature: the journey to the metropolis offers only disappointment and experiences of alienation which in turn can be used as a justification for presenting a contrasting idyllic vision of the homeland. There are traces of such a binary opposition in *Le Baobab fou* but it is a reading that cannot be pursued with any consistency. What Ken finds in the West is a conception of life stripped of its spiritual, sacred dimensions. Her references to 'back there, in the village' are evocations of a time and a place where a sense of 'the sacred' still held sway but she is well aware that the desacralisation that characterises Western life-styles is progressing rapidly in post-colonial Africa too. While colonialism and neocolonialism are openly condemned as having instigated the process which leads Ken to lose her bearings ('le colonialisme, . . . avait créé la distorsion des esprits pour engendrer la race des sans repères' (p. 85) [Colonialism . . . had created the spiritual distortion that brought into existence the people stripped of their bearings], she refuses to lay the blame entirely at the door of the colonial enterprise. She comments, for example, 'Le colonialisme avait tout ébranlé . . . Mais je . . . refusais de croire que le colonialisme en était la seule cause.' (p. 64) [Colonialism had undermined everything. . . But I . . . refused to believe that colonialism was the only reason for it all.] So understanding the postcolonial predicament in starkly ideological or political terms is not enough, mainly because it fails to take into account the deeply personal nature of the crisis she describes. Hence, throughout the novel French schooling ('l'école française') is evoked alongside the traumatic departure of the mother as being implicitly causally connected with her own disorientation and confused sense of selfhood.

The ambivalence of Ken Bugul's views reflects her refusal to simplify complex problems and present them in terms of binary oppositions. The narrator-protagonist in *Riwan* is an older Ken Bugul, an educated woman who has returned to her native Senegal after a disorientating period spent in Europe. She is an *évoluée*, a person who has been exposed to and/or embraced Western values by virtue of education and often first-hand knowledge of the West, yet she not only embraces many of the traditions such a person might normally be expected to have rejected, including polygamy and *mouridisme* (the term used to describe the powerful religious fraternities that operate within Senegalese society), she is content to become the twenty-eighth wife of the Serigne (the religious leader) of the region where she lives. The narrator's complicity with the customs and values of her native land can also be detected in the ethnographic tone of many passages in the novel, where she presents detailed accounts of various rituals and practices that shed light on the social dynamics underpinning polygamy and *mouridisme*. In particular, the novel explains how the Serigne's power is based on the blind subservience of his disciples to the *Ndigueul*, the unwritten code of conduct and beliefs that constitutes the ethical imperatives of their lives: the order. Yet in this novel too, for all the overarching explanations of social customs and traditional cultural practices, the choice the narrator makes is a deeply personal one. The decision to become the wife of the Serigne is also a way of rejecting the Western model of monogamous marriage that, in Ken Bugul's opinion, leads to a possessive, proprietorial, highly exclusive relationship between the sexes and ends up obliging any wife to see every other woman as an enemy and a rival. Marriage to the Serigne, on the other hand, is seized upon by the narrator as an opportunity to reconcile herself with her past and recompose her shattered sense of selfhood:

> Ainsi le Serigne m'avait offert et donné la possibilité de me réconcilier avec moi-même, avec mon milieu, avec mes origines, avec mes sources, avec mon monde sans lesquels je ne pourrais jamais survivre. J'avais échappé à la mort de mon moi, de ce moi qui n'était pas à moi toute seule, De ce moi qui appartenait aussi aux miens, à ma race, à mon peuple, à mon village et à mon continent.   (pp. 167–8)

> [Thus the Serigne had offered me and given me the possibility of reconciliation with myself, with my milieu, with my origins, with my beginnings, with my world without all of which I would never be able to survive. I had escaped the death of my own selfhood, that self that didn't belong to me alone. The self that also belonged to those close to me, to my race, to my people, to my village and to my continent.]

Ngandu's belief that autobiography typically involves catharsis (see above) would seem to be borne out by the early writings of Ken Bugul. Having exorcised her own demons through the autobiographical trilogy, she frees herself to deal with related themes and issues in a far less personalised way in the later novels. Novels like *La Folie et la mort* (2000) and *Rue Félix-Faure* (2004), for example, deal with abuses of power at various levels within African society, notably as they impact upon women, the poor and marginalised, or vulnerable groups in general. In the first of these novels, madness is the privileged metaphor deployed to illustrate the ills of postcolonial African states where corruption, exploitation and despotism have turned relationships into a mascarade. Descending into real madness or assuming feigned madness seem to be the only options available to the characters in this novel, although neither ploy can ultimately ensure their survival in a system without any internal checks and balances to protect the weak. *Rue Félix-Faure* is also a novel that speaks from within Africa, exploring the world of religious sects and false spirtualism that exerts a hold over its victims, mainly women. The *moquadem* (leader of a religious sect) can be read as an inauthentic, desacralised, almost a pastiche version of the Serigne of *Riwan*. Unlike the latter, who works for good and incarnates social order, the *moquadem* of *Rue Félix-Faure* is a destabilising force within society, transmitting leprosy to his victims. Ken Bugul's interrogations of her own life, and more latterly of contemporary African society, are both equally disturbing, primarily because they are sincere interrogations asking questions to which she herself has no clear answer.

Chapter 3

Oceania – Middle East

Overview

It is something of a commonplace in postcolonial criticism to divide the world into metropolitan centres and colonial or postcolonial peripheries. The centre–periphery metaphor provides a useful image for describing what is essentially a power relationship, one of domination and control, rather than a seriously spatial one. Yet space and geography are not totally irrelevant to the way it functions. The metaphor also includes perhaps the notion of the centre as a privileged vantage point. Itself always visible to the outside world, always the focus of attention, it struggles, at times, to focus its vision over long distances and those situated at too great a distance from the centre may well fall from view. Hence the islands of the Indian Ocean (the Arabian Sea as the Indians themselves call it) often refer to themselves as the periphery of the periphery. Geographically distant and scattered, the francophone presence in the Indian Ocean also emerges from a chequered history that evolved in a remarkably fragmented and *ad hoc* fashion.

When dealing with the francophone presence on the large continental land masses of Canada, sub-Saharan Africa or even the Maghreb, there is little alternative but to resort to generalisations that blunt the edges of the cultural and linguistic differences that distinguish Acadia, for example, from Quebec, Congo from Senegal, or the Moroccan Berber from the Tunisian Jew. When dealing with the francophone presence in the Indian Ocean, the opposite is the case. Heterogeneity and diversity impose themselves as the starting point for discussion while forms of hybridity and creolisation (the intermingling of cultures and races) are not merely acceptable models for conceptualising identity, they are the standard model. The notion of some pure cultural origin located in a pre-colonial, pre-transportation era does not even function as a myth in the way vaguely remembered African roots did for the former slave populations of the Caribbean islands. The Djiboutian writer Abdourahman A. Waberi ironically refers to this absence of founding myths as one of the reasons why his homeland is of so little interest to the wider world : 'Nous sommes en peine de mythes capables d'attirer sur nous les yeux du monde. Nos voisins s'étaient inventé ... les noces métissées du roi Salomon et la reine de Saba ... On fait grise mine, nous, à côté.'[1] [We are a little short of myths capable of drawing the attention of the eyes of the world upon us. Our neighbours invented ... the mixed marriage of King Solomon and the Queen of Sheba for themselves ... We look quite boring by comparison.] Nor, in modern times, has the homogenising potential of *francophonie* imposed itself over other ethnic, linguistic, religious or cultural lines of affiliation that link the various communities present in the region. It is simply one strand of a composite identity that remains a matter for ongoing negotiation.

This is the message Mauritian poet Khal Torabully has reiterated through a series of collections of poetry that outline the concept of 'coolitude': 'Coolitude: parce que je suis créole de mon cordage, je suis indien de mon mât, je suis européen de ma vergue, je suis mauricien de ma quête et français de mon exil.'[2] [Coolitude: because I am creole through my rigging, I am Indian through my mast, I am European through my yardarm, I am Mauritian through my journey and French through my exile.] Coolitude acnowledges rather than stresses the poet's Indian origins. It is a strand of identity that Torabully always seeks to exploit in combination with other influences rather than as an exclusive, defining influence. One commentator has summed up this poetics as 'constitutive of a new perspective on Indian identities characterised by multiple crossings: crossings between cultures, heritages, places, generations, gender, historical assertions and mythical references'.[3]

The geographical dispersal of the Indian Ocean islands and their contrasting histories repeats and echoes the multiple cultural origins of their inhabitants, populations that have been formed from waves of voluntary or involuntary immigration. Madagascar, 'la grande île', was peopled originally by the successive arrivals of groups of Africans from the eastern seabord and Indonesians during the first millennium. Islamised Arab traders arrived in the course of the tenth century, possibly by way of the Comores, which have remained largely Muslim islands with strong cultural ties with East Africa. The earliest French presence dates from 1643, although the island was used only as a source of supplies for vessels heading further east, and later as a source of slaves for the plantations in La Réunion and Mauritius, until the 1890s when the French began systematic colonisation. By that time Madagasacar was an island that had been successfully unified by an indigenous monarchy with a single language and a cohesive cultural identity. By contrast, the Mascareignes were uninhabited until relatively late and only permanently settled in the course of the seventeenth (La Réunion) and eighteenth (Mauritius) centuries when

French colonisers and African and Malagasy slaves arrived in greater numbers. Following the abolition of slavery, indentured labourers from the Indian sub-continent were brought to the islands and now form substantial elements of the populations of both, particularly Mauritius.

MAURITIUS

The year 1768 saw two imports into the island of Mauritius, 'l'île de France', from the metropolis. Both would have a lasting impact on the evolution of liter-ary life there. The arrival of the first printing press coincided with the arrival of Bernardin de Saint-Pierre, a young engineer embarking on a two-year stay on the island. He would go on to publish two texts that helped mould French and European perceptions of Mauritius as an exotic location while rankling with the local population. The Rousseauesque inspiration of Bernardin's *Voyage à l'île de France* (1773) and *Paul et Virginie* (1788) did not prevent the author from voicing serious reservations about the inhuman treatment of the slaves who worked on the plantations. Bernardin's writings and the discussion of them by elite society in Mauritius can be seen as a very French-francophone debate that is merely a curious sideshow as far as the mainstream cultural life of metropolitan France is concerned. The printing press would facilitate the development of newspapers and reviews throughout the nineteenth cen-tury. It was in the columns of publications like these, rather than through the highly imitative, 'francotropiste' poetry of supposedly 'great Mauritian poets' like Léoville l'Homme, that the quest for a local literature began. (The term 'francotropisme' was coined by the Mauritian critic Jean-Georges Prosper to refer to the obsessively francophile attitude of Mauritian writers.)

A literature of local inspiration and dealing with local realities would take a considerable time to emerge, all the more so perhaps because the defence of French culture by the francophone elite became more entrenched as a reac-tion to the cession of the island to British control in 1815, and later, as a result of insecurity in the face of changing demographic trends. It is almost as though Mauritian writers, collectively (from Robert-Edward Hart to Malcolm de Chazal), had felt the need to invent an alternative fiction of origins based on the pseudo-scientific, fantastical notion of a lost continent (Lémurie) before a later generation was able to exorcise its links with France sufficiently to exam-ine its true origins in the cultural and ethnic intermixing of recent history. Nowadays, writing from Mauritius reflects these hybrid elements of Mauritian society, both through the ethnic origins of the writers themselves (Kahl Torab-ully, Ananda Devi or Shanez Patel for example), or through a concern to explore aspects of sociocultural diversity on a thematic level (Carl de Souza or Nathacha Appanah).

Ananda Devi (Mauritius, 1960–)

Hailed as a child prodigy in 1972 following the publication of a prize-winning short story written when she was an adolescent schoolgirl, Ananda Devi's work has continued to attract substantial critical attention ever since. A first collection of short stories, *Solstices*, was published at her own expense in 1976 (subsequently republished by L'Harmattan in 1997) and a second collection, *Le Poids des êtres* (1987), came out in Mauritius a year before her first novel, *Rue la poudrière* (1988), was published by Nouvelles Editions Africaines. Françoise Lionnet has argued convincingly that Ananda Devi consciously subverts the referential codes that would allow her to be read as a Mauritian or a francophone writer. There is a hybrid quality to *Rue la poudrière*, for example, including the way the book is packaged and presented, that makes it difficult to place it within 'an unambiguous literary or cultural framework'.[4] This claim is consistent with the frequently stated view that in her work she represents the 'other Mauritius', not the tropical paradise of French tourist brochures but as Delphine Chaume expresses it in a recent number of *Le Magazine Littéraire*, 'les multiples univers qui s'y côtoient, se déchirent, se nourrissent réciproquement'[5] [the multiple worlds that rub shoulders there, mutually tearing each other apart and sustaining each other].

Yet even though the fictional worlds she creates express the diversity of traditions and cultures cohabiting on the island, she herself would claim that there is an underlying unity to her work that comes from her own experience of life on Mauritius and her sensibilities as a woman of Hindu origin. In a recent interview she explained her attachment to Mauritius in the following way:

> Je dirais donc que, très profondément, c'est la présence de l'île en moi qui me pousse à écrire – mais c'est l'île revée dont je parle toujours, l'île mystique qui a enveloppé et guidé mes débuts d'écrivain. Là-dessus sont venus se greffer les histoires à proprement parler, la société telle qu'elle était ou telle que je la voyais, et les personnages sont venus habiter cette île en porte-à-faux avec la vraie en créant l'illusion que je racontais le pays véritable.[6]

> [I would say then that, in a very deep way, it's the island's presence within me that motivates me to write – but what I'm always talking about is the imaginary island, the mystical island that protected and guided my first steps as a writer. The stories themselves then came and

grafted themselves on to this dreamed-up island, as did society as it was
or as I saw it, and then characters came to inhabit this island that was
out of step with the real island, thus creating the illusion that I was
narrating the real place.]

The confusion between the world of everyday reality and the world of the
imagination, between the prosaic and the mystical, has been a characteristic
of francophone Mauritian literature since Robert-Edward Hart's *Le Cycle de
Pierre Flandre* (1928–36), through the unclassifiable writings of Malcolm de
Chazal and down to the present day.

In the case of Ananda Devi, critics have tended to present the mystical dimension she so frequently plays upon in her writing as being somehow associated
with her Indian origins. This is surely a reductionist response to a complex
aspect of her work, particularly since 'the mystical' is merely one type of 'other
worldliness' discernible in her novels and stories. Equally common in her writings are various examples of madness and psychic alienation that can readily be
understood within a Western tradition of psychiatric discourse. It hardly needs
pointing out that the psychiatrist Octave Mannoni, who had himself worked
for a while in Madagascar, published a groundbreaking study of the psychology of colonialism, *Prospero et Caliban* (1950), that was a forerunner to Frantz
Fanon's seminal *Peau noire masques blancs* (1952) which dealt with the psychiatric disorders that colonialism brought in its train. The emphasis on madness,
like the appeal to Indian cultural traditions, should not be neatly attached to
any distinct and discrete strand of Ananda Devi's cultural make-up: they feed
into and upon each other, confirming the postcolonial emphasis on the interconnectedness of the multiple layers that make up identity. Nevertheless, the
appeal to Eastern mysticism and Indian mythology is undeniably a feature of
Ananda Devi's work, particularly in relatively early novels such as *Le Voile de
Drapaudi* (1993) or *L'Arbre fouet* (1997). More often than not, however, this
source of inspiration is not presented as an escape route for beleaguered characters struggling to cope with modernity and its multiple forms of oppression.
It is itself interrogated as one of the constraints bearing down on characters
and perhaps as one of the forms of their marginalisation and alienation.

The stories, the society and the characters she refers to when speaking of the
'imaginary island' of Mauritius combine together to build up an unremittingly
bleak portrait of Mauritian society. Foremost among the preoccupations she
revisits time and again in her writings is the destructive nature of key human
relationships, whether these be interpersonal (parents and children), intereth-
nic (between the various communities inhabiting the island) or between the
sexes. The condition of women and their struggle to seize and maintain control

of their own bodies and their own sexuality is a particularly important leitmotif of her novels, although it could be argued that women figure so prominently for the simple reason that they are archetypal examples of the marginalised, oppressed beings that increasingly haunt her work.

The various stories that make up *Le Poids des êtres* can be seen as so many explorations of dysfuctional relationships: accounts of intimacy, for example, are invariably stories of hatred rather than love stories. Children figure prominently, representing childhood as a magical place but only temporarily so, and often retrospectively, since child deaths and infanticide are the painful norm and recur insistently. Happiness and joy are only ever fleetingly glimpsed before hatred, violence and decay intervene to destroy them. The failure of relationships between adults, as individuals or within the family unit, mirrors a breakdown on the more general level of social interaction. The most vicious illustration of this theme is that presented in 'Le Fuyard' where the unnamed protagonist is portrayed from the outset as a madman on the run. It transpires that his crime has been to murder his newly married wife, Marie-la-chauve [bald-headed Marie], herself an outcast disfigured by illness whom he had expressly chosen to marry, pursuing an inverted form of reasoning, out of hatred and a desire for vengeance. His wife's offence is a shared rather than an individual offence: she and other women persistently mock the menfolk who have returned from university studies to a life that offers them no prospect of useful employment or functionality. The killer's madness cannot simply be explained away as an acute form of postcolonial alienation, but the narration invites the reader to interpret the madness as a form of deviancy that has direct correspondences with the dysfunctionality of society at large. The murder itself, while clearly being a matter of choice, and undeniably of premeditated choice at that, is also portrayed as an atavistically 'male thing', a characteristic of men in general: 'Il n'était plus conscient que de son droit de vie et de mort sur la femelle de l'espèce, et, formidable, empli de sa propre grandeur, il choisissait de prodiguer la mort.' (p. 151) [He was no longer conscious of anything other than his right of life and death over the female of the species, and superb, filled with a sense of his own greatness, his decision was to dole out death.] The story closes with a scene that echoes the movement from the specific to the general that the murder has already illustrated. Racked with hunger and desperate for human company after days on the run, the killer stumbles into a village where he is confronted and attacked by an aggressive farmyard cock. He kills the bird in a macabre fashion by biting off its head. This in turn triggers a violent reaction from the villagers who, having discovered him in the act (literally red-handed, one might say) proceed to avenge themselves by committing an act of collective murder. The narrator bleakly concludes: 'voilà tout ce qu'il y a de vrai en l'homme, un brûlant désir de violence et de destruction' (p. 156) [there we have all that is true about men, a burning desire for violence and destruction].

In *Rue la poudrière* the destructive nature of relationships is again illustrated with unrelenting insistence. The narrator, Paule, is sold into prostitution by her own alcoholic father, Edouard, for a small bottle of rum, while the pimp who controls her, Mallacre, exerts a magnetic power over her that is partly sexual and partly mystical. Her mother, Marie, is a violent and cruel woman who engages in witchcraft, infanticide and bizarre esoteric practices suggestive of voodoo rituals. Her own fate is to fall pregnant when she unwittingly accepts a client who turns out to have been her own father. From her destroyed childhood onwards, through her life as an 'enslaved' prostitute to the final apocalyptic scene where she sits and awaits the end having ingested a poisonous concoction of herbs, Paule's life is portrayed as a descent into ever more extreme forms of marginalised existence that are increasingly equated with madness. In this novel, as in the earlier stories, specific experiences and events are narrated as instances of deviancy and transgression that have a wider, universal significance.

In different ways, madness is also a key theme of later novels such as *Pagli* (2001), *Soupir* (2002) or *La Vie de Joséphin le fou* (2003). 'Pagli' is the creole word for 'mad woman' and the novel, like *Rue la poudrière*, is a first-person narrative account of one woman's journey into ever more extreme forms of marginalisation and isolation. Daya (the narrator's real name) is isolated within an Indian family setting that has seen her betrothed as a child to a man who rapes her when she is a mere thirteen years old. Her response is to accept the planned marriage as an opportunity to wreak her revenge on the man she loathes. Simultaneously, her personal quest for control of her feminine identity and, indeed, of her own body, leads her into a love affair with Zil, a fisherman whose frequent absences allow him to figure as a shadowy, almost mystical being. He is present in memory and as a symbol as much as, in any effective way, as a lover. The two poles of Daya's being are thus identified as, on the one hand, a revolt against the oppression she suffers at the hands of the husband and the wider family circle who inhabit 'la maison de sucre glace' [the icing sugar house], and, on the other, a self-affirming passionate love affair with Zil. They correspond, of course, to two contrasting perceptions of the island of Mauritius: the tourist brochure, 'icing sugar' image of the island that conceals from view a violent, conflictual world of oppression and exploitation, and Daya's highly subjective perception of the island ('mon île, mon Zil' (p. 87) [my island, my Zil]) as a place of refuge. The psychiatric home ('l'asile'), in which the family would like to confine Daya, belongs to a universe that she rejects. So is Daya mad after all? Phonetically, the 'asile' proposed by the family is redundant; she might need no cure if they could accept that she already belongs to Zil ('mais je suis déjà à Zil' (p. 112) she says when the family mentions the psychiatric home). Daya's madness, then, is a consequence of the clash between two world views that has acted like an explosion to shatter her sense of selfhood. Is this a metaphor for the unequal encounter between cultures orchestrated by colonialism? The novel closes with Daya buried alive in a wall of mud as torrential rain transforms the chicken coop, where the family have locked her away, into a deathtrap. This pitiful destiny (Daya means 'pity') can be summarised, as Daya herself does at one point, in remarkably few words: 'Je vois toutes ces moi disséminées dans le temps et je les saisis toutes; née, violée, mariée, voilée, aimée, enfermée – tout cela en même temps.' (p. 57) [I see all these selves disseminated through time and I seize them all: born, raped, married, veiled, loved, locked away – all that at the same time.]

Soupir is in many ways a more ambitious novel in the sense that it addresses madness from a collective rather than an individual angle. The novel is structured as a succession of texts dealing with individual characters who, ostensibly, are only vaguely linked. It is only towards the close of the novel that the real relationships of paternity and reciprocal exploitation and betrayal become clear. The novel closes with an horrific scene of collective rape perpetrated on the person of the disabled woman, Noëlle. Collective madness, linked as ever to violence and rape, would seem in this instance to be proposed as a founding myth of the island of Rodrigues where the novel is set. *La Vie de Joséphin le fou*, similarly, deals with madness, murder and the destruction of young lives. The eponymous Joséphin (Zozéfin-fouka in creole), is a strange, almost amphibian creature who has fled the brutal world of men and the neglect and abuse he had suffered at the hands of his prostitute mother and her clients to seek refuge among the eels and fishes, living in a marine environment of shoreline and submarine caves. The welcoming sea (*la mer*) thus acts as a direct substitute for the mother (*la mère*) who refused to nurture him and allowed him to grow into manhood in a state of savage nature. The narrative consists of an interior monologue in which readers learn that he has sequestrated two girls, Solange and Marlène, in a vain attempt to capture and share something of the beauty and music of their young lives. But Joséphin belongs to an alien world. Excluded from culture by the destruction of his childhood and deprived of reason by the isolation he has endured, he is beyond community. His insanity is the marker of his difference and it translates itself into the violent destruction of the two girls with which the novel closes.

Eve de ses décombres (2006) reworks the now familiar basic ingredients of rape, murder and male brutality but this time in an urban setting evocative of inner-city deprivation more readily associated with the cities of metropolitan

France than the Indian Ocean. The narrative is made up of contributions from four adolescents – Sad, Savita, Clélio and Eve – which provide four different perspectives on the events leading to Savita's murder and its aftermath. The neighbourhood they inhabit, Troumaron, is a dumping ground for the wretched of the earth and serves as a backdrop for the individualised versions of despair and hopelessness that each of the adolescents projects into their narrative. The crime itself confirms their disorientation in a world where adults have not only failed to provide a nurturing, protecting environment in which they might grow, but actually constitute the danger and the imminent threat to the young. The fact that the crime has been perpetrated by a male teacher on a pupil merely underscores the sense that society as a whole has abdicated its responsibilities to the young and the vulnerable, but perhaps especially that atavistic, predatory male instincts have triumphed over the veneer of cultural conditioning. Nor is the crime itself part of an act of sexual aggression, committed in the heat of the moment. The sexual abuse is practised not on Savita but on her friend, Eve, a young woman so pyschologically damaged that she has chosen to embrace degradation rather than resist it. Savita is killed because she has witnessed the teacher and Eve together and the teacher eliminates her to protect his reputation: the reality of these wasted young lives must not be allowed to tarnish the image that the rich and powerful seek to project. It is fitting, then, that Savita's body should be consigned to a dustbin near the block of flats where she lives, discarded like so much rubbish. Her final words to Eve were, 'Promets-moi de ramasser mes morceaux.' (p. 85) [Promise to pick up my pieces.] She, like her friends, is acutely conscious even before her death that she is a shattered personality, split into shards by the violent, alienating environment of a postcolonial slum and the exploitative treatment meted out by its patriarchal, adult guardians. These are the 'décombres' [rubble] of the novel's title from which Sad promises to extricate Eve: both the physical rubble of the urban ghetto in a developing country and the metaphysical rubble of postcolonial alienation.

LA RÉUNION

Like Mauritius, La Réunion emerged only relatively recently from the literary orbit of France and this in a context where debates about the status of creole as a language have both fed upon and fed into wider debates about creole identity and creole culture. However, unlike Mauritius, La Réunion has been a French *département* since 1946, so any campaign to promote creole culture is difficult to dissociate from a politics of separation and autonomy. In terms of literary, rather than political history, however, the contemporary concern for a Réunionnais creole cultural identity have generally been traced back to the appearance of *Zamal,* a collection of poetry published in Paris by Jean Albany, in 1951. The lyrical quality of these poems nevertheless predominates and for all their links to subsequent, more politicised campaigns on behalf of *créolité,* they can also easily be read as variations on the exotic that has been characteristic of the work of earlier generations of Réunionnais poets. With Boris Gamaleya's *Vali pour une reine morte* (1973) the political dimension of the creole inspiration became far more apparent.

The exploration of creole identity has also proved to be an important element in the prose writings of, for example, Monique Agénor, Jean-François Samlong and Axel Gauvin. But in their work, the defence of creole culture is never constructed as a simple antithesis to metropolitan French language or culture. There is no Manichean opposition between French and creole for the simple reason that French is itself one of the major building blocks, linguistically and culturally, of creole culture. It is perhaps for this reason that authors born in France but choosing to write texts inspired by childhood memories of time spent on La Réunion (the case of Jean Lods), or choosing to take up residence on the island and work there (the case of Daniel Vaxelaire), are so readily incorporated into the island's literary culture.

Axel Gauvin (La Réunion, 1950–)

The first part of Axel Gauvin's *L'Aimé* (1990) is taken up with a dramatic account of the sudden arrival of a physically and emotionally damaged young boy, Ptit-mé, at the home of Margrite Bellon, at the very moment a cyclone prepares to strike the small community perched in the mountains of La Réunion. For the rest of the novel, the boy will be enveloped in a cocoon of love and tenderness (hence the title of the novel), but the chaotic disorder of the storm that marks his arrival can be read as a symbol of the ever-present threat posed by the violence of the natural world, the precariousness of existence and the concealed trauma of the boy's own dark past. Once Ptit-mé has entered her life, Margrite's every effort will be directed to first saving and then nurturing her orphan grandson. The forces against which she struggles include the harsh natural surroundings of the island, the indifference and incompetence of the medical services at the hospital, the difficulty of making ends meet on her low income, the intransigent bureaucracy of the education service which refuses to accept the boy in school, and eventually her own failing health and the illness that she will only overcome, in the end, by taking her own life. The act of suicide which closes the novel is less an indication that circumstances have defeated Margrite than a final affirmation of her devotion to the boy, since her own disappearance will free him from the responsibility of caring for an ill and ageing woman.

In the event, in *L'Aimé*, the conflict between the constructive forces that are figured in Margrite's mothering of Ptit-mé and the destructive forces of the surrounding world is not presented as a head-on clash. The novel is composed of multiple narratives and the threat of entropic disorder is not confined merely to the narrative present (Margrite's battles on behalf of Ptit-mé) but distributed across many of the mini-narratives that, taken together, build up a portrait of the everyday life and experiences of Réunionnais people over several generations. At various points in the novel, Gauvin enters the private world of his characters through their memories, recollections, desires, regrets, fears and anxieties. The colourful characters from Margrite's own family history (for example, her father, Antoine-Joseph, or her eccentric uncle, Calixte) and the nostalgia she feels for Vincendo, the village in which she grew up, are evoked on numerous occasions: the quirkiness of the characters betokens chaotic individuality while Vincendo shines like a beacon of peacefulness and order in a changing world. Similarly, it is by way of access to the inner thoughts and memories of Margrite's husband, Gaétan Bénard, that a picture of his personality is communicated. His anticolonial, anticlerical attitudes endure into the narrative present of course, but they are represented most clearly in a narrative past through recollections of his younger days in the colonial service in Madagascar, or through the account of his love affair with Esther that began as a plan to seduce a 'bigote' and therefore as a conscious attack on the church itself but which ironically developed into a real love affair. Even in the narrative present, the most dynamic activity Gaétan undertakes is calling up memories of his younger days, many of which involve what is quite literally a *re-membering*. Gaétan is impotent but he manages to achieve erection when he begins to undertake regular car journeys, accompanied by Ptit-mé, to revisit the locations where, in his prime, he had enjoyed amorous escapades with various sexual partners. But perhaps the most striking example of these mini-narrative threads that run through the novel is the piecemeal reconstruction of Ptit-mé's own traumatic experience prior to being taken into the care of Margrite. It is presented in dribs and drabs throughout the novel as Ptit-mé's nightmares gradually dredge up the memories of the traumatic early childhood he has suppressed. Within this narrative, his mother is a witchlike evil spirit (*la loule*) who kills her own daughter while in an alcoholic stupor, drives her husband to his death and finally tries to kill Ptit-mé too. Memories, whether of remembered pain, remembered desire or remembered pleasure, play a far more important role in this novel than anything the present has to offer by way of action or incident.

In *L'Aimé*, then, the motor of the narrative is quite clearly the tension that exists between the affective world of interpersonal relations and the disturbing forces that threaten its stability or permanence from all sides. Inscribed in the margins of this universal theme (order threatened by disorder) are quite specific ideological positionings, embedded in the attitudes of characters and in the situations they live through. Margrite and Gaétan belong to the class of 'petits blancs', white folk but of peasant status, living in relatively impoverished conditions. In departmentalised La Réunion, the 'petits blancs' are on a par with a range of other racial groups of African, Malagasy, Indian and Chinese extraction, that together form the highly creolised bedrock of the social order. Her lowly social status is in evidence on each occasion that Margrite is obliged to engage with the urban, institutionalised world of officialdom: hospitals and schools; precisely areas where she confronts official *francophonie*. This is the world inhabited by a range of characters who are deficient in human empathy and understanding: 'Sans soutien', the modern, sophisticated yet incompetent nurse who almost kills Ptit-mé by failing to ensure that the penicillin he needs is at the required temperature; the hospital director who shields her when her incompetence is discovered; Gabriel, Gaétan's right-minded, highly conservative civil-servant son; the unhelpful schoolmistress who refuses to allow Ptit-mé into the school, Laken, the dreaded doctor who is totally devoid of compassion and basic human kindness. The striking exception to this rule is Dr S., the man who saves Ptit-mé's life and in due course tends Margrite herself when she falls ill. He alone, among the educated elite represented in the novel, has the human qualities that are the indispensable basis of social cohesion in the community. These repeated examples of encounters with officialdom highlight contrasting approaches to life and contrasting value systems that amount to a subtle yet pervasive valorisation of creole culture and an indictment of 'French' ways.

Through the character of Gaétan, the novel proposes a rather more direct thread of anticolonial discourse. His aloofness from the colonial enterprise is evident whenever he reminisces about Madagascar, while his passion for the natural history of the island and his respect for its people demonstrate that his attitude was never grounded in the blind cultural imperialism of colonialism. Among the papers discovered after his death are a photograph of the Malagasy lover with whom he had cohabited during his time on the island and a document attesting to the restitution to the Malagasy people of a salt mine to which Gaétan had been granted the concession. The strength of his anticolonialist views is comically exploited in the scene where he finally achieves an erection: Gauvin portrays him talking to his penis as it becomes increasingly tumescent. At the final stage of erection Gaétan's new-found sexual potency is associated with virulent anticolonial language:

Enfin à dureté ligneuse, en bois (comme on dit en créole), l'insulter, le traiter de 'chien méchant', de 'Thiers', de 'Guy Mollet', lui donner le nom d'autres impérialistes, ceux de 'Gallieni', de 'Bugeaud', car Gaétan bandait anticolonial:

– Mon salaud, je vais t'en donner moi, de la Mission civilisatrice! il pensait . . . Je vais t'en donner, moi, de la Grandeur de l'Empire français.

(p. 134)

[Finally when it became a hard straight line, wooden (as we say in creole), he insulted it, called it a 'nasty dog', 'Thiers', 'Guy Mollet', gave it the names of other imperialists, 'Gallieni', 'Bugeaud', because Gaétan's hard-on was anticolonialist:

– You bastard, I'll give you a taste of a 'civilising mission'! he thought . . . I'll let you have a piece of the Glory of the French Empire.]

The two poles that can be identified in *L'Aimé*, on the one hand the tenderness and warmth of human relationships and, on the other, the turbulence and violence of the ambient natural, social and political environment, are a recurring structuring device in Gauvin's novels. From text to text either of these poles may dominate the narrative, but the counterbalancing presence of the other pole is always implicitly or explicitly discernible. In *Faims d'enfance* (1987) for example, the theme of nourishment is omnipresent since the privileged setting is the school refectory in which the various characters gather every day for lunch. Food, especially the typical dishes of creole cuisine, provides comfort to the ravenous children who seem to attend school solely in order to eat. Echoing views he had already expressed in *Du Créole opprimé au créole libéré* (1977), in which he castigates the education system of La Réunion as unfit for purpose, Gauvin implies in *Faims d'enfance* that the authorities are content to maintain the population in the most abject state of intellectual impoverishment, the real hunger perhaps of the novel's title. There are multiple connections linking *Du Créole opprimé au créole libéré* and *Faims d'enfance*. Although the essay focuses essentially on language policy, arguing forcibly that an insistence on French as the language of instruction in La Réunion is an obstacle to meaningful education, it also demonstrates that this has highly political consequences: 'le monopole du français bâillonne le peuple . . . [Il] est un des moyens de l'oppresssion coloniale et de la domination du peuple réunionnais.'[7] [the monopoly of the French language gags the people . . . (It) is one the means by which colonial oppression and the domination of the Réunionnais people are effected.] The narrow pedagogical focus thus opens out on to wider political and cultural perspectives. In so far as the essay implicitly equates a defence of the creole language with the view that creole culture and the creole personality are themselves intrinsically valuable, it can be seen as precursor of the more culturally focused *Eloge de la créolité* that would be published just over a decade later by Caribbean writers.

Faims d'enfance echoes the valorisation of creole culture that is implicit throughout Gauvin's essay in that food acts as a master metaphor for culture and cultural nourishment in the novel. Not only do the children learn nothing in the 'French' school, their sole reason for attending is their hunger for creole food. Moreover, the school remains a fundamentally creole community: efforts to counter the creole influence and assimilate the children to French values are half-hearted and inadequate. In this respect, food is a cultural marker that allows Gauvin to contrast the spiciness of creole cuisine with the blandness of 'nourriture zorèy' [metropolitan French food]. Nothing that is served up to the children can wean them away from their natural taste for creole food-stuffs. Moreover, any attempts the school makes in this direction are narrowly functional and self-serving, as when food is used to blackmail the children in order to enlist them in the political process in support of the incumbent mayor, Maisonneuve. Indeed, the blackmailing and social divisiveness that the election process introduces into the school community are the only visible signs of Frenchness on offer. They are negative or vacuous, as when the children are made to mouth the words of the *Marseillaise,* an anthem they do not know, as a sign of the support they do not feel (pp. 174–5). All these examples echo Gauvin's argument that France is not serious about assimilating the Réunionnais, merely intent on ensuring their subservience within a system that remains colonial in all but name. In La Réunion as in the Caribbean, the valorisation of creole culture begins with self-acceptance and the possibility of feeling good about oneself. This 'self-directed' love (creole to creole) is underscored in the novel through the burgeoning relationship between Baya, the Malabar boy, and Lina, the creole girl. This is yet another example of the tenderness of creole relationships contrasting with the destructiveness of the (on this occasion) political forces that surround them. The novel closes as Baya and Lina finally come together, combining in their efforts to save Lina's brother, Ara, who has greedily ingurgitated food laced with needles: Maisonneuve's revenge on the school for his defeat in the elections.

In Gauvin's fourth novel, *Cravate et fils* (1996), the caring, nurturing role is assumed by the narrator, Laurent, an itinerant nurse who devotes himself wholeheartedly to the service of the community and in particular to saving his suicidal friend, Mmon, the eponymous Cravate fils. The destructive forces that Laurent is confronting can be figured as the illnesses, the disease and the range of pathological conditions he treats, as well as the miserable social conditions that favour their development.

By way of contrast, in *Train fou* (2000) it is the anarchic violence unleashed by the 'zorèy' [metropolitan Frenchman], Bernard Montcorbeil, that dominates the narrative while Maxime Grondin's efforts to save his friends from the clutches of the Frenchman prove ineffectual. *Train fou* is possibly Gauvin's most political novel to date. The protagonist is an egotistical, career-driven, self-serving Frenchman who has recently arrived in La Réunion to take up a post in the administration of the island's Water Company. After a bout of heavy drinking, evicted from the reception he had been attending, he loses his way and ends up in the bar-boutique of Cheung-to where he continues drinking heavily with a group of creole characters: Pan, Noiseau and Parle-Pas. Bernard leads the trio down to the ocean on an absurd quest to discover whether seawater is still salty out at sea, away from the shore. At this point, Bernard's recollections of a carnivalesque initiation march he had led through the Latin Quarter in his student days begin to confuse past hatreds with present anger. Gauvin's prose reflects Bernard's chaotic mental state as deep-seated racist attitudes are liberated by the alcohol he has consumed. The procession on the shore ends in an orgy of violence and death in which the three Réunionnais lose their lives. Noiseau is killed by a car as he attempts to cross a road, while Bernard drowns Pan in a pool close to the shore before breaking the neck of the only witness to his crime, Parle-pas.

There is a powerful allegorical dimension to this narrative that speaks to the dynamics of colonial power relations. Bernard's domination of the characters he will go on to kill invites questions about who exactly is superior to whom. His supposed 'superiority' amounts to little more than a favourable position in economic and technological hierarchies. In absolute terms, he is neither more civilised nor more cultivated than they are, and, in the course of the novel, as Gauvin provides details of the biography of each 'creole' character in turn, the difficulties and precariousness of their lives as well as the strong bonds of solidarity and mutual assistance that they show to each other are far more likely to win the respect of readers than the petty-minded, self-seeking individualism that epitomises the character of Bernard. Pan's admiration for the 'vazabé' [foreigner] is exemplified when Bernard exclaims 'Putain': with trenchant irony Gauvin develops this into a symbol of French cultural supremacy:

> Meilleur marqueur de civilisation, y a pas. De même qu'un petit pipi suffit pour poser la frontière du royaume des rats, de même un 'Putain!' marque mieux qu'un Grévisse, qu'un Bescherelle, qu'un Bled, la frontière entre France et non-France, Culture et inculture, Etre et néant.
>
> (p. 74)

[No better way of marking out a civilisation. Just like a few drops of pee are enough to mark out the boundary of the kingdom of rats, so a 'Bloody hell!' works better than any Grévisse, any list of conjugations, any French grammar to mark the boundary between France and non-France, culture and culturelessness, Being and nothingness.]

Bernard's contempt for his victims combines sexual and racist resentment and a hatred that is deeply atavistic. Bernard is portrayed as a physically powerful male, eliminating weaker potential rivals whose humanity he questions anyway. But most strikingly of all, next morning when Bernard awakens on the beach he has no recollection of what he has done. His actions have been obliterated from his mind as the alcoholic haze dissipates. This amnesia seems to suggest that the frenzy of violence he has indulged in can simply be forgotten, written off, have no consequences, just as the crimes of colonisation are so often ignored by selective metropolitan historiography. The insignificance of the deaths he has perpetrated suggests the voicelessness that is characteristic of all victims of historical processes. History after all is written by the conquerors not the vanquished.

MADAGASCAR

The relative cultural unity of Madagascar prior to the arrival of Europeans extended to an extremely rich oral tradition. As throughout mainland Africa, it included folk tales, fables, proverbs and riddles but a number of types of oral performance specific to Madagascar had also developed. In the High Plains of central Madagascar, the local population practised *hain-teny*, a form of popular poetry that was structured as a verbal joust, a lovers' quarrel, between two 'opponents'. Formally, *hain-teny* drew on a range of conventionalised rhetorical resources while still requiring a high degree of improvisation and spontaneity. They were frequently used as a means of resolving disputes within the community and, originally at least, had served a real social function as a poeticised form of litigation. A second type of oral practice peculiar to the island was the *kabary*, the set-piece rhetorical performance that was an essential element of any major ceremony: birth, circumcision, marriage or funeral. The *kabary* was a highly conventionalised and tightly structured speech that proceeded by allusion, drawing on a wide range of references to capture the interest of the audience. Alongside this flourishing and sophisticated oral tradition there also existed a written literature. The Arab traders who had settled in the island had brought writing with them and thus made possible the gradual development of an embryonic pre-colonial literature consisting mainly of chronicles, historic texts, accounts of major events and royal speeches. The replacement of Arabic script by Latin script in the first decades of the nineteenth century allowed the development of the printing press. From the 1860s onwards a number of Malagasy newspapers and periodicals began to appear. At the time of the annexation of the island by the French in 1896, Madagascar was already relatively sophisticated in terms of 'literary' practices and endowed with an infrastructure capable of supporting rapid further development.

In Madagascar, then, it is difficult to see the military conquest of 1896 in terms of a *mission civilisatrice*. It was more easily presented in terms of a 'modernising mission' and in reality this meant that the military conquest was accompanied by a campaign for cultural domination too. Gallieni, the first governor-general, made a knowledge of French a prerequisite for any official post in the administration and consciously used schooling through the medium of French as a strategic weapon in his efforts to bring the island under French control. Jean-Joseph Rabearivelo, the leading francophone literary figure of the early decades of the twentieth century, was equally at home in the two cultures as he was working in either language. His writings reflect this bicultural background. They include early collections of poetry reminiscent of the French Parnassian movement, a novel, *L'Interférence*, written in 1928 but only published in 1987, that explores the complexities of the various ways colonial values 'interfered with' Malagasy society, and, towards the end of his life, a number of bilingual works and translations into French of traditional Malagasy poetry. His biculturalism can hardly be viewed as an example of the successful fusion of two traditions, however. On the contrary, Rabearivelo is generally viewed as a poet who suffered rejection by both cultural communities. He committed suicide at the age of thirty-four in an act that has been interpreted by many as an act of despair born of cultural alienation, but also as having been 'staged' for public consumption.

One of Rabearivelo's final acts before his suicide was to send a message through which he 'passed on the torch of poetry' to a man who was to have a considerable influence on the literary and political life of the island for the remainder of the twentieth century, Jacques Rabemananjara. A man of strong convictions, Rabemananjara's work reflects the same cultural self-confidence and desire for self-affirmation that had fuelled *Négritude*. A friend of Senghor and Alioune Diop, he worked with both to create the review *Présence Africaine*. Some of his most powerful and original poetry was written during the ten years he spent in prison following the rebellion against French colonial rule in 1947: *Antsa* (1948), *Lamba* (1956) and *Antidote* (1961). In the years since independence, the publication of literature in French went through a period of decline as policies of 'malgachisation' were implemented. More recently, however, notably through the work of the poet David Jaomanoro and prose writers Michèle Rakotoson and Raharimanana, a new generation of franco-phone authors has emerged.

Raharimanana (Madagascar, 1967–)

In an open letter to his friend, the Congolese poet and novelist Alain Mabanckou, published in *Africultures* in 2004, Raharimanana considers in some detail the quandary of many francophone writers who find themselves obliged by circumstances to opt for a life of 'voluntary' exile, often in Europe or the USA, while remaining deeply committed in their writings to the countries they have left behind. The urgency of the need to write and the impossibility of being able to do so are inextricably linked: the postcolonial conditions that he is intent on denouncing also include that generalised 'conspiracy of silence' that renders criticism and denunciation impracticable. This is how Raharimanana explains it:

> Déjà, nos premiers pas dans l'écriture furent imprimés sur des sables mouvants, fin de règne des grands dictateurs et institutionnalisation de l'imposture 'démocratique'. Des tapages et des exubérances tropicaux, nous passons maintenant aux silences des magouilles des nouveaux maîtres de l'Afrique. Silence imposé. Silence organisé . . . nous avons quitté nos pays puisque nous voulions contourner ce silence. Aucune possibilité de publication. Aucune possibilité de vie littéraire. Aucune possibilité de se construire comme nous l'entendions . . . mais nous savons très bien que la faille d'où a surgi notre écriture provient du pays.[8]

> [Already, our first steps as writers were taken upon quicksands, the end of the era of great dictators and the institutionalisation of that sham called 'democracy'. We've moved on from all that tropical noise and hullabaloo to shady dealings carried out in silence by Africa's new masters. A silence they impose and organise . . . we left our homelands because we wanted to avoid this silence. No possibility of being published. No possibility of literary life. No possibility of making anything of ourselves in the way we understand the term . . . but we know full well that the wellspring from which our writing pours forth is located in our homeland.]

This is the postcolonial predicament par excellence. Wishing to write about social injustices, political and cultural oppression, the new forms of asymmetrical power relations that have replaced the cleavages of colonial rule, the silencing of memory, the hijacking of history and so many other of the ravages of modernity to which his homeland is subjected he finds, paradoxically, that it is only in the former colonial centre, France, that he can enjoy the civil freedoms and have access to the technical infrastructure that allow him to be published at all. Even more paradoxically, as his commitment to addressing such burning issues translates itself into a body of postcolonial literature that defies incorporation into the national literature of 'la plus grande France' [the greater France], it is precisely the machinery of official *francophonie* that acts as a vehicle for the promotion and dissemination of his work. Questioned at the annual *Salon du Livre* in Paris in 2006 about how he personally 'inhabits the French language' Raharimanana replied, 'L'écriture en français, pour le moment, demeure un carrefour de malentendus. Le terme d'écrivain francophone appartient plus aux critiques qu'aux écrivains.'[9] [For the moment, writing in French remains a crossroad of misunderstandings. The term francophone writer is one used by the critics rather than by writers.]

Raharimanana's departure for France in 1989 occurred in circumstances where state censorship was bearing down upon him very heavily. His first play, *Le Prophète et le président*, deals with a powerful cocktail of sensitive themes: madness, corruption and the politics of development, personalising them by direct allusions to the president. The play was in rehearsal at the *Alliance française* in the capital, Antananarivo, when a combination of death threats to members of the cast and intense diplomatic pressure were sufficient to ensure the play never made it to the stage. Fortuitously, two months later Raharimanana was awarded the Radio France Internationale prize in its annual short-story competition and a grant allowing him to pursue his studies in France. The story in question, 'Le Lépreux', was later incorporated into his first published collection of stories, *Lucarne* (1996).

The twelve texts that make up this collection take the reader into a universe where extremes of violence, cruelty, depravity, the wanton exercise of power, and sexual lubricity are represented as constituting the norm of human interaction. As the title of the collection suggests (*Lucarne* means 'skylight'), these stories provide openings through which light (perhaps lucidity) is allowed to illuminate brief moments in the lives of the innumerable victims of the violence endemic in all forms of postcolonial oppression. Traditional notions of character and plot have little relevance to the way Raharimanana operates. Instead he creates an atmosphere that intermingles images of sensual luxuriance, putrefaction and decay with flashes of cruelty, pain and suffering. In the story that opens the collection, 'Par la nuit', there are details to suggest that the sexual coupling that is described occurs in the midst of the rotting detritus of a marketplace at night, but it is not clear whether animals or humans are involved. Equally disorientating is 'Ruelles' where events appear to unfold in the fevered brain of a character in a hospital bed. Consciousness ebbs and flows, events drift in and out of focus. The result is that the images of violence, or the atmosphere of threat and danger that they conjure up, cannot be explained or understood, only re-experienced through the power of the language. The title story, 'Lucarne', illustrates the fact that the fragility and precariousness of social relations is generalised. The violence targets not only the poor and vulnerable, women, children and the infirm; it indiscriminately touches all sections of society. On this occasion, a corpse uncovered in a rubbish skip by a forager is cynically used as bait in an ambush. It is laid out in the road so that the car driver who eventually happens along stops the vehicle, horrified at the prospect of driving over a body, and this moment of 'weakness' allows the predator to strike, killing and robbing his wealthy victim. Such shocking acts of violence and disregard for human life are omnipresent, as they are in his second collection of stories, *Rêves sous le linceul* (1998),

Nour, 1947, Raharimanana's first full-length novel, is a far more ambitious undertaking than these atmospheric shorter texts if only by virtue of the fact that it pursues a clearly discernible narrative project, that of connecting the rebellion against French colonial rule in 1947 to the wider history of 'la grande île', Madagascar. The structure of the work is complex, since it draws on a variety of texts and voices that echo through the various sections of the novel building up a composite picture of Madagascar from its origins to the suppression of the 1947 rebellion in which, it is calculated, 100,000 Malagasy people lost their lives. Historical focus is thus provided by the traumatic date of 1947, the end of history beyond which the tale cannot progress, while the focus of the narrative is provided by an unnamed character, an insurgent who has escaped the massacre to seek refuge on the island of Ambahy. From there he orchestrates the various voices and snippets of text that make up the narrative. Each of the seven nights he spends on the island (the seven sections of the novel) opens with his own semi-delirious reflections on the failure of the uprising and the loss of his beloved Nour. His thoughts are punctuated by the obsessive image of *Dziny*, the spirit of the Malagasy children who, in earlier times, had preferred to throw themselves from the cliff tops rather than live in captivity. Other voices that visit him include that of Konantitra, a timeless spirit who feeds into the narrative tales of the first origins of Madagascar and the arrival of Arab traders in the fifteenth century. The perspective of the waves of missionary activity that preceded colonisation is provided by quotations from the journals of two sets of priests who sought to evangelise the natives in the early 1700s and early 1800s. The history of internal struggles among Madagascar's own rival kings and queens before its eventual unification in the late eighteenth century is sketched through Nour's recollections of her own family history, notably memories of the enslavement of her forebears. Memories of the Madagascar of more contemporary times are provided by the rebels, Siva, Jao and Benja, while the narrator's own experience as a 'tirailleur' (soldier in a French colonial regiment) in the service of Pétainiste France (Maréchal Pétain was the head of the French government that collaborated with the German forces occupying France during the Second World War) offers a powerful critique of the notion of the *mission civilisatrice* that was still used as a justification for colonial rule. The links between this discredited point of view and the Nazi ideology of Aryan racial purity could hardly be clearer. Hence, these passages evoking his work in the railway yard at La Jonquière, from whence Jews were dispatched to the death camps of Germany, echo many of the themes of Aimé Césaire's *Discours sur le colonialisme* (1955). The mosaic of texts, memories, voices and dreams that make up this disturbing novel underline the fact that the history of Madagascar has consistently been marked by slavery and oppression. Raharimanana's commitment to his native land is channelled through writings that bring this tragedy to the attention of the wider world.

THE MIDDLE EAST

The countries of the Middle East where the French language has played an important role as a vehicle of culture did not gravitate into the French sphere of influence as a result of colonial conquest. The success of French as the language of predilection of certain communities, particularly in Lebanon and in areas of Egypt, was not, for all that, totally dissociated from a situation of domination and oppression by foreign rulers that characterises colonial societies. From the early sixteenth century onwards France had assumed the role of 'protector' of the Christian communities of the Middle East, particularly the Maronites of present-day Syria and Lebanon. This historic link is largely the basis for French influence in the region in modern times and accounts for the strong affective bonds that link francophone communities in the Lebanon to the metropolis. A significant number of French schools were established in the region in the course of the nineteenth century, consolidating the importance of French as an unofficial *lingua franca* alongside Arabic. When Lebanon became an independent state in 1920, it was placed under French mandate until the Second World War. Throughout the recent, troubled history of the country, the link with France has been seen by many Lebanese as one of the few remaining bulwarks against the country's incorporation into an enlarged Syria. In Egypt, too, links with France have been the result of choice rather than coercion. Some knowledge of French had already been established as a result of trade and diplomatic links before the real expansion of French influence came with the Napoleonic expedition of 1798. Although the expedition only lasted three years its legacy was far more enduring. A significant number of French engineers and scientists remained behind working on various projects, some of which continued for several decades. Links had also been established between French religious orders and the Egyptian Christian communities. As in Lebanon, this missionary activity led to the establishment of a large number of French schools and eventually to the creation of whole francophone communities.

Amin Maalouf (Lebanon, 1949–)

In recent decades, the military conflicts that have ravaged Amin Maalouf's country of origin, Lebanon, have been fuelled by religious, ethnic and political rivalries that have a strong identitarian component to them. At the risk of stating the obvious, the cycle of violence that perpetuates itself in the 'battlefields' of the Middle East can be seen as one channel through which an *exclusive* view of identity and difference violently expresses itself. The various factions and interest groups define themselves by those elements of social and cultural life (religion, ethnicity, nationality) that mark them out as different from their neighbours and set them apart as essentially 'other'. Framed in this way, the defence of any given identity or tradition simultaneously constitutes an attack on all other identities and traditions. The consequence, very frequently, is armed conflict, even though armed conflict can never provide a solution to these antagonisms; on the contrary, it perpetuates them since it is one of the most visible and dramatic ways through which they can be expressed. Maalouf's increasingly impressive *œuvre*, composed largely of novels and historical writings, can best be characterised as an ongoing attempt to demonstrate that alternative approaches to identity and difference are nevertheless available, and that they too have a long and respectable history within the region.

Maalouf's first published book, *Les Croisades vues par les Arabes* (1983), recounts the Crusades of the twelfth and thirteenth centuries from an Arab perspective. Events that have been glorified as part of a grand narrative of Western historiography are presented here from an entirely different perspective to that normally to be found in Western history books. Maalouf's painstaking reconstruction of events draws on Arab sources, Arab eye-witness accounts and Arab chronicles, all contemporaneous with the invasions by the *Franj* (Westerners), and this makes it possible for another version of this history to be heard. Where the dominance of one historiographic tradition has effectively silenced other voices (at least within the Western tradition), Maalouf's narrative redresses that imbalance and opens up a space for rethinking the *Franj*–'Arab' confrontations in a more nuanced way. Edward Saïd's seminal work on Western representations of the Orient, *Orientalism* (1978), frequently cited as one of the founding texts of postcolonial studies, could be seen as something of a theoretical blueprint for Maalouf's project. Saïd argues that the Orient is largely a construct of Western discourses on, and Western representations of, an idea of the Orient. That idea is nourished from generation to generation by texts, documents, narratives and fantasies that tell us more about the imaginary of the West, and Western stereotypes, than they do about any real Orient that can be located in time and space.

Maalouf does not, of course, pursue such abstract arguments in his book. Nevertheless his account of the Crusades has a similar trajectory to Saïd's work. It demonstrates the complexity of the various confrontations that collectively go under the name of Crusades and ensures that they cannot be interpreted through a simple binary opposition pitting 'us' against 'them', essentialised 'Christians' versus essentialised 'Muslims'. All such binaries melt away as Maalouf explains how the successive waves of invasions by the barbaric *Franj* were perceived and experienced by the local populations within the region, how the 'success' of the Crusaders was not so much a consequence of military prowess as a result of internal weaknesses within the Islamic culture they were attacking, and how the brutal atrocities perpetrated by the Crusaders were often matched by equally brutal responses from the 'Arabs'. As Maalouf's account unfolds, readers are obliged to acknowledge that the identity of the participants in the conflict is consistently being problematised. The 'Arabs', for their part, are in actual fact, more often than not, Turks, Kurds, Africans or Jews rather than people with cultural or even linguistic links with the Arabian peninsula. As for the Crusaders themselves, the 'Christian' label that attaches to them and their mission is constantly at odds with their behaviour and indeed their motives. These complexities are fully explored but never in order to serve as a basis for judgement. Instead they seem to be suggesting that earlier historical judgements have been arrived at rather too hastily and on the basis of rather restricted evidence.

One of Maalouf's strengths as a writer is his ability to produce gripping narratives: a gift that is as evident in his history of the Crusades as it is in his autobiographical journey into his family origins (*Origines* (2004)) or in his non-fictional writings (*Les Identités meurtrières*). It also goes a good way to explaining the success of his novels which, with the exception of the futuristic setting of *Le Premier Siècle après Bérénice* (1992), all tend to have an important historical element to them. Indeed they are often close to the genre of historical romance since they frequently explore key moments when the history of Europe and the Middle East comes into contact, physically or intellectually (the early sixteenth century in Europe in *Léon l'Africain* (1986), the mid nineteenth century in *Le Rocher de Tanios* (1993)). Others examine the lives of important historical personalities (the Persian poet, Omar Kayaam, in *Samarcande* (1988) or Mani, the founder of Manicheism, in *Les Jardins de lumière* (1991)).

The fact that Maalouf's work generally explores historical events, or romances the lives of historical personalities, ultimately tells us little of substance. As his history of the Crusades demonstrates, there are innumerable ways of writing history. For Maalouf, however, capable of drawing on his deep knowledge of both Western and Middle Eastern languages and cultural traditions, at some level it usually involves an attempt to present to readers alien cultural worlds, experiences and systems of belief. In this respect, the journeys of Hassan al Wazzan, the eponymous Léon in *Léon l'Africain*, are a case in point. Born towards the close of the fifteenth century in Grenada, Hassan's wandering existence begins with his dramatic departure into exile as he experiences at first hand the *Reconquista* [reconquest] of Andalusia by the Spanish crown in 1492, the moment when the Catholic monarchy of Isabelle and Ferdinand expelled the Muslims from southern Spain. Hassan's childhood in Fes is followed by other exotic displacements to Timbuktu, Cairo, Constantinople, Mecca and Rome and a variety of roles as rich trader, ambassador or adviser to the papacy. He is in Cairo at the decisive moment in Egyptian history (1517) when the Mameluke dynasty is ousted by the Ottomans, just as he is in renaissance Rome at the moment the imperial forces of the Emperor Charles V sack the town (1527). If Hassan survives these multiple adventures it is because of his cultural flexibility. He is open to other cultures and beliefs while no single strand of his own composite identity ever dominates sufficiently, or for sufficiently long, to prevent him from wandering into further adventures where yet further transformations and adaptations will be required of him. Something of a cultural chameleon, Hassan's autobiography concludes with the following words of advice to his son:

> Lorsque l'esprit des hommes te paraîtra étroit, dis-toi que la terre de Dieu est vaste, et vastes Ses mains et Son cœur. N'hésite jamais à t'éloigner, au-delà de toutes les mers, au-delà de toutes les frontières, de toutes les patries, de toutes les croyances.   (p. 473)

> [When it seems to you that men are narrow-minded, remind yourself that God's earth is vast, and vast are His hands and His heart also. Never fear to continue on your way, beyond the seas, beyond the frontiers of territories or beliefs.]

The novel for which Maalouf was awarded the Prix Goncourt, *Le Rocher de Tanios*, also interweaves fiction and historical events, this time the intervention by the European powers to stifle the political ambitions of the future viceroy of Egypt, Mehemet Ali, in the Lebanon of the 1830s. Tanios, the young boy who is called upon to play a part in these important events, has nothing of the hero about him. It is true that Tanios serves the forces of 'progress' by helping to oust the Emir, the symbolic figurehead of the arbitrary, exploitative system of rule that has typefied the politics of the region for generations Yet he is not in any real sense an *agent*, deciding on, and pursuing, a course of action to which he is personally committed. On the contrary, he illustrates a position between cultures and systems of belief. His accidental role in the ceremony of dethronement secures his reputation in his native land, but he himself is painfully aware that he has been caught between conflicting cultures, belief systems and material interests, a plaything of political forces over which he has no control. The novel closes with the mysterious disappearance of Tanios at the very moment when he is ideally placed to profit from his new-found reputation as a political miracle-worker. Apparently, what Tanios cannot accept is the single-minded (narrow-minded?) outlook required of the politician. He is aware of the complexity of competing cultural (and political) forces and the most plausible explanation for his departure is that to remain behind would constitute a betrayal of that complexity. In this respect, Tanios, like Mani in *Les Jardins de lumière*, can be seen as a vehicle for Maalouf's own overriding preoccupation with openness and open-mindedness where cultural exchange and intercultural relations are concerned.

Albert Cossery (Egypt, 1913–)

Over a period of almost sixty years, Albert Cossery has constructed a remarkably compact fictional universe in which the same preoccupations and the same themes recur insistently. With the exception of *Une ambition dans le désert* (1984), all of his work is explicitly or implicitly set in his native Egypt. In addition, more often than not the historical setting of his writings can most easily be associated with the emerging nationalism of the Egypt of the 1930s rather than the post-Second World War period of Egyptian politics, marked by the complex geopolitics of the Suez crisis and its aftermath, and later by the Arab–Israeli conflict that has continued down to the present day. (Egypt had been proclaimed a republic in 1952 following a coup d'état led by Nasser, who later became president of the country. Nasser pursued policies of rapid modernisation and reform, including the nationalisation of the Suez canal, a decision that sparked a military response from French, British and Israeli forces and looked for a while as though it might lead to conflict between the USA and USSR. Nasser positioned Egypt as a non-aligned state, playing the superpowers off against each other, while pursuing doctrines of pan-Arabism within the region.)

It could be argued that Cossery's decision to remain in what might be described as a private 'time warp' comes from a need to write about what he knew from first-hand experience, but it is probably closer to the truth to say that the sociopolitical content of his work is always explored on a symbolic level rather than against a backdrop of real-life politics. It is certainly true that the Egypt Cossery knew best was that of the 1930s since he had left his native land in the early 1940s and took up residence in Paris in 1945. He has occupied the same hotel room in the sixth *arrondissement* ever since. His first return trip to Egypt was a relatively fleeting visit for the funeral of a family member some fifty years later, in the mid 1990s. What is striking about *Les Couleurs de l'infamie* (1999), the novel which the ageing Cossery published a few years after that visit (thus breaking a silence of some fifteen years), is that it is so precisely in tune with his earlier work in terms of themes, style and philosophical outlook. There is a clear political dimension to what may well be his last novel, but as is the case with all his earlier writings, from *Les Hommes oubliés de Dieu* (1941) onwards, it has little if anything to do with a critique of contemporary political events. Instead, his aim throughout his writing career would seem to have been to describe the people and places of Egypt through an ongoing reflection on power relations at work within society. This is an archetypal theme of postcolonial literature. But Cossery's originality lies in his persistence in seeing politics as indissociable from philosophical, ethical and even aesthetic considerations.

Reading Cossery can be rather like taking alternating looks through a microscope and a telescope. The big picture, the universal themes of human suffering, poverty, social inequality and survival in the face of grinding adversity, can only be grasped through the detailed portrayal of individual lives and destinies. Conversely, no detail can ever be deemed insignificant. The quirky absurdities and peculiarities exhibited by the assortment of highly idiosyncratic characters he describes all have a contribution to make to the wider canvas he paints depicting a society built on irreconcilable differences. The disempowered and hungry rub shoulders with the rich and powerful. The near destitute, living in appalling conditions, exposed to violence and promiscuity, move in the same landscapes and cityscapes as the businessmen and government officials who swindle and exploit them.

The tragedy of the lives of the downtrodden is frequently narrated through appeals to comic effect. Laughter punctuates the narratives, whether it be laughter born of joy or the laughter born of despair, the ironic laughter of social satire or the laughter triggered by the incongruities so common in postcolonial settings. As a general rule, however, laughter functions as an assault on power. In *La Violence et la dérision* (1964) the power of the Governor who rules the town is challenged from two different angles. The approach of the dissidents, Karim and Heykal, is to refuse to take seriously the grotesque abuses of power characteristic of the Governor. They treat the tyrant with the contempt they feel he deserves and, rather than seeking to overthrow him, they simply laugh at him and seek to expose him to ever more general public ridicule through a clandestine poster campaign. These tactics contrast sharply with those of the 'pure' revolutionary, Taher. His methods are those of the terrorist and include political assassinations and bombings. As the narrative progresses and Taher develops his plot to assassinate the Governor, Cossery makes it clear that he sees the ideological confrontation between tyranny and revolution as a fruit-less contest between two contrasting yet similar examples of the same logic. Heykal's opinion of Taher is:

> il [Taher] ne pouvait briser le cercle dans lequel l'avait enfermé le pouvoir sanguinaire. Il jouait le jeu de l'honneur et du déshonneur, comme on lui avait appris à le faire. Il n'en sortirait jamais. Il était plus prisonnier que dans une cellule, car les mythes sur lesquels il fondait son action étaient les mêmes dont usait l'adversaire . . .   (pp. 141–2)

> [he (Taher) couldn't break the circle within which he had been trapped by the bloodythirsty tyrant. He was playing the game of honour and dishonour in the way he had been taught to play it. He was trapped forever. He was less free than he would have been in a real prison cell because the myths on which he based his actions were the same as those used by his opponent . . .]

By contrast, Heykal believes that responding to violence with violence simply shows tyrants that they are being taken seriously. The strategy he adopts is to show them their behaviour is, in fact, derisory, and to laugh at them. This displacement of the battlelines sees Heykal competing with the Governor not for the chance to exercise power but in pure buffoonery: the world is transformed into a playground and politics an occasion for ever more clownish behaviour.

Karim and Heykal are variations on a recurring theme. They belong to a long list of characters who illustrate Cossery's highly individualistic world view, embodying his anarchic, yet undoubtedly elitist belief that the powerful, the wealthy and the influential people of this world pursue ambitions that he would dismiss as clownish and derisory. True distinction lies in refusing to have any truck with such grubby profiteering attitudes. Hence his novels are peopled by 'aristocratic' characters whose distinction is only incidentally related to social status and is more accurately linked to their social attitudes or philosophical outlook. Gohar in *Mendiants et orgueilleux* (1955) is a typical example of this archetypal figure. The trajectory of Gohar's life is one of increasing withdrawal from the bustle of the world into a private universe inhabited in accordance with an ethic of extreme abnegation. Formerly a respected philosophy teacher, Gohar has turned his back on the 'establishment' and the pursuit of worldly possessions, electing instead for a life of utter poverty among the poor. After murdering a young prostitute of his acquaintance in a fit of drug-related madness, Gohar comes to interpret his terrible action as a final step down the road away from his former life of bourgeois respectability. Nour El Dine, the homosexual policeman who is charged with the investigation, represents the world Gohar has left behind. As the novel progresses, it becomes increasingly apparent that the policeman's real quest is not to identify the killer (Gohar makes no secret of the fact that he is the culprit) but to decide whether he too can embrace the ethic of simplicity practised by Gohar and his circle. Paradoxically, it is the beggars, prostitutes and drug addicts who represent not a social elite but an elite nevertheless since they are portrayed as figures of absolute, uncompromising integrity. They epitomise all that is dignified in the human condition.

The social battlelines drawn up in this novel reappear throughout Cossery's fiction. He frequently depicts, on the one hand, an underclass of beggars, prostitutes, drug-dealers and the teeming masses of the urban poor seeking to eke out an existence in appalling material conditions. Their world is nevertheless a place where solidarity, good humour and an anarchic sense of life's absurdity lock the people into a common ethic of survival. Ranged against the common people, exploiting them and oppressing them, are the forces of the establishment: the government, officialdom in all its forms, landlords, employers, businessmen, the wealthy, in short all those who have possessions and positions to protect. The 'aristocratic' characters straddle these two worlds and occupy the ambiguous terrain that separates them.

On occasion, they are defectors from the wealthy classes who refuse to take their place in a social order they despise. Teymour, the protagonist of *Un Complot de saltimbanques* (1975), is a case in point. During the years he spent as a student in the West he had dedicated himself to a life of hedonistic idleness, refusing to study for the diploma he eventually buys before returning home. The buying of the diploma may be an example of 'imposture' [fraud] but it is a transparent act of deception in a world where the rule of law and the protection of established order are portrayed as the real 'imposture', perpetrated on the common people and designed to maintain them in a state of subservience to their political masters. Teymour and his friends' pursuit of pleasure is consistent with their total rejection of an established order, but the terms in which Cossery develops the narrative draw constantly on parallels between 'play' and political dissidence. The group's anarchic behaviour is perceived by the world of official-dom as a plot to overthrow the government: play, laughter, pleasure-seeking, giving free rein to the imagination, all these are forms of liberation that Cossery endows with a political significance: the 'conspiracy of street performers' of the novel's title denotes a serious form of oppositional politics.

On other occasions, the 'aristocrats' may in fact be beggars and thieves from the underclasses but they have achieved a degree of lucidity that sets them apart from their fellow men. Ossama, the thief in *Les Couleurs de l'infamie*, is more an artist than a criminal. The compromising letter he finds in the wallet of one of his wealthy victims, the corrupt property speculator Suleyman, is seized upon not as a way to extort money or advantage out of the businessman but as a source of amusement. Ossama and his associates use the letter to entice Suleyman to a meeting during which they are able to confirm their conviction that it is members of the ruling classes, ministers and businessmen, who are the true social parasites, organising theft on a grandiose scale. The confronta-tion between Suleyman and Ossama resolves nothing. It simply exposes the breathtaking extent of Suleyman's corruption.

This absence of resolution is typical of Cossery's work. The sense of revulsion he feels at the miserable living conditions and the poverty endured by the common people is clear. But his refusal to accept political action as a way of attacking injustice leaves him nowhere to go in his search for a solution. His characters either refuse to acknowledge the world at all, as is the case in *Les Fainéants dans la vallée fertile* (1948) where an entire family's most ardent wish is to spend their lives sleeping, or they embrace playful anarchic responses to oppression, displacing politics into the realms of fantasy. Cossery's treatment of social injustice, deprivation, oppression and the unequal distribution of power within society is highly original. His focus on ethics and aesthetics rather than politics knocks the whole debate slightly off kilter, but the underlying thirst for change that motivates all his writings cannot be questioned for all that.

Chapter 4

Canada

Overview

The contention that francophone literatures form not merely a subgroup of metropolitan French literature but are distinctive in kind, by virtue of their postcolonial status, requires particular scrutiny in the case of Quebec.[1] The argument is easier to make in the context of those regions of the world (the Maghreb, sub-Saharan Africa, the Caribbean and so on) where an oppressed, indigenous population (or a 'transplanted' one, in the case of the Caribbean) has struggled to stake out a distinctive space of cultural expression, albeit through the medium of French. Usually such efforts were part and parcel of decolonisation struggles and involved forms of cultural self-affirmation that challenged the centre–periphery model upon which present-day 'official' *francophonie* (like colonialism itself) is constructed. This standard version of the narrative that portrays the centre–periphery model being challenged and overthrown appears to be of questionable relevance to Quebec. Yet on closer examination it transpires that a similar challenge to the centre–periphery power relationship is precisely what does occur in francophone Quebec, even if the struggles involved in bringing about that revolution sometimes take on forms that bear little resemblance to those that occurred in other regions of the world. Fundamentally, however, the issues remain the same. The patterns of power relations and status that often characterise the postcolonial context, and which are inscribed in a variety of ways in postcolonial literatures, are omnipresent in Quebec society and literature, as are the range of issues to do with identity, language, gender and intercultural dynamics. Yet in Quebec the roles often seem to be assigned in rather 'unorthodox', paradoxical and sometimes confusing ways.

One of the difficulties in making the case for Quebec as a postcolonial society can be linked precisely to the argument that historically and demographically Canada is so dissimilar to other former colonial societies. There is the obvious fact (so often underplayed) that the francophone population descends from a population of colonisers who themselves effectively dispossessed native American tribes and whose very presence on the continent was a contributory factor

138

to the destruction of indigenous First Nations cultures, even if there was no 'colonisation' of them as such. The racial difference that usually divides the metropolitan coloniser from the indigenous colonised is not applicable to the Quebec context either. It is applicable to another historiography, that of the First Nations, but one that has little relevance to the specifically francophone issues that concern us here.

Such caveats are worth making at the outset because they provide a backdrop against which any discussion about the francophone presence in Canada must eventually be viewed. They are also relevant because they relativise the process we are witnessing when we see *Québécois* casting themselves in the roles of 'colonised' or 'nègres blancs' [white niggers].[2] Clearly, these self-designations are largely metaphorical. They may be justified in so far as they serve to illustrate the position *Québécois* occupied, until fairly recent times, as inferior partners in a relationship characterised by the cultural, economic and political domination of francophone Canadians by an encircling anglophone world. Yet they are essentially an allegorisation of a complex set of relationships that evolved not between coloniser and colonised but between two groups of colonisers: the 'successful' British and the rather 'less successful' French. The latter found themselves cut off from the mother country with the collapse of the first French empire in the mid eighteenth century and condemned thereafter to a struggle for cultural survival in a world ruled by British interests.

The experience of French-Canadians following the conquest by the British was fraught with anxieties. Indeed, the struggle for survival of a francophone presence of any sort in Canada hung in the balance for much of that period. On the one hand, the psychological trauma arising from a sense of having been not only defeated but abandoned by France should not be underestimated. It coloured future relations between the former colony and the mother country with a degree of ambivalence: maintaining the connections with France was fundamental to the French-Canadian sense of identity, yet it was fraught with the insecurities of any non-reciprocated relationship. But the more pressing question following the conquest by the British centred on maintaining a way of life that was under the immediate threat of linguistic and cultural absorption by the powerful anglophone presence. Ultimately, the isolation and self-sufficiency of rural life played in the favour of francophone communities. The church played a key role too, as a mediator with the British authorities on the one hand, and ultimately as a guardian of the traditional, conservative values that would ensure continuity: a respect for family and community, a narrow conception of social order and a strong sense of rootedness in the land.

The harsh conditions of life experienced by the majority of francophone Canadians over the long decades between the ceding of *la Nouvelle-France* to England in 1763 and *la Révolution tranquille* [the Quiet Revolution] two centuries later form the specific context from which francophone literature emerges, firstly as a literature of survival and subsequently (and quite belatedly) as a literature of self-affirmation. The passage from the one to the other neatly sums up what is effectively a rejection of the centre–periphery model on which *francophonie* rests. In survival mode, French-Canadian literature kept its eyes turned towards France, which was seen as a repository of the traditions, values and linguistic orthodoxy that provided an identitarian model and fuelled literary ambitions. In self-affirmative mode, as the Quiet Revolution gathered pace, the 'French-Canadian' epithet mutated into the self-consciously nationalist designation *Québécois* and all eyes are turned inwards (towards Montreal rather than Paris). Such a switch in focus involved a reconfiguration of power relations: France ceased to occupy its central position as a legitimising force in cultural life and was consigned to a cultural and linguistic periphery in so far as the preoccupations of an increasingly self-confident and nationalistic Quebec were concerned.

In many ways, this division of the literary history of Quebec into a 'before' characterised by the dominance of metropolitan 'French' influence, and an 'after' characterised by a more autonomous, home-grown focus on local preoccupations, illustrates the inadequacy of the term 'francophone' in describing a key feature of the evolution of that literary history. The term 'francophone' can be used to describe with equal accuracy, on the one hand, those literary productions from the period when French-Canadians were struggling to survive as a distinct cultural community in North America, and on the other, the writings that, from the 1960s onwards, mark a break with the past, experiment with new forms, ideologies and voices, and, in short, assume the agency that indicates the arrival of a new literature on the scene. It thus fails to discriminate between the types of writing that implicitly sought to maintain cultural dependency on the metropolis and those that, in the first instance, sought to contest such dependency before, in due course, apparently forgetting it had ever existed at all.

The current dynamism of the Quebec literary scene is in marked contrast to the dearth of activity following the arrival of Europeans on the scene. There was some semblance of embryonic literary activity in the early decades of the seventeenth century but the texts concerned have a historical rather than a literary interest. They include accounts of journeys and expeditions, notably the *Relations Jésuites* (a series of reports of the missionary and other activities undertaken by Jesuit priests, published in Paris from 1632 onwards) and occasional histories and personal accounts of first-hand experiences in the colony. Moreover, as one commentator has suggested, it is debatable whether writings by 'expatriate Frenchmen should be regarded as the origins of French-Canadian literature'.[3] Lord Durham's dismissal of the francophone community of Lower Canada as 'a people with no history and no literature' in his 1839 *Report* to the British government may reflect the arrogant dominance of the anglophone community, but it no doubt contained more than a grain of truth in its portrayal of a demoralised, rather inglorious francophone community.

The decades that followed Lord Durham's *Report* saw a burgeoning activity in both history and literature that it is tempting to cast, with the benefit of hindsight, as a conscious rebuttal of his opinions. A major contribution was François-Xavier Garneau's *Histoire du Canada depuis sa découverte jusqu'à nos jours*, a three-volume work completed in 1848. Garneau consciously anchored his account in francophone experience and emphasised the need to resist British dominance. His efforts to portray French-Canadians as possessed of distinct qualities (resilience, gravity, perseverance) are a transparent attempt to define, in essentialist terms, a model of French-Canadian identity to which the francophone communities of Canada could subsequently align themselves. In this respect, Garneau had considerable influence on the writers who emerged in the second half of the century. *Les Anciens Canadiens* (1863) by Philippe Aubert de Gaspé (senior), for example, looks back with unashamed nostalgia to the days before the conquest, portraying them as a golden age of French rule. Equally influential as a guide and as self-appointed guardian of the literary scene in his day was Henri-Raymond Casgrain. A great admirer of Garneau, Casgrain was one of the chief organisers of literary life through his work as founder of the 'mouvement littéraire du Québec', his influence in literary 'salons' and through the review he helped create in 1861, *Les Soirées Canadiennes*. He was also a theoriser of that activity. His *Le Mouvement littéraire en Canada* (1866) provides a highly prescriptive definition of literature as a vehicle for essentially religious values and beliefs that associated patriotism with social and political conservatism.

This cocktail of conservative, not to say reactionary, values and beliefs fed into and nourished the dominant literary form of the second half of the nineteenth century, the *roman du terroir*. From the mid nineteenth century to the outbreak of the Second World War, these novels actively promoted a transparent ideology of social and religious values that amounted to what was virtually a political campaign on behalf of a lifestyle centred on working the land, raising a family, adhering to the tenets of Catholicism and refusing modernity, more often than not represented by the allurements of urbanised life and industrialisation. The focus on peasant values has much in common with the regionalist writings of metropolitan France; but in the Canadian context, rather than being a marginal strand of literary activity, they were the core of literary output. The reason why this should be so is all the more apparent if one bears in mind the fact that the binary oppositions frequently evoked or implied in the *roman du terroir*: agriculture/industrialisation, country/city, rootedness/exile, sedentary/nomadic, peasant virtues/urban vices (alcoholism, unemployment, moral degeneracy), Catholic beliefs and values/religious agnosticism and so on, can all be seen as relevant to a single, overarching, identitarian opposition between patriotic French-Canadian values and British values. In such a scheme, to embrace peasant values is to contribute to the construction of the notion of the patriotic French-Canadian, while to display ambivalence in respect of such values is to undermine that identity and risk personal and collective perdition. In short, for almost a century the *roman du terroir* provided the only model available through which francophone identity could be negotiated. Patrice Lacombe's *La Terre paternelle* (1846) is an early example of the genre, while novels such as Antoine Gérin-Lajoie's two-part novel, *Jean Rivard* (1874 and 1876) can be seen as variations focusing on the colonisation of new territories.

Louis Hémon's *Maria Chapdelaine* (1916) allegorises some of the ideological meanings that are frequently expressed through attitudes to the land. In this novel, three suitors gravitate around the eponymous heroine, each representing a distinct relationship to the earth. François Paradis, the trapper, has an avowed distaste for working the same piece of land year in year out, preferring a nomadic existence that harks back to the spirit of the first pioneers. Symbolically, the impermanence that his constant displacements underscore is confirmed when he fails to reappear after a dangerous journey into the wilds in the depths of winter. The direct antithesis of Paradis's choice of a wandering existence is the sedentary lifestyle of the peasant farmer and it is figured in the novel by many incidental characters, but especially by Eutrope Gagnon. The third option involves a refusal of the nomadic/sedentary opposition represented by Paradis and Gagnon. Instead, the third suitor, Lorenzo Surprenant represents the temptation of voluntary exile and migration away from the monotony of the countryside to the modernity of the manufacturing towns of the United States. At the close of the novel, Maria's various options revisit her as so many voices, each offering a different potential future. Her decision is less the choice of a particular suitor, in the event Eutrope Gagnon, than an acquiescence to the destiny spelled out by a third voice, that of Quebec itself: 'la voix du pays du Québec, qui était à moitié un chant de femme et à moitié un sermon de prêtre' (p. 239) [the voice of the Quebec countryside, that was half a song sung by a woman and half a sermon delivered by a priest]. The device of the disembodied voice allows the novel to close with a panegyric to the conservative values that are so characteristic of the *roman du terroir*: respect for traditional forms of worship, for the French language so jealously preserved, and for the multiple connections with a certain idea of French identity that is increasingly translated into lived experience in a constrained and somewhat negative form, as 'un devoir de témoignage' [the duty of bearing witness to the past] and a refusal to change. The closing pages of the novel reveal more than a hint of gritty resignation in Maria's decision to stay and work the land with Gagnon. Her attitude of self-abnegation and concern for the durability of the community are portrayed in a positive light by Hémon, but they could equally well be seen as mere stubbornness and a refusal to embrace new ideas or pursue personal aspirations.

Many of the novels that followed in the wake of *Maria Chapdelaine* confirm the importance of the fundamental option that structures this particular novel: the opposition between the 'habitants' and the 'coureurs de bois', the sedentary agriculturalists and the nomadic trappers. Displacement, whether voluntary or through the force of circumstances, is frequently the means by which the ideal of rootedness in the land is threatened, negated or subjected to various forms of attenuation and renegotiation. Hence in Ringuet's *Trente Arpents de neige* (1938) the pastoral ideal recedes as the true harshness of life on the land is foregrounded. For the protagonist, Euchariste Moisan, the attempt to eke out a living on the soil ends in failure and exile to the city. Similarly in Germaine Guèvremont's *Le Survenant* (1945) it is the arrival of the stranger, the nomadic character without roots, that disturbs the static equilibrium of the community, opening up the closed horizons and prising open the closed mentalities of the inhabitants, albeit without pushing the boundaries back too far or too rapidly. Indeed so measured and restrained is the impact of Venant that it is possible to see him as representing not so much one strand of the conflict between sedentary and nomadic lifestyles as a synthesis of them both. His general competence as an agricultural worker complements his philosophical commitment to rootlessness. Moreover, in the eyes of Didace Beauchemin, Venant increasingly functions as a substitute for his own feckless and cowardly son, Amable. In a context that places so much emphasis on filiation and the transmission of values, Venant thus comes to figure as the ideal of the French-Canadian identity. Fittingly, he continues to do so even after his departure so that he embodies not only the contradictions inherent in the ideal he represents but also its material *absence*. Rather than challenge the ideological foundations of the *roman du terroir*, *Le Survenant* reinforces their claim to relevance.

This reading of *Le Survenant* demonstrates the extent to which the dominant ideology of the period was able to stifle dissension by incorporating it and absorbing it into a renegotiated version of the French-Canadian identity. Indeed the *roman du terroir* was one of the chief vehicles through which the ideology was disseminated; these novels did not simply portray aspects of

French-Canadian identity, they were one of the means by which that identity was constructed and reinforced. The fate of Albert Laberge's novel, *La Scouine* (1918), is an example of what could happen when a truly dissident voice emerged. His portrayal of peasant family life is a scathing condemnation of a degrading, degenerate milieu in which lust, alcoholism and greed are commonplace. The myth that sustained the national self-image was directly threatened by this text which is, thematically at least, more reminiscent of Zola's *La Terre* than of any pastoral idyll. The multiple forces of conservatism saw this as a dangerous message, so its serialised publication in *La Presse* was halted and the novel was never made widely available to the public until the 1960s.

The absence of any space for dissident voices is of course a consequence of the underlying insecurity of the society from which this literature was emerging. The influence of Casgrain, referred to above, and the deep-seated suspicion of the clergy with regard to the production and consumption of any literature whatsoever combined to create a highly prescriptive view of what literary activity entailed. These ideological and societal constraints no doubt go a long way to explaining why the poetry of the period was so often concerned with private worlds and subjective experiences. The 'Ecole littéraire de Montréal' created in the mid 1890s by a group of artists and intellectuals, notably the painter Charles Gill, was a loose grouping which had the potential to mount a challenge to the prevailing order. However, many of those associated with the group, Emile Nelligan for example, were greatly influenced by French Parnassian and Symbolist poets. Writers with such a conception of the purposes and status of their art were far too preoccupied with the world of the imagination and their own sensibilities to engage in a battle with the prosaic guardians of public morality, whom they deliberately refused to confront. Nelligan's trajectory as a poet was brief but brilliant. His poetry was heavily influenced by a post-Romantic philosophy that preferred retreat into the seclusion and consolations of Art to the vicissitudes of the world. In many ways, his life came to corroborate these very sources of inspiration and mirror the themes his poetry explored: shortly before his twentieth birthday he was hospitalised with a mental illness and he spent the remaining years of his life in various asylums. Despite the brevity of his writing career (and perhaps partly because of it), Nelligan has assumed an iconic status in Quebec poetry. His melancholic rejection of the world demands to be read first and foremost as an aesthetic response to experience, yet it can be mapped on to more mundanely political and social concerns. This probably explains why Nelligan has remained such an influential figure among contemporary writers such as Réjean Ducharme.

Nelligan's emblematic exile and retreat into a private world was expressed through his poetry before it was confirmed in his life as a result of health problems. A few decades later a remarkably similar fate lay in store for another very significant poet, Hector de Saint-Denys Garneau, whose brief and tragic life also fuelled the myth of the 'poète maudit'. The poetry of Saint-Denys Garneau is highly introspective and obsessed with images of sterility and impotence, very often expressed in counterpoint to a disappointed longing for the playful innocence and lightness of childhood. Even before the publication of *Regards et jeux dans l'espace* (1937) at the age of twenty-five, Saint-Denys Garneau was living as a virtual recluse in the family manor-house having been diagnosed with a life-threatening medical condition. The thematic insistence to be found in his work on inner exile, existential anguish, alienation, silence and solitude thus seems entirely consonant with his own, sadly neurotic preoccupations. As with Nelligan, Saint-Denys Garneau's fundamentally aesthetic preoccupations can be interpreted as providing a poetic parallel to a sociopolitical agenda. The impossibility of writing, the absence of poetry in the world and the consequent exile of the poet to a private universe can all be read as a comment on the sclerosis of literary activity during the period of 'la grande noirceur', the decades from the economic crisis of the 1930s to the end of the Duplessis government in 1959. In this respect, Saint-Denys Garneau belongs to a generation of poets, many of them associated with the review *La Relève*, founded by Robert Charbonneau in 1934, that sought an aesthetic response to the crushing conservatism of life under the Duplessis régime.

The tensions that were building during these decades are generally perceived as coming to a head in the Quiet Revolution when the stranglehold on cultural life exerted by the clergy and the forces of social conservatism was finally broken. But the rapid changes that came about after the death of Maurice Duplessis in 1959 had been long in the preparation. The seeds of an alternative to the established order are already germinating in the work of the poets considered above. In the late 1940s another group of painters and poets heavily influenced by Surrealism, notably Paul-Emile Borduas, signed a manifesto, *Refus Global*, that prefigures the open revolt of the 1960s. Throughout the late 1940s and 1950s, the post-war transformation of French-Canadian society into far more industrialised and urbanised patterns of existence is reflected in the novel, at least in terms of the renewal of the themes it treated, if not in terms of formal inventiveness. Gabrielle Roy (with *Bonheur d'occasion* (1945) and *Alexandre Chenevert: caissier* (1954)), Roger Lemelin (with *Les Plouffe* (1949)) and André Langevin (with *Poussière sur la ville* (1953)) are among the many novelists who explored directly sociological and psychological themes, focusing for the first time on the urban working and lower-middle classes, often in order to reveal the spiritual vacuity, alienation and loneliness of the lives their characters led. Similar changes were taking place in the theatre too, in the work of Gratien

Gélinas (*Ti-coq* (1948)) and, slightly later, of Marcel Dubé (*Un simple soldat* (1958)).

The literature of the decade preceding the Quiet Revolution increasingly demonstrated the mismatch that existed between, on the one hand, the reality of what it meant to be a French-Canadian and, on the other, the sustaining mythological representations that had been projected and nourished for so many decades by a coalition of conservative forces in both church and state. In so far as the cultural life of the francophone communities of Canada is concerned, what was truly revolutionary about the Quiet Revolution was the sea-change that occurred in such a very short period of time, in the way French-Canadians viewed themselves. What might be called the 'official' ideology of French-Canadian identity was swept away to be replaced by the franker, more self-confident, more forward-looking self-image of the *Québécois*. A new sense of individual and collective identity emerged that could be characterised as much by its readiness to jettison the past as by its aspirational dimensions, the latter often translated into the politics of Quebec nationalism (in the writings of Hubert Aquin, Jacques Godbout or Gaston Miron, for example) but also present in broader sociocultural activity that focused on accurately representing Quebec to its people (through song, theatre, comedy and cinema, for example). The break with the past is clearest in the new-found emphasis on individual freedom often expressed as a rejection of the values associated with family and local community life, including the strict attitudes to sexual mores defended by the Catholic church. Women in particular had suffered under the old dispensation, limited in the social roles available to them and by the lack of personal freedoms they were able to enjoy. But what was new about the emerging *identité québécoise* was the way it directly linked cultural expression and lived experience. The new-found freedom was partly a freedom to address the history of their own sense of alienation and confront their own moral inadequacies: for example, their submissiveness with regard to British political and economic power, their relative cultural impoverishment, and their failure to champion their distinctive cultural heritage, not a heritage viewed as a relic of an irrelevant past relationship with France but seen rather as one of the building-blocks of a dynamic, evolving cultural life.

Not surprisingly, language had a key role to play in the ways this new-found sense of identity was negotiated, in the first place, and then in the ways it expressed itself. On one level, of course, the state and status of the French language in Canada has long been a hot political issue with its own history of policy measures, provincial or national governmental initiatives and legal frameworks. But in terms of cultural production, from the early 1960s onwards the state and status of the varieties of French spoken and written in franco-phone communities of Canada came to be used increasingly as a metonymic device for engaging with more general issues relating to Quebec identity. The debate about the use of *joual* in works such as Michel Tremblay's *Les Belles-Sœurs* (1968), set in eastern Montreal, was a catalyst for a new approach to many of these issues. It has much in common with debates about the status of creole or Africanised French in other geographical and cultural contexts. To think of Tremblay's recourse to *joual* in terms of a promotion of this working-class dialect of Quebec to the status of a literary language is to frame the issue in a skewed way because it accepts the basic premise that there exists a hierarchy of idioms and, by extension, of subject matter worthy of treat-ment. This view in turn is somehow linked to a conception of what may be considered as appropriate ingredients of serious art and inevitably, in the Que-bec context, such hierarchies (and the value judgements implicit in them) are imported from France rather than home-grown. In fact, Tremblay's portrayal of the inhabitants of eastern Montreal quite naturally incorporates, or rather is freighted through, a portrayal of the language such characters use. It is dif-ficult to see how such a portrayal, located within the culture it depicts, could have used any other idiom. This is comically confirmed through the charac-ter of Lisette de Courval, a relatively minor character in the play whose sense of social superiority is based on the fact that she has visited France and who believes herself to speak a purer version of French than her neighbours. Her linguistic snobbery is, of course, totally unfounded and is undermined by her own use of language and (presumably) her accent: 'A Paris, tout le monde perle bien. C'est du vrai français partout . . . C'est pas comme icitte . . . c'monde-là, c'est du monde *cheap*.' (p. 42) [In Paris, everybody talks proper. They talk proper French everywhere . . . Not like round 'ere . . . All this lot are common as muck.]

Tremblay's plays did not launch the debate about the use of *joual* as a means of expressing *Québécois* cultural realities, they simply gave these matters a greater prominence in the eyes of the wider world. In fact, the debate about language had been a key vector from the very beginning of the cultural awakening of Quebec in the post-Duplessis era, notably in reviews like *Liberté* (founded in 1959) and *Parti Pris* (founded in 1963). Contributors to the latter publication, in particular, were conscious of the links between their own situation as *Québécois* and the wave of decolonisation movements around the world. Writers like Jacques Godbout, a regular contributor to *Liberté*, located the debate in the specifically literary context of the writers' need to have at their disposal a language appropriate to their needs:

Et tout ce que les écrivains québécois tentent, avec plus ou moins d'habileté, de dire aux écrivains français d'Europe, c'est que la langue française littéraire est trop polie, trop cultivée, trop usée, trop étiolée, trop instruite, trop codifée, trop propriété privée, trop correcte pour l'usage que nous voulons en faire. Nous avons besoin . . . d'un français plus souple et plus fou et plus utile que le leur, nous avons besoin d'un français plus sauvage, le québécois, pour nous civiliser.[4]

[And all that Quebecois writers are trying to say, with a greater or lesser degree of talent, to French writers from Europe, is that literary French is too polished, too cultured, too worn-down, too insipid, too well-educated, too codified, too 'private property', too correct for the use we want to put it to. We need a French language that's more flexible and madder and more useful than theirs, we need a wilder, less domesticated French, Quebecois, in order to civilise ourselves.]

The insistence by writers like Godbout that French effectively needed to be decolonised in order to function as a tool for representing the life and people of Quebec goes some way to illustrating why language questions have such importance in any discussion of Quebec identitarian politics. Yet simply adopting a more appropriate idiom was hardly an effective way of addressing the underlying alienation that was such an acutely felt part of the experience of being a *Québécois* for so many people. The Quiet Revolution was also a struggle for agency by a population that needed to counter political and economic domination at the hands of the British and to recognise, finally, that it had for decades been clinging to a bankrupt relationship with a distant and indifferent *mère-patrie*. Significantly, both resistance to British domination and cutting the umbilical cord with France had a linguistic dimension, indeed were inconceivable outside a framework of linguistic action and activity. There were various strands to this activity of resistance and reconquest of a cultural space. The hybrid political/poetic work of Paul Chamberland, *L'Afficheur hurle* (1964), and the texts and poems that Gaston Miron worked, reworked and performed before publishing them in a single volume, *L'Homme rapaillé* (1970), are two examples of texts that gave voice to the existential anguish of 'l'homme *agonique*'. The neologism 'agonique' is untranslatable but includes, semantically, notions of near-extinction, of 'being on the threshold of death', as well as the notion of a down-trodden, ignominious state, that could be associated with the plight of the 'colonised' *Québécois*, and, formally, evokes the notion of a person literally cut off from the 'hex-agon' of metropolitan France. It was through such creative and liberating work on language that Miron and the poets of the 'Hexagone' group sought to rally resistance and effect social and political renewal. Michèle Lalonde's 'Speak White', first performed in 1968 and published in 1974 is another example of the double-barrelled poetical/political approach that took language as its subject and used poetry as a vehicle for expressing a political message.

Many of the *Québécois* writers active in the 1960s and early 1970s saw the opportunities that their new-found freedoms afforded them as having a clear political dimension and were naturally committed to the cause of Quebec nationalism. With the passage of time, however, the alliance between the political and the poetical loosened. The election of the Parti Québécois to power in 1976 ensured that measures to protect and safeguard the status of French could be actively pursued through legislative channels, a notable example being *la Charte de la langue française* (Bill 101) voted in 1977, which sought to make French the language of the state and the institutions of Quebec. The rhetoric of alienation and resistance was no longer appropriate to a context in which the francophone population was largely in charge of its own affairs. Whether or not the failure of nationalists to secure the outcome they sought in the two referenda on independence held in 1980 and 1995 can be seen as evidence of a waning interest in the politics of nationalism is debatable. But what is certainly the case is that the dynamism of Quebec literature was no longer automatically coupled with the urge to carve out a new collective *identité québécoise* once a share of political power had been won. The complexities of identity and their multiple connections with language and literary form could now be explored through more subjective areas of experience rather than harnessed to a collective, national mission.

From the early 1970s onwards, feminist concerns had come to occupy an increasingly prominent place in the cultural landscape, notably through the writings and other activities of Nicole Brossard. She had co-founded the review *La Barre du jour* in 1965 to provide an outlet for a new type of literature by a new generation of writers. Within a few years the focus had switched to an exploration of 'l'écriture au féminin' [writing in the feminine] and Brossard's own work had become resolutely feminist. This rich vein of writing includes influential works by Yolande Villemaire, Louky Bersianik and Madeleine Gagnon, and the later writings of Marie-Claire Blais. In many respects 'l'écriture au féminin' merely reinforces one of the most characteristic aspects of Quebec literature, the dominant contribution that has been made by women writers throughout the twentieth century. Feminist preoccupations naturally found an outlet in the theatre too; *La Nef de sorcières* (1976), written by a collective of women actors and writers (including Blais and Brossard), stages a range of neglected women's voices. Perhaps more schematic than dramatic, the play highlights the marginalisation that women frequently undergo. Denise Boucher's *Les Fées ont soif* (1978) takes similar feminist concerns into a highly controversial religious context. A statue of the Virgin Mary eventually comes to life as the play goes on and the liberated, desacralised Virgin joins the two main characters, Marie, the wife, and Madeleine, the prostitute, in a symbolic dance that suggests a new dawn for women. The play's powerful mix of religious and social critique caused a scandal that continued into the mid 1980s.

In the aftermath of the Quiet Revolution, the question of *identité québécoise* had been posed in terms largely concerned with carving out a collective identity. In the later decades of the century, the very concept of a common identitarian project seems to fade increasingly into insignificance as identity questions assume a far more individualistic flavour. The considerable body of feminist writings are one strand of this tendency. The women writers mentioned above are far more concerned about their status and position in society *as women* than they are about what it means to be *québécoise*. A similar shift can be detected in the works that emphasise and invite scrutiny of both writing as a process and language as an artistic medium. Brossard's 'l'écriture au féminin' is one version of this, but it can be perceived most clearly in the recourse to linguistic inventiveness that is typical of writers commonly bundled together as working a 'postmodern' vein: the puns and word-plays that abound in Francine Noël's *Maryse* (1984), for example, or any of the plays and novels of Réjean Ducharme illustrate this tendency.

Linguistic playfulness is one aspect of what Lise Gauvin has termed 'la surconscience linguistique' [the overconsciousness about language] that she sees as typical of contemporary Quebec literature. But it is also a marker of the progress towards a more general cultural decolonisation of Quebec that had occurred, albeit unevenly, by the 1980s; the willingness to play with the 'French' language equates to a taking possession of it, a seizing of ownership and a determination to treat it with the degree of respect or disrespect one happens to deem appropriate. These shifts with regards to attitudes to French language almost exactly parallel what Gauvin sees as having happened in respect of the trajectory of Quebec literature as a whole. Both are examples of forms of decolonisation. Gauvin argues as follows:

> il s'agit d'une littérature qui, dès le début, est hantée par la conscience de son statut, qui cherche à se constituer en littérature nationale et ne le devient qu'au moment où elle met fin à ses énoncés programmatiques, au moment où elle laisse dans l'ombre le qualificatif et se conçoit comme littérature avant d'être québécoise.[5]

> [it is a literature that, from the very outset, is haunted by an awareness of its own status, a literature that is seeking to constitute itself as a national literature and only succeeds in doing so when it abandons its programmatic pronouncements and begins to think of itself as literature first and foremost, allowing the adjective 'Quebec' to slip into the background.]

The very fact of highlighting linguistic playfulness as evidence of Quebec literature's independence and growing self-confidence should make it clear that playfulness in this sense is not to be associated with gratuitousness. For example, Tremblay's inventiveness with regard to popular speech is something of an aesthetic necessity given his aim of representing the experience of distinct communities and social groups, while Ducharme's linguistic playfulness has an anarchic dimension that is closely allied to derision and despair. It is their particularity and individuality that makes them so effective in helping *Québécois* to call into question the ideologies of *québécité* or militant nationalism. The links they entertain with postmodernism are no doubt located here, in this refusal of the grand narratives of national emergence and the conviction that the individual and the local are the privileged sites of cultural expression.

One major consequence of the shift in emphasis away from the national to the individual is a generalised acceptance that identity is never a given and is always to be negotiated and renegotiated. The contemporary literary scene in Quebec is thus marked by a certain cosmopolitanism and recent works frequently explore intercultural relations. This is as true of writers born in Quebec like Jacques Poulin (*Volkswagen Blues* (1988)) as it is of 'migrant writers', those born elsewhere who have migrated to the province and pursued successful careers there, such as Régine Robin (France), Ying Chen (China), Marco Micone (Italy) and Emile Ollivier or Dany Laferrière (Haiti). The journey undertaken by the protagonist Jack in *Volkswagen Blues* is a journey through both the space and temporality of North America and involves a quest that is informed by encounters with texts as much as encounters with different locations. His search for his brother, Théo, is conducted in the company of a 'métisse', la Grande Sauterelle, who provides the narrative with a contrapuntal 'Indian' perspective focused on the history of the vanquished First Nations rather than the official histories, French and British, that tell the stories of their conquerors. This approach to constructing the narrative ensures that it is nourished from a variety of different cultural sources and, in the end, the reality Jack uncovers is that of a North America that is geographically and historically constrained by the monocultural historiographies that seek to contain it. At the close of the novel Jack sets off to return to Montreal, alone, but with a broader sense of the mulitple sources of his own cultural identity.

The various migrant francophone writers who have based themselves in Quebec in recent decades often explore similar tensions in their own cultural make-up. For example, Régine Robin's Jewish background serves as a marker for radical alterity in much of her work, particularly *La Québécoite* (1993), while Ying Chen, born in Shanghai, explores notions of cultural difference through the linguistic exile that 'inhabiting' another's tongue inevitably entails. Through the success of such works the francophone literature of Quebec demonstrates how far it has travelled. From the tentative search of early writers for the means to create a national literature, unavoidably reliant on French linguistic and aesthetic norms, it now positions itself within a postcolonial, transcultural perspective, where a refashioning of the French language is both the process whereby the works come into being and the product they have set themselves to create.

Gabrielle Roy (Manitoba, 1909–1983)

With the benefit of hindsight, the contemporary reader may well conclude that what is most striking about Gabrielle Roy's celebrated novel, *Bonheur d'occasion* (1945), is the fact that it mounts no more than a rather perfunctory challenge to the prevailing orthodoxies of the 1940s. The novel is so often painted as an important precursor to the Quiet Revolution that was to follow some fifteen years later that one tends to expect a more fully fledged assault on the ideological underbelly of Duplessis's Quebec. Instead, what the novel actually delivers is a fiction drawing on the conventions of the realist novel and a meticulously crafted portrait of a specific social group in a specific place at a specific moment in history: the working classes of Montreal during the Second World War. In this respect then, it attempts to represent, and to a limited extent theorise, social conditions from the bottom up. Far from illustrating an ideological position by inventing a yarn to fit it, Roy's method involves the close observation of social conditions and providing an accurate account of them to her readers.

The emphasis on observation as a key method recalls the techniques favoured by the naturalist school of nineteenth-century France and, indeed, the novel has a thoroughly Zolaesque flavour about it on a number of levels. Firstly, the world inhabited by Florentine and the two men in her life, Jean Lévesque and Emmanuel Létourneau, is a world that bathes in an all-pervasive sense of the 'predetermined' that is so typical of the naturalist novel. By and large the fate of the various characters appears sealed from the outset. They live in a world where money and jobs are scarce, where opportunities for self-improvement are rare and where the war looms large as a constant reminder of some impending doom or inescapable destiny. Secondly, Roy, like Zola, portrays in some detail the everyday world of the workplace with its tools, mechanical contraptions and divisions of labour as well as the urban infrastructure: the streets, tramways, railways, bars and restaurants where ordinary people spend their time. Between these two extremes, between the macrocosm of historically determined social conditions and the microscosm of harsh, day-to-day experience, Roy, similar to Zola in this respect too, draws the reader into a greater awareness of the forces at work within society. She does not draw direct political conclusions from the disparate strands of social critique that can be discerned in the novel, but nor is this writing that is unaware of the link between the material misery of the poor and the broader, often economic, forces that bear down upon them. Roy's other writings confirm the fact that her interest in politics is limited. So even in this most political of her writings there is a marked tendency to extrapolate from experience not in the direction of the need for social or political reform but towards the instructive parallels she feels can be drawn between material conditions and the moral sphere. The material poverty of French-Canadians as the war approached parallels the state of moral indolence and despair, and the lack of moral direction, that are omnipresent in the novel.

The happiness referred to in the novel's title, *Bonheur d'occasion*, is suggestive from the outset that the reader is entering a fallen world. It translates literally as 'second-hand happiness', but it also has connotations of the opportunistic, of 'making do', contenting oneself with what is possible rather than striving after an unattainable ideal. For these reasons the title provides a useful key to understanding the love story that one might assume to provide the ostensible storyline of the novel. But it applies equally well to the wider social drama the novel portrays, that which deals with the disappointed aspirations of a whole generation of French-Canadians. As far as the love plot is concerned, despite her passionate feelings for Jean Lévesque, Florentine falls back on a tactical, loveless marriage to his friend, Emmanuel, purely in order to secure a future for herself and her unborn child. Her decision is partly an acceptance of reality (Jean is consumed with ambition and callously indifferent to Florentine's feelings) and partly a calculated trade-off (years of living in want have taught her the value of security and material comfort).

If love is absent from Florentine's world and effectively denied to her by circumstances beyond her control, the same is true of work for a whole range of characters in the novel. Work is valued both in and for itself, as a principle, but also in terms of the individual jobs that are mentioned throughout the novel. Emmanuel declaims at one point, 'l'argent n'est pas la richesse. La richesse, c'est le travail, c'est nos bras, c'est nos têtes à nous autres, la grande masse' (p. 63) [money isn't wealth. Wealth is work, for us, the great masses, it's our arms, it's all our heads, together]. The absence of work brings in its train the squalor, the filth, the misery and the lingering smell of poverty that are constantly referred to throughout the novel. It is the precariousness of the world of work, the high rates of unemployment, the impossibility of finding any work at all for so many young men, such as Boisvert, Alphonse and Pitou, Emmanuel's former classmates, that eventually oblige more and more men to enlist in the armed forces and go to war. They do so not out of any sense of commitment to an ideal (equivalent to 'love' in Florentine's frame of reference) but for opportunistic, pragmatic reasons, simply to occupy themselves or to secure a regular income for a spouse and family. This is the case of Azarius, Florentine's father, who, like so many others is 'saved by the war' after years of unsuccessfully trying to scrape a living to support his family. By way of contrast, Emmanuel's principled commitment to fighting the war is seen precisely in terms of an ideal and of 'love': 'subitement il avait cru comprendre une chose épouvantable . . . c'est que pour faire la guerre, il fallait être rempli d'un amour, d'une passion véhémente, il fallait être exalté par une ivresse' (p. 316) [suddenly he had understood an awful truth . . . in order to fight the war you had to be filled with love, with a burning passion, you had to be intoxicated by an ideal]. On both axes, in the world of work as in the world of love, the happiness secured comes at a high price, and it is not even true happiness for all that, merely a second-hand version of it.

Jean Lévesque provides a bridge between the two worlds of love and work, as he does between the two readings proposed here. His self-absorbed character allows him the emotional space to feel little more than a passing curiosity for Florentine, as much inspired by a mild interest in her origins as it is by her person. When he is eventually lured to her home he is more deeply affected by the smell of poverty and misery than by their love-making. This impresses itself upon his mind so strongly that any further commerce between the couple becomes impossible for him. She inhabits a world he has left behind in the ruins of his childhood and his ambition is fired by a determination to ensure he never returns. Lévesque thus figures as an extreme example of the compromises that characters are drawn into as they seek to secure their futures, be it through a loveless marriage of convenience, or donning a soldier's uniform. Lévesque is an extreme character in his professional life too. His single-mindedness sets him apart from the masses. The war may offer an escape route of sorts to many unemployed workers but Lévesque, by contrast, recognises very early on in the novel that the war offers opportunities for rich pickings, a chance to rise quicker and higher than would otherwise have been possible. In conversation with Emmanuel, he makes his personal vision clear: 'toi, tu crois que c'est les soldats qui changent le monde, qui mènent le monde; et moi, bien moi, je crois que c'est les gars qui restent en arrière et qui font de l'argent avec la guerre' (p. 67) [you think that it's soldiers who change the world, who decide where the world is heading, and me, well I think that it's the blokes who stay behind and make money out of the war].

Critics have suggested that Lévesque is the only character in the novel who embodies any real spirit of revolt, but this is to confuse social conscience with strength of character and dynamism. Lévesque is certainly dynamic and determined to succeed at any cost but his lack of interest in the plight of his fellow men makes him little more than an egoistic monster whose personal ambition is the only force that drives him. It is easy to contrast him with the other, rather pathetic, often feckless and generally unambitious male characters who people the novel. In a comment that captures a general mood, Emmanuel says of his trio of former classmates, 'Chez eux, il avait trouvé la véritable expression tourmentée, blagueuse, indolente, de sa génération.' (p. 53) [In them, he had discovered the feckless, facetious, truly tormented face of his generation.] Lévesque displays more energy than these characters, but he channels it into a career that will allow him to benefit from the system (the war) rather than challenge it or revolt against it. It is left to the female characters in the novel to exert themselves so as to ensure the survival of their families and the community. It is Florentine's salary, earned as a waitress, that keeps the Lacasse family financially afloat, just as it is the ingenuity of her mother, Rose-Anna, in managing and marshalling these meagre resources that ensures their survival. It is Rose-Anna too who undertakes the annual search for new lodgings and thus literally ensures the family have a roof over their heads.

Bonheur d'occasion is generally considered as one of the first novels to break with the dominant tradition of the *roman du terroir* and to deal with the realities of daily life in an urbanised, industrialised setting that was the experience of increasing numbers of French-Canadians. In this respect, the novel marks a break with the past but it does not go very far down the path of envisaging, much less demanding, the reforms that would be required in the years ahead. It pinpoints many of the problems confronting the urban poor of francophone Canada but the portrayal itself, like the characters it depicts, seems to be groping towards an understanding of the nature of the predicament. In the final pages, storm clouds are gathering on the horizon, suggesting perhaps that the novel, for all its length, has merely served as a prelude to a drama yet to unfold.

Roy's next novel was also based in an urban setting, *Alexandre Chenevert: caissier* (1954). As was the case with *Bonheur d'occasion*, this novel too has a 'pre-political' feel to it. It provides a wealth of material drawn from a close observation of lived experience that could be used to substantiate and justify political conclusions which are never, in the event, formulated. The eponymous antihero of the novel, Alexandre, is an anxiety-ridden, obsessive character whose life in the mechanistic, highly commercialised world of Montreal is lived as a form of absolute alienation. At much the same time that Fanon was writing in *Peau noire masques blancs* about the alienating effects of colonisation on blacks, Roy explores similar psychic phenomena in terms of pure 'mal de vivre' and ascribes them to the stresses of modernity. Alexandre works in a cage at a bank, worries constantly about the ills of the world (melting ice caps, the fate of the Palestinians, the Berlin blockade) and about his own state of health. He is capable of only the most superficial relationships, even with his own wife, Eugénie. At one point in the novel Alexandre follows the advice of his doctor and escapes from Montreal to spend a few days in a rented cabin in the woods. The life of carefree self-sufficiency enjoyed by the family of farmers who own the place seems to offer the prospect of an alternative lifestyle: for a brief interlude Alexandre dreams of becoming a backwoodsman in what would have been a highly symbolic return to nature. But his vision falters and fades away immediately upon his return to the city. The commercial advertising hoardings, the electrified statues of Christ and the saints that 'sell' religion to the masses, the bustle and aggressiveness of city life all reclaim him like a familiar illness he can neither live with nor live without. Roy explores the raw material of Alexandre's life and eventual death (he even worries about the cost of his coffin and headstone), leaving the reader in little doubt that his morbidity is a consequence of his alienation from forms of social organisation to which he cannot adapt, yet she resists any temptation to claim it has a wider metaphysical significance or holds a broader political message.

Somewhat paradoxically, the techniques of social realism and the pessimistic tone that distinguish Roy's best-known works, *Bonheur d'occasion* and *Alexandre Chenevert: caissier*, are not characteristic of the vast majority of her writings. The more personal tone that characterises her later works, often semi-autobiographical in nature and rooted in her own experience, is already in evidence in the novel she published in 1950, *La Petite Poule d'eau*. Critics have frequently suggested that Roy, born in Manitoba and therefore outside the mainstream cultural life of Quebec, was all the better equipped to observe and give an account of life in the province. In respect of her other, more pastoral works, the obverse claim is often made: that she delved into her own memories and personal experiences to describe the towncapes and landscapes of her earlier years, the austere natural beauty of the northern Canadian provinces and the distinctive characters who inhabit them. The 'pastoral' vein in Roy's work tends to celebrate the landscapes, the flora and the fauna of the regions she portrays, but this documentary approach is not unrelated to the ethnographic tendency that runs throughout her work, from the early reports on 'Peuples du Canada', 'sortes de portraits de communautés ethniques'[6] [sorts of portraits of ethnic communities] that were collected together and published in *Fragiles Lumières de la terre* (1978), to many of the tales in *Rue Deschambault* (1955). In this latter collection the father of Christine, the narrator, works for the Ministry of Colonisation settling communities of immigrants in the open spaces of Manitoba and Saskatchewan. The father consciously participates in the process of nation-building while displaying the same respect for diversity and harmony between cultures that is illustrated by Joseph-Marie, the Capuchin friar of *La Petite Poule d'eau* and which Roy herself undoubtedly shared. But just as she stopped short of a truly political analysis in the two 'urban' novels so she never seriously interrogated the full ramifications of the colonisation that is portrayed in terms of progress in her 'pastoral' works. Her faith in the goodness of humankind, her longing for harmony between men and with nature, the value she placed on fraternity and social solidarity are all, no doubt, exemplary character traits. But in an age when postcolonial scepticism about the progressive nature of such intercultural relations invites us to interrogate them with a little more rigour, it has become apparent that they are not, perhaps, a recipe for exemplary literature.

Anne Hébert (Quebec, 1916–2000)

Although Hébert's first published work, a volume of poetry entitled *Les Songes en équilibre*, dates from 1942, she began writing both poetry and novellas as early as the 1930s. Born in the year in which Louis Hémon published *Maria Chapdelaine* (1916), her writing career thus spans well over half a century. Her imposing presence as a figure on the Quebec literary scene over so many decades (she died in 2000 in Montreal) is due in no small part to the fiercely independent nature of her practice as a writer. It is certainly true that her work defies attempts to be 'pigeon-holed' in the categories associated with the recent, often stormy literary history of Quebec

Hébert's international standing as a poet and novelist is therefore founded not on any role(s) that can be assigned to her within a history of the dynamic emerging literature of Quebec, but on the uncompromising literary qualities of her writing. Often profound and complex in its structure and orchestration, her prose writing frequently has poetic qualities that make special demands of her readers. To enter the fictional universes she constructs, readers are required to draw heavily on their own internal resources, their experience, sensibility and imagination. This intimate side of Hébert's work exists in tension with the frequently extreme nature of the subject matter she explores. Her prose writings, in particular, foreground scenarios of family life and small communities yet the relationships that unfold within them are typically racked by torments of passion and violence as the grand themes of love, death, solitude and revolt are played out. The intimate and the universal are interwoven, interdependent facets of the worlds she deploys, since such grand themes are meaningless unless their exploration is rooted in the personal and particular. Hence her characters have bodies, souls and libidos that make them individual exemplars of humanity while they also occupy a place in recognisable social and economic hierarchies. They are sexually preoccupied, gendered beings with a historical baggage of linguistic, religious and community affiliations to weigh them down. It is from within (and against) these various types of determinism that they confront the overarching existential questions of the human condition, as they seek to define their own place in the world and battle with their personal demons.

The tension between the intimate and the universal in Hébert's work allows her much scope to examine more topical issues as well as those grandiose questions about the human condition that *also* preoccupy her. Her novels may be about destructive passions and the cycles of decay and renewal that characterise the human condition, but they can also be read as denunciations of the material and spiritual poverty that are so often a feature of life in communities where the dead hand of tradition has never been challenged, where women are subjected to the stultifying oppression of patriarchal authority, and where convention and the pressure to conform override all other ethical considerations. Yet her treatment of the larger questions to do with the human condition is usually rooted in the specific, historical and geographical context of Quebec. Hence the landscapes and the physical environment of Quebec figure largely in almost all of Hébert's work as does the broader historical canvas of relationships between francophone and anglophone communities, between Canada and the USA, and between the new world and the old world of Europe. Hébert is undeniably a Quebec writer but tangentially so. She does not engage directly with debates about Quebec identity, about linguistic or cultural alienation, about abandonment, exile or the dangers of assimilation. There is no conscious effort to illustrate such topics through her fiction. Instead she comes to these issues from the other direction: she writes about human experiences (childhood, love, desire, death, loss) with a sensibility and an imaginary that is rooted in Quebec life. It is through the process of writing about such experiences that she comes to engage with the more politically focused postcolonial agenda of other contemporary Quebec writers.

Hébert's first novel, *Les Chambres de bois* (1958) is an enigmatic, highly original work that is as much a prose poem as a novel in the generally accepted sense of the term. The text provides only a skeleton of a narrative and the bare bones of characterisation and plot. Where a traditional novel might provide a dramatisation of events, sociological detail and/or psychological depth, Hébert, in this novel, seems intent on producing a minimalist narrative in which her true subject is the mood and atmosphere in which her characters move. There are identifiable characters from identifiable social backgrounds, notably Catherine, the working-class protagonist who marries Michel, the tormented, cultured aristocrat. Their relationship is more metaphysical than physical and, over time, it comes to a crisis point when Michel allows his sister, Lia, to join the couple in the stiflingly restricted space of the family home, the eponymous *Chambres de bois*. Catherine's isolation is exacerbated by the alienating exclusivity of the relationship between the siblings and she consequently falls ill. The self-absorbed, introspective world of Michel and Lia is associated with a world of high culture (books, piano, painting) from which Catherine is excluded, and it is only when she manages to escape from the claustrophobic atmosphere generated by Michel and Lia that she is able to recover her health and begin a more life-affirming relationship with Bruno. At the close of the novel, while Catherine has finally freed herself from the 'strange love' that was all Michel could offer her, Michel himself is living in a state of spiritual and emotional isolation, abandoned by his sister who has betrayed the 'childhood pact' that appears to be the foundation of their relationship. The language of this novel is beautifully evocative and yet restrained and austere.

As with all of Hébert's work the potential for symbolic interpretations of *Les Chambres de bois* is enormous. The narcissistic, incestuous relationship of Michel–Lia evolves against a background of involvement with 'high culture' that is also associated with material dispossession (the loss of 'la maison des seigneurs' (p. 31) [the house of the overlords] through the fault of Lia) and emotional betrayal. All of these elements can be assigned a meaning and a value in an allegorical account of French-Canadians' relationship with France. (The ceding of Canada to the British through the Treaty of Paris in 1763 was a traumatic moment of betrayal and abandonment for French-Canadians who nevertheless continued to look to France as a repository of linguistic and cultural standards.) On an entirely different level, the novel can be read as a symbolic reworking of events that occurred in Hébert's own family life. Her cousin, the well-respected poet Hector de Saint-Denys Garneau, withdrew from public life at the age of twenty-two and spent his final years living as a virtual recluse in the manor house of Sainte-Catherine de Fossambault. His own poetry had evolved from an initial preoccupation with the ludic world of childhood innocence to a sombre, introspective and metaphysically anguished vein of writing after he had been diagnosed with a life-threatening heart condition. He died at the age of thirty-one in 1943. There are clear thematic correspondences between the later work of Saint-Denys Garneau and Hébert's own writings, many of which surface in this novel, and it would not be unreasonable to suggest that Catherine's rejection of Michel in the novel is reminiscent of Hébert's own need to move out of the orbit of her elder cousin's influence.

Hébert's next published novel, *Kamouraska* (1970), also focuses on a female character seeking to shake off the shackles that prevent her from achieving a form of self-realisation. The vagueness of setting and context that allows readers of *Les Chambres de bois* to allegorise Catherine's experience, and read into it a more generalised critique of women's dependency on men, gives way in *Kamouraska* to a specific individual drama played out in a specific geographic and historical setting. The key events of the novel are presented through a series of flashbacks, retrospective memories and imagined reconstructions mainly emanating from and channelled through the consciousness of the female protagonist, Mme Rolland/Elisabeth d'Aulnières. These are supplemented (and occasionally challenged and contradicted) by witness statements and other reported accounts of the events that took place in January 1839, when Dr George Nelson, Elisabeth's lover, drove from Sorel to Kamouraska and murdered her brutish husband, Antoine Tassy. Elisabeth herself is an accomplice to the murder in that she incited Nelson to eliminate Antoine after an earlier attempt to poison her husband, through the offices of her maid, Aurélie Caron, had failed.

On one level, this is the stuff of high romantic drama: it is a tale of thwarted love that leads to a crime of passion, vicariously committed by Elisabeth, albeit performed by the dashing young doctor. A symphony of colour (the distinctive black of Nelson's horse, the white glare of the snow, and the red of the spilled blood of Tassy) underscores the account of the murder provided by Elisabeth as she later reconstructs a mental image of how events unfolded. Significantly, the murder leads nowhere. It is an end in itself, a very public explosion of violence that serves only to release the tension under which the lovers are living but providing no solution to their dilemma, no liberation for Elisabeth and no prospect of a shared future together. It is an irrational act that contains within itself no horizon beyond its own realisation. Nelson's subsequent flight across the US border to Burlington cuts him off forever from Elisabeth, who remains unsure as to whether this constitutes an act of betrayal or a case of *force majeure*.

On a very different level, however, the real drama of the novel lies not in the 'kernel' event provided by the bloody murder of Tassy but in the wider, domestic drama of Elisabeth's life. Her condition as a woman is inescapably one in which any appetite for life is constrained and circumscribed by the crushing need to conform to the limited range of roles that society allows. This is the permanent reality of her condition. The temporal framework within which the narrative unfolds (a series of flashbacks from a narrative present) emphasises this point. The Elisabeth of the narrative present is Mme Rolland, ostensibly a dutiful wife and mother whose second marriage to a respected businessman has allowed her to reintegrate into society after her acquittal. She has saved her reputation by playing the role of a devout and devoted wife, and bearing M. Rolland a further eight children. As Elisabeth watches her husband on his death-bed slowly succumb to the terminal illness from which he is suffering, her reflections repeatedly express the *impasse* of her condition:

> Je n'ai plus qu'à devenir si sage qu'on me prenne au mot. Fixer le masque de l'innocence sur les os de ma face. Accepter l'innocence en guise de revanche ou de punition. Jouer le jeu cruel, la comédie épuisante, jour après jour. Jusqu'à ce que la ressemblance parfaite me colle à la peau.   (p. 249)

> [All that's left to me now is to be so well-behaved that they take me at face value. Fix the mask of innocence on the bones of my face. Accept innocence as a form of revenge or punishment. Day after day, play the cruel game, keep up the exhausting pretence. Until the perfect resemblance melds with my skin.]

Nothing has changed for Elisabeth. As she simultaneously witnesses the death of both her husbands (one before her eyes and one through her mind's eye), the lesson she draws from her experience is the overwhelming constancy and power of hypocrisy in social relations. Even an event as dramatic as the (vicarious) slaughter of her husband never seriously inflects the course of her life or the expectations that society places on her. The tears she sheds at the close of the novel are interpreted by other women present as a sign of her devotion to her dying husband but they can, of course, equally be read as the 'sincere' tears shed by a woman who realises that she has failed to break her shackles and is now condemned to die of her thwarted 'hunger for life' and solitude.

Just as *Kamouraska* has as its kernel the 'reconstruction' of a brutal murder, so *Les Fous de Bassan* (1982) is a reconstruction of the disappearance of two adolescent girls that turns out to have occurred in a similarly violent, murderous manner. Although the later novel includes an element of suspense that is absent from *Kamouraska*, both novels are primarily concerned with an investigation of relationships between characters rather than unmasking, much less condemning, the killer(s). In *Les Fous de Bassan*, the narrative structure is complex and again involves a dual time frame. The narrative is supplied from a number of different sources, written interventions in the form of notebooks or letters, from characters living in the community of Griffin Creek where the drama occurred in August 1936. Some of these are contemporaneous accounts of the events of that summer, including contributions from the two murdered adolescents, Nora and Olivia Atkins, while two contributions, that of the pastor,

Nicholas Jones, and the letters of Stevens Brown, are dated 1982. In his final letter, Stevens Brown admits to having killed Nora before raping and killing her cousin, Olivia, and disposing of their bodies in the sea. The letter describes the fit of rage that engulfs Brown as he becomes a plaything of elemental, destructive forces and embarks on a passionate frenzy of violence.

Just as the murder of Tassy in *Kamouraska* is a largely irrational act, disconnected from calculating motivations or practical objectives, so the murder of the two cousins has no cause or purpose commensurate with its violence. It is a gratuitous act of evil motivated poetically rather than rationally. The frustrated sexual desire of Brown and the emerging sexuality of the young girls are an undercurrent, as is the constraining ethical and moral environment of a small, isolated, somewhat inbred, patriarchal community. Yet it is not suggested that these in any way account for Brown's actions. When the storm breaks upon him it is questionable whether he is agent or acted upon, just as it is questionable whether the storm he experiences as he performs the murders is internal or external. Either way, Brown can be seen as a conduit for the destiny of the community who collectively share the guilt his acts bring in their train.

But examining the (absent) motives of the murderer may be the wrong place to look for a deeper understanding of these sombre events. Viewed phenomenologically, the death of the two girls is simply a horrific yet banal example of what some men do to some women. Elisabeth d'Aulnières's hunger for life is perhaps an avatar of the blossoming sexuality and vitality of Nora and Olivia Atkins. Stevens Brown snuffs them out in a text through which Hébert ensures they continue, nevertheless, to shine. An almost exactly equivalent process is described in one of Hébert's earlier poems:

> Il y a certainement quelqu'un
> Qui m'a tuée
> Puis s'en est allé
> Sur la pointe des pieds
> Sans rompre sa danse parfaite
>
> A oublié de me coucher
> M'a laissée debout
> Toute liée
> Sur le chemin
> . . .
>
> A oublié d'effacer la beauté du monde
> Autour de moi
> A oublié de fermer mes yeux avides
> Et permis leur passion perdue[7]

[There is certainly someone
Who has killed me
Then gone away
On tiptoe
Without losing his step in his perfect dance

Who has forgotten to lay me down
Who has left me standing
All tied up
On the path
. . .

Who has forgotten to wipe away the beauty of the world
From around me
Who has forgotten to close my hungry eyes
And allowed their lost passion]

The woman killed in this poem has not been obliterated by her male killer. While his forgetfulness suggests indifference and carelessness about the fate of his victim (thus trivialising the killing), the corpse is paradoxically able to comment on the event from the half-life/after-life position of abandonment to which the male has relegated her: she remains in an upright position, still aware of the beauty of the world and her hungry eyes still open. This unhappy victim has much in common with the accomplice to murder, Elisabeth d'Aulnières, and the victims of murder, Olivia and Nora Atkins, in that the life of each of them is threatened (or taken) by a male-dominated, convention-ridden, life-denying social structure.

With *Le Premier Jardin* (1988) Hébert's interest in social masks and role-playing is once again a prominent feature of the narrative, but this time it is developed within a more clearly postcolonial thematics of origins, roots and identity and linked to the *topos* of the return to the native land after a period of exile. Flora Fontanges, an ageing actress, returns to her native Quebec for two reasons: she has received an invitation to create the role of Winnie in Beckett's *Oh! les beaux jours* [*Happy Days*] at the same time as a call for help from her daughter, Maud. The return to Quebec provides Flora with an opportunity to revisit key sites in her personal past and reflect on the multiple identities she has previously assumed: first as Pierrette Paul (an orphan), then as Marie Eventurel (following her adoption), and finally as Flora Fontanges. In addition, her profession as an actress has allowed her to assume a wide range of dramatic roles and identities (Ophelia in *Hamlet*, Phèdre, and Fantine in *Les Misérables*, among others). As she reveals more and more details of her private past, it becomes clear that the childhood experience of needing to play a role in order to win the approval of her adoptive parents (and beyond them of the all-powerful grandmother, guardian of family values) provides an originary script that she will continue to repeat into adult life: the existential necessity to live in the ephemeral present of a rootless, provisional identity. Indeed, her decision to flee from her parents and from Quebec to pursue an uncertain career as an actress is clearly presented as a revolt against pressures to conform and accept a planned marriage (to the worst dancer on the social circuit). Her departure for Europe is thus a life-affirming gesture that freed her to invent the identity (and name) of her choosing.

The return to Quebec is also an occasion to revisit key sites in the historical past of the city and reflect on the contribution of a range of women to the construction of the 'national' identity of Quebec. As Flora visits a range of tourist attractions she spontaneously and dramatically enters the lives of a succession of female characters associated with them and who peopled Quebec's past. These include, among others, Marie Rollet who planted the eponymous 'first garden' in the city of Quebec shortly after its founding, the 'filles du Roi' who were sent to *Nouvelle France* in the late seventeenth century to work and provide children for the colony, to the maids of the bourgeois families of late nineteenth-century city. The personal and historical pasts eventually fuse as Flora reincarnates/remembers her own experience of December 1927 when she was saved from the flames as the orphanage in which she lived was burned to the ground. This fusion of the two pasts in a creative act of memory echoes the motto of Quebec Province, 'Je me souviens' [I remember], and frees Flora to move on to her next role. But the conclusion of this novel is not an apotheosis. Flora's journey (and her talent) have highlighted the unglorious contributions of women to the 'making' of Quebec yet the full irony and bathos of the journey's end is underscored by the role she has been preparing: Beckett's Winnie, an absurd old woman demonstrating the 'inanité de toutes choses' (p. 187) [inanity of all things]. At the close of the novel Flora leaves Quebec with a new contract in her pocket and the prospect of playing Madame Frola in Pirandello's *Chacun sa vérité*. It would seem that truth, like identity, is never fixed and remains eternally negotiable.

Marie-Claire Blais (Quebec, 1939–)

For almost half a century Marie-Claire Blais has been an important presence on the Quebec literary scene and a prolific writer of poetry, plays and novels. In the course of her long career she has won eight major international prizes for her work. It has been argued, however, that this longevity does not necessarily correspond to an evenly distributed output, in terms of either 'quality' or quantity, and it remains the case that her early novels, especially *La Belle Bête* (1959) and *Une saison dans la vie d'Emmanuel* (1965), have attracted, and continue to attract, particular attention from critics. One early commentator acidly complains about the slimness of many of the early volumes published, suggesting that collectively they have the weight of only a single fully fledged novel.[8] *La Belle Bête* was published when Blais was only twenty and it immediately caught the eye of the influential American critic, Edmund Wilson. Its publication coincided with the end of the Duplessis era, 'la grande noirceur', that marked the beginning of the Quiet Revolution, and, like *Une saison dans la vie d'Emmanuel*, it has been seen as offering a portrait of life in the 'dark' days of the 1940s and 1950s, albeit not a realist one. The impact these novels had is undoubtedly linked to their topicality: they contributed to that critique of society and expressed the mood of revolt against conventional values that signalled the dismantling of old orthodoxies. But it is also the case that Blais's highly idiosyncratic poeticisation of the realities she describes marked her out as a new and distinctive voice on the Quebec literary scene.

Already, in her first novel, *La Belle Bête*, Blais adopts a tone that intermingles elements of poetic symbolism and realist narrative. The setting is a hybrid world reminiscent of the landscapes to be found in the fantasy world of the fairytale ('La Belle et la Bête' is an obvious intertext here), while including the trains, ploughs and agricultural implements of the rural farmsteads of contemporary Canada. The characters share a similarly ambiguous status. They are to an extent crude allegorical representations of stock emotions and characteristics and yet Blais portrays them in sufficient detail and with sufficient context to enable readers not to abandon reading strategies that are appropriate for realist novels. Blais thus treads a fine line between portraying characters that are 'believable' and characters that are merely caricatures. Patrice, the beautiful yet empty-headed youth (both 'beau' and 'bête'), is a synonym for self-absorbed physicality. Isabelle-Marie, his sister, is his ungracious antithesis: physically unprepossessing and riddled with the anger and cruelty born of jealousy. Louise, the mother is a superficial, shallow creature whose own beauty is mirrored in that of her son. Equally superficial is Lanz, the town-dwelling dandy she chooses as a husband. The drama that binds this family is a highly schematic interplay of primal emotions, more often than not figured in a series of binary oppositions and violent contradictions: love/hate, beauty/ugliness, good/evil, idiocy/lucidity. Although death and destruction play a large part in the novel, however, they are not counterbalanced by any sense of renewal or renaissance. The dynamic force for evil throughout is Isabelle-Marie, whose hatred for her family, contempt for her mother and jealousy of Patrice lead her to disfigure the latter by plunging his face in boiling water and, in a bleak dénouement, to destroy the family home and farmlands by an act of arson.

Motivations for actions do not flow from any psychological depths since Blais's purpose is to demonstrate the all-pervasive shallowness and superficiality of the universe in which her characters move. Louise is attracted to Lanz, the dandy, for his looks, sophistication and urbanity, so when he is killed by Patrice's charging horse the lack of substance to the man is expressed through a type of hyperbole: his body literally disintegrates, demonstrating that his whole persona was a purely artificial construction, even down to the golden cane he constantly carried with him:

> Patrice suivait la canne d'or qui s'enfuyait comme un glaive en fusion, et aussi, ce qu'on n'avait jamais remarqué, la perruque de Lanz qui quittait son crâne. De plus, mêlée aux taches de sang, la barbe fausse de Lanz s'égrenait.   (p. 93)

> [Patrice followed the golden cane that was vanishing into the distance like a melting sword, and also, something they had never noticed before, Lanz's wig was slipping away from his skull. What is more, mixed up with the spattered blood, Lanz's false beard was falling apart.]

The attraction Louise feels for Lanz is based on surfaces, just as her admiration for the physical beauty of Patrice can be seen to be literally skin-deep since it instantly disappears the moment he is disfigured. Louise's summary rejection of Patrice once he has lost his good looks parallels the equally summary rejection of Isabelle-Marie by her husband, the blind Michael Livani, when he regains his sight to discover that she is not the beautiful bride she had assured him she was. Mirrors and reflections abound in this novel creating a world of surfaces which repeat *ad infinitum* the superficiality and lack of depth of Patrice, Louise, Lanz and Michael. The only characters who do not share the real or metaphorical blindness that leaves them at the mercy of the attractions of physical beauty are Isabelle-Marie and her daughter, Anne, whose revolt against the world of surfaces is born out of, and fuelled by, their own physical ugliness. For all that, Isabelle-Marie is not portrayed as a lucid 'heroine' in a world of otherwise blinkered characters. Before her hatred boils over into her final act of destructive revolt there is a point in the novel when she is clearly prepared to join the herd and live a life based on deception and false claims about her own supposed beauty. In this respect, then, all the characters in the novel are, to a greater or lesser extent, locked into a single drama: their sense of self-worth depends entirely on the approval of others and the relationships they enter into are fundamentally narcissistic, involving only spurious forms of exchange.

La Belle Bête is an unremittingly dark novel, peopled by monstrous characters whose very monstrosity has ensured that they have tended to monopolise the attention of readers. Yet scope for other, less character-focused, readings of the novel certainly exists. Not least among these must be Lucien Goldmann's attempt to interpret the novel (along with *Une saison dans la vie d'Emmanuel*) as an allegory of the sociological conditions existing in Quebec at the time.[9] Perhaps a more fruitful approach than Goldmann's is to recognise the symbolic power of the peculiar imaginary deployed by Blais in this novel. Given that the narrative unfolds in a rural setting and portrays a family (however dysfunctional), it can be argued that Blais was consciously writing against the whole *roman du terroir* tradition. The values that dominate in the *roman du terroir* are systematically flaunted in this text: there is no appeal to notions of rootedness in the soil, to physical labour and the battle for daily survival, to the importance of family ties and the overpowering influence of the church as an arbiter of conduct and morality, or to any sense of a community living in contact with the rhythms of the natural world. Instead Louise is a wealthy landowner whose farmlands are as much an investment as a home; she is attracted to urban sophistication and inhabits a thoroughly secular universe; her rejection of her children equates to a dismantling of her family and threatens continuity and transmission across generations; her superficiality and individuality are the antithesis of the notions of depth and durability associated with tradition. Thus the burning of the house and fields at the close of the novel can be seen as the inevitable destruction of a social order that had, in any event, nowhere to go.

If the symbolism of *La Belle Bête* can be seen as offering a critique of the society of the day, *Une saison dans la vie d'Emmanuel* has also frequently been portrayed as a sort of 'anti-*roman du terroir*'. But whereas the earlier novel displays a crisis in values and a breakdown in transmission, the later novel seems to be pointing up the sorry fact that the baby, Emmanuel, has little chance of escaping the fate that he shares with previous generations of his family. In the opening pages of the novel, Grand-Mère Antoinette makes it clear that the only future open to the baby is that he will go on to take his place within the precarious universe that Blais is about to portray: 'Tu feras comme les autres, tu seras ignorant, cruel et amer . . . ' (p. 8) [You'll do just like the others, you'll be ignorant, cruel and bitter . . .] The grandmother follows this harsh prediction with other equally dismissive comments that help set the tone of the novel, leaving no illusions as to the quality of family life in the household: 'Les nouveau-nés sont sales. Ils me dégoûtent' [New-born babies are dirty. They disgust me]; 'tu pleures vainement, tu apprendras vite que tu es seul au monde' [you're crying for nothing, you'll soon learn that you're all alone in the world]; whereupon Emmanuel purportedly realises, 'que cette misère n'aurait pas de fin, mais il a consenti à vivre' (p. 10) [that this miserable condition would never end, but he consented to go on living].

The grandmother is the dominant figure in the household, eclipsing both the self-effacing, nameless mother and the ineffectual father. It is she who assumes the role of archetypal parent to the gaggle of semi-delinquent children: Héloïse, Jean le Maigre, Pomme and le Septième. Her dominance, resilience and the dynamism she exercises in the running of the home tend to disguise the extent to which she is a largely negative force. As is so often the case where the depiction of maternal figures in Quebec fiction is concerned, the grandmother represents the durability of traditional values. She is the guardian of a system of values based on a Catholic moral universe. Her respect for the church and for clergymen is evidenced above all in her readiness to argue that children should be entrusted to the novitiate (Jean le Maigre) or the convent (Héloïse). But her faith also blinds her to the risk posed by the defrocked novice, the monstrously sado-masochistic Théodule Crapula, whose murderous paedophile tendencies almost seal the fate of le Septième towards the close of the novel.

The values that Grand-Mère Antoinette defends are not so much actively promoted as vigorously defended in a constant rear-guard action. She stands as much for the principles of permanence and durability as she does for any particular ideological belief. So her beliefs are harnessed to the maintenance of a certain status quo within society: she does things the way they have always been done and is resistant to change. This is perhaps the key characteristic of her world view. Hence the annual cycle of pregnancies and childbirths that women are obliged to endure, the high rates of infant mortality, the overcrowding, the physically harsh living conditions and the attendant health problems, the lack of educational or vocational opportunities for the children, all these are considered as constituting the unchanging norm. So much so that at the close of the novel she feels able to look back with satisfaction on the long winter that has been the first season in Emmanuel's life. Despite the death of Jean le Maigre, despite Héloïse's engagement as a prostitute in the *Auberge de la Rose Publique*, despite the fact that Pomme has lost three fingers in an accident at the shoe factory where he and le Septième have taken employment (signalling the effective end of any childhood they ever had), despite the fact that le Septième has narrowly escaped death by strangulation at the hands of Crapula, despite this catalogue of stunted hopes and disappointed aspirations, the grandmother remains complacently unruffled: 'L'hiver a été dur, mais le printemps sera meilleur . . . Mais oui, tout va bien, disait Grand-Mère Antoinette, en hochant la tête de satisfaction.' (p. 165) [Winter has been hard but spring will be better . . . Ah yes, everything is fine, said grandmother Antoinette, nodding her head with satisfaction.]

In contrast to the solidity and permanence that Grand-Mère Antoinette embodies, the family consists of a 'deluge of children' that flit in and out of focus. The home seems incapable of containing them and when they are indeed indoors they overflow into attics and cellars, just as they occasionally overflow from their beds and under the kitchen table. We learn that Emmanuel is the sixteenth child his mother has borne but the family as a whole lacks any clear definition as a group, partly because several of their number have already died (Pivoine, Léopold), partly because the girls tend to blend into background insignificance (the little As: Héléna, Maria, Roberta) and partly because nameless, older brothers have already passed into the anonymous world of adulthood, appearing only in the evenings to eat their supper and smoke their pipes. The children who succeed in emerging from this indeterminate mass to be portrayed as individuals within the narrative (Héloïse, Jean le Maigre, Pomme and le Septième) react to the various forms of deprivation they endure by seeking solace in a range of activities: poetry, religion, delinquency, alcohol consumption, precocious sexual activity and serial attempts at suicide. What these different examples of 'deviant' behaviour have in common is that they are all attempts to feed the spiritual, physical and emotional appetites of the children concerned. It is the family's inability to provide nourishment in this wider sense that defines its dysfunctionality.

Various institutions provide an alternative to the family, either as a replacement, when deviant behaviour calls for some form of punishment, or as an alternative, when the physical or mental health of the child warrants an appeal to a 'spiritual' order of response. Jean le Maigre and le Septième spend time in a 'maison de correction' [reform school] and yet another reforming institution, *Notre-Dame-de-la-Miséricorde*, before Jean le Maigre enters the novitiate to train for the priesthood. Héloïse spends time in a convent before entering the institutionalised world of Madame Enbonpoint's brothel. It is through the character and experience of Héloïse that the parallels are drawn between sexual desire and religiosity, on the hand, and between the two institutions of the brothel and the church, on the other.

In these two early works, then, the dysfunctionality of individuals and the family can be read as an allegorisation of the dysfunctionality of society at large. Despite their poetic, oneiric qualities they contributed directly to the attack on the official, French-Canadian ideology that the Quiet Revolution eventually overthrew. It is difficult to make such overarching claims about Blais's subsequent writings. In recent works she has explored a number of broadly philosophical and ethical themes: human suffering, death, war, disability, unconventional sexuality, and political extremism. Somewhat paradoxically, the importance of the issues she frequently treats in these works has not been seen as having the broad significance that can be ascribed to the two earlier novels.

Jacques Godbout (Quebec, 1933–)

Novelist, film-director, journalist, poet, essayist and cultural commentator, Jacques Godbout has been an immensely influential figure in the cultural life of Quebec since the beginnings of the Quiet Revolution in the early 1960s. Just as he has made use of a variety of media to engage in debates, so he has been active in developing structures and organisations within which to progress them. Co-founder of the review *Liberté* in 1959, he has also been active in the *Mouvement laïque de langue française* and was the first president of the Union des Ecrivains Québecois. Godbout's personal commitment to the nationalist cause in Quebec does not always transfer into his literary production in very obvious ways. A political discourse of sorts can usually be traced through his novels, but the 'Quebec issue' is usually overshadowed by his anxieties about, for example, the political and cultural hegemony of the United States in world affairs, the interconnections between language, culture and power, or simply the role of the writer in society. It is far easier to pigeon-hole Godbout as a political activist than as an artist.

His first two novels, *L'Aquarium* (1962) and *Le Couteau sur la table* (1965), are generally accepted as having been heavily influenced by the French *nouveau roman*, and are formally innovative in that they eschew any linear development of plot or any traditional notion of characterisation involving psychological depth. The narrator-protagonists of both novels are erratic, remarkably fluid characters with no 'essential' characteristics. Nomads within their own skins, they are dispersed characters fretfully seeking some sort of unity to underpin their actions. However, in an oblique way, largely through the contexts and the settings in which they operate, a political significance can be ascribed to their situations. It is as though with each novel the pull that is dragging them back within the orbit of Quebec nationalism increases. The first-person narrator of *L'Aquarium* is a member of a diverse community of expatriates who share the same residence (the aptly named *Casa Occidentale*), in an unnamed tropical country where a revolution is brewing, fomented by the local independence movement. Such a context of decolonisation is clearly relevant to the prevalent mood of Quebec at the time the novel was written, but Godbout never exploits this connection directly in the novel. Hence, despite invitations to join the revolutionary cause, the narrator remains aloof and indifferent to the promptings of the intermediary, Gayéta. His indifference to the politics of his situation confirms his status as one of the so-called 'escargots' [snails] that inhabit the aquarium of *Casa Occidentale*, an artificial environment and microcosm of Western life, isolated within the enveloping colonial world. One critic's assessment that '[b]oredom and cruelty, cowardliness and moral irresponsibility, reign supreme' in this novel is confirmed when the narrator secures his own flight to safety using money stolen from a dead colleague, whose lover he has also appropriated.[10]

L'Aquarium includes a sustained critique of Western values and civilisation exemplified as much by the amorality of its narrator as by events in the novel. Indeed the novel itself could be seen as an example of the decadence it describes. In *Le Couteau sur la table* the narrator displays the same inability to extricate himself from the englobing morass of catastrophic world events (often figured in the novel as journalistic, factual snippets of information supplied by newspapers, radio or TV) or to find a way of acting upon the world in a sustained and coherent way. He bemoans the frivolity of his existence ('il y a tant de choses graves dont il faudrait s'occuper, tant de fascismes!' (p. 57) [there are so many serious things we should be dealing with, so many forms of fascism]) as he drifts between lovers: Patricia, the rich anglophone heiress, and Madeleine, the working-class, francophone girl, who represent the two poles of the cultural identity available to him. His sense of his own futility is expressed in terms of fear: 'j'ai peur, là, au creux du ventre, de crever sans avoir fait un seul geste qui soit humain, sans laisser derrière moi autre chose que moi qui refroidis, moi qui pourris' (p. 50) [I have this fear, here, in the pit of my stomach, of dying without ever having done a single thing that was human, without leaving behind me anything other than me, growing cold, me, rotting]. Just as *L'Aquarium* concludes with a theft and a flight to a new life with the narrator selfishly leaving behind the group of 'friends' whose existence he had shared, so, in the closing stages of *Le Couteau sur la table*, the narrator commits fraud to fund his escape to a new life in the United States, following the death (accident or suicide?) of Madeleine. But in this case the novel goes on to demonstrate that the 'new life' is merely a whirlwind of false identities, pointless, criss-crossing journeys and insignificant love affairs, that appears to be a speeded-up, condensed version of his former, futile life. The final section marks a dramatic shift as the narrator arbitrarily opts to commit himself to the terrorist activities of the Quebec Liberation Front. The knife which, earlier in the novel, is poked in the air to emphasise some point in an idle, dinner-table discussion about some catastrophe or other can now remain on the table since, for the narrator at least, the talking appears to be over.

Salut Galarneau! (1967), Godbout's third and most widely acclaimed novel, is a far more accessible and light-hearted work than his previous novels. The protagonist, François Galarneau, is the first of Godbout's narrators to reside in Quebec and offer a view of the francophone community there 'from the inside'. A hot-dog salesman having dropped out of formal education at an early age, Galarneau is nevertheless a poet in his spare time and has ambitions to write the ethnography of Quebec. His anticlerical, anti-English, anticolonialist, anticonsumerist opinions are typical of the views that fed into the demands for reform in the post-Duplessis years of the Quiet Revolution, although his non-conformist, often naïve attitudes increasingly set him apart from the mainstream. His views are often delivered in humorous, throw-away lines. When grilling sausages, for example, he imagines that priests are burning ('Quand je fais griller des saucisses, je m'imagine que c'est des curés qui brûlent' (p. 42)), or, when he imagines setting up an empire of hot-dog outlets to counter 'English' commercial supremacy in Quebec he comments, 'Je ne suis pas séparatiste, mais si je pouvais leur rentrer dans le corps aux Anglais, avec mes saucisses, ça me soulagerait d'autant.' (p. 120) [I'm not a separatist, but if I could stick my sausages up those English, I'd be all the happier.]

Galarneau's decision to write is already bearing fruit when his partner, Marise, triggers a crisis in his life by having an affair with his brother Jacques, a successful script-writer. It is this betrayal that leads him to decide to retreat into isolation. He cuts himself off from the world by having a wall built around his house and devotes himself to introspection and to writing. His tête-à-tête with himself comes to focus increasingly upon either the commercials he watches on his television screen or upon his dreams of recreating the solidarity with his brothers that he had known in childhood, when their group had been known as 'les vampires'. Godbout's own obsession with the language of advertisements and their role in contemporary culture is well documented and has been the theme of many pieces of journalism from his pen. In the preface to a collection of such pieces, *Le Murmure marchand*, published in 1984, Godbout wrote: 'Je crains en effet qu'imperceptiblement le chant des marchandises, ou même la publicité "sociétale", soient à notre civilisation ce que la pensée philosophique était à nos pères . . . il y a dans les objets et leur aura publicitaire une odeur de mort culturelle.'[11] [I'm actually quite frightened that, imperceptibly, the clamour of 'goods for sale', or even commercial advertising, have become for our civilisation what philosophical thought was for our forebears . . . there is in consumer goods and the aura of publicity surrounding them a reek of cultural death.]

In splendid isolation behind his wall, Galarneau is amazed at the fact that the television continues to bombard him with invitations to acquire consumer goods. His writing comes to incorporate lists of the products and the accompanying messages that he sees on the screen. These advertisements, rather than the substantive programming (cultural programmes, variety shows and documentaries) they interrupt, tell the real truth about people on the outside. So his desire to write ethnography appears to be realised in his rewriting of lists of household goods, cleaning aids, toothpastes and deodorants that progress across his screen. If commercialism is the poisonous threat for Galarneau (this is, after all, the world inhabited by the perfidious seducer that his brother Jacques has become), the antidote seems to be located in some form of reconnection with the community he had known in childhood, a time when constructive action to change the world still seemed an option. Hence in the closing section of the novel Galarneau comes to oppose 'writing' ('écrire.') to 'life in society' ('vivre') and realises that they cannot be seen in the starkly confrontational terms that his isolation behind the wall has figured. This leads to his decision to leave the house and seek a synthesis in 'writing/living': 'Je sais bien que de deux choses l'une: ou tu vis, ou tu écris. Moi je veux *vécrire.*' (p. 157) [I know that both ways are not possible: either you live, or you write. Personally I want to *wrive.*]

In subsequent novels, *D'Amour, P. Q.* (1972), *Les Têtes à Papineau* (1981) and *Une histoire américaine* (1986), for example, the writer as protagonist becomes a standard device for structuring the narrative. In *D'Amour, P. Q.* the very processes involved in the production of the text become the prime elements of the novel's intrigue. The author, Thomas d'Amour, employs Mireille to type his text but the secretary proves an increasingly recalcitrant scribe and challenges the language, style and content of the writing. She subverts the production processes, both physically (as typist) and artistically (as critic) and eventually takes over the co-authorship of the text, as her relationship with d'Amour develops into a love affair. This is fitting as there are repeated suggestions throughout the novel that writing a book involves making love with language. In the struggle for control over the production of the narrative, d'Amour and Mireille oppose distinctive opinions as to what literature is, to whom it should be addressed, the purposes it serves, and above all from what types of linguistic material it should be created. These were urgent questions for the rapidly evolving literature of Quebec at the time, even if their treatment by Godbout in this novel is burlesque and frequently mocking in tone.

The competition between Mireille and d'Amour is naturally played out on the battlefield of language and their interactions in dialogue, as well as the written texts they produce, provide examples of a range of registers and styles that amount to a display of linguistic virtuosity by Godbout. Since Mireille's language is a colourful and aggressive form of *joual*, contrasting starkly with d'Amour's poetic and rather abstract version of standard French, linguistic style and register are endowed with a clear political significance in this novel.

Ultimately, though, the struggle between Mireille and d'Amour is a competition between two cultural systems. As the novel progresses a conservative high culture, associated with European traditions, is ousted by a more 'authentic', indigenous low culture that speaks to, and for, the ordinary people of Quebec in their own language. In the later stages of the novel Mireille and d'Amour become characters in the narrative and assume roles as militants organising a 'cellule d'amour' of the 'Front de libération du Kébek' (p. 127). But this overt political content is merely a sign (like the renaming of d'Amour as 'Tarzan' rather than 'Thomas') of the contest between cultures that is the real political battle outlined by the novel. At the close of the novel, when interviewed on TV, d'Amour makes it clear that the carnival is over and that the old hierarchical roles of author and secretary should be re-established. He contends that 'la littérature est un produit inutile, gratuit comme l'amour' (p. 153) [literature is a product without a purpose, as gratuitous as love], while Mireille maintains that the novel was about 'class struggle' and refuses to accept that words belong to authors. The struggle has not been resolved but the novel serves to clarify some of the stakes involved.

Written in 1981 shortly after the referendum in which Quebec voted to remain within Canada, *Les Têtes à Papineau* is more of a circumstantial text than any of Godbout's other novels. It is a tale of a man with a single body and two heads, Charles and François, clearly representing the anglophone and francophone components of Canadian identity. Godbout struggles to develop this striking initial idea into a full-length narrative. Papineau's decision to undergo an operation fusing the two heads into a single head is clearly an allegory for the contemporary political scene and Godbout's jaundiced reflection on the failure of the Parti Québécois to win the sovereignty vote, thus condemning Quebec to the union with anglophone Canada. Interest in the outcome of Papineau's operation is maintained, to an extent, by the promise that the last chapter will be written after the operation (the referendum). In the event, this chapter is never written but is replaced by a letter, in English, explaining that it cannot be written since Papineau no longer understands French. It is worth remarking in passing that the signature at the bottom of the closing letter replaces François with a capital F, thus eliding the French element of Papineau's identity at a stroke.

The distrust of the ever-encroaching presence of anglophone language and culture surfaces again in *Une histoire américaine*, but this time in a broader context than the internal politics of Quebec. The plight of the *Québécois* Gregory Francœur, imprisoned in California on trumped-up charges of rape and arson, is the occasion for a reflection on the global power and influence of the USA and of the cultural poverty that is masked by the American dream. References to Ethiopia, where Godbout worked for three years in the late 1950s, feed into the novel at frequent intervals and form a counterpoint to the Californian setting in which Francœur is conducting his research on 'happiness', prior to his arrest. The critique of Western values that runs through *Une histoire américaine* appears to have brought Godbout full circle as a novelist, reconnecting as it does with the themes of *L'Aquarium*, a novel that was also undoubtedly nourished by his Ethiopian experience.

Réjean Ducharme (Quebec, 1942–)

The fact that the 'Quiet Revolution' was quiet does not mean that its causes or its consequences were benign or painless. It was fuelled by a deep sense of alienation, resentment and frustration among French-Canadians that was all the more painful in that they could hardly ignore their own complicity in the 'oppression' they were suffering, even if only because it was plausible to view them (and for them to view themselves) as lacking the resolve or the pride to do anything about their situation. This was the landscape into which Réjean Ducharme burst 'meteor-like', in the words of one critic, with the publication of his first novel *L'Avalée des avalés* (1966).[12] The political and cultural maelstrom of the early 1960s carried an emotional and psychological charge that should not be underestimated, and it was these latter aspects of the Quebec experience that can be posited as the privileged subject treated by much of Ducharme's writing. His characters are generally 'damaged goods', alienated, marginalised beings from dysfunctional families or communities, often following trajectories that imply self-destruction. They are also beings who display an explosive linguistic energy and poetic power that is often judged by critics to contain within it a similarly auto-destructive urge. Lise Gauvin, for example, has suggested, 'On peut lire l'ensemble de l'œuvre de Ducharme comme une recherche pour faire éclater le sens des mots, les pousser hors de leurs limites convenues.'[13] [One can read the whole of Ducharme's work as an attempt to explode the meaning of words, to push them beyond their conventional limits.]

Bérénice Einberg, the child protagonist–narrator of *L'Avalée des avalés* pushes this iconoclastic approach to language to the limit by creating a new, personal language, 'le bérénicien'. The playfulness of the text is evident in the few ludicrous examples she provides: 'Mounonstre béxéroorisiduel' and 'spétermatorinx étanglobe' are apparently synonymous expressions, we are told, but Bérénice stops short of explaining their meaning (p. 337). Unless, of course, their meaning has already been made clear earlier when she has explained the origins of the language itself. Bérénice is so frustrated by the

inadequacy of the insults available to her in the common language that she has
to invent a new form of expression with which to refute the adult world: 'Je
hais tellement l'adulte, le renie avec tant de colère, que j'ai dû jeter les fonde-
ments d'une nouvelle langue.' (p. 337) [I hate the adult world so much, reject
it with so much anger that I had to lay the foundations of a new language.] This
passage combines two recurring features of Bérénice's world: her detestation
of adults and the retreat into a solipsistic world as a strategy of self-protection.
'Tout m'avale' (p. 9) [Everything swallows me] writes Bérénice, in the opening words of the novel. When she sheds further light on this notion of 'being
swallowed' a few pages later, she does so by expounding a highly personal philosophy that involves manipulating 'reality', through a radical process of tunnel
vision and a dynamic reinvention of the world around her:

> Il faut trouver les choses et les personnes différentes de ce qu'elles sont
> pour ne pas être avalé. Pour ne pas souffrir, il ne faut voir dans ce qu'on
> regarde que ce qui pourrait nous en affranchir. Il n'y a de vrai que ce
> qu'il faut que je croie vrai, que ce qu'il m'est utile de croire vrai, que ce
> que j'ai besoin de croire vrai pour ne pas souffrir.   (p. 33)

> [In order not to be swallowed you have to take things and people as
> being different from what they really are. So as not to suffer, you must
> see in whatever you are looking at, only those things that are capable of
> freeing you from their hold on you . . . Nothing is true other than what I
> have to believe to be true, than what it is useful for me to believe true,
> than what I need to believe true in order not to suffer.]

Later, in the New York section of the novel, when Bérénice revolts against
her uncle, Zio, she adopts a very similar strategy of refusing to believe that he
exists at all once he is out of sight. This absolute rejection of Zio, who functions
as a surrogate form of the paternal authority that she has already rejected, is
Bérénice's way of asserting her freedom. Elsewhere freedom is figured through
her reflections on the notion of 'possessing'. Ownership, 'having' a dog, for
example, ultimately means having the power to control, even destroy the object
or creature concerned. This explains an enigmatic remark she makes about the
private language, 'bérénicien': 'En bérénicien, le verbe être ne se conjugue pas
sans le verbe avoir.' (p. 337) [In Berenician, the verb to be cannot be conjugated
without the verb to have.] In Bérénice's scheme of things, to 'have' is to have
ownership and power. The defining feature of the private language, conjugating
having and being, is that it allows Bérénice to have control over being itself.
This control over existence can be exercised in two ways: by the imagination,
either positively as she reinvents reality through poetic energy and word-play,
or negatively, as in the examples above, when she refuses to acknowledge the

existence of whatever or whomsoever she considers 'unacceptable'. Freedom can also be exercised through destruction, which is the extreme stage of ownership and 'having'. In Bérénice's system one is either swallower or swallowed, and freedom lies in swallowing while resisting being swallowed:

> Voilà ce qu'il faudra que je fasse pour être libre: tout avaler, me répandre sur tout, tout englober, imposer ma loi à tout, tout soumettre ... Mais j'aime mieux tout détruire. Je ne sais pas pourquoi. C'est plus désintéressé, plus rapide, plus joli. Ça me donne plus envie de rire, si vous voulez.   (p. 216)

> [That's what I have to do to be free: swallow everything, spread myself out over everything, cover everything, impose my law on everything, bring everything under my control ... But I prefer to destroy everything. I don't know why. It's more disinterested, quicker, prettier. It makes me want to laugh more, if you like.]

Bérénice's revolt hinges on her refusal to join the world of adults, and her loyalties seem to be limited to other children: a brother, Christian, whom she adores and a friend, Constance Chlore, whom she refers to as Constance Exsangue after her death mid-way through the novel. Her narrative spans the period of her adolescence when she is in open revolt against her parents. Since her mother is a Catholic and her father a Jew it can neatly be seen as encompassing a revolt against the whole Judaeo-Christian tradition. Her turbulent behaviour leads her father to 'exile' her, first to the home of an uncle in New York and finally to Israel, where she participates in the Arab–Israeli conflict. The final scene of the novel describes her under enemy gunfire she has recklessly provoked, surviving only by using the body of a friend, Gloria, to shield herself from the bullets that rain down on her. She is still free, still refusing responsibility, but perhaps finally entering the adult world she has resisted for so long.

The theme of childhood as a privileged, poetically charged universe is common to all of Ducharme's early novels and some of his theatrical works (for example, *Ines Pérée et Inat Tendu* (1976)). His next two published novels, *Le Nez qui voque* (1967) and *L'Océantume* (1968), also have child narrators, while subsequent novels like *L'Hiver de force* (1973) and *Les Enfantômes* (1976) are narrated by characters who idealise childhood and have many child-like characteristics. The first three novels have particularly close thematic links in that the child characters form tightly bonded couples that function as cocoons protecting them from the adult world. The friendship between Bérénice and Constance Chlore in *L'Avalée des avalés* is echoed by that between Mille Milles and Chateaugué in *Le Nez qui voque* or Iode Ssouvie and Asie Azothe in

L'Océantume. The fierceness of the loyalty displayed in these friendships is epitomised by the strategy adopted by Mille Milles and Chateaugué when they fuse their individual beings into a single entity they name Tate. In each novel, the power of the imagination of these child characters is the key weapon in their armoury as they do battle with the adult world in an attempt to stave off the ineluctable process of physical and sexual maturation, and soften the anguish that is associated with the loss of innocence and purity.

If the preoccupation of these characters is a Peter Pan-like refusal to enter adulthood, there is nothing childlike about their sophistication as users of language or in their knowledge of what Gilles Marcotte has described as '[le] littéraire comme institution'.[14] All the novels engage in intertextual play with poets. Emile Nelligan, Saint-Denys Garneau, Lautréamont and Rimbaud are favoured 'interlocutors'. All were 'poètes maudits' whose works contained a strong element of revolt and challenged literature as an institution. The emphasis Ducharme frequently places on writer-narrators and depicting the act of writing itself (one that resurfaces in later texts such as *Dévadé* (1990) and *Gros Mots* (1999)) is perhaps simply another avatar of the engagement with 'literature'. Mille Milles, for example, describes the physical details of the writing process and the pact between himself and Chateaugué is sealed not in blood but through the imbibing of black ink, a gesture which finds echoes in *L'Avalée des avalés.* Like Mille Milles, André Ferron in *L'Hiver de force* is self-consciously a writer, but whereas the former is writing to note the events that are leading up to his projected death by suicide, the latter is a scribe of the everyday futility of existence in a consumer-orientated society. *L'Hiver de force* opens with André and his partner, Nicole, recognising the mediocrity of their lives and with his decision to record it in writing: 'On va se regarder faire puis je vais tout noter avec ma belle écriture.' (p. 17) [We're going to watch the things we do then I'm going to write it all down in my neat handwriting.] Marcotte has argued convincingly that Ducharme's narrative ('récit' not 'roman') is itself intended to be as transient and ephemeral as the the world the couple inhabit: 'Ils vivent l'extrême du banal, du consommable, de l'actuel, du quotidien ... Pourra-t-on lire *L'Hiver de force*, dans vingt-cinq ans, sans un arsenal de notes explicatives?'[15] [They live at the extreme point of the banal, the consumable, the current and the everyday . . . Will anyone be able to read *L'Hiver de force*, in twenty-five years' time, without an arsenal of explanatory notes?]

Ducharme's work plays with language, plays with literature and plays with life. The acerbic social comment that is part and parcel of his work cannot easily be systematised or bent to serve any particular coherent political or ideological purpose. It is delivered in bits and pieces, contradicted, restated and repackaged in ways that are self-reflexively subversive. Ducharme has even made a fiction of his own identity by his refusal to give interviews or engage with the intrusive media attention that surrounds successful writers. Many of the prizes he has received have been accepted *in absentia* or by third parties. Only two photographs of the author are in common circulation and there can be no certainty that these are truly likenesses of Réjean Ducharme. Given his fascination with onomastics, it is fair to wonder whether his name is not a pseudonym. It would be more accurate to say 'additional' pseudonym, since Réjean Ducharme is also known as Roch Plante, an artist who makes pictural and sculptural artefacts (named 'trophoux' from the collapsing of the words 'trophées' [trophies] and 'fous' [mad] to suggest a new meaning, literally 'too mad') from the discarded everyday objects he finds in the streets of Montreal. The ludic, postmodern, magpie mentality of Roch Plante is entirely consonant with the verbal fireworks of his *alter ego*, Ducharme.

In her analysis of Ducharme's *Dévadé* (1990), Lise Gauvin makes a surprising remark: 'Il faudrait citer chacune des phrases du roman pour donner une idée adéquate de la gamme des styles adoptée par le narrateur.'[16] [We would need to quote each and every one of the phrases in the novel in order to give an adequate idea of the range of styles adopted by the narrator.] This is to propose a strange sort of criticism indeed: one that directs the reader back to the entire work under consideration in a gesture that seems very much like an abdication of the critic's function. Yet, faced with a text by Ducharme, the critic cannot fail to be disarmed by a sense that any secondary discourse engaging with it is doomed to miss the point. The Ducharmian text cannot be reduced, explained, summarised, critiqued, analysed, without the critic in some sense betraying it. His writings share a bizarre quality, which is that, for any given text, the whole is never *more* than the parts that constitute it. Meaning is not accumulated over time or through experience in the Ducharmian universe, nor is it subject to the 'value-added' insights that characterise the Proustian experience, allowing insignificant places and incidents to be flooded with significance. Ducharme is an archaeologist of the ephemeral present and each phrase of his text is a 'stratum' to be explored *in situ* for its poetic and emotional resonances, the insights it provides into society's underbelly, or its subversive transgression of cultural codes and institutions, including 'literature' itself.

Chapter 5

The Caribbean

Overview

None of the current inhabitants of the francophone Caribbean territories (with the exception of some 4,000 or so descendants of assorted Amerindian tribesfolk in Guyane) are indigenous to the region. The Amerindian tribes (Caribs and Arawaks) that circulated in the region at the time of the arrival of the Europeans were annihilated within a few generations of the establishment of French settlements in Martinique and Guadeloupe in the 1630s. As land was cleared, the Caribs were unceremoniously transported to the inhospitable shores of nearby Dominique to make way for the colonisers. The subsequent creation of a plantation economy by the white planters was only made possible by the slave trade that operated for over two centuries and led to the influx of hundreds of thousands of black slaves from West Africa. In the nineteenth century the demographic mix in the region was further enriched by the immigration of indentured labourers from the Indian subcontinent and by Levantine traders. All of these elements (including mixed-raced descendants of the now extinct Amerindian tribesfolk) have contributed to the physiological mix that constitutes the Caribbean population. Consequently, the vast majority of the current inhabitants descend from peoples who have all arrived in the last four centuries from a variety of 'elsewheres': from Europe, Africa and more recently various parts of Asia.

It is not surprising then that literature from the French Caribbean obsessively explores issues relating to identity. Indeed, the interrogation of identity and how, in a context dominated by oral traditions, it may usefully be reconstituted and configured in literature are omnipresent and urgent preoccupations among francophone Caribbean writers. These questions are an energising component of the foundational texts of Aimé Césaire and the *Négritude* movement just as they underpin the more nuanced positions of Edouard Glissant's exploration of the concept of *antillanité*, and the work of those arguing in favour of *créolité*, particularly Patrick Chamoiseau and Raphaël Confiant. Glissant's concept of 'Tout-monde' (elaborated in texts like *Poétique de la relation* (1990) and *Tout-monde* (1993) among others), itself echoed by Chamoiseau's 'totalité-monde', frequently evoked in *Ecrire en pays dominé* (1997), are among the most recent avatars of this same identitarian concern. Although these more recent explorations of identity tend to conceptualise it in a deterritorialised, almost context-free, way, thinking about identity issues has more generally involved a consideration of origins, roots, affiliations and genealogies, and these are frequent thematic preoccupations of the literature of the region.

The urgency of the question of identity in a Caribbean context is most dramatically illustrated by reference to that imposing historical scar on world history that was the slave trade. *La traite* brings the identity question to the very forefront of any discussion of Caribbean literature for two main reasons. Firstly, it accounts for the physical displacement of millions of individuals, over a period lasting more than two centuries, an experience that involved the brutal severing of all ties with the human and spiritual communities they had inhabited and in which their sense of selfhood was rooted. In a recent interview Patrick Chamoiseau draws a parallel between the plight of the African slave, arriving bereft on the shores of the Caribbean and obliged to reconstitute an identity from the disparate elements available, and the emerging literature of the region which involves a similar effort to constitute a 'new', albeit problematic, subjectivity:

> l'esclave africain, l'Africain qui avait été arraché à la côte occidentale de l'Afrique, qui a été précipité dans le gouffre du bateau négrier et qui a été fracassé dans la plantation américaine, qu'est-ce qu'il a dû faire? Il a dû recomposer un 'moi' et un 'je' à partir de tous les éléments qui étaient à sa portée: des traces africaines mais aussi des traces amérindiennes et ce qu'il a pu récupérer des valeurs dominantes. Donc tout le processus d'émergence de cette littérature et de cette résistance, c'est un processus de constitution d'un 'je' nouveau, d'un 'je' problématique.[1]

> [the African slave, the African who had been snatched from the west coast of Africa, who was thrown into the abyss of the slave boat and who was smashed on the American plantation, what did he have to do? He had to reconstitute a 'self' and an 'I' using all the elements that he had to hand: traces from Africa but also from Amerindian sources and what he was able to hang on to from the values of the master culture. So the whole process of the emergence of this literature of resistance is a process through which a new 'I', and a problematic 'I', is constituted.]

But as well as effectively erasing the cultural identity of the slave, the process of enslavement also had an ontological dimension: those engaged in the slave trade sought to justify the practice by refusing to recognise the very humanity of the slaves in question. Hence the slaves were doubly despoiled: in their bodies and in their souls. Categorised as 'movable chattels' by the *Code noir* of 1685, slaves were considered mere 'property' whose every activity, including sexual reproduction, could be harnessed for the economic advantage of their masters. The middle passage across the Atlantic marked a severing of social, cultural and family connections with African roots that was, of itself, a catastrophe of incalculable consequence for the individuals concerned. But there can be little doubt that this trauma was compounded by the denial of their humanity that was not only inscribed into the legal conception of their status, as enshrined in the *Code noir*, but was reinforced on a daily basis by the inhuman and degrading experience that life as a slave on the plantations inevitably entailed.

The identity vacuum that was a consequence of slavery and plantation life could not simply be conjured away by removing the cause. The 1848 decree finally granting freedom to the slaves (an earlier 1794 decree having been repealed by Napoleon in 1802) marked an official scotching of the specious argument that blacks were not fully human and thus simultaneously (and at the stroke of a pen) freed them to aspire to fully fledged French citizenship. The brutality of this (absence of) transition from technically subhuman status to that of individuals entitled to claim citizenship is itself significant: effectively the stick of slavery was replaced by the carrot of assimilation. Where slavery had meant a denial of any identity other than as a piece of property belonging to a master, freedom, on the other hand, came in a very specific form and with an implicit requirement, that of moulding oneself to correspond as closely as possible to French political and cultural norms. However welcome it may have been, the abolition of slavery could not undo history or reverse the traumatic severance from their cultural roots in Africa that continued to haunt slaves and the descendants of slaves. To an extent, abolition may have compounded the identitarian problems by offering the liberated slaves the single, perhaps equally alienating, option of aspiring to be like their former masters. The condition of the black population, before and after the abolition of slavery, then, remained a condition of fragility and insecurity.

This insecurity about identity was not merely a fact of life for the transplanted slaves and their offspring. There seems every reason to suppose that it affected all social groups and all levels of the social hierarchy that emerged over the generations. The importance attached to skin colour and attendant notions of purity of the 'blood' provide the clearest examples of this identitarian anxiety at work. At the top of the social hierarchy, the white *békés* defined themselves to themselves largely by insisting on exclusivity in a range of social practices (clubs, culture and leisure activities, educational provision, and so on), but the 'rule' of intermarriage within the white elite was the lynchpin of the system. Sexual exclusivity applied only to women, of course, since they were the effective guardians of the family line and therefore of racial 'purity'. The white masters, by contrast, could father children on Amerindian women (in the early days of settlement) or on black slaves and servants without jeopardising the 'purity' of the family line. In due course, the mixed-race offspring (mulattos) would emerge as the professional middle classes (often doctors, lawyers, administrators and teachers) who throughout the nineteenth century mounted an increasingly significant political challenge to the unreconstructedly 'aristocratic' tendencies of the *békés*.

The racial prejudice that determined social relations from the seventeenth century onwards gradually translated itself into a generalised obsession, affecting all levels of society, with the notion of 'purity' of the blood and its visible correlate the colour of one's skin. These are dangerous generalisations, of course. Yet Frantz Fanon's analysis of what could be called the 'lactification complex', particularly his critique of Mayotte Capécia's novel *Je suis Martiniquaise* in *Peau noire masques blancs*, corroborates the view that various forms of valorisation, from a basic sense of self-worth to social status, were linked to skin colour.[2] Hence, the concern of various sections of society to 'blanchir la race' [whiten the race] by selecting a partner with lighter skin pigmentation than themselves, became a widespread phenomenon. Obversely, while male *békés* or mulattos were free to cross colour boundaries in choosing occasional, temporary or unacknowledged sexual partners, the institutionalisation of such relationships, through marriage or other forms of more or less permanent cohabitation, would lead to ostracism from the group. Leaving aside the double standards in evidence here (including the different behaviours expected of men and women), what is striking is the general acceptance of the notion, commonly shared by blacks themselves, that procreation also involved 'progression' or 'regression' in a racialised hierarchy. The aspiration to 'whiten the race' becomes synonymous with the aspiration to progress from savagery to civilised values. The fact that such an impulse (not to say 'programme') necessarily mobilises the participation of all sections of society is an indication of the extent to which racist perceptions had been internalised by blacks and coloured people. Having learned to see themselves through the dehumanising gaze of their white masters and been condemned to occupy a lowly position in the social hierarchy even after abolition, blacks inevitably suffered from low self-esteem and a negative sense of their own self-worth. (When contracted labourers from the Indian subcontinent (Coolies) began to appear in the Caribbean in the 1850s, they in turn suffered from racist treatment at the hands of the population already settled there, blacks, mulattos and *békés* alike. They, in turn, quickly came to occupy a position at the very bottom of the social hierarchy.) 'Race' cannot therefore be seen as merely one aspect of the identitarian anxieties in the Caribbean; historically it has functioned as an important marker of identity, but a marker that clearly implicates the whole cultural system.

Négritude, antillanité and créolité

Literature is, of course, one of the most powerful tools available for challenging dominant cultural systems and francophone Caribbean writing emerges in the 1930s as a literature which contests the dominant value systems of white (racist) colonial culture. The backlash against the racially motivated oppression of blacks had begun to gather force in the 1920s in the United States with the Harlem Negro Renaissance and the work of campaigners like Marcus Garvey and W. E. B. Dubois who sought to counter the racism of North American society by celebrating black cultural achievements. Paris proved to be the crossroads where these new ideas could enter French cultural consciousness. In the early 1930s *La Revue du monde noir* published a number of texts by Harlem Renaissance poets, many of whom spent time in Paris during this period. This work quickly found an echo in the work of young poets and intellectuals from the francophone 'diaspora' then studying in France: Aimé Césaire, Léopold-Sédar Senghor, Léon-Gontran Damas, Birago Diop and many others. Through a series of, often short-lived, publications (*Légitime Défense* (1932), *L'Etudiant noir* (1935)) the ideological content of what came to be known as the *Négritude* movement became more radicalised and focused. The driving force behind the 'movement' was a desire to counter the message of worthlessness that had been applied to black people and had denied the very existence of any distinctive black culture. Drawing on the work of ethnologists like Leo Frobenius whose work on African civilisation had argued the existence of a specifically black sensibility, *Négritude* appealed to the notion of a universal 'black essence' and a brotherhood of black peoples. The argument that black culture had a specific contribution to make to humanity was simultaneously a promotion of a new conception of civilisation and a rejection of the dominant world view promoted by the West, according to which Western values were generally presented as universal. The positive side of its message reverberated through the colonial world as a model and an example of a newly self-confident, liberating discourse that empowered other oppressed minorities to proclaim their own worth and distinctiveness. The critique of Western (colonial) domination it also conveyed fed into forms of counter-hegemonic resistance that shaped the decolonisation struggles of subsequent decades.

As this summary illustrates, *Négritude* contains within it both a cultural and a political dimension and it is useful to distinguish these in order to understand both the significance of the movement itself and the various criticisms that have been levelled against it since the 1930s and 1940s. In its day, the prime impact of *Négritude* within the Caribbean was as a channel through which blacks could begin to counter the dominant colonial discourse and the consequences that flowed from it: their sense of disconnectedness from history and of inhabiting a cultural void, the alienating pressures of assimilation to French norms and values, low self-esteem and negative self-image. Whatever literary merits 'le grand cri nègre' of the *Négritude* poets may have had, it also functioned politically as a form of resistance to these negative effects of colonial domination and humiliation. So this was a moment in history when poetry could rightly be considered to be a form of direct political action, rather than a reflection on, or even incitement to, such action. When judged in these terms (as direct political action) *Négritude* can be seen as a necessary, preliminary phase of a fight for recognition that has since come to adopt more sophisticated intellectual positions than Césaire, Senghor and their companions could have contemplated.

At the time there was a far more pressing need: that of proclaiming loud and clear the message that black culture had been systematically ignored, undervalued and denigrated by the West. In the Caribbean, the powerful rhetorical appeal to the notion of a common African ancestry and the coherence of black civilisations served an immediate purpose in that it could potentially resonate with large sections of the population. But it was also a mythopoeic enterprise in the sense that the African past that was being valorised as a cultural model and exemplar was, in reality, to be found nowhere in the Caribbean. There could be no concrete foundation, in terms of lived cultural experience, to this appeal to African roots. So when, in Césaire's play *Et les chiens se taisaient* (1958), Le Rebelle evokes 'le vieil amadou déposé par l'Afrique au fond de moi-même' (p. 77) [the old tinder that Africa deposited in the depths of my being], the phrase can only have a symbolic power even though it has frequently been interpreted literally. In his own book on Césaire, Raphaël Confiant glosses this oft-quoted line as follows: 'C'est oublier que cet "amadou", ces éléments culturels africains sont passés par le tamis (ou l'enclume) de la culture française et caraïbe, qu'ils ont été broyés, recomposés, refondus dans le magma colonial antillais.'[3] [This is to forget that this 'tinder', these African cultural elements, have been through the sieve (or under the anvil) of French and Amerindian culture, that they have been crushed, reconstituted, recast in the colonial magma of the Caribbean.]

Yet the notion of a return, even a metaphorical return, to an original, spiritual homeland was never voiced by Césaire himself. Indeed, the native land of his *Cahier d'un retour au pays natal* (1939) was Martinique not Africa, and the return he evokes is from the French metropolis back to the island, not from a peripheral colonial territory to an African motherland. By the time the poem was published in 1939 three centuries had passed since Martinique had been colonised by the French and the first African slaves had begun to arrive in the Caribbean. In such circumstances the notion of 'return' could only operate with any credibility on a metaphysical level, as a return to values and cultural roots located in a distant time and place. It is worth emphasising here that the authenticating source of experience in such a scheme (that which validates and valorises it) remains external, vaguely African, but certainly located elsewhere. Just as colonial discourse was validated by reference to metropolitan France, so the counter-discourse of the *Négritude* poets and writers was validated by reference to a rather vague notion of African origins. In this respect, the similarities between the two discourses are striking.

Nevertheless the focus on the black African component of the Caribbean racial mix could function as a rallying point for all the oppressed sections of Caribbean society, irrespective of their actual racial origins in any given instance. This accounts for the wider political impact of the movement and its potential to serve as a rallying cry for oppressed peoples around the world. Colonised peoples in Indo-China or the Maghreb, or indeed in any other of the regions under the control of European imperialism, could just as easily associate their own struggles for freedom with the revolutionary message of the *Négritude* poets. The movement did not address the Caribbean with a direct message that the rest of the world could read figuratively. In point of fact, it required an equally figurative reading for those in the Caribbean too, for the simple reason that by the 1930s Caribbean culture was itself a highly creolised, new culture, incorporating Amerindian, European, African, Indian and Levantine elements. By looking to an increasingly distant past and appealing to a single strand (the African) of this complex network of traditions *Négritude* was not offering an accurate account of reality. More than that, it was effectively ignoring and undervaluing the various other cultural traditions that have been interwoven into creole culture.

An earlier version of this criticism, and one of the earliest forms of critique applied to the *Négritude* movement, was that it operated within a confrontational framework, insisting on the value of 'blackness' as a way of opposing white oppression. In so doing it deployed essentialist arguments about 'black culture' or 'Africa' that were ostensibly the same in kind as those that had been deployed by the whites to justify the slave trade and plantation life. The binary opposition that underpins such arguments has been generally decried by postcolonial critics not only because of its appeal to crude essentialisms but also because it is so easily reversible. Hence the claim of one of Confiant's characters, in *Bassin des ouragans*, that 'la négritude . . . n'est, comme chacun sait, que la manière noire d'être blanc' (p. 41) [as everyone knows, *Négritude* is only the black man's way of being white]. Sartre was among the first to point out the essentialist nature of the logic of *Négritude* when he referred to it as 'un racisme anti-raciste' [an anti-racist racism] even while seeking to justify it by appeal to a version of the dialectic: he argued that *Négritude* was the natural antithesis to the theses of colonial oppression and was therefore one moment in a historical process that would be superseded in the fullness of time. In the same essay Sartre goes on to describe *Négritude* as 'le temps faible d'une pro-gression dialectique' [the minor proposition in a dialectic] and concludes 'il vise à préparer la synthèse ou réalisation de l'humain dans une société sans race' [it aims to prepare for the synthesis or humanity's culmination in a raceless society].[4]

Négritude has also been criticised in rather less abstract terms for being an intellectual rather than a popular movement. There is certainly some truth in this claim since its germs were in the literary salons of the left bank in Paris. It can also be categorised as one manifestation of the 'French' taste for literary 'schools' and *côteries*, a damning criticism indeed since it assimilates the movement to a metropolitan literary tradition that Césaire, Senghor and Damas were actively seeking to challenge and resist from outside.

As the weight of these criticisms tends to suggest, the *Négritude* movement led into a *cultural* impasse, partly because it replicated arguments that theoretically more sophisticated postcolonial critiques have had little trouble deconstructing and debunking, but partly too because its intellectual roots and its language were unavoidably drawing on a French rather than a Caribbean tradition. If we look beyond *Négritude*'s iconoclastic purposes it is not too difficult to identify ways in which Césaire's poetry, for example, can be viewed as imitative of French models (surrealism) and even as being innovative in ways that French readers could appreciate and understand. André Breton's famous 'discovery' of Césaire's work through a chance reading of *Tropiques* (the review Césaire had co-founded in Martinique with his wife, Suzanne, in 1941) is a case in point. Praise from a poet of such considerable reputation and stature as Breton ensured that Césaire was effectively catapulted to literary stardom. Yet the very power such a 'seal of approval' could exert confirms the extent of the colony's reliance on metropolitan France in matters of literary and aesthetic taste. The example illustrates how 'approval from the centre' (guaranteeing the widespread dissemination of the work) and 'opposition to the centre' (the predominant theme of the work) are two sides of the same coin. Even efforts to formulate resistance to the power of the metropolis are themselves incorporated into the overarching pattern of subservient relationships that characterise all encounters between the metropolis and the colony. Dependency and resistance are inseparably interlocked.

One of the central threads running through this discussion of *Négritude* has been the contention that its central message, the valorisation of black culture, was 'delivered' in a way that unconsciously continued to valorise French culture and language. The problem is not really that *Négritude* had been conceptualised and articulated through the French language and therefore from within the 'world view' freighted by that language. After all, other important texts that tackle the question of Caribbean identity, including Glissant's *Le Discours antillais* (1981) and *Eloge de la créolité* (1989), jointly authored by Jean Bernabé, Patrick Chamoiseau and Raphaël Confiant, are also written in quite standard forms of French yet do not attract the same criticism. The problem is rather that the failure to identify language as a key vector in their own attacks on colonialism and Western values left the *Négritude* writers open to the charge that, despite the revolutionary nature of their message, they were fundamentally embroiled with, indeed perhaps even a part of, the very culture they were attacking.

Le Rebelle in Césaire's *Et les chiens se taisaient* cries out at one point: 'laissez-moi crier à ma suffisance le bon cri saoul de la révolte, je veux être seul dans ma peau, je ne reconnais à personne le droit de m'habiter' (p. 50) [let me have my fill of screaming the good old drunken scream of revolt, I want to be alone in my skin, I concede to no one the right to inhabit my person]. Le Rebelle, at once archetypal slave and colonised subject, feels himself inhabited by the 'other' through the multiplicity of ways the power of the 'other' is exercised upon him, constraining him physically, mentally and spiritually to live through and for the 'master', whether *béké* or coloniser. For Edouard Glissant as well as the authors of *Eloge de la créolité*, this 'living through and for the other', this 'being inhabited by the other' is synonymous with adopting the language and culture of the other. Whereas Césaire's Rebelle cries his revolt to express his refusal of the other, *Eloge de la créolité* identifies the continuing presence of the other within the very cry of revolt itself: 'Car si, dans cette révolte négriste, nous contestions la colonisation française, ce fut toujours au nom de généralités universelles pensées à l'occidentale et sans nul arc-boutement à notre réalité culturelle.' (p. 21) [For if we were challenging French colonisation through this black revolt, it was always in the name of universal general principles, conceived in a Western fashion, and with no foundation in our own cultural reality.]

It was on this question of cultural reality that *Négritude* was eventually subjected to its most incisive and lasting challenges, firstly through Edouard Glissant's switching of the centre of gravity from Europe to America as he developed the concept of *antillanité*, and subsequently through those writings that have adopted a rather more narrow approach by arguing in favour of the specifically creole dimension of Caribbean culture. Both concepts (and they have much in common) have shaped the identitarian quest implicit in francophone Caribbean literature over recent decades and deserve to be examined in some detail.

Like *créolité* the concept of *antillanité* takes as its starting point the everyday lived experience of life in the Caribbean. This conscious choice to focus on the 'here and now' of Caribbean life has two important consequences. It bespeaks a refusal to interpret political, economic and cultural realities within structures that derive their coherence from colonial relationships of the past (and their extension into the present). In the case of the francophone Caribbean, instead of looking to France for models to imitate, for approval and reassurance, and for the material and financial assistance to protect standards of living and determine the parameters of social interaction, proponents of *antillanité* begin by looking inwards rather than outwards, locating the key to understanding Caribbean realities in the population and geography of the Caribbean itself. Expressed in terms of human psychology this means advocating self-assurance, self-reliance, autonomy and responsibility for one's actions while focusing upon the local before the regional, the regional before the national and the national before the international. Translated into macro-political terms, *antillanité* is predicated on the assumption that the Caribbean *départements d'outre mer* (Martinique, Guadeloupe and Guyane) should strive to secure independence from France, develop their own economic bases and assume full responsibility for the consequences of these ambitions. Whatever the cost of such a move, it is the prerequisite for the cultural revival that Glissant calls for, through a diverse body of writings in which politics and poetics are interwoven in mutually sustaining arguments.

Naturally, therefore, the ideas that contribute to the concept of *antillanité* have a cultural as well as a political dimension. Indeed it is instructive to see the relationship to culture in two distinct ways. *Antillanité* has implications for the way cultural life is (or could be) conducted. Creole culture in the French Caribbean should develop its own distinctive styles, modes and forms of expression that are grounded in the local, concrete and everyday experience of the artists concerned. The key relationships for a dynamic culture are those that exist, firstly between people meaningfully engaged in productive activity, and then between the people and the space they inhabit, including the layerings of temporal 'space' that structure the popular imaginary through the workings of memory. Hence alongside French creole culture, *antillanité* presupposes the development of a diversity of different but distinctive cultures in the anglophone, hispanophone or Dutch-speaking territories of the Caribbean. But culture is vital to the concept of *antillanité* in a second way in the sense that, for intellectuals like Edouard Glissant, the driving force for change is itself not political or economic but cultural. His wide-ranging analyses of Caribbean discourse may draw heavily on social, political and economic arguments yet they are angled in such a way as to demonstrate how these determine the present state of culture in the region. Hence the shift in emphasis he advocates does not target specific aspects of political or social policy; he proposes no programme for change other than a shift in cultural attitudes, exhorting the peoples of the Caribbean to re-engage with their local environments, look to their own resources and assume responsibility for *producing* their own histories, their own lives and their own futures.

In much the same way, the 'reality' that is the only reference point for the authors of *Eloge de la créolité* is not mediated through French culture or language, or indeed through the prism of *Négritude*. They argue that a realistic assessment of the everyday experience of the vast majority of inhabitants of the so-called 'francophone' Caribbean must give priority to the common language and culture that has emerged over more than three centuries of co-presence in the region, creole. French is merely one component of creole language and culture. It has interacted with other less prestigious but equally important cultures and languages: the various African components championed en bloc by *Négritude*, but also an Amerindian substratum and more recent accretions from Indian and Levantine sources. Various syncretisms have operated in all the areas one would expect to be actively at work in any dynamic cultural system, and have created a composite mosaic of creolised culture: language, belief systems, art, oral traditions, cuisine, agricultural practices and so on. In his book on Césaire, Confiant summarises some of these as follows:

> toutes ses pratiques culturelles [du peuple martiniquais] s'exprimaient, jusqu'aux années soixante en tout cas, en créole; qu'elles relevassent du domaine économique (coup de main agricole, pratique de la senne), de l'art (chants, contes, comptines), du jeu (combats de coqs, jeu de dés-serbi), du magico-religieux ('séances' divinatoires).[5]

> [until the 1960s at least, all their cultural practices [the Martinican people's] were expressed in creole; whether they belonged to the sphere of economics (the agriculturer's 'helping hand', communal fishing), of art (songs, stories, children's rhymes), of games (cock fights, dice games, serbi) or of magical/religious activity (fortune-telling).]

He concludes that the black African 'a perdu son africanité (comme le Gaulois sa celtitude) mais il ne s'est pas fondu pour autant dans la francité de son maître. Il a réussi à recréer une culture nouvelle, médiane, à recréer une identité, à réinstaurer une différence, une originalité.'[6] [has lost his Africanness (just as the Gaulois had lost his Celticness) but has not, for all that, been absorbed into the Frenchness of his master. He has managed to recreate a new, mid-way culture, reconstruct an identity, re-establish a difference, a form of originality.]

Part of the difficulty faced by those arguing in favour of *créolité* is that they must combat the general perception of creole language and culture as lacking any prestige. The early efforts of a poet like Gilbert Gratiant to use creole for literary purposes (especially from 1935 onwards, at exactly the period when the *Négritude* poets were meeting in Paris) made little headway against the overwhelming power of French. It should be remembered that throughout the latter half of the nineteenth century, non-*békés* had fought for the right to schooling and access to French, the language of the masters, while the traditional *béké* view on the matter had always been to discourage their slaves (and later, their labourers) from gaining access to any educational opportunities whatsoever. The ability to speak, and *a fortiori* to write, French was consequently generally admired and highly prized. Indeed, this admiration for eloquence in French goes a long way to explaining the peculiar importance André Breton's comment about Aimé Césaire's poetry had for Martinicans: 'un Noir qui manie la langue française comme il n'est pas aujourd'hui un Blanc pour la manier.'[7] [a black man who uses French in a way that not a single white man alive today knows how to use it]. Conversely, the low esteem in which creole was generally held during the first half of the twentieth century is forcefully conveyed by L.-G. Damas in the poem 'Hoquet', published in *Pigments*. The poem also demonstrates how attitudes to language impact on the individual's sense of selfhood as well as a range of socialisation processes.

> Taisez-vous
> Vous ai-je ou non dit qu'il vous fallait parler français
> le français de France
> le français du français
> le français français
>
> Désastre
> parlez-moi du désastre
> parlez-m'en   (p. 37)
>
> [Be quiet
> Have I, or have I not, told you that you must speak French
> French from France
> The Frenchman's French
> French French
>
> What a disaster
> Tell me about the disaster
> Tell me about it]

The conflict between French and creole played out in the poem goes far beyond the purely linguistic dimension to embrace the whole personality of the individual, and by extension his place within culture. 'Hoquet' is a practical illustration of Fanon's contention, 'Parler une langue, c'est assumer un monde, une culture.'[8] [To speak a language is to take on a whole world, to assume a culture.]

In contrast to the 'bonnes manières à table', the 'leçon de vi-o-lon' [good table manners, vi-o-lin lessons] and other expectations laid upon the son in 'Hoquet' by his mother, the list of characteristic creole cultural activities mentioned by Confiant above is clearly made up of unpretentious, even vulgar, everyday activities that are the antithesis of high culture. But the authors of the *Eloge* would argue that this is precisely why creole culture can claim authenticity: it is the means by which the people actually engage with, and seek to act upon and interpret, the world they collectively inhabit. Creole culture has emerged as a culture of survival and owes much to the practice of *bricolage*, the cobbling together of disparate elements to create a new way of inhabiting a specific landscape and meet specific challenges, not least that of connecting the past to the present. Hence the emphasis among *créolité* authors upon modes of resistance to colonial oppression that Confiant describes as 'compère lapinesque' [Br'er Rabbit-like]: the stubborn, cunning, unimpressive, mundane forms of resistance to domination that find no place in written histories.[9] Hence too their scepticism with regard to history based on the glorification of heroic figures, Toussaint Louverture, Louis Delgrès and others, since the historiographic model such accounts embrace belongs to an alien, Western tradition.

The whole impetus of *créolité* is to reject such determinisms, those interpretative grids that are implicitly part and parcel of any cultural system, be it *francité* or *africanité*, and which are the structuring mechanisms of a specific world view. *Créolité* focuses instead on the here and now, the minutiae of daily experience. The authors of the *Eloge* claim to be motivated by 'le seul désir de nous connaître nous-mêmes, dans nos tares, dans nos écorces et dans nos pulpes, en rêche nudité' (p. 39) [the simple desire to know ourselves as we are, in our defects, in our superficiality and in our inner depth, in our stark nudity] and their method is firstly to observe: 'Voir notre existence c'est nous voir en situation dans notre histoire, dans notre quotidien, dans notre réel.' (p. 38) [To see our existence is to see ourselves contextualised in our history, in our daily lives, in our reality.] Hence there is a tendency for the interrogation of creole identity, as it surfaces in the novels of Chamoiseau and Confiant, for example, to involve dramatised portraits of everyday life in low-life rural and urban Martinican settings, the 'quartier Texaco', Terres-Sainvilles or the 'morne Pichevin', since these are the spaces in which creole culture flourishes. There is an ethnographic aspect to such writing that is evident, in particular, in texts like Chamoiseau's *Chronique des sept misères* (1986). The portrait of the *djobeurs* working in the three markets of Fort-de-France bears a close resemblance to what James Clifford has termed 'salvage' ethnography, an attempt to save in the text examples of language (the 'paroles de djobeurs' which figure as an annexe to the 1988 Folio edition, for instance) and behaviour that otherwise risk being lost 'in disintegrating time and space'.[10] The multiple narrators of Chamoiseau's chronicle (Didon, Sirop, Pin-Pon, Sifilon and Lapochodé) close the text on a rather ruefully lamenting tone, bemoaning the closure of the markets and the passing of their trade: 'nous disons et redisons ces paroles, ces souvenirs de vie, avec la certitude de devoir disparaître' (p. 240) [we tell and re-tell these stories, these memories of lives, with the certainty of having to disappear from the scene].

One of the paradoxes of *créolité* is the fact that modernity appears to pose such a serious threat to the way the 'vécu réel antillais' [lived reality of the Caribbean] is conceived. It is almost as if the weight of uncaptured history is so great, and the desire to identify its traces in the present so overwhelming, that barely a glance is directed towards the future. The emphasis is placed squarely on understanding how diversity has produced difference, and the key to the composition of this particular form of difference that is creole culture lies in the past. The alienating other of the past (France, colonial discourse, Western values) exerted pressure to reduce diversity through assimilation to French linguistic and cultural norms. The affirmation of creole culture can be seen as a response to such pressures. Yet modernity has not seen them diminish. On the contrary, the thrust of Glissant's argument in *Le Discours antillais* (echoed in Confiant's *Aimé Césaire* and Chamoiseau's *Ecrire en pays dominé*) is that departmentalisation has accelerated assimilationist tendencies and that globalisation is an incredibly powerful force working to effect cultural homogenisation. The ultimate threat to *créolité* is modernity in the form of rampant globalisation. The response of *créolité* authors has been to assign 'capitalist' globalisation to the dustbin of unicity, seeing it as the product of the nation-state mentality that gave rise to colonialism and has now moved up a level to play itself out on a cybernetically connected world stage. In direct opposition to this version of globalisation, they proselytise on behalf of an essentially metaphysical form of globalisation that draws on an ethos of diversity as evinced in the writings of Victor Segalen, designated under such names as 'Tout-monde', 'diversalité', 'mise-en-relations'.

The 'vécu réel antillais' that reveals *créolité*, then, is not the daily experience of everyday reality as decanted through the television screens of third-millenium Martinique or Guadeloupe. It is a selected and selective 'reality' that contributes to a specific discourse of counter-modernity, in which the local, the improvised and the marginal are assigned intrinsic value. This explains why the period of isolation from Pétainiste France, under the governorship of Admiral Robert (in Martinique) and Sorin (in Guadeloupe), is such a frequently cited reference point. The islanders suffered real hardship as a consequence of being cut off from the metropolis but survived relatively unscathed by managing to reactivate community-based systems of self-help, reviving dying skills and developing a high degree of self-reliance that was independent of mainstream (pro-Vichy) structures. Possibly for the first time in the history of the French Caribbean, the population was thrown back on to its own resources and assumed a degree of agency (and managed a type of productivity) that was inconceivable in normal circumstances. This experience of survival through *bricolage* and *débrouillardise* in a prevailing mood of dissidence feeds directly into the conception of creole culture as 'a warts and all' counter-culture.

The authors of the *créolité* movement (both those who signed the *Eloge* and those associated with its general aims, including Simone Schwarz-Bart, Daniel Maximin and others) derive much of their inspiration from the seminal work of Glissant. A cursory glance at the footnotes to the *Eloge* shows how frequently the authors appeal to Glissant to illustrate their points or to support, clarify and contextualise their arguments. Their indebtedness to Glissant is not, however, matched by a corresponding sympathy for *créolité* on his part. This can be explained partly by Glissant's reluctance to be associated with a movement that lays itself open to being interpreted as another type of cultural essentialism. But more importantly, Glissant's much more general concern that the Caribbean should open up to a diversity of relationships and participate in global forms of creolisation, leaves him with no particular reason to invest in the restricted form of cultural and linguistic proselytising that characterises *créolité*. J. Michael Dash has argued that Glissant's real achievement has been to provide 'a way out of the temptation to relapse into identitarian thought. His vision of inexhaustible hybridity is an ideological breakthrough.'[11] Perhaps the key difference lies precisely here: in the very inexhaustibility of Glissant's conception of creolisation as an ongoing process without *parti pris* as to where the process might lead. Despite Confiant's contention that *créolité* is not an ideology – 'la Négritude est une idéologie . . . tandis que la Créolité est la prise en charge d'une réalité historique et anthropologique (en perpétuel mouvement) que personne ne peut contourner ni invalider'[12] [*Négritude* is an ideology . . . whereas *Créolité* is the acceptance of a historical and anthropological reality (in perpetual motion) that no one can ignore or invalidate] – it clearly invests heavily in the promotion of a specific culture as well as specific cultural practices.

Promoting the creole language, the mother tongue of the vast majority of the population in the 'francophone' Caribbean, is obviously the foremost among these cultural practices, and the one that concerns us here in this discussion of the region's literature. Language becomes the particular focus of concern in two different sections of the *Eloge*, the first entitled 'L'enracinement dans l'oral' [Roots in oral culture] and the second, 'Le choix de sa parole' [Choosing one's idiom] (pp. 33 and 43). Where the two converge is in their common effort, not so much to oust French as a medium of expression as to creolise it and thereby claim ownership of it. This creolisation involves contending with a number of difficulties. Firstly, there is the fact that creole belongs to a fundamentally oral tradition. While it is a relatively simple matter to acknowledge that creole identity is freighted through the the oral culture – 'l'oralité est notre intelligence, elle est notre lecture de ce monde, le tâtonnement, aveugle encore, de notre complexité' (p. 33) [orality is the way we understand the world, it is the way we read the world, the as-yet blind groping towards grasping our own complexity] – it is rather more difficult to imagine how creole might be standardised in a written form capable of replacing French in that function. Unless and until such a substitution is possible, the cleavage 'oral/written' will continue to correspond to the identitarian cleavage 'creole/ French', which casts French in the Western imperialist role and creole in the roles of resistance, dissidence and metaphorical *marronnage*. (The word *marron* refers to the runaway slave who refused to submit to plantation life and took to the woods and hills. *Marrons* often lived in small, autarchic, fiercely independent communities rejecting Western civilisation in all its forms.) The *Eloge* apparently recognises this when it pursues Glissant's argument that, whereas in the West the evolution from orality to literature saw a smooth transition, in the Caribbean this was not the case: 'Ici, ce fut la rupture, le fossé, la ravine profonde entre une expression écrite qui se voulait universalo-moderne et l'oralité créole traditionnelle où sommeille une belle part de notre être.' (p. 35) [Here, the break was complete, there was the gulf, the deep ravine between a written expression that sees itself as modern and universalising, and traditional creole orality in which a generous part of our being still slumbers on.] The oral/written cleavage historically corresponds to a division between two distinct cultures.

The real question that flows from this difficulty is not so much how to arrive at a standardised written form of creole (because any amount of work on the language alone can do little to bridge the cultural gap that it represents), as how to integrate into literature the creole identity that has been repressed, suppressed and treated with contempt over such a long period of time. The *Eloge* more or less opens with the argument that no such integration has yet taken place, hence the provocative statement: 'La littérature antillaise n'existe pas encore. Nous sommes dans un état de prélittérature: celui d'une production écrite sans audience chez elle.' (p. 14) [Caribbean literature does not yet exist. We are in a state of preliterature: one in which we have literary production without an indigenous audience.] The point is well made in respect of the whole period of pre-*Négritude* literature stretching back into the eighteenth century, written with metropolitan audiences in mind and slavishly adhering to aesthetic and literary fashions emanating form the metropolis. As the French critic Daniel Delas has pointed out,

> Les premiers écrivains antillais des années romantiques n'ont d'autre ambition que de se faire connaître et reconnaître en France ... Leur poésie – car ils sont presque tous poètes – répète à satiété les clichés de l'exotisme à la mode, celui de la nonchalante doudou créole étant particulièrement insistant. D'où la qualification péjorative de *doudouisme* qui s'attache à eux.[13]

> [The first Caribbean writers of the Romantic period had no other ambition than to be recognised and make their names known in France ... Their poetry – for they were almost all poets – endlessly repeats fashionable exotic stereotypes, that of the carefree creole 'doudou' was particularly prevalent. Hence the pejorative term 'doudouism' that was applied to their work.]

He goes on to cite Poirié Saint-Aurèle, Daniel Thaly (frequently an object of ridicule in Confiant's novels) and Gilbert de Chambertrand as examples of such imitative *doudouist* literature that, from generation to generation, can be seen embracing Romantic, Parnassian and Symbolist themes. But the point made in the *Eloge* must also be read as applying to *Négritude* and post-*Négritude* literature too. However carefully chosen and diplomatic the language used, the claim in the *Eloge* that *créolité* is the child of Césaire's *Négritude* rings rather hollow:

> L'Assimilation ... s'acharnait à peindre notre vécu aux couleurs de l'Ailleurs. La Négritude s'imposait alors comme volonté têtue de résistance tout uniment appliquée à domicilier notre identité dans une culture niée, déniée et reniée ... C'est la Négritude césairienne qui nous a ouvert le passage vers l'ici d'une Antillanité désormais postulable et elle-même en marche vers un autre degré d'authenticité qui restait à nommer. La Négritude césairienne est un baptême, l'acte primal de notre dignité restituée. Nous sommes à jamais fils d'Aimé Césaire.   (p. 18)

> [Assimilation ... insisted on depicting our experience through a palette of colours from elsewhere. At the time, *Négritude* made its presence felt in the form of a stubborn will to resist, completely bent upon bringing our identity back home, as a culture that was rejected, denied and

refuted . . . It was Cesairean *Négritude* that opened the door for us, allowing us entry to the here and now of a Caribbean culture that was henceforth thinkable and was itself moving towards a greater degree of authenticity that had yet to find a name. Cesairean *Négritude* is a baptism, the inaugural act of our restored dignity. We are forever the sons of Aimé Césaire.]

Elsewhere, Confiant for one has described Césaire as as 'un assimilationniste qui s'ignore' [an assimilationist without realising it], thus rather contradicting the careful chronology set out in the *Eloge* and placing Césaire's work firmly back in the category of 'prélittérature'.[14]

These considerations about 'orality' and the fact that creole remains essentially a spoken language, have already brought us to the heart of the second major difficulty faced by the authors of the *créolité* movement, namely how to work upon the French language so as to make it an appropriate tool for expressing creole realities. The problem has been illustrated on a very practical level by Confiant when he describes the difficulties he encountered as a young man intent on embarking on a literary career. Working on a text about a runaway slave, *Les Aventures de Dambo, le fier nègre-marron*, the young Confiant experienced a sudden attack of writer's block when he attempted to switch from narration to a dialogue in which his protagonist uses the word 'wolf'. Confiant suddenly realised, 'cette variété d'animaux n'existait pas aux Antilles' [this kind of animal didn't exist in the Caribbean] and a gulf opened up between the language available to him and his own lived and imagined experience:

> Un nègre-marron, voire le plus banal des personnages antillais, pouvait-il vraiment employer l'expression 'faim de loup'? Quant à 'automne de ma vie', cela te fit franchement rire, à la réflexion. Ici-là, point de printemps, d'été, d'automne et d'hiver. Seulement deux saisons, foutre! Deux: le carême pendant lequel le soleil s'amuse à brûler la terre et les humains, et l'hivernage qui déverse ses avalasses de pluie et ses cyclones en septembre . . . les pages qui précédaient ton dialogue avorté . . . étaient . . . bardées d'expressions qui n'appartenaient aucunement à l'expérience particulière des Antillais.[15]

> [Could a runaway slave, that most obvious of West Indian characters, really use the expression 'faim de loup' (ravenously hungry)? As for 'the autumn of my days', on reflection the expression made you burst out laughing. Here there was no spring, summer, autumn, winter. Only two seasons, what the hell! Two: 'carême' during which the sun takes pleasure scorching the earth and human beings, and 'hivernage' with its downpours and its September hurricanes . . . the pages that had preceded your stillborn dialogue . . . were . . . full of expressions that in no way matched the specific experience of West Indians.]

Confiant's illustration of the inadequacy of French as an appropriate linguistic tool is typically light-hearted and self-deprecatory.

Chamoiseau, for his part, has approached the same problem in a way that highlights the power relations that are always at work whenever 'choice' of language is at issue. *Ecrire en pays dominé* opens with the following question: 'Comment écrire alors que ton imaginaire s'abreuve du matin jusqu'aux rêves, à des images, des pensées, des valeurs qui ne sont pas les tiennes? . . . Comment écrire dominé?' (p. 17) [How can you write when, from the moment you wake to the moment you drift off into sleep, your imagination is feeding on images, thoughts, values that don't belong to you? . . . How can you write while dominated?] By naming creole a 'langue dominée' and French a 'langue dominante' he willingly politicises the literary problem of finding a language ('langage') adequate to the task of expressing the duality of creole and French cultures. This is a matter of creating an idiom between the two languages and drawing simultaneously on the two cultural traditions: 'Quand j'écris je dois faire en sorte, pour exprimer vraiment ce que je suis, de mobiliser, de ramener le conteur créole à côté de tous ces écrivains qui me sont donnés par la littérature française. Je construis mon langage entre langue créole et langue française.'[16] [When I write, in order to truly express who I am I have to act in such a way that I mobilise, and bring back to life, the creole storyteller alongside all those writers that French literature has bequeathed me. I build my idiom between the creole language and the French language.] The process described here as a personal quest for an idiom is, however, only a starting point. It involves an initial type of creolisation that can (and logically must) be envisaged as belonging to the larger context of global creolisation that is 'totalité-monde'. Chamoiseau has explained the literary dimension of the notion thus:

> Lorsqu'on rentre dans cette réalité composite, lorsqu'on plonge dans cette histoire, dans ces événements, dans cette complexité langagière et qu'on rencontre les Amérindiens, les Africains, les Européens, on rentre dans un processus d'une complexité inouïe . . . Nous comprenons désormais que toute littérature est située en face, non pas d'une langue ou au centre d'une langue, mais en présence de toutes les langues du monde.[17]

> [When we enter this composite reality, when we plunge into this history, these events, into this linguistic complexity and we encounter Amerindians, Africans, Europeans, we are entering a process of incredible complexity . . . We then begin to understand that all literature is positioned not in relation to a single language or within a language but in the presence of all the languages of the world.]

The difficulties experienced by Confiant and Chamoiseau in finding an appropriate literary idiom through which to 'construct a literature' echo many of the elements of an earlier analysis of the same questions in *Le Discours antillais*. In the section entitled *Poétiques*, Glissant draws a distinction between 'poétique naturelle' [natural poetics] and 'poétique forcée' [constrained poetics] and suggests that the latter can be identified wherever 'une nécessité d'expression confronte un impossible à exprimer ... La poétique forcée ou contre-poétique est mise en acte par une collectivité dont l'expression ne peut jaillir directement, ne peut provenir d'un exercice autonome du corps social.' (pp. 402–3) [a need for expression comes face to face with the impossibility of expressing ... Constrained poetics or counter-poetics is the strategy adopted by a collectivity whose self-expression can find no spontaneous outlet, cannot result from the autonomous activity of the social group.] The blockage that Glissant identifies has its origins in the lack of autonomy within the social group and, in his view, it is by working on these sociopolitical issues, rather than on the promotion of creole in speech or in writing, that progress towards a solution will be made. In the meantime, the tensions that accumulate as a result of the blockage cannot find a 'natural' outlet and the dilemma of the francophone writer, as identified by Confiant and Chamoiseau, remains clearly a fundamentally linguistic project: 'Il faut frayer à travers la langue vers un langage, qui n'est peut-être pas dans la logique interne de cette langue.' (p. 402) [We have to find a path through language towards an idiom that is perhaps at odds with the internal logic of that language.]

In a sense, almost a century of francophone Caribbean literature has been a working and reworking of the same dilemmas, paradoxes and contradictions. Césaire's efforts to 'negrify' the French language prefigure the present-day efforts to integrate creole identity within a type of literary expression that betrays none of the composite elements that contribute to its make-up. However much *créolité* and *antillanité* succeed in transcending *Négritude* conceptions of identity, challenging *francité* (and French as its medium of domination), and broadening the claim to relevance of creolisation as a global process, francophone literature from the Caribbean region remains largely entangled in a familiar nexus of identitarian concerns.

Aimé Césaire (Martinique, 1913–)

Aimé Césaire has assumed iconic status as one of the most influential figures of francophone literature, possibly as much for the impact his work has had on the evolution of ideas as for the undoubted intrinsic literary qualities of his poetry and drama. It is certainly the case that accounts of Aimé Césaire's career tend to focus at least as much on the various roles he has played, as a founding figure of the *Négritude* 'movement', as co-founder of the influential Paris-based review *Présence Africaine* in 1947, as mayor of Fort-de-France, or as *député* to the French National Assembly from 1945 to 1993, as on any detailed analysis of his literary output. Indeed, it is debatable whether any objective appraisal of his literary work is currently possible such has been the weight of his influence as a vector of change in the political and ideological landscape of his times. In a sense Césaire's own identity has become inseparable from the messages that readers have identified in texts such as *Cahier d'un retour au pays natal*, *Discours sur le colonialisme* (1955) or *La Tragédie du Roi Christophe*. The brilliant academic career he pursued in the 1930s saw the young black man of modest origins successfully negotiate entry to the prestigious Ecole Normale Supérieure in Paris. His apparently effortless ascension of the academic hierarchy was subsequently matched by a seemingly equally effortless entry into political life and elected office, thus illustrating through his own biography and the political activism of his public life the main theses that can be derived from *Négritude* and the anticolonial writings of later decades.

The parallels between the life and the work are ultimately a distraction, however. The early poetry, published in *Tropiques*, and the frequently reworked text of the celebrated *Cahier d'un retour au pays natal* (the poem in which he recounts his homecoming to Martinique) can be 'used' as an archive of source material for an understanding of the ideological 'content' of *Négritude*, but such a 'use' is, to an extent, a 'misuse'. As A. James Arnold has explained, 'Because it is a political poem, some commentators have read it as a document, passing over the significance of its poetic fabric.'[18] His own analysis of the *Cahier* successfully adopts a more balanced approach. He identifies a ternary structure in the poem, composed of:

> an initial revolt against an intolerable present; a recollection of childhood and early youth that calls up images both fascinating and revolting, culminating in the recognisation [sic] of an awful personal reality; and finally a shorter movement that swells with the surge of vital force renewed.[19]

The poem's forward progression through these various moments is punctuated by switches of rhythm from aggressive, staccato passages to more nuanced, lyrical periods. The tone of the 'narrative voice' also switches from impelling instances of direct address to the reader, through less subjectively inflected passages of comment and allusion with a clear sociohistorical dimension, on to the more triumphal mood of self-assertion that marks the final sections.

The imagery deployed by Césaire, for all the debt the poem owes to surrealism, is marked by landscapes (perhaps 'mindscapes' would be more accurate) that are tropical rather than French. It is not necessary to evoke the rhythms of the tom-tom, or suggest that lexical items provide echoes of an ancestral African world, to support the view that the poem has a powerful musicality and verbal richness.

Yet none of these formal aspects of the poem exist in isolation, divorced from the signifying intent of the author. Césaire's purpose is not merely to deconstruct the racism that has underpinned the historical contacts between blacks and Europeans, or even to correct it by means of a counter-discourse.

> Eia pour ceux qui n'ont jamais rien inventé
> pour ceux qui n'ont jamais rien exploré
> pour ceux qui n'ont jamais rien dompté
>
> mais ils s'abandonnent, saisis, à l'essence de toute chose
> ignorants des surfaces mais saisis par le mouvement de toute chose
> insoucieux de dompter, mais jouant le jeu du monde   (*Cahier*, p. 47)
>
> [Eia for those who have never invented anything
> for those who have never explored anything
> for those who have never tamed anything
>
> but they surrender themselves, transfixed, to the essence of all things
> ignorant of surfaces, but transfixed by the movement of all things
> with no interest in taming, but playing the world's game]

The historical European view of blacks as culturally impoverished is not denied in these lines. On the contrary, the view is accepted as accurate but with the proviso that it function as a signifier of radical *difference*. By accepting the view proposed by the white (racist) dominators Césaire is able to effect a reversal of values: the blacks' indifference to technological advances, geographical exploration, the subjugation of nature or the conquest of other lands, in short the range of activities that define imperialism, is not some congenital defect but a sign of cultural difference that can be adjudged superior. Black cultures engage with the world in other ways, but ways that are more in tune with, and respectful of, the essence of things: 'the world's game'.

Potted versions of *Négritude* for general consumption have frequently done a disservice to Césaire. They have blunted much of the subtlety and many of the nuances of his appeal to African values as a way of countering the alienating discourses of imperialism. Perhaps chief among the many misrepresentations that have resulted from popularisation is the suggestion that Césaire idealises the pre-colonial African past, or expresses nostalgia for a return to such origins.

As the lines from the *Cahier* quoted above illustrate, the assertion of self-worth is based not on a glorification of an African civilisation but on a refusal to recognise the accuracy of European civilisation's self-proclaimed worth, and *a fortiori* its supposed universal significance. The self-affirmation and political contestation discernible in the *Cahier* are two phases of the same argument, as the more overtly political *Discours sur le colonialisme* demonstrates:

> On me parle de progrès, de 'réalisations', de maladies guéries, de niveaux de vie élévés au-dessus d'eux-mêmes.
>
> Moi, je parle de sociétés vidées d'elles-mêmes . . . de terres confisquées, de religions assassinées, de magnificences artistiques anéanties, d'extraordinaires *possibilités* supprimées . . .
>
> Pour ma part, je cherche vainement . . . où l'on m'a entendu prêcher un quelconque *retour*, où l'on m'a vu prétendre qu'il pouvait y avoir *retour*. (pp. 19–22; Césaire's italics)

> [They talk to me about progress, about 'projects completed', about illnesses cured, about standards of living raised above their own.
>
> I talk about societies emptied of their being . . . of lands confiscated, of religions massacred, of artistic splendours demolished, of extraordinary *possibilities* wiped out.
>
> For my own part, I wonder in vain . . . where they have heard me preaching about a supposed *return*, where they have seen me claim that there could be any *return*.]

Being clear about the details of historical domination as a precondition for moving forward is not the same thing as seeking to put the clock back and start again.

The 1960s saw Césaire turn increasingly to the theatre as a form of literary expression with a triad of plays often grouped together on the basis of their preoccupation with decolonisation. *La Tragédie du Roi Christophe* (1963) was followed by *Une saison au Congo* (1966) and *Une tempête* (1969). The last of the three is a reworking of Shakespeare's play *The Tempest* that recentres that canonical European text in a colonial setting. Themes that are already present in the *Cahier* (but which have achieved a wider circulation through the writings of Frantz Fanon) are developed in this text, notably Césaire's casting of Caliban as a dispossessed, colonised subject struggling for his freedom and that of his island homeland, and the alienating power of the dehumanising gaze of Prospero, the colonial oppressor. Caliban declaims:

> Et tu m'as tellement menti,
> menti sur le monde, menti sur moi-même,
> que tu as fini par m'imposer

une image de moi-même:
Un sous-développé, comme tu dis,
un sous-capable,
voilà comment tu m'as obligé à me voir   (p. 88)

[And you have lied to me so much,
lied about the world, lied about me,
that you've ended up imposing upon me
an image of myself:
Under-developed, as you call it,
Under-skilled,
that's how you've forced me to see myself]

Of the three plays, *La Tragédie du Roi Christophe* has the richest resonances both as a postcolonial (scrutinising the political and discursive practices that have enabled imperialist patterns of domination) and a post-colonial (situated *after* the period of colonisation) text. Set in post-independence Haiti, this play examines not Caliban's dilemma as to how to wrest his freedom (psychological and material) from the colonial master, but the more thorny issue that faces Christophe is how to use that freedom once it has been won by the force of arms. There are echoes of Fanon once again in this play, particularly from such writings as 'Mésaventures de la conscience nationale' [Pitfalls of national consciousness] in *Les Damnés de la terre* (1961). But as Régis Antoine has suggested, the list of diffuse influences on Césaire's thinking when writing the play can be extended to include a range of contemporary political and literary intertexts: 1960 had been the year when numerous African countries had achieved independence and were grappling with similar problems.[20]

One of the key axes of the play is an exploration of the pragmatics of organising a national culture ('nation-building') in a post-colonial setting. Christophe's response to the problem is marked by ambivalence. He sets the nation to work, more as a matter of principle than as a practical way of achieving any specific outcome. Work is an end in itself, the means by which Christophe intends to raise his people from the mire into which colonial oppression has consigned them. The parallels between Christophe's tyrannical vision and the despotism of so many post-independence African leaders could hardly be clearer. The content of his programme (work, work, work) is intended to confirm the distinctiveness of blacks and to prevent them from behaving like whites: 'Il est temps de mettre à la raison ces nègres qui croient que la Révolution ça consiste à prendre la place des Blancs et continuer, en lieu et place, je veux dire sur le dos des nègres, à faire le Blanc.' (p. 84) [It's time to teach a lesson to those blacks who think the Revolution is about taking over from the whites and continuing in their place, I mean on the backs of the blacks, and acting like whites.] There is a certain irony about this insistence on *difference* from a man whose conception of freedom leads him to instigate a new form of servitude for his people that so closely resembles the slavery of colonial rule. But irony is in fact the structuring principle of the second major axis the play explores. In the forms of government with which Christophe chooses to surround himself, the ceremonies and the paraphernalia of court life, imitation, parody, carica-ture and mimicry of both European models and theatrical representation itself, are omnipresent. Homi K. Bhabha has identified mimicry as 'one of the most elusive and effective strategies of colonial power and knowledge', arguing that if 'colonialism takes power in the name of history, it repeatedly exercises its authority through the figures of farce.'[21] Césaire's play seems to appropriate (in advance) this critical discourse on colonialism and demonstrate how in a similar, but not *quite* the same, way it illuminates the postcolonial desire and 'will to power' of Christophe himself.

In recent decades Césaire's position and significance as a cultural icon and dominant figure in the emergence of francophone Caribbean literature have been challenged, particularly as a consequence of the refocusing on creole language and culture that has resulted from the work of Glissant and the authors of the *créolité* movement. Martin Munro, among others, has argued that such attacks are unfair. While recognising that Césaire and his generation's 'quest to disalienate the colonised self . . . seemed to open up new layers of alienation for themselves', he argues (as would Césaire too) that the historical context left little alternative but to fight oppression with the only tools available at the time and the creole language was not one of them.[22]

Frantz Fanon (Martinique, 1925–1961)

In the case of influential figures like Aimé Césaire, who have achieved success in both political and literary spheres of activity, it is understandable that critics often choose to interrogate the way political commitment manifests itself (or not) in their writings. When critical judgement is harsh (as when Confiant describes Césaire as a 'génie littéraire . . . nain politique'[23] [literary genius . . . political dwarf]) the poet always has the option of insisting that the literary work speaks only for and of itself. Frantz Fanon's life and writings allow no such easy distinction between the political and the literary. They fuse into a composite whole: his life and his writings are inextricably linked to the same project of denouncing and resisting colonialism and the racism that underpins it. Fanon's two most important texts, *Peau noire masques blancs* and *Les Damnés de la terre* (1961), are not only political in content, they emerge from the same impulse to act in and on the world: they are political actions as much as they are literary texts.

Peau noire masques blancs is something of a hybrid text that draws on Fanon's personal experiences of life in France (he had left his native Martinique at the age of eighteen in 1943 to fight with the Free French forces against Nazi occupation) and his professional knowledge of psychiatry to produce a passionate denunciation of the relationship between blacks and whites as it is staged through the colonial encounter. In this first period Fanon's anticolonialism is deeply imbued with the self-affirmatory theses of *Négritude* allied to the personally empowering philosophy of existentialism. Fanon's originality, however, was to articulate these ideas within a framework provided by the psychiatric discourses of alienation, neurosis, desire and therapy. The various sections of the book describe aspects of the psychopathology of the black, how inter-racial desire is perceived and inscribed within colonial culture, and how the negative image of blacks projected by the colonial masters is internalised and incorporated into black consciousness. Fanon's political activism is motivated by his refusal of the various forms of external determinism to which blacks (and, by extension, colonial peoples more generally) are subjected. One feature of Fanon's analysis is that the black/white relationship may be understood in terms of irreducible binary oppositions. But this is a Manichean universe of double consciousness, representations, images and masks, not the thesis/antithesis of a classic dialectic. The book's power lies in the demonstration itself and it is not a major weakness that Fanon leaves himself with nowhere to go. The book concludes with the rather generalising, woolly language of exhortation: 'Que jamais l'instrument ne domine l'homme. Que cesse à jamais l'asservissement de l'homme par l'homme. C'est-à-dire de moi par un autre. Qu'il me soit permis de découvrir et de vouloir l'homme, où qu'il se trouve.' (p. 187) [May instruments never be allowed to dominate man. May the enslavement of man by his fellow man cease for ever. That is to say, my enslavement by another. May I be allowed to discover my fellow man and to want him, wherever he is to be found.]

On completing his medical studies in Lyon, Fanon was appointed head of the psychiatric department at a hospital in Algeria. He remained in post for three years (1953–6) during which time, in 1954, the growing Algerian resistance to French rule was formally declared a war by the FLN (Front de Libération Nationale). Fanon's experience in Algeria has generally been seen as the cause of a second phase of political radicalisation. His involvement with the FLN deepened as the war took hold and he eventually resigned from his post to devote himself full time to the anticolonial struggle. His letter of resignation to the resident minister was published posthumously in 1961 alongside a selection of his journalism and other writings, under the title *Pour la Révolution africaine*. Typically, Fanon makes the connection between the psychological state of alienation and the dehumanising effects of political oppression, even interpreting the normally political question 'What status for Algeria?' as a diagnostic question, and replying in the terminology of psychiatric medicine:

> Si la psychiatrie est la technique médicale qui se propose de permettre à l'homme de ne plus être étranger à son environnement, je me dois d'affirmer que l'Arabe, aliéné permanent dans son pays, vit dans un état de dépersonnalisation absolue.
> Le statut de l'Algérie? Une déshumanisation systématisée.   (p. 51)

> [If psychiatry is the medical technique that seeks to provide man with the wherewithal to no longer be at odds with his environment, I am obliged to make it clear that the Arab, permanently alienated in his own country, lives in a state of absolute depersonalisation.
> The status of Algeria? A state of systematic dehumanisation.]

Fanon's radicalisation is nowhere more in evidence than in the sections of *Les Damnés de la terre* devoted to 'violence'. The binary opposition that characterises the black/white relationship in *Peau noire masques blancs* is not *resolved* in the later text, it is simply transcended through a purifying violence that is envisaged as eliminating the terms of the problem while ushering in the national unity that Fanon identifies as the basis for post-colonial harmony: 'L'homme colonisé se libère dans et par la violence' (p. 118) [Colonised man liberates himself in and through violence] and 'La violence du colonisé . . . unifie le peuple.' (p. 127) [The violence of the colonised subject . . . unifies the people.] This messianic tone is, of course, of its time and of its context: the active military struggle to throw off colonial rule. It undoubtedly contributes in no small measure to the importance Fanon assumed as an inspiration to decolonising efforts around the world during the 1960s and after. Yet any attempt to evaluate even such an iconic text as this (published in the year of Fanon's untimely death from leukaemia with a resounding endorsement from Sartre by way of preface) has to dig beneath mere rhetorical effect. In a detailed argument based on events in the post-independence Guinea of Sékou Touré (whom Fanon frequently quotes in *Les Damnés de la terre*), Christopher Miller has demonstrated how the discourse of violence in Fanon's essays 'allowed Sékou Touré – like any other ruler – to relativise and liquidate' his own opponents.[24]

Robert J. C. Young begins his discussion of Fanon's impact on what he calls the 'theoretical practices of the freedom struggles' by drawing a distinction between anglophone and francophone activists. He argues that the former tend to focus on 'the objective realm' of history, economic and social realities and material conditions whereas the latter tend to counterbalance their interest in such questions with a subjective 'concern for the human attitudes towards them'.[25] How do colonial subjects live the experience of colonialism and with what effects? are key questions in such an approach. Young's emphasis on the subjective realm of experience echoes Homi K. Bhabha's point, in *The Location of Culture*, that Fanon's resistance to colonial oppression was not merely an attempt to inflect the course of Western history but a challenge to its 'historicist idea of time as a progressive, ordered whole'. Bhabha goes on:

> There is no master narrative or realist perspective that provides a background of social and historical facts against which emerge the problems of the individual or collective psyche . . . It is through image and fantasy . . . that Fanon most profoundly evokes the colonial condition.[26]

Fanon did not organise his analysis of the colonial condition in accordance with the rules of evidence-based, academic scholarship from within a tradition of Western rationalism. The evidence to which he most frequently alludes is drawn from 'the heterogeneous assemblage of the texts of history, literature, science, myth'.[27] Facial expressions, bodily gestures, physical attitudes, overheard conversations and moments of unguarded comment are all recycled in Fanon's analyses. Moreover, he himself is physically implicated, as both subject and object, within the double consciousness of racism and colonial oppression he describes. It is because of the nature of this challenge to a post-Enlightenment Western order of reason and language that Fanon has come to assume such a significant place in postcolonial theory.

Patrick Chamoiseau (Martinique, 1953–)

Patrick Chamoiseau, born in 1953, is of a generation for whom the Césairean imagery of black cultural self-affirmation no longer seems an appropriate vehicle through which to express the cultural reality of life in Martinique. Where Césaire had seen only black culture, and had trumpeted the fact to the world as a powerful message of liberation, Chamoiseau and the *créolité* movement see creole culture, and deduce from it a model for an innovative way of conceiving intercultural relationships on a global scale. Black culture and the dominant values of French culture are merely two of the component elements of *créolité*, not definitive statements of an essentialised state of culture that has pretensions to universality. The fundamental difference between the two generations can be captured in attitudes to language. However much Césaire's poetry may have 'negrified' the French language (or creolised it, according to René Depestre[28]), his respect and admiration for it never faltered. By the same token, he was unable to conceive of creole as a vehicle for cultural expression. With the generation of Chamoiseau (through the enabling efforts of a range of writers, poets and dramatists from Gilbert Gratiant, through Sonny Rupaire, Daniel Boukman, to Simone Schwarz-Bart, to name but a few) the reverse was the case. French for Chamoiseau remains a valued and valuable tool, and the literary culture freighted through the language remains an indispensable point of reference for his work. Yet it is the creole language that provides the structuring principle of the imaginary that he has chosen to explore and French provides no access to that particular universe.

Chamoiseau's conviction that the creole language provides unique access to a specifically creole sensibility is a key tenet of his 'theoretical' writings, from *Eloge de la créolité* and *Lettres créoles* (1999), written in collaboration with Raphaël Confiant, to that hybrid mixture of genres that is to be found in *Ecrire en pays dominé*. The same conviction can also be identified as a key preoccupation of his fictional and autobiographical writings, both thematically, in that it influences the type of stories he chooses to write about, and formally in that the interface between the oral and the written itself becomes a space to be explored and a subject to be investigated. There are many similarities here with the work of Edouard Glissant, who must be considered as something of a *maître à penser* for Chamoiseau. The emphasis on creole as a linguistic raw material has allowed Chamoiseau to cast himself as a scribe, a 'marqueur de paroles' transcribing the words dictated to him and in so doing ensuring access to the creole universe. The invention of such a persona may be connected with Chamoiseau's lived experience, for example in recording the actual words of *djobeurs* who figure in his first novel, *Chronique des sept misères*, or in his manifest interest in creole storytellers, but it is ultimately a convenient fictionalisation that serves to obscure as it simultaneously illustrates what is a very literary function: his fiction is a representation of a reality that is partly observed and partly imagined – it is not reality simply and directly transcribed. In his preface to the Folio edition of *Chroniques des sept misères*, Glissant refers to the 'talent romanesque de Chamoiseau' [Chamoiseau's talent as a novelist] and comments on the invention of 'the scribe' in terms of those eminently unobservable worlds of the past and the future – memory and future action:

Dans l'univers multilingue de la Caraïbe, il nous avertit lui-même qu'il se considère comme un 'marqueur de paroles', 'oiseau de Cham' ou 'Chamgibier', à l'écoute d'une voix venue de loin, dont l'écho plane sur les lieux de notre mémoire et oriente nos futurs. C'est reconnaître qu'il marche à cette lisière de l'oral et de l'écrit où se joue une des perspectives actuelles de la littérature. (p. 6)

[In the multilingual universe of the Caribbean, he himself tells us that he considers himself as a 'transcriber of words', 'bird of Cham' or 'Cham-gamebird', listening to a voice that comes from afar, whose echo hovers over those places inhabited by our memory and which also shapes our futures. This is to recognise that he operates at the boundary between the oral and the written, where one of the contemporary approaches to literature is being played out.]

Examples of the creative and dynamic power of creole are naturally rooted in, and routed through, characters and situations. The early works, including the two autobiographical volumes of his childhood experiences *Antan d'enfance* (1990) and *Chemin d'école* (1994) abound in colourful character portraits that are sketched partly through linguistic performances. These may typically be set in the everyday contexts of the market place, the street, and the home or school, but they also frequently include instances of creole historiography: attempts to evoke a distant past through 'memory' or through stories and tales. The conscious effort to delve into a personal or collective memory as a way of maintaining contact with, perhaps even of reimagining, the formative influence of the past, is a hugely important dimension of creole culture and is entirely in keeping with its status as a non-written culture whose modes of transmission are opaque. The 'dix-huit paroles rêvées d'Afoukal' transmitted to Pipi in *Chroniques des sept misères* are a case in point (pp. 151–68). Afoukal, the archetypal 'ancestor', 'speaks' to Pipi in his dreams, not to reveal the where-abouts of the treasure Pipi seeks but to transmit a different form of 'treasure', the invaluable memory of the humiliations and suffering of the slave trade and of life on the plantations in the days before abolition.

Solibo Magnifique (1988) plays on the notion of linguistic performance, this time in the guise of 'storytelling', at every conceivable level and includes among its themes an exploration of the interface between the spoken word and the written text. The mysterious death of Solibo, a master storyteller, in the midst of a public performance while the Carnival is in full swing, is literally a silencing of the oral performance. The police investigation that follows quickly becomes a murder enquiry. The arrival of the police marks the irruption of bureaucratic modernity into the creole universe of storytelling: it evokes the realm and the logic of the written word (witness statements, interrogations, police reports). The presence of the novelist, the 'scribe', 'oiseau de Cham' himself, in the midst of the audience at the time of the death complicates matters, adding another dimension to the range of tensions between the oral universe and literature. His presence at the 'scene of the crime' also builds on the exchanges between the authorial persona and Solibo that punctuate the text and shed further light on the tensions that exist between the two worlds. Indeed, the novelist becomes a prime suspect for the putative murder of Solibo (who else could be more deserving of suspicion in respect of the death of a fictional character than the author of the text?), thus maintaining the antithetical nature of the orality/literature relationship. Yet silence is only suspicious in literature. In the oral tradition it is an integral part of the process of creating and conveying meanings. At one point the policeman, Bouafesse, expresses surprise at the fact that none of the audience realised something was amiss when the 'storyteller' suddenly went quiet:

> Toutes les dépositions furent les mêmes: un silence est une parole. On attendait à l'aise même, car de la parole tu bâtis le village mais du silence ho! c'est le monde que tu construis . . . Qui a peur du silence par ici? Le silence sonne et résonne, et signifie autant que la voix . . . la parole du conteur, c'est le son de la gorge, mais c'est aussi sa sueur, les roulades de ses yeux, son ventre, les dessins de ses mains, son odeur, celle de la compagnie, le son du ka et tous les silences.   (p. 137)

> [All the statements agreed: silence is an act of language. We waited, quite happily even, because with words you build the village but with silence ho! you build the world . . . Who's afraid of silence around here? Silence booms and echoes, and has as much meaning as words . . . the story-teller's language is the noise from his throat, but it's also his sweat, the way he rolls his eyes, holds his stomach, it's the movements of his hands, his smell, that of the audience, the sound of the music and all the silences.]

So if literature ultimately supplants, eliminates and silences orality, it is through a process of impoverishment: meanings are lost along with the oral tradition. The close of the novel confirms this pessimistic conclusion. Cham realises that all his efforts to *fix* the words of Solibo in a written version of his 'parole' catch nothing of the true performance: 'je compris qu'écrire l'oral n'était qu'une trahison, on y perdait les intonations, les mimiques, la gestuelle du conteur . . . il était clair désormais que sa parole, sa vraie parole, toute sa parole, était perdue pour tous – et à jamais (pp. 210–11) [I understood that writing orality was nothing but a betrayal, in doing so you lost the intonation, the facial expressions, the gestures of the storyteller . . . it was clear now that his words, his true words, the whole of his words, were lost to everyone – and for evermore].

The structuring of the narrative in *Texaco* (1992) also relies heavily on models of oral performance. The novel opens with a series of accounts, from the point of view of a number of witnesses, of an attack perpetrated on the person of the young town planner whose job it will be to co-ordinate the destruction of the shantytown of Texaco and the rehousing of its inhabitants. Hit on the head by a stone thrown by one of the local residents, the young man is taken to the *case* of Marie-Sophie Laborieux to be looked after. It is from this encounter that the whole of the novel will develop, as Marie-Sophie realises that the imminent destruction of the neighbourhood of Texaco can only be averted if she succeeds in winning over the support of the young man: 'j'avais soudain compris que c'était moi, . . . avec pour seule arme la persuasion de ma parole, qui devrais mener seule – a mon âge – la décisive bataille pour la survie de Texaco' (p. 41) [I had suddenly realised that it was I . . . with the persuasive power of my speech as my only weapon, who – at my age – was going to have to wage the decisive battle for the survival of Texaco]. The novel is ostensibly the oral performance of Marie-Sophie, as she recounts the origins of Texaco and the stories of its inhabitants. But as in earlier texts, the authorial persona, 'Oiseau de Cham', figures as the addressee of the narrative which is thus staged as an account made to the author (Chamoiseau) of the story told by Marie-Sophie to the character (the town planner). This complex distribution and layering of narrative roles matches the equally complex interconnections between 'Histoire et histoires', the history of Martinique and the stories of the rich variety of characters that inhabit the narrator's world.

The dimension of creole life that *Texaco* explores more fully than any of the earlier texts is that of habitat. The 'chronological milestones' with which the novel opens periodise the history of Martinique according to the type of homes the population inhabited and the building materials from which they were constructed. Hence place assumes a crucial importance in this novel as first Esternome, the narrator's father, undertakes the conquest of 'l'En-ville' [the urban space] and then Marie-Sophie herself struggles for the survival of the creole space of Texaco. Place in both cases represents far more than a physical environment. Just as the landscape becomes a key character in the novels of Glissant, so in this novel place is invested with meanings and memories so that the occupation of a living space is the quintessential gesture of a culture and reflects the cumulative history and experience of the inhabitants. This is the message Marie-Sophie must convey to the town planner if she is to succeed in saving Texaco (and by extension the creole culture that Texaco represents). But if her 'explanation' is largely an exposition of the past, her personal 'story' intertwined with island's history, the significance of creole culture is far broader. The town planner gradually appreciates this, as one of his notes to the 'marqueur de paroles' indicates: 'La ville créole restitue à l'urbaniste qui voudrait l'oublier les souches d'une identité neuve: multilingue, multiraciale, multi-historique, ouverte, sensible à la diversité du monde.' (p. 282) [The creole town is a reminder to the town planner, who would prefer to forget it, of the roots of a new identity: multilingual, multiracial, multi-historical, open, sensitive to the diversity of the world.]

This definition of creole culture as prospective rather than retrospective informs all of Chamoiseau's more recent writings, in which the diversity of creole culture becomes a transcultural, transhistorical model for global relationships. It would be mistaken, however, to see Chamoiseau's 'diversalité' as some sort of harmonious utopia dominated by mutual respect, and tolerance of cultural difference. Adlai Murdoch's reading of *Solibo Magnifique* gives a clue as to why this is the case. He writes: 'any reading of *Solibo Magnifique* must come to terms with the slave-based phenomenon of *marronnage*, or marooning, and with the figural role of the maroon, or runaway slave, as an identitarian icon of rebellion and liberation for the Caribbean diaspora.'[29] Solibo's oral performances, like the creole culture they express, are intrinsically incitements to rebellion with regard to the dominant (written) cultures of the West. Adlai Murdoch's insight informs us that *créolité* is always a form of dissidence. The figure of the *marron* takes centre stage in *L'Esclave vieil homme et le molosse* (1997) and in this text, the runaway's eventual death is staged in a remote, forest location that represents not only the antithesis of the ordered, cultivated *béké* plantation but links him to the Carib past that predated the arrival of the slaves on the island. The *marron* and the Carib tribes suffered the same fate at the hands of Western domination. 'Diversalité', then, is a discourse of resistance. The 'warrior' of *Ecrire en pays dominé* has much in common with the protagonist of *Biblique des derniers gestes* (2002), M. Balthazar Bodule-Jules, who is referred to as 'un grand guerrier' [a great warrior] in the closing lines of the novel (p. 852). Chamoiseau's 'warrior' embodies this duality, simultaneously defending creole diversity and resisting the cultural imperialism of monocultural, monolingual uniformity. As Chamoiseau commented in a recent interview:

> aujourd'hui nous avons à faire face à une domination silencieuse, invisible: quelque chose qui transforme notre imaginaire et qui crée des processus de standardisation et d'uniformisation, donc de perte de la diversité . . . Donc la nouvelle forme de résistance devient celle du guerrier: c'est cette manière de s'opposer à tout ce processus de négation de la diversité.[30]

[today we are confronted with a silent, invisible form of domination: something that is transforming our imaginary and is creating processes of standardisation and uniformisation, therefore of loss of diversity . . . So the new form of resistance becomes that of the warrior: this is the way to counter the whole process of the negation of diversity.]

Raphaël Confiant (Martinique, 1951–)

Raphaël Confiant's career as a writer can be seen as reflecting some of the key themes he explores within his work: inhabiting two languages, creole and French, which pull him in very different directions, his writing both illustrates the strategies he has adopted to come to some sort of resolution of this antagonism, and provides a commentary on them. Passionately committed to promoting the creole language and representing the culture it expresses, Confiant began by publishing texts in creole at his own expense throughout the early 1980s. He had, in fact, some five creole publications to his name before venturing to write in French. In *Eloge de la créolité*, along with his co-authors, he bemoaned the fact that Caribbean literature did not yet exist and described the current situation as 'un état de prélittérature: celui d'une production écrite sans audience chez elle, méconnaissant l'interaction auteurs/lecteurs où s'élabore une littérature' (p. 14) [a state of preliterature: one in which we have literary production without an indigenous audience and where there is none of the interaction between authors/readers on which a literature is built]. This statement has often been read as a provocation: 'What about Césaire?' we might ask as we read it. Yet it also reflects the more serious notion of 'manque' [lack/loss] that is a characteristic of a cultural anxiety about roots, among people who have all experienced some form of uprooting. The notion of 'manque' recurs throughout *Le Discours antillais* and Celia Britton has also identified it as a recurring trope in Glissant's fiction. She uses the expression 'lack of language' to explain how Glissant's characters confront the same notion:

> The 'lack' of language is not just a question of missing items – words that do not exist . . . It is also the fact that the language they do use is experienced by them as lack, blighted by a kind of nothingness because it has no real connection either to its speakers or to the reality it is supposedly expressing.[31]

Confiant's decision to write in French can be seen as a response to another version of such a 'lack of connection' as Britton identifies here. It would appear to be motivated by his practical need to connect with a readership rather than any weakening of his commitment to creole. Encouraged by his friend Patrick Chamoiseau to make the switch, he nevertheless agonised over a decision that he partially lived as a betrayal: at one point he even attempted to burn the manuscript of his first novel in French, *Le Nègre et l'amiral* (1988); it was rescued from the flames by his wife.

Since the appearance of that first novel, Confiant has proved a prolific writer, publishing more than twenty novels and narratives as well as substantial studies of Aimé Césaire and creole literature (*Lettres créoles*), the latter co-authored with Chamoiseau. The rate at which these texts have appeared is itself impressive but what should not be underestimated, in the case of Confiant, is the great range he possesses as a writer. His *œuvre* includes a number of novels that are linked in so far as they present the same groups of characters, albeit at different moments in Martinican history: *Le Nègre et l'amiral* recounts the years of penury during the Second World War; *La Vierge du grand retour* (1996) involves many of the same characters, this time living through an episode that occurred in 1948, when a statue of the Virgin Mary arrived in Martinique on a small boat that had seemingly crossed the ocean; many of the group also figure in *L'Allée des soupirs* (1994), *Le Meurtre du Samedi-Gloria* (1997) and *L'Archet du colonel* (1998), although in all these novels they act more as a framing device for the narratives and their presence is incidental to the main storyline. In addition to this core group of texts, Confiant has written novels that focus on specific moments and aspects of Martinican history: *Nuée ardente* (2002) recounts life in the island's capital, Saint-Pierre, prior to its destruction in 1902 when the Mont Pelé erupted; *Le Barbare enchanté* (2003) centres on the brief period spent on the island by the painter Paul Gauguin; *La Panse du chacal* (2004) explores a specific aspect of creole identity that is frequently ignored and treated dismissively: the dimension contributed by Tamoul immigrants.

Alongside these 'mainstream' novels Confiant has also written two autobiographical works (*Ravines du devant-jour* (1993) and *Le Cahier de romances* (2000)) as well as a series of shorter, essentially comic narratives that portray the anarchic world of modern-day Martinique. Four have appeared to date: *Bassin des ouragans* (1994), *La Savane des Pétrifications* (1995), *La Baignoire de Joséphine* (1997) and *La Dernière Java de Mama Josépha* (1999). All are narrated by Abel, whose chaotic universe provides an ideal form of cover from which Confiant is able to pour scorn on various aspects of modernity. The corrosive humour of these texts contains a good dose of 'auto-derision' [self-mockery], as though Confiant uses them to adopt a more destructive and free-wheeling critical voice than that which figures in his novels. In terms of structure too they are less carefully crafted works that appear to have been dashed off spontaneously and somewhat whimsically: the narrative thread is not so much dictated by unfolding events as by the fertile imagination of Abel. Above all, the distinguishing characteristic of these narratives is their engagement with the modernity (the world of consumer goods, motorways, tourists and contemporary life) that is generally ignored by the texts exploring creole culture, associated as it usually is with the plantation life of earlier decades.

It is nevertheless this culture that is the chief preoccupation of Confiant's work and the universe he has sought to portray from text to text in both his French and creole texts. It is no coincidence that his first French novel, *Le Nègre et l'amiral*, is set during the difficult years of the Second World War since the hardship suffered by the islanders has a foundational quality about it: it acted as a fillip to self-awareness and helped raise the population's consciousness of themselves as creoles, a people with a distinctive culture of their own. Chamoiseau has remarked on the fact that Caribbean literature has no foundational myth on which to draw: 'On n'a pas de mythe fondateur; on n'a pas de discours de genèse . . .'[32] [We have no founding myth; we have no discourse of origins.] Yet in a sense, the period the islands spent under the Pétainist governership of Robert and Sorin can be seen as a counter-myth that 'founds' creole culture. The key to such a reading lies in the double estrangement that isolation from France implied. Firstly, the Vichy government's capitulation to the Germans and the subsequent years of collaboration by the Pétainist régime were at odds with the patriotic groundswell of opinion in the Caribbean. During the First World War inhabitants of the Caribbean colonies had enthusiastically paid *l'impôt du sang* [the blood tax] that was required of them by France in defending national integrity. On this occasion, however, official French policy demanded the exact opposite reaction from them. It is little wonder therefore that the notion of *francité* was undermined and to an extent fractured. The decision taken by several characters in the novel who choose to go into 'dissidence' by seeking to rejoin the Free French Forces in Dominique (Rigobert, Amédée Mauville and others) is not simply a political act of resistance, it is a declaration of their independence from a certain 'official' version of Frenchness. *La mère patrie* is no longer seen as the monolithic force it had previously represented. A second consequence of the isolation from France, more mundane but equally significant, is also portrayed in the novel. The lack of contact with Europe resulted in very real material hardship, hunger and deprivation. After the event, the islanders could realise with some pride that they had fended for themselves by falling back on practical networks of mutual help and solidarity outside the loop that connected them to the distant metropolis. The struggle for daily survival that the novel depicts through the portrait of colourful inhabitants of Le Morne Pichevin (Rigobert, Philomène, Carmélise and many others) is a celebration of creole culture as an autonomous, functioning system.

The portrait Confiant paints in *Le Nègre et l'amiral* is not overly concerned with such abstractions, however; it is a down-to-earth illustration of creole culture in action, depicted through the day-to-day experiences of a broad range of characters. The universe of Le Morne Pichevin is a crude, low-life world of dubious morals (sexual promiscuity, casual prostitution and violence are commonplace), distinctive leisure activities (dicing, gambling, cock-fighting, tafia [rum] consumption) and parallel forms of social organisation (each suburb is regulated by the authority of a 'major' [strong-arm man] who periodically fights with the others to establish or maintain the pecking-order). Despite the generalised lawlessness and petty criminality, relationships within this microcosmic community adhere to a strong common ethic in which mutual respect and group solidarity are constantly in evidence. There are clear limits to behaviour and clear hierarchies of authority, albeit marginalised from 'official' systems of regulation and control. But this is merely the general framework within which the characters evolve. The full flavour of the creole culture they embody is to be located in the stories of their lives and loves that Confiant narrates with both pathos and humour, frequently drawing on a creolised version of French that mirrors the composite, highly imaged and therefore highly mediated world of Martinique, in which the familiar becomes strange while the unfamiliar has an eerie recognisability about it. The creole universe Confiant describes is fundamentally and unpretentiously surreal. As one character remarks following André Breton's departure from the island:

> A quoi bon le surréalisme? . . . Il suffit de regarder la réalité de ce pays les yeux bien écarquillés et quasiment à chaque pas, on bute sur des hommes qui se muent en chien ou en oiseau et sur des arbres qui se mettent à jouer des partitions musicales. La vie d'ici est surréaliste en elle-même, messieurs. La décrire telle quelle suffit, non pas avec le regard de l'étranger assoiffé d'exotisme comme le font nos poètes régionalistes, mais avec notre propre regard, celui des vieux nègres, des djobeurs, des joueurs de sèrbi, des charbonnières, des coulis balayeurs de rue . . .   (p. 356)

> [What good is surrealism? . . . You only have to look at the reality of this country with your eyes wide open and practically at every step, you come across men who transform into dogs or birds, and trees that begin to play musical scores. Life itself here is surrealist, gentlemen. Simply describing it as it is is sufficient, not as seen through the eyes of our regionalist poets, hungry for exoticism, but as seen through our own eyes, those of old blacks, hired hands, women coal carriers, Indian street sweepers . . .]

Many of the theoretical positions championed in *Eloge de la créolité* can be recognised here. The opening question challenges the very idea that European criteria are useful for evaluating Caribbean realities. The aestheticising canons of Surrealism are emptied of significance by the claim in this passage that every-day life offers a form of 'surreality' in its own right. The reversal effected here poeticises the everyday and justifies Confiant's constant emphasis on present-ing daily life in its unmediated forms. It also highlights the self-sufficiency of the internally generated vision (the 'vision intérieure' of the *Eloge* (p. 23)) that connotes both autonomy and self-acceptance. The French gaze (and the gaze of the regionalists assimilated to a French perspective) looks for poetry in the wrong place; its adherence to a 'French' imaginary blinds it to the poetry before its eyes. The creole gaze, by contrast, finds poetry everywhere because its vision is in harmony with a creole imaginary.

This dichotomy cannot be read as a simple binary opposition, however. The boundaries between the two perspectives on the world outlined here are porous, as the liminal mulatto character, Amédée Mauville, constantly illustrates. The passage quoted above is written in standard French because that is the idiom in which Amédée composes his 'Mémoires de céans et d'ailleurs' from which the comment is taken. Amédée belongs to one of the leading mulatto families of Fort-de-France, but on his return from his studies in France he finds it impos-sible to assume the role(s) that his position in society and his education have mapped out for him. He breaks with the 'society' and class into which he was born, refuses to take up a teaching post at the Lycée Schœlcher and pursues the bewitching Philomène into the creole milieu of Le Morne Pichevin. His integration into that milieu only jars when viewed from a 'French' perspective in which identity is associated with exclusion and an intolerance of difference. From a creole persepective Amédée's migration is not only tolerated it is *neces-sary* since creole identity is forged through such examples of the absorption of different forms of otherness. Amédée is part and parcel of the complex, com-posite whole that is creole culture. Just as the language is shared by all levels of creole society from *béké* to *couli*, (and has been constructed as an amalgam of all their varied contributions), so the culture itself has to be a mosaic in which *all* elements are represented.

Indeed, Confiant seems at pains to ensure that the mosaic of creole culture he presents is fully representative and he achieves this in a variety of ways. Within individual texts he uses devices such as intercalated narratives, often involving switches in narrative perspective and narrative voice. Amédée's 'Mémoires' are one case in point but other such intercalations frequently occur in other texts. *L'Archet du colonel* is particularly inventive in this respect as the third-person narration is interrupted by various distinctive 'documents' including a draft of a historical novel by Amédée, itself composed largely of various fictional 'cahiers' that take up the story of events in the post-Revolutionary Caribbean from the point of view of celebrated historical characters such as Delgrès,

Ignace and Pélage. The effect is one of transhistorical *collage* that allows an effective interrogation of official 'History' against a backdrop of a wider range of (often occulted) stories of resistance to colonial domination and subsequent assimilation. The staging of 'languages' and idioms is a key element of what might be seen as an attempt to creolise Caribbean historiography. But Confiant also tries to ensure that he illustrates the full mosaic of creole culture as he moves from text to text. Individuals from different social classes and all racial and cultural groups are depicted in their evolution through time in his narratives. This is not a case of tokenism and reflects a concern to demonstrate that ultimately the overlapping, intertwining identities cannot be disentangled to reveal any originary truth. The novel that explores such issues in greatest depth is undoubtedly *Eau de Café* (1991) in which the narrator seeks to unravel the enigma surrounding the identity of the symbolically named Antilia. His project is doomed to failure: the more he delves into the complicated genealogy of Eau de Café and that of his own step-mother, the birth mother of Antilia, the more it becomes clear that he is delving into an entanglement of ever-expanding narratives that bring no clarity whatsoever. Confiant's wish to represent all elements of the creole mosaic in his work stems from a concern to include all the stories that constitute the oral archive, but simply for their own sake, not so much as a way of explaining the present but perhaps simply with a view to demonstrating and celebrating the richness of the diverse, often mysterious origins of creole culture.

Edouard Glissant (Martinique, 1928–)

Edouard Glissant is probably the most original and influential francophone intellectual to emerge from the Caribbean in the course of the twentieth century. He has had a direct and palpable influence on the work of many of his contemporaries, including such major figures as Chamoiseau and Confiant. In a rather more diffuse way, his ongoing attempts to define an Antillian poetics can be seen as having helped ignite the flames of the *créolité* movement that provided the context within which any number of contemporary writers have grounded their work. The distance he quickly put between himself and the movement's identitarian proselytising has perhaps been equally influential. His scepticism about campaigns in favour of creole have not diverted attention away from the importance of creole language and culture, they have merely ensured that a more realistic appraisal has been made of the place creole occupies in Caribbean cultural life. This has helped to move the debate on to a different level and enriched its potential for inflecting attitudes to intercultural relationships. Glissant's refusal to essentialise Caribbean identity (the reproach frequently directed at *Négritude* and the underlying temptation the *créolité* movement has had to resist) is a key feature of his methodological approach.

Glissant's influence made itself felt locally through the work of the Institut Martiniquais d'Etudes, which he founded in the mid 1960s, and then more widely through 'essays' like *Le Discours antillais* and various works on poetics, particularly *Poétique de la relation*. Indeed, this general contribution to the theorising of cultural relations has been so important that it has tended to overshadow the significance of the substantial body of poetry, theatre and fiction he has produced alongside it. By way of entry into these complex, often rather hermetic, writings it is helpful to bear in mind that Glissant has little time for the notion of *understanding*. In 'Le chaos-monde, l'oral et l'écrit', Glissant elaborates on his reasons for being wary of the concept. His argument is developed by reference to the etymology of the French words *comprendre* and *compréhension* but Glissant would no doubt enjoy any increase in the opacity of the argument when it is developed in relation to the English word *understanding*, not least because 'under-standing' could be used to include a line of argumentation about hierarchies of knowledge, as they 'stand' in a position of inferiority or superiority to each other. The argument Glissant actually pursues is as follows:

> La question posée est la suivante: dans la magnifique perspective des cultures occidentales organisées autour de la notion de transparence, c'est-à-dire de la notion de compréhension, 'com-prendre', je prends avec moi, je comprends un être ou une notion, ou une culture, n'y a-t-il pas cette autre notion, celle de prendre, d'accaparer? Et le génie de l'Occident a été de nous faire accepter cela . . . moi je dis que ce génie est un génie trompeur, parce que dans *comprendre* il y a l'intention de prendre, de soumettre ce que l'on comprend à l'aune de sa propre mesure et de sa propre transparence.[33]

> [The question is as follows: from the magnificent perspective of Western cultures, organised around the notion of transparency, that is to say the notion of comprehension, 'com-prehend', I take with me, I comprehend a being or a notion or a culture, is there not also that other notion, of taking, of seizing for oneself? And the genius of the West has been to make us accept this . . . for my part, I say that this genius is a spirit that leads us into error, because within 'comprehend' there is the intention to seize, to submit the thing one comprehends to measurement by one's own yardstick and see it in the light of one's own transparency.]

Readers who set out to 'understand' his poetry, his fiction or his theoretical writings on a purely rational level, then, set themselves an objective that he would probably have difficulty sanctioning. The paradox here is evident. Readings, one way or another, are attempts to make sense of texts and this present brief engagement with Glissant's work is an attempt to argue that there exists a certain coherence to his writings that can be illuminated through commentary. This paradoxical starting point is useful nevertheless because it foregrounds the internal tensions that run through the whole of Glissant's *œuvre*: he consciously resists transparency and repeatedly extols the virtues of opacity, he generalises about the inadvisability of dealing in generalisations, he theorises about the insufficiency of theories, in short he resists the very medium of writing through which he works.

The 'transparency' Glissant so strongly objects to is at one and the same time linguistic and conceptual: it involves the reduction of diversity to a singular, unified epistemological frame of reference that is both monocultural and monolinguistic. By way of direct contrast, the opacity he champions is a positive attribute of 'otherness', its radical and irreducible difference. Glissant would argue that Western culture seeks to reduce perceived 'difference' by schemas through which it may be 'understood' (and thereby eliminated). The first footnote in *Le Discours antillais* reads: 'L'Occident n'est pas à l'ouest. Ce n'est pas un lieu, c'est un projet.' (p. 14) [The West is not 'to the west'. It is not a place, it's a project.] His own approach is to advocate respect for the opacity of 'otherness', appreciating it in its radical difference, and thus preserving diversity. His poetics of 'Relation' is characterised by a willingness to engage with radical otherness rather than seek to tame it through various strategies of assimilation. As Glissant explains, 'je n'ai pas besoin de comprendre un peuple, une culture, de la réduire à la transparence du modèle universel pour travailler avec, les aimer, les fréquenter, faire des choses avec.'[34] [I don't need to understand a people, a culture, I don't need to reduce it to the transparency of a universal model in order to work with them, to love them, to spend time with them, to do things with them].

As these comments on transparency and opacity indicate, Glissant's elaboration of a poetics is constantly informed by a politics of anti-imperialism. It is also predicated on a Marxian conception of culture as indissociably linked to, if not determined by, material conditions of life. So before turning our attention to Glissant's literary work, it is worth pursuing in a little more detail his analysis of the alienation that in his view characterises life in Martinique.

Glissant begins *Le Discours antillais* with a section entitled 'La dépossession' [Dispossession] in which he focuses on the multiple ways the inhabitants of the island have been obliged, coerced and duped into forms of fragile and insecure relationships with the land they inhabit. This lack of security can be traced back (or forwards) through historical circumstances such as slavery, plantation life, assimilation and departmentalisation, and invested with a socioeconomic rationale, but for Glissant it evokes a fundamentally cultural relationship: one which links the individual to the space he/she inhabits:

> Que l'espace martiniquais ne soit pas vécu globalement comme sécurisant par les Martiniquais, il est à peine besoin de le montrer. Ce n'est pas l'espace ancestral; le traumatisme de l'arrachement à la matrice originelle (l'Afrique) joue encore sourdement. Le rêve du retour à l'Afrique, qui a marqué les deux premières générations importées, a certes disparu de la conscience collective, mais il a été remplacé dans l'histoire subie par le mythe de la citoyenneté française: ce mythe contrarie l'enracinement harmonieux ou non de l'homme martiniquais dans sa terre.   (pp. 148–9)

> [It is hardly necessary to show that Martinicans do not, on the whole, enjoy a secure relationship with the space they inhabit. It is not the ancestral space; the traumatism of being snatched from the original womb (Africa) remains as a dull ache. The dream of the return to Africa that marked the first two generations of slaves has certainly disappeared from the collective consciousness, but it has been replaced, in the history they have endured, by the myth of French citizenship: this myth prevents Martinicans from feeling rooted, for good or ill, in their own soil.]

The uneasy relationship Martinicans (and by extension French Caribbeans in general) maintain with the space they inhabit is only one of the many forms of alienation that Glissant is at pains to identify throughout *Le Discours antillais*. Taking Martinique as his main source of examples, he argues that the economic, social and cultural history of the island has continued to reinforce an alienating disequilibrium among all sections of society. Former slaves (and, later, indentured workers from the Indian subcontinent) form the lower and most precarious strata of society. Their lingering sense of belonging to a homeland (Africa/India) from which they have been irreversibly cut off was eventually replaced by the pull exerted by metropolitan France itself (another distant mythical space), firstly as it offered the benefits of French citizenship and more recently, since departmentalisation in 1946, the more tangible benefits of social protection, health care and education. Glissant forcibly argues that the middle class (largely mixed-race mulattos) that emerged as a political force in the late nineteenth century quickly became a simulacrum with no real function in any effective power structures, as real power and decision-making is (and always has been) located elsewhere, in metropolitan France. What is true for political power has always been true of the economic realities of the plantation economy. The wealth of many *béké* families is not disputed, but Glissant argues that they have never evolved very far beyond the 'pillaging' mentality that characterised their original relationship with the island. They remain opportunistic profiteers who have never exercised control over the system of production; indeed, the logic of the colonial system demanded that the functional role of the *béké* was to act as agents for the transfer of wealth to the metropolis.

For Glissant, the incorporation of Martinique, Guadeloupe and Guyane into the French state when they became *départements d'outre mer* in 1946 marks the apotheosis of the colonial relationship: assimilation has been pushed to the extreme limit at which the absorption of the colony into the metropolis becomes possible. This swallowing up of the three Caribbean territories (along with La Réunion in the Indian Ocean) has subsequently been denounced by Glissant as 'une des formes les plus pernicieuses de colonisation: celle par quoi on *assimile* une communauté' (p. 21) (Glissant's italics) [one of the most pernicious forms of colonisation: that through which one *assimilates* a community]. Politically and economically the process is tantamount to zombification. It encourages a mentality of dependency that locates all forms of agency and initiative elsewhere, in the metropolitan space. Glissant's analysis has the Caribbean operating as a non-productive machine for transforming French state subsidies into private capital that is re-exported out of the region. The people themselves function only as consumers, incapable of assuming responsibility for their own lives in any meaningful or creative way. A bleak analysis indeed.

In *Le Discours antillais* identitarian issues are examined through social, economic, political and psychoanalytical models and theories to reveal types of alienation that are ultimately cultural in nature. To the extent that culture can be understood as the myriad ways in which a people interacts with its environment and thereby forges a sense of itself as a community, it is clear that the very concept of culture in the French Caribbean is particularly complex and problematic. The two key elements of the view of culture proposed here, 'environment' and 'community'/'people', are infinitely unstable in the Caribbean context. The monolithic, controlling presence of France makes this inevitable. Glissant's argument is that Martinicans can only begin the process of forming a community that is free, responsible and productive if it reverses the process of deculturation that is synonymous with assimilation to French norms and values. The closest Glissant comes to suggesting how this might be achieved in practical terms is to recommend an organic engagement with the Caribbean space and Caribbean partners. Thus the vision of *antillanité* he proposes involves a new way of inhabiting the Caribbean space rather than a new version of Caribbean identity. In more recent writings, *Poétique de la relation* and *Tout-monde* in particular, he has insisted more on strategies for escaping the impasse of the various forms of alienation identified in earlier work. Interrelatedness and tolerance of difference are key concepts of 'Relation' but they are invested with a philosophical almost mystical significance as they are deployed in a context of non-linear time and with an appeal to new ways of thinking about ontology: 'being' and 'existence'.

The poetry and fiction he has produced alongside his theoretical work interact with it in a variety of ways: his novels and poems stage many of the theoretical ideas and concepts, illustrate them, interrogate them and at times seem to act as the laboratory from which they emerge. The interrelatedness of 'Relation' that is stressed in later writings is nevertheless present from the outset in his fiction, in the sense that his novels are best viewed not as individual entities (singular, self-standing narratives) so much as periodic forays into a single imaginary archive. Michael Dash touches on this in his book on Glissant, when he writes of the early novels, *La Lézarde* (1958), *Le Quatrième Siècle* (1964) and *La Case du commandeur* (1981), 'There is a sense in which each work is a provisional utterance elaborating earlier themes and anticipating future ideas.'[35] But the point deserves to be made far more strongly than this that all his fiction prior to *Sartorius: le roman des Batoutos* (1999) reworks a relatively limited number of narrative events involving a relatively restricted number of characters. *La Lézarde* begins the cycle with an almost contemporaneous account of the political (and therefore in the context of Glissant, cultural) awakening of a group of Martinicans at the time of the 1946 elections. The action of the second novel, *Le Quatrième Siècle*, predates that of *La Lézarde* but sheds light on the intertwined family origins of many of the characters already presented in that novel.

Le Quatrième Siècle could be read as a genealogy of the Longoué and Béluse 'families' stretching back over six generations and starting with the arrival of the two 'ancestors' in Martinique in 1788, but the narrative resists such a way of reading history just as it ultimately works against the possibility of energising the narrative by appeal to stereotypical notions of conflict (Manichean, binary oppositions). The antagonism between the *béké* master, Laroche, and the runaway slave, Longoué, is marked by mutual respect as much as by more violent, conflictual emotions. Similarly, the antagonism between Longoué, the 'nègre marron' [runaway slave], and Béluse, the 'nègre de bitation' [plantation slave] (underscored by the antithetical strategies they adopt on arrival: absolute resistance from one [*marronnage*] and ostensible submission from the other), is real, but its cause is lost in an African past that can only be the subject of conjecture. The eventual merging of the two family lines in the person of Papa Longoué (whose mother is a Béluse) further complicates matters by evoking fusion where radical difference seems to be required. The 'lignées désordonnées des Longoué ou des Béluse, des Targin ou des Célat'[36] [chaotic lineages of the Longoué or the Béluse, of the Targin or the Célat] as they surface and undergo further development in *Malemort* (1975) or *Tout-monde*, confirm the view that the interrelatedness of the two families illustrates not legitimising lines of affiliation but chaotic exuberance. 'Les branchages de noms ne sont pas de généalogie, ils font brousse dans le Tout-monde' remarks Glissant in a comment on the names of characters in *Tout-monde* (p. 605) [the branching out of names does not make a family tree, it forms the undergrowth of 'Tout-monde']. The same is true of the recurring cluster of 'families' and the recurring group of principal characters (Longoué, Mathieu, Thaël and Mycéa), around which his fictional universe gravitates.

The chaotic profusion of this fictional universe is underscored by a cyclical rather than linear conception of time. The past and the future are not related sequentially partly because they are not conceived of as separate entities (any more than characters are portrayed as distinct individuals with characteristic features). The future repeats the past and echoes elements of it, just as the past contains the seeds of the future within it, and sets off reverberations that echo through the coming generations. Hence the past and the future interact the one upon the other rather like intermittent pulses of energy. Papa Longoué is a visionary (from a line of visionaries), capable of predicting the future (for example, when he foresees the danger of dogs to Valérie in *La Lézarde*, p. 83) but equally important is his role as guardian of the communal memory. Yet the traces of the past he uncovers for Mathieu (in *Le Quatrième Siècle*, in particular) seem to have been imagined or envisioned, perhaps 'predicted', from the present. This complex interweaving of time frames means that events are not simply narrated from a stable perspective. The frequency of references to dates in the novels provides a framework within which the narratives can be anchored, but dates ultimately also serve to set up a tension with the fundamental temporal instability that is the atmosphere in which events bathe, as they drift in and out of focus from text to text, repeating themselves, modifying themselves, and acquiring symbolic significance as they do so. The most poignant example is probably the recurring sequence of violent deaths recounted in *Malemort* (pp. 117–36). The bodies that rise and fall, punctuating Martinican history with their movement, form an unbroken and presumably unending chain, suggesting a single fatal event doomed to repeat itself. Time becomes the central character here, not the unindividuated victims of 'colonial' violence.

Similarly, landscape, trees and rivers constantly and persistently figure as constitutive elements of the human reality Glissant's writing seeks to evoke. The imagined land and the real land (of *Pays rêvé, pays réel* (1985)) are interdependent in the whole of Glissant's fictional output. In a colloquium held in Montreal in 1974, and reported in *Le Discours antillais*, Glissant explained the link thus:

> Le rapport à la terre, rapport d'autant plus menacé que la terre de la communauté est aliénée, devient tellement fondamental du discours, que le paysage dans l'œuvre cesse d'être décor ou confident pour s'inscrire comme constituant de l'être. Décrire le paysage ne suffira pas. L'individu, la communauté, le pays sont indissociables dans l'épisode constitutif de leur histoire. Le paysage est un personnage de cette histoire.   (p. 343)

> [The relationship with the land, a relationship all the more under threat to the extent that the community is alienated, becomes such a fundamental element of discourse that landscape in the work ceases to be a mere setting or a confidant and is inscribed as constituting being itself. Describing the landscape is no longer sufficient. The individual, the community, the land are indissociable within the moment in time at which they produce their story. Landscape is a character in this story.]

If Glissant's poetics of diversity explains the 'logic' of his insistence on the interconnectedness of time, Caribbean landscape and a certain conception of 'being', language too has a role to play in elucidating its distinctiveness. The interface between the oral traditions of creole culture and the written tradition of French culture is the space where Glissant's involvement in literary activity is conducted, as a search for an appropriate idiom ('un langage'):

> Mon langage tente de se construire à la limite de l'écrire et du parler; de signaler un tel passage . . . J'évoque une synthèse, synthèse de la syntaxe écrite et de la rythmique parlée, de l''acquis' de l'écriture et du 'réflexe' oral, de la solitude d'écriture et de la participation au chanter commun.
> (*Le Discours antillais*, pp. 439–40)

> [My language seeks to constitute itself at the limits between writing and speech; to point out the passage from the one to the other . . . I foreground a synthesis, the coming together of the syntax of writing and the rhythms of speech, of what is 'accumulated' in the written form and the 'instinct' of the oral, of the solitude of writing and the participation in a common melody.]

It is also an interface that he attempts to incorporate *dramatically* into his fiction. Within his texts, a range of linguistic registers, styles and varieties attest to this effort, as does 'le cri' that frequently echoes through the Caribbean landscapes he evokes, bearing witness to this concrete facet of creole experience that is 'la parole créole'.

Ernest Pépin (Guadeloupe, 1950–)

The *créolité* movement has generally been associated with the island of Martinique although the writings of Ernest Pépin, from neighbouring Guadeloupe, share many of the interests and ideas the movement has sought to promote. As is so often the case, Ernest Pépin began his writing career by publishing poetry before turning his attention to narratives and the novel. As Daniel Delas has remarked, 'son œuvre en prose reste celle d'un poète, tant elle est marquée par l'amour de la langue'.[37] [his prose writings remain those of a poet, so much are they marked by a love for language]. It is certainly the case that the originality of Pépin's work lies not so much in the way he structures his narratives or in the fact that he provides fresh or original insights into the range of issues that preoccupy his fellow Caribbeans; the interest his work has aroused is related far more to a particular type of engagement with language as a material to be worked upon. His texts are heavily 'creolised' and, in this respect, bear some resemblance to the writings of contemporaries like Confiant and Chamoiseau. His first novel, *L'Homme-au-Bâton* (1992) hypostatises an important point made by Confiant about the creole language: 'le lexique créole est structuré à partir du vocabulaire de la sexualité'[38] [the lexis of creole is structured on the vocabulary of sexuality]. The hypersexuality of the protagonist of the novel can thus be understood as representing a collective, rather than an individual subjectivity, not only because he corresponds to the popular Caribbean imaginary in terms of sexual activity, but also because the creolisation of French through which he is portrayed itself involves a constant appeal to sexual imagery. It is almost as though what motivates the narrative for Pépin is not so much an ostensible storyline, an unfolding drama, as certain features of language that he wishes to exploit and lay bare. These features of language seem to generate the narrative, control its tempo and determine its direction.

The point can perhaps be more clearly understood by reference to his second major novel, *Tambour-Babel* (1996), where the interrelationship between registers of language and the narrative thread is a central feature of the work. Reduced to its bare essentials, the storyline of *Tambour-Babel* is not particularly striking. It centres on the Guadeloupian tradition of the *tanbouyès*, virtuoso drummers who form a loose-knit community and who practise their art in occasional ceremonial gatherings, *lewoz*. The human drama is supplied by the predicament of Eloi, an exceptionally gifted drummer whose son, Napo, considers that he has not inherited his father's gift. Against the wishes of his wife, Hermancia, Eloi decides to transmit the knowledge he possesses to the hypocritical, scheming Bazile who, in due course and as Hermancia has predicted, ruthlessly supplants his former mentor. When Eloi's gift eventually deserts him he is left a broken man in the eyes of the whole community. It is at this point that Napo chances to undergo a spiritual transformation and emerges from a series of mystical encounters with a magical figure, 'le Commandeur', having acquired the skill as a drummer to metaphorically destroy his father's tormentor and assume his own, 'rightful' place as a master of the art of *tanbouyè*. This rather simplistic story of jeopardised cultural transmission from father to son, of battle between the righteous Napo and the hypocritical Bazile, even when overlain with a veneer of moral rectitude, is really a pretext for the main purpose of the novel, that of serving as a panegyric to the art of drumming. The tradition is portrayed in the text as the creole art *par excellence*, mainly because of the myriad rhythmical and musical influences it is capable of absorbing and internalising. It is also clothed in a certain mystery and prestige by virtue of its mystical links with African origins: it is portrayed as providing a bridge to a past that has otherwise been lost. But these rather abstract comments on the cultural context in which it is possible to place the art of drumming are also something of a side-show. The real heart of the novel lies in the set-piece passages of purple prose in which Pépin dramatises and depicts some of the virtuoso drumming performances. Paradoxically but inevitably, the text displays Pépin's own linguistic (literary) virtuosity as the only means available to convey a sense of the musical virtuosity of the fictional performances. And, naturally, drumming not only lays claim to sketching something like an ethics of *créolité* (as illustrated by the sententious pronouncements of 'le Commandeur', pp. 188–9), it also assumes all the attributes of a language in its own right. Or rather, to the extent that it offers a principle for incorporating, ingesting, hybridising, in short for *creolising*, a range of distinct styles of 'language', drumming is the 'tambour-babel' that gives the novel its title.

In *Le Tango de la haine* (1999) Pépin displays a similar linguistic virtuosity as he embroiders on an equally 'thin' storyline: the failed marriage of Nika and Abel. As in the earlier novel, several sections are narrated by different characters, partly in order to provide contrasting perspectives on the same material, but partly, too, in order to enrich the novel with the co-presence of contrasting linguistic worlds. The 'voice' of Nika may contrast quite starkly with the 'voice' of Abel at times, but ultimately the distinction between the two can be located in the verbal delirium that seems to be the outlet for Nika's hatred of her former partner. Given that both Abel and Nika are fundamentally amoral characters who only acquire some sense of moral responsibility (almost as a matter of narrative expediency) as the novel progresses, there is no human drama whatsoever in this text. The novel opens with a 'déclaration de haine' and little of substance has changed by the end. Indeed, the very persistence of Nika's lust for revenge comes to mark it out as a form of madness, an obsession that constantly feeds upon itself. Pépin's spasmodic attempts to link his narrative to a wider discourse on Caribbean life and claim a general significance for the mutually destructive relationship he describes are unconvincing. Towards the close of the novel, for example, Abel muses, 'N'était-ce pas ce monde-là où chacun se voulait sur une scène, à la vue de tous, où chacun s'imaginait être une puissance à lui tout seul ... qui nourrissait la haine de Nika?' (p. 221) [Was it not this world they inhabited in which everyone wanted to be centre stage, in full view, in which everyone saw themselves as a power in their own right ... that was feeding Nika's hatred?] But the striking aspect of this argument is that it mirrors Pépin's own practice as a writer: the verbal virtuosity he displays (in this particular novel, largely in standard French), is both self-celebratory and self-conscious, an end in itself and the apparent purpose of the work.

Maryse Condé (Guadeloupe, 1937–)

Despite their many differences the identitarian discourses of *Négritude*, *antillanité* and *créolité* all share at least one common characteristic: they all tend towards a similar goal of identity *construction*. Each proposes a theoretical model that gives value to a possible version of Caribbean identity and acts as a form of therapy against the alienating discourse of (post)colonial domination. Maryse Condé's entire output as a creative writer resists being subsumed into such projects of identity construction. Her constant preoccupation is the *deconstruction* of the various subject positions available to the francophone Caribbean individual, particularly women. This approach finds its vindication perhaps in the fact that francophone Caribbean literature has been largely dominated by male writers. Simone Schwarz-Bart (especially the novels *Pluie et vent sur Télumée Miracle* (1972) and *Ti Jean L'Horizon* (1979)) stands out as a notable exception, but one that confirms rather than tests the rule.

The fact that Condé has chosen not to engage with the grand identitarian 'narratives' that other writers espouse does not mean that she has other aims than to resist the alienating discourses of oppression, or that curing the ills they continue to cause is of no interest to her. Quite the contrary. But what characterises her own approach to dealing with such fundamental issues is her distrust of the materials with which she is expected to work. She interrogates the tools at her disposal, ironises about the categories that received wisdom offers her, and deconstructs the cultural and discursive frames of reference within which identity is supposedly located. Indeed, as Jeannie Suk has suggested, her independence, not to say truculence, with regard to some of the theoretical debates that her work engages with, has brought her a degree of 'notoriety':

> She has gained some notoriety for her tendency to react to and contest in her writing an array of contexts, traditions, and issues: for example, debates about Antillean literary culture (*Négritude, antillanité, créolité*), feminism, race, identity, Africa, and postcolonial literature.[39]

Condé's writings frequently invite yet defy attempts by critics to seek parallels with her own biography. Having spent long periods of her life outside her native Guadeloupe, which she left at the age of sixteen in 1953, Condé lived in France, England, West Africa and the United States, before finally returning to Guadeloupe in 1986. Whether any of these travels can be seen as definitive periods of 'exile' or 'return' is debatable, of course, but they inevitably feed into the creative sensibility of the author. Françoise Lionnet has set great store by such 'nomadism' and has argued that it represents a fusing of individualism with a new version of humanism.[40] Whether 'nomadism' has any intrinsic merits, or indeed whether one needs to have travelled at all in order to feel attuned to the fluid conception of identity it implies, are debatable points. Where Lionnet is far more convincing, however, is in her appeal to anthropologists and cultural critics like Dominique Schnapper, Edouard Glissant and James Clifford to corroborate a view of identity as, respectively, 'ongoing creation', 'relation', 'conjectural rather than essential'.[41]

Condé's fictions are often described as 'quests' for identity and, at some level, anxieties about identity are certainly an omnipresent feature of her writing. Rosélie Thibaudin, protagonist of *Histoire de la femme cannibale* (2003), one of her most recent novels, is 'seeking herself' in much the same way that Véronica Mercier did in Condé's first novel, *Hérémakhonon* (1976). Yet these quests have no substantive external goal. Both Rosélie and Véronica are involved in journeys of self-discovery, trying to understand the significance of where they have been as much as trying to decide where the onward journey should take them. Véronica's journey from Guadeloupe to Africa via Paris is less an itinerary as such than a coding of the three geographical elements that give shape to the 'cultural nightmare of perpetual unbelonging', that one critic has identified as her predicament.[42] The journeys that have led Rosélie from Guadeloupe to Capetown are not depicted as a matter of active choice: agency is a male prerogative in her experience. After studies in France she has simply followed the various men in her life, first to West Africa, then New York and finally to the Cape. Place is of no significance to Rosélie. She lives in South Africa because her partner Stephen brought her there, and she remains even after his murder because, even in his grave, he alone represents 'home' to her: 'mon seul pays, c'était Stephen' [my only country was Stephen] she remarks at one point (p. 43).

For both these female protagonists the unfolding narratives provide scope for inner journeys where it is less the landscapes through which they pass than the maps by which they navigate that are subjected to scrutiny. Véronica has to come to recognise that her search for ancestral roots in Africa has been a (necessary) detour, side-tracking her from a confrontation with the unresolved dualities of her own sexual, class and racial origins that may allow some form of resolution of her 'identity problem'. Her journey has provided an opportunity, not to find the roots of her alienation but to re-examine the *terms* in which the problem of identity is couched. At the close of the novel she leaves for Paris, not 'cured' but having reached 'a new form of knowledge'.[43] This almost exactly matches the trajectory of Rosélie's experience in the novel written more than thirty years later. Rosélie is led, almost despite herself, to delve into the private life of her partner after his brutal death, a process which obliges her to re-evaluate her experience. This is partly a matter of hermeneutics, a reinterpreting of the significance of her own past as she discovers that the man to whom she had surrendered control of her life had been a self-obsessed manipulator of others, and a practising homosexual. Like Véronica, however, in order to move forward Rosélie must first throw away the old grids of interpretation and remap her existence afresh. She needs to go back to the beginning and start again. The 'identity problem' in her case had involved a constantly repeated experience of feeling excluded or invisible; she is assigned to oblivion through what she sees as the double negative of her race and her gender. Stephen's dismissal of such feelings as figments of her imagination had led her to constantly deny and repress them. Her dependency on Stephen (his colonisation of her?) is thus closely linked to her own complicity with the control he exercised, and her acceptance of the limited range of roles he allowed her to play. At the close of the novel, Rosélie decides to remain in Capetown, no longer as a mark of fidelity to Stephen but to pursue her own career as a painter. This may smack of 'strategic essentialism' (appealing to the very stereotypes and essentialist arguments that have been deployed as a means of oppression, in order to counter that oppression),[44] a way of resolving an 'identity problem' rather than as a provisional, enabling tactic in an ongoing negotiation of identity. But for Condé the close of both novels signals only a partial and provisional closure, a stage in the evolution of the 'quests for identity' she describes.

In her reading of *Hérémakhonon* (1976) Gayatri Spivak has cautioned against the sort of reductive analysis that is based on character study.[45] Spivak's own impressive analysis of how time is 'staged' within the novel enables a more nuanced reading of the text as a conflict of '"mémoires" subalternes' [subaltern 'memories'], a reference to the subaltern status accorded to women, particularly in Indian society where much of Spivak's work has been conducted. Yet the focus on characters as part of any analysis of Condé's work seems justified to the extent that their day-to-day experience, often rooted in the failures of family and community life, are frequently among the structuring devices she employs. Her work exploits the tensions that are set up when any attempt is made to inscribe basically unheroic, human experiences within a wider context of historical significance. This explains why she is equally at home in writing historical epic on the grand scale, as evidenced by the success of the best-selling novel *Ségou* (1984 and 1985) and the epic sweep of *La Vie scélérate* (1987), as she is in writing personalised accounts of individual lives. Nor need the two genres be seen as distinct. Their hybridisation is another way of exploiting the same tensions: *Moi, Tituba sorcière . . .* (1986) is an account of the life of the eponymous heroine, caught up in the hysteria of the Salem witch hunts at the end of the seventeenth century. The fate of Tituba is sealed, not by her involvement in withcraft, however defined, but as a victim of the march of History embodied in the narrow perceptions of 'otherness' that a dominant, puritanical Christian ethos permitted.

Likewise *Les Derniers Rois mages* (1992) intermingles the everyday and the historical in bathetic counterpoint. In this case, an historical event, King Béhanzin of Dahomey's period of exile in Martinique (1894–1906), lives on in the confused memories of his descendants. Their ritualistic commemoration of the king's death each December, and other attempts to hang on to the royal connection through acts of memory, are a celebration of an essentialised conception of identity. Royal blood is, after all, a defining characteristic. But with the passage of time it becomes increasingly difficult to hang on to the historical significance of the connection with the past. For the king's great-grandson, Spéro, modernity, the demands of daily life, and a catalogue of failed relationships empty the historical connection of any meaning. Memories fade, texts and testimonies are dispersed, while the doubt grows as to whether the real legacy of the king was not his callous and unexplained abandonment of the son he had fathered while exiled on the island: 'Roi africain ou pas, le papa de Djéré s'était comporté comme tous les autres nègres de la terre. Il ne s'était pas occupé de son enfant. Il l'avait laissé derrière lui à la charge de sa seule pauvre maman.' (p. 20) [African king or not, Djéré's father had behaved just like all the other negroes on earth. He hadn't taken care of his child. He'd left him behind to be looked after by his poor mother all alone.] Spéro's own worries about his parenting skills echo through the second part of the novel, 'C'est vrai qu'il avait été un mauvais père?' (pp. 197, 209 and 235) [Is it true he'd been a bad father?], confirming that identity is negotiated in the ethical contexts of interpersonal and family relations as much as through lines of blood.

Traversée de la mangrove, the first novel Condé wrote following her return to Guadeloupe in 1986, has also been read as a novel primarily concerned with 'the dynamics of identity'. Many critics have pointed to the novel's structural similarities to Faulkner's *As I Lay Dying*, since the narrative is composed of a series of distinct testimonies from the various villagers of Rivière au Sel as they attend the wake of one Francis Sancher/Francisco Sanchez. There are echoes too of García Marquez's *Chronicle of a Death Foretold* since the death of the protagonist that will dominate the narrative is a 'given' at the outset. The mystery surrounding Sanchez's death pervades the various interventions but it is overshadowed by the mystery surrounding his identity. Lionnet describes him as:

> Neither hero nor antihero, Sanchez is an 'everyman': an archetypal inhabitant of the Caribbean archipelago, with his uncertain origins; his multiple geographic, emotional, and sexual attachments; his adventurous, rebellious nomadism; and the fragility that often characterises a dissatisfied intellectual.[46]

Unsurprisingly, the overlapping, contradictory testimonies that reconstitute some of the fragments of the man's life serve to shed as much light on the collective identity of the village as they do on the person of the interloper whose death unites and divides them in equal measure. The key to Sanchez's identity would seem to lie in the obscurity, indeterminacy and absence of roots that are characteristic of the man. Like paths that lead into the mangrove swamp ('traces' in Antillean French) the testimonies are partial contributions to a whole picture that can never be grasped in its entirety, just as the mangrove swamp can never be traversed, without destroying the swamp itself. In the words of Vilma, 'On ne traverse pas la mangrove. On s'empale sur les racines des palétuviers.' (p. 192) [One does not cross the mangrove swamp. One is impaled on the roots of the mangroves.]

On two occasions in *Le Cœur à rire et à pleurer* (1999), in those true tales from her childhood, Condé describes how her attempts to write about people close to her caused not the expected pleasure but acute pain. The first example was her response to a school assignment requiring a description of her best friend, the second was a pen portrait of her mother, written on her own initiative as a birthday gift (pp. 40–3 and pp. 82–5). Both had catastrophic effects. Her description of her friend, Yvelise, as neither pretty nor intelligent, was adjudged to have been motivated by nastiness rather than honesty. It almost destroyed the friendship. Similarly, the long text she prepared and recited to her mother to mark her birthday was the cause of a rift which, in the text ironically entitled 'Bonne fête, maman!' [Happy birthday, mummy!], contains no moment of closure, no scene of reconciliation: 'C'est comme ça que tu me vois?' (p. 84) [Is that how you see me?], her mother asks before leaving the room in tears. These early instances of writing are arguably symptomatic of something fundamental in Condé's approach to her creative work: the urge to tell her version of the 'truth' overrides all other considerations. It would be disingenuous to see these incidents as examples of a childhood blindness to the effect her words have on her audience. Rather, the effect is precisely what motivates the writing: Condé writes at the interface between conflicting perspectives on personal, collective, Caribbean and ultimately human identity, in ways that are intended to disturb and unsettle.

Haiti

The literary evolution of Haiti, like the social and political history of the island, often appears to be radically out of synchronism with the rest of the Caribbean and the wider world beyond. The early and historic distinctions of being the first colony to win independence from France, the first modern nation to free itself from slavery and the first army to inflict a miltary defeat on Napoleonic forces (as early as 1804) left Haiti in a position to engage with the opportunities and the pitfalls of autonomy decades before the conquest of Algeria had even taken place and many decades before the vast French empire in sub-Saharan Africa had begun to be carved out. The attempt to identify a distinctive cultural identity, not to speak of appropriate forms of social and political organisation, thus began at the very beginning of the nineteenth century in Haiti. The interrogations that would feed into debates about *Négritude, antillanité, créolité, québécité* and so on throughout the twentieth century were already being formulated in the decades following independence in Haiti.

The natural urge to shower praise on those who had fought for the island's freedom was part of a self-affirmatory tendency that paradoxically drew heavily on an admiration for French civilisation and French culture. By associating themselves with the high culture of France Haitians were able to counter racist prejudices about the inferiority of blacks and the backwardness of black culture. So Haitian respect for 'book culture' stems in part from these rather inglorious motives. By imitating French literary models, including the highly stylised rhetoric and the Neoclassical imagery of the time, and showing a slavish respect for correct usage in speech and writing Haitians were demonstrating to the world that they should and could command respect. The poetry of Jules-Solime Milscent, published in the review he founded in 1817, *L'Abeille haytienne*, is characteristic of this vein of imitative writing. Only gradually did self-affirmation begin to look inwards, towards the tropical landscapes and lifestyles of Haiti, rather than to France. The idea of a literature dealing with *le vécu haïtien* was a subject for debate as early as the 1830s: it was proposed, for example, by writers such as the Nau brothers through a newspaper they had founded in 1837, *Le Républicain*. It was not until much later in the century, however, that Oswald Durand, who is credited with writing the first poem in creole, 'Choucoune', produced significant work celebrating the everyday realities of life on the island. His poetry, including 'Choucoune', also exposes some of the social and racial prejudices that inform later Haitian writings:

> Gnou p'tit blanc vini rivé,
> P'tit barb'roug', bell' figur' rose,
> Montr'sous côté, bell chivé . . .
> Malheur-moin, li qui la cause! . . .
> Li trouvé Choucoun' joli . . .
> Li parlé francé, Choucoun' aimé-li . . .[47]

> [A little whiteman came along,
> With a reddish beard and a pink face,
> A pocket watch and fine soft hair,
> He's the cause of my despair! . . .
> He thought my Chicoune pretty . . .
> Spoke French to her and Chicoune loved him.]

The invasion of Haiti by American troops in 1915 was seen by Haitians as a reversal of the overthrow of colonial rule that was the wellspring of national pride. Naturally it inflected the literary preoccupations of the island quite dramatically. In the years leading up to the take-over a flourishing literature had begun to develop in both poetry and the novel. During the latter years of the century a group of poets taking their inspiration from the French Symbolists had begun to publish in *La Ronde*, replaced after 1915 by *La Nouvelle Ronde*. The direction chosen by these poets, among them Etzer Vilaire, and later Georges Sylvain and Etienne Laforest, was away from an engagement with Haitian realities towards a literature inspired by an exaggerated love of things French and the vaguely mystical abstractions in vogue in the Paris rather than the Port-au-Prince of the day. This was certainly one way of expressing their contempt for the American invaders, but the craving for endorsement from France in matters of literary and linguistic taste must clearly be viewed as a form of voluntary subservience to the spectre of the former colonial masters. A different, practically antithetical, type of political commitment was in evidence in prose writings, particularly in a series of articles published by the hugely influential Jean Price-Mars and later collected in a single volume, *Ainsi parla l'Oncle* (1928).

Price-Mars has often been cited as one of the forebears of Césairian and Senghorian *Négritude*. His views were articulated in a series of articles and conferences that proved highly controversial, not so much for their appeal to a notion of Haitian cultural authenticity as for the fact that they identified its roots in popular culture. He sought to rehabilitate the originary African culture that formed the bedrock of Caribbean culture by arguing that it was merely different from, rather than inferior to, European culture. This argument was not itself unacceptable to the elite of Haitian society. What was far more difficult for them to accept was the suggestion that the popular Haitian culture of the masses, including voodoo practices (which Price-Mars argued constituted a religion rather than a set of superstitions) and the whole oral tradition of folk tales, proverbs and riddles, was equally respectable. Price-Mars's ideological positions on Haitian cultural authenticity had a distinctly popular political content that made few concessions to the island's established elites. While they continued to look to France for inspiration and approval, Price-Mars looked to the masses and recognised the African roots evident on their culture. The duality that is evident in these diverging views found expression in one of the most celebrated poems of the period, Léon Laleau's 'Trahison', from *Musique Nègre*:

> Ce cœur obsédant, qui ne correspond
> Pas avec mon langage et mes costumes,
> Et sur lequel mordent, comme un crampon,
> Des sentiments d'emprunt et des coutumes
> D'Europe, sentez-vous cette souffrance
> Et ce désespoir à nul autre égal
> D'apprivoiser avec des mots de France
> Ce cœur qui m'est venu du Sénégal? (p. 9)

> [This restless heart that corresponds neither
> To my language nor my way of dressing,
> And into which are biting, like a vice,
> Borrowed feelings and customs borrowed
> From Europe, can you not feel this pain
> And this despair, comparable to no other,
> That comes from taming with French words
> A heart that came to me from Senegal?]

Price-Mars's thinking fed directly into the *indigéniste* movement of the 1930s and 1940s. *Indigénisme* is often summarily dismissed as equating to the novel of Haitian peasant life and peasant values. In fact it was a more eclectic movement that readily combined with other ideological currents, including *noirisme* and strands of surrealist and Marxist thinking. *La Revue Indigène*, published briefly from 1927 to 1928, provided a melting pot for these diverse ideological encounters. *Noirisme* proved to have the longest political legacy. It combined the black nationalist outlook gaining ground in the USA with a radicalised version of Price-Mars's appeal to African roots, translating them into a racially based politics that would eventually provide an ideological foundation for the long period of dictatorship of *Papa Dok* Duvalier. In literary terms, these ideas found their most convincing developments in the poetry of Clément Benoit, Frank Foucher, Jean-François Brierre and Jacques Roumain, but especially in a number of influential novels, particularly Roumain's *Gouverneurs de la Rosée* (1944) and Jacques Stephen Alexis's *Compère Général Soleil* (1955). Roumain's dual background as a militant Marxist and trained anthropologist is in evidence in the novel that set the tone for the whole *indigéniste* movement. The protagonist, Manuel, is engaged in a rural version of a workers' struggle to overcome factionalism among the peasantry and improve difficult working conditions. The triumph of the proletariat is ensured once Manuel discovers a spring that will allow them to irrigate the land. But a newly discovered awareness of the need for solidarity among the peasants is required before their triumph is sealed. The novel ends on an optimistic note despite the murder of Manuel. Interwoven with this rather schematic Marxist scenario are scenes of daily life typical of the rural setting Roumain elected to present: details of voodoo ceremonies, wakes, cock fights and collective agricultural working practices. Linguistically too the novel is innovative in its exploitation of a hybrid language that is recognisably French but which draws on the resources of rhythms, syntax and lexis of creole.

Jacques Stephen Alexis came to prominence as a student activist militating against the régime of President Lescot in 1946. A contributor to the newspaper, *La Ruche*, along with the poets Carl Brouard and René Depestre, the group succeeded in overthrowing the government. Alexis's deep commitment to politics is reflected in *Compère Général Soleil*, a novel that has many similarities with *Gouverneurs de la Rosée*, not least through its portrayal of awakening political consciousness, this time in the milieu of the urban proletariat. The protagonist, Hilarion, like Manuel is assassinated but the suggestion is that his struggle against the forces of oppression has opened up channels of resistance that will be pursued by a new generation of workers. The novel is a historical account of life in Port-au-Prince in the late 1930s and as such portrays a specific moment in the political life of Haiti. In subsequent works, *L'Espace d'un cillement* (1959) and the collection of short stories *Romancero aux étoiles* (1960), for example, Alexis's political commitment seeks to express itself through an aesthetic of magical realism which he considered as emanating from a peculiarly Haitian view of the world.

The coming to power of the Duvalier régime in 1957 led to an exodus of writers and intellectuals fleeing into exile, largely in France, Africa, the USA and Canada. Much of the literature of the Haitian diaspora that was subsequently written in exile exemplifies the transcultural preoccupations that began to appear in second- and third-generation 'immigrant' writers in the metropolitan centres of former colonial powers. Their cultural 'otherness' as exiles in foreign lands could be (and no doubt was) assigned an exotic value by their various host communities. In many cases, however, it was channelled into writing that insisted on highlighting the exchanges that occur whenever there is cultural contact. Such an emphasis on reciprocity favours mutual interaction between the observer and the observed, or at very least allows the exile to expose the host community's blind spots, the points where cultural differences become dramatically significant. Certain texts by Haitian 'expatriates', Roger Dorsinville (Senegal), Jean-Claude Charles or Louis-Philippe Dalembert (France), Gérard Etienne or Dany Laferrière (Quebec), tap this vein to great effect. Other texts, sometimes from the same writers, exploit the space and freedom of exile to recreate the horrors of Haitian political and social violence under Duvalier: Marie Chauvet (in the USA), René Depestre and Jean Métellus (in France), Gérard Etienne and Emile Ollivier (in Quebec).

Given the readiness with which the Duvaliers hunted down and murdered any intellectuals displaying a tendency to write 'committed literature', it is not surprising that writers who chose to remain in Haiti gravitated towards a type of literary expression that would not bring them into direct conflict with the régime. By and large this meant poetry rather than prose, especially the novel, and increasingly work in creole rather than French. As early as 1962, a group of young poets founded *Haïti littéraire* through which they published a highly personal type of poetry in a style that probably escaped censure because it proved a little too hermetic for Duvalier's henchmen, the *tontons macoutes*. Many of their number, including Anthony Phelps and Roland Morisseau, eventually preferred a life of exile in Canada. René Philoctète, another member of the group tasted exile only to return to Haiti and join the *spiralisme* movement with Frankétienne and Jean-Claude Fignolé. *Spiralisme* would claim to be a type of writing practice rather than a literary aesthetic. It offered a form of response to the Duvalier dictatorship, but rather than directly countering the *noiriste* ideology underpinning the régime, it proposed instead a commitment to writing as an anarchic activity enacting fundamentally poetic forms of rebellion and chaos whilst simultaneously rejecting all forms of authority and all forms of constraint. Frankétienne's imposing but unclassifiable work, *L'Oiseau schizophone* (1993), is typical of the movement's conscious mixing of literary genres, levels of consciousness, styles of writing and linguistic innovation.

In a pertinent comment about where recent decades have left Haitian literature Daniel Delas evokes the violent clashes of the Duvalier years and the profound wounds they have inflicted on Haitian society before concluding:

> on pourrait affirmer à bon droit que la littérature haitienne a plus de points communs avec la littérature africaine d'après les indépendances – presque partout confrontée aux dictatures les plus sanglantes – qu'avec la littérature des Antilles françaises, 'protégées' de ces perversions politiques par le statut départemental.[48]

> [we would be quite within our rights to claim that Haitian literature has far more in common with African literature of the post-independence period – confronted on every hand with the bloodiest of dictatorships – than with the literature of the French Caribbean islands, sheltered from political perversions of this sort by their status as French *départements*].

The chronological 'regression' Delas seems to be sketching here is an ironic reversal of the chronological 'advantage' Haiti had enjoyed in earlier times, following its own independence in 1804. Yet the movements, migrations and various types of cultural exchange that the creation of a Haitian diasporic literature has brought in its train seem somehow more contemporary, and closer too to the transcultural concerns of Glissant and Chamoiseau than any postcolonial interrogations of identity ever could be.

Conclusion

One of the key premises of this book has been that the term 'francophone literature' can be conceptualised as a branch of postcolonial literature, rather than as being somehow connected to the national literature of France. In his important book, *Postcolonial Criticism*, Nicholas Harrison has argued that the term 'francophone literature', 'freighted as it is with confused assumptions about "representativity", French, literature and national identity, is redundant'. He comes to this conclusion because he believes that the ways in which languages are shared across space and time are too complex to be explained in terms of 'a general identity'.[1] So what Harrison is really baulking at is the notion of a general francophone identity, not the complexity of the overlapping histories or the diversity of subject positions that may be discernible within any given francophone text. Whether or not it is preferable to think of the body of texts discussed here as forming a single literature or several distinct literatures, then, remains an open question. But it is not one that simply disappears when we choose to approach the literature with the preoccupations of postcolonial theory uppermost in our minds.

In the book that is generally accredited with having launched the discipline of postcolonial studies, *Orientalism*, Edward Saïd's argument centres on discursive practices. The Orient comes to be constituted as an object of Western discourse through the practice and performance of various types of discourse *about* the Orient. Postcolonial theory has never shied away from the circularity of this argument even though it has fuelled some of the fiercest criticism of postcolonialism as an area of enquiry about the developing East (or the South), based in universities located in the West (or North), that is overly preoccupied with texts and theoretical discourse rather than practical problems and the implementation of solutions. Yet Saïd's insight remains as valid as ever. The discourses that constitute and sustain 'official' *francophonie*, that seek to posit it as the very type of 'general identity' that Harrison presumably finds inappropriate and inadequate, can only be exposed by the very reasoning that Saïd invokes in his work on Orientalism.

One of the great dangers of appealing to postcolonial theory as a way of approaching francophone literature, however, is that too much emphasis may be placed on the first term (postcolonial) and that the second term (literature) will be forgotten completely. In other words, we would do well to remember that francophone literature is not only postcolonial, it is also literature. To forget this is to risk creating a classificatory ghetto for any text of non-metropolitan origin. And if we wish to obviate this risk, the way to do so is to seek to examine francophone texts first and foremost as examples of literature. Postcolonial theory provides the tools for reading texts in ways that expose the interconnectedness of political, economic and cultural dimensions of their textuality. What we do not yet have is a postcolonial poetics that will allow the *literarity* of francophone texts to be the dominant strand of enquiry when it is deemed appropriate.

The tendency, still relatively prevalent within French academia, loosely to identify francophone literature as an exotic offshoot of a national literary scene alone capable of generating criteria of taste and value will be increasingly challenged as the world becomes ever more globalised. The forces that led to the rise of national literatures in post-Enlightenment Europe have been irredeemably weakened in recent decades. The future for French literature is not to cast itself as the vaguely mystical expression or representation of a national spirit that is itself becoming more of a fiction with each passing day. Its future is more likely to lie in the problematisation of its own multilayered identities and overlapping histories thus connecting with the more mainstream preoccupations of francophone literature. Such a process had been predicted as early as 1899 by Léopold de Saussure in his *Psychologie de la colonisation française*:

> A la limite l'assimilation risque même de se faire dans le sens inverse de celui qui se trouve officiellement préconisé. Ce n'est plus le colonisateur qui intègre le colonisé dans ses institutions, ses croyances et ses mœurs, mais ce sont les institutions, les croyances et les mœurs de l'Europe qui, remodelées par les mentalités locales se transforment, s'altèrent et se dégradent au contact des mentalités indigènes.[2]

> [Assimilation even runs the risk of working in the opposite direction to that which is expected in official circles. It is no longer the coloniser who integrates the colonised native into his institutions, his beliefs and his system of morals, it is these same European institutions, beliefs and moral systems which, re-defined by local influences, are transformed, altered and degraded through contact with the world view of the natives.]

Almost a century later this idea was reiterated by the American-based, Ghanaian academic K. A. Appiah, in terms that unfortunately echo, albeit ironically, the old imagery of contamination, 'If there is a lesson in the broad shape of this circulation of cultures, it is surely that we are all already contaminated by each other', he writes.[3] The richness and diversity of francophone literature today would argue that it is high time that the contact across cultures that it makes possible should be viewed in terms of enrichment rather than contamination.

Notes

Introduction

1. David Murphy, 'De-centring French studies: towards a postcolonial theory of Francophone cultures', *French Cultural Studies* 13.2 (2002), p. 168.
2. Quoted in Gabrielle Parker, 'The Fifth Republic and the Francophone Project' in Kamal Salih (ed.), *French in and out of France: Language Policies, Intercultural Antagonisms and Dialogue* (Oxford and Bern: Lang, 2002), p. 14, n.11.
3. Marie-Louise Pratt, *Imperial Eyes: Travel Writing and Transculturation* (London and New York: Routledge, 1992).
4. 'Sony Labou Tansi face à douze mots', *Equateur*, 1 (1986), p. 30.
5. L'abbé Grégoire, *Rapport sur la nécessité et les moyens d'anéantir les patois et d'universaliser l'usage de la langue française*, 9 prairial, an II; read to the Convention 16 prairial, an II. Barère's speech to the convention is dated 8 pluviôse, an II.
6. Raoul Girardet, *L'Idée coloniale en France de 1871 à 1962* (Paris: Seuil, Pluriels, 1972), p. 413.
7. Robert J. C. Young, *White Mythologies: Writing History and the West* (London and New York: Routledge, 1990), p. 43.
8. Bart Moore-Gilbert defines postcolonial criticism as 'a more or less distinct set of reading practices' in *Postcolonial Theory: Contexts, Practices, Politics* (London: Verso, 1997), p. 12, while Jeannie Suk describes the postcolonial as 'a practice of reading' in *Postcolonial Paradoxes in French Caribbean Writing: Césaire, Glissant, Condé* (Oxford: Oxford University Press, 2001), p. 19.
9. Amin Maalouf, *Les Identités meurtrières* (Paris: Grasset et Fasquelle, Le Livre de Poche, 2005 [1998]).

1 The Maghreb

1. Elleke Boehmer, *Colonial and Postcolonial Literature: Migrant Metaphors* (Oxford and New York: Oxford University Press, 1995), p. 3.
2. Albert Camus, 'Le malaise politique' in 'Chroniques Algériennes' (Actuelles III), *Essais* (Paris: Gallimard, Pléiade, 1965), p. 950.
3. Peter Dunwoodie, *Writing French Algeria* (Oxford: Clarendon Press, 1998).

4. Bernard Mouralis, *Littérature et développement: essai sur le statut, la fonction et la représentation de la littérature négro-africaine d'expression française* (Paris: Silex, 1984), p. 18. The connection between the Algerianist movement and the point made by Mouralis is identified in Dunwoodie's book.

5. See Albert Memmi, Introduction to *Anthologie des écrivains maghrébins d'expression française* (Paris: Présence Africaine, 1965), p. 12.

6. Camus, 'Algérie 1958' in 'Chroniques Algériennes' (Actuelles III), *Essais*, p. 1012.

7. Ibid., p. 1013.

8. Abdelkébir Khatibi, *Le Roman maghrébin: essai* (Paris: Maspero, 1968).

9. Tahar Bekri, 'De l'étoile secrète au printemps blessé', *Notre Librairie*, 108 (January–March 1992), p. 93.

10. Mouloud Feraoun, *L'Anniversaire* (Paris: Seuil, Points, 1989 [1972]), p. 54.

11. Ibid., p. 55.

12. Ibid., p. 39.

13. Ibid., pp. 93–102.

14. Mouloud Feraoun, *Jours de Kabylie* (Paris: Seuil, 2003 [1968]), p. 110.

15. Ibid.

16. Jean Déjeux, *La Littérature maghrébine de langue française* (Ottawa: Editions Namaan, 1973), p. 141.

17. Khatibi, *Le Roman Maghrébin*, p. 27.

18. Ibid., p. 28

19. Peter Hallward, *Absolutely Postcolonial: Writing between the Singular and the Specific* (Manchester and New York: Manchester University Press, 2001), p. 189.

20. Khatibi, *Le Roman maghrébin*, p. 115.

21. Albert Memmi, *Portrait du colonisé* précédé de *Portrait de colonisateur* (Paris: Gallimard, 1985, [1957]), p. 130.

22. Interview in *Afrique-Action*, 13 March 1961.

23. Interview in *Témoignage Chrétien*, 7 February 1958.

24. Quoted in Déjeux, *La Littérature maghrébine*, pp. 148 and 171.

25. Interview in *Afrique-Action*, 13 March 1961.

26. Interview in *Jeune Afrique*, 324 (26 March 1967).

27. Khatibi, *Le Roman maghrébin*, pp. 102–3.

28. Ibid., p. 30.

29. Nicholas Harrison, *Postcolonial Criticism: History, Theory and the Work of Fiction* (Oxford: Polity, 2003), p. 98.

30. Ibid., p. 100.

31. Quoted in Debra Kelly, *Autobiography and Independence: Selfhood and Creativity in North African Postcolonial Writing in French* (Liverpool: Liverpool University Press, 2005), p. 150.

32. Albert Camus, Preface to *La Statue de sel*, p. 9.

33. 'Loin de décrire une fatalité, Agar énonce en vérité les conditions d'une libération' [Far from describing inexorable fate at work, Agar sketches the conditions for a liberation]: Albert Memmi, Preface to the 1963 edition of *Agar*, p. 16.

34. Rachid Boudjedra, *Lettres algériennes*, (Paris: Grasset et Fasquelle, le Livre de Poche, 1997 [1995]) p. 76.

35. In Yacine Alim, 'L'ami de ceux qui titubent', *El Watan*, 18 December 2004.

36. Rachid Boudjedra, 'La fascination de la forme', *Le Matin*, 24 June 2003.

37. Rachid Boudjedra, 'L'écriture est une jubilation', *La Nouvelle République*, 6 January 2005.

38. Assia Djebar, 'Idiome de l'exil et langue de l'irréductibilité', www.remue.net/article. php3?id'article=683, consulted 9 March 2006.

39. Khatibi, *Le Roman maghrébin*, p. 62.

40. Réda Bensmaïa, '*La Nouba des femmes du mont Chenoua*: introduction à l'œuvre fragmentale cinématographique' in Sada Niang (ed.), *Littérature et cinéma en Afrique francophone: Ousmane Sembène et Assia Djebar* (Paris: L'Harmattan, 1996), p. 164. Author's italics.

41. Anne Donadey, *Recasting Postcolonialism: Women Writing between Worlds*, Studies in African Literature (Portsmouth, NH: Heinemann, 2001) p. 45.

42. Harrison, *Postcolonial Criticism*, p. 117.

43. Charles Bonn in Charles Bonn and Farida Boualit (eds.), *Paysages littéraires algériens des années 90: témoigner d'une tragédie?* (Paris: L'Harmattan, 1999), pp. 8–9.

2   Sub-Saharan Africa

1. Sartre wrote the preface to Senghor's celebrated *Anthologie de la nouvelle poésie nègre et malgache* (Paris: Presses Universitaires de France, Quadrige, 1985 [1948]), under the title 'Orphée noir', pp. ix–xliv. For a more detailed discussion of *Négritude*, see Chapter 5 below.

2. The article appears under the initials A. B. (Alexandre Biyidi) in *Trois écrivains noirs* (Paris: Présence Africaine, 1954).

3. Ahmadou Kourouma, *Je témoigne pour l'Afrique* (Grigny: Editions Paroles d'Aube, 1998), pp. 8–9.

4. Chidi Amuta, *The Theory of African Literature: Implications for Practical Criticism* (London: Zed Books, 1989), p. 197.

5. Bernard Magnier, *Notre Librairie*, 87 (April 1987), p. 14.

6. Guy Tirolien, Preface to *Tribaliques* (Yaoundé: CLE, 1991).

7. 'Réinventer la logique à la mesure de notre temps', *Equateur*, 1 (1986), p. 34.

8. Quoted by Nicolas Martin-Grenel, *Rires noirs* (Paris: Sepia, 1991), pp. 33–4.

9. Pius Ngandu Nkashama, 'L'autobiographie chez les femmes africaines', *Notre Librairie*, 117 (April–June 1994), p. 137.

10. Boniface Mongo-Mboussa, 'Ken Bugul ou la passion de la liberté' in *Désir d'Afrique* (Paris: Gallimard, Continents noirs, 2002), p. 109 (Ken Bugul's italics).

3   Oceania – Middle East

1. Abdourahman A. Waberi, *Rift, Routes, Rails* (Paris: Gallimard, Continents noirs, 2001), pp. 13–14.

2. Khal Torabully, *Cale d'étoiles, Coolitude* (Ile de La Réunion: Alizées, 1992), p. 105.

3. Véronique Bragard, *International Journal of Francophone Studies* 8. 2 (August 2005), p. 220.

4. Françoise Lionnet, *Postcolonial Representations: Women, Literature, Identity* (Ithaca and London: Cornell University Press, 1995), p. 52.

5. Delphine Chaume, *Le Magazine Littéraire*, 451, (March 2006), p. 60.

6. 'L'écriture est le monde, elle est le chemin et le but', www.indereunion.net/actu/ananda/intervad.htm, consulted 18 December 2006.

7. Axel Gauvin, *Du créole opprimé au créole libéré: défense de la langue réunionnaise* (Paris: L'Harmattan, 1997), p. 70.

8. Raharimanana, 'Sortir du bois', *Africultures*, 59 (18 May 2004).

9. *Le Magazine Littéraire*, 451 (March 2006), p. 52.

4 Canada

1. Although there are almost one million francophones in Canada outside Quebec (including, in particular, substantial numbers in New Brunswick and Ontario), they inevitably form a linguistic minority and in no case do they represent more than 5 per cent of the population of a province. Throughout this chapter 'Quebec' is therefore used to refer not only to the city and province of Quebec but also to the francophone diaspora in Canada.

2. The idea that the *Québécois* should be considered a 'colonised' people was developed at some length by the group of intellectuals writing for *Parti Pris*, a journal founded in 1963. *Nègres blancs d'Amérique* (1969) was the title of an influential essay by Pierre Vallière.

3. Belinda Jack, *Francophone Literatures: An Introductory Survey* (Oxford: Oxford University Press, 1996), p. 64.

4. Jacques Godbout, *Liberté*, 93 (May 1974), p. 33. Quoted in Lise Gauvin, *Langagement: L'écrivain et la langue au Québec* (Montreal: Boréal, 2000), p. 39.

5. Gauvin, *Langagement*, p. 38.

6. Gabrielle Roy, *Fragiles Lumières de la terre: écrits divers 1942–1970* (Montreal: Stanké, 1982 [1978]), p. 9.

7. Anne Hébert, *Poèmes* (Paris: Seuil, 1960), p. 51.

8. Gérard Tougas, *La Littérature Canadienne-Française* (Paris: Presses Universitaires de France, 1960), p. 193.

9. See Lucien Goldmann, *Structures mentales et création culturelle*, (Paris: UGE, 10/18, 1970). pp. 353–4.

10. Maurice Cagnon, *The French Novel of Quebec* (Boston: Twayne, 1986), p. 75.

11. Jacques Godbout, *Le Murmure Marchand 1978–1984* (Montreal: Boréal, 1984), pp. 7–8.

12. Ben-Zion Shek, *French-Canadian and Québécois Novels* (Toronto: Oxford University Press, 1991), p. 72.

13. Gauvin, *Langagement*, p. 170.

14. Gilles Marcotte, *Le Roman à l'imparfait: La 'Revolution tranquille' du roman québécois* (Quebec: Hexagone, 1989 [1946]), p. 119.
15. Ibid., p. 120.
16. Gauvin, *Langagement*, p. 174.

5 The Caribbean

1. Unpublished interview with Patrick Corcoran and Lorna Milne', 'Mosaïques festival', Institut français du Royaume-Uni, 4 May 2005.
2. See Frantz Fanon, *Peau noire masques blancs* (Paris: Seuil, Points, 1986 [1952]), pp. 33–50.
3. Raphaël Confiant, *Aimé Césaire: une traversée paradoxale du siècle* (Paris: Ecriture, 2007 [1993]), p. 111.
4. Sartre, 'Orphée noir', pp. xl and xli.
5. Confiant, *Aimé Césaire*, pp. 112–13.
6. Ibid., pp. 113–14.
7. André Breton, 'Un grand poète noir', postface to Aimé Césaire, *Cahier d'un retour au pays natal* (Paris: Présence Africaine, 1983 [1939]), p. 80.
8. Fanon, *Peau noire masques blancs*, p. 30.
9. Confiant, *Aimé Césaire*, p. 113.
10. James Clifford, 'On Ethnographic Allegory' in James Clifford and George E. Marcus (eds.), *Writing Culture: The Poetics and Politics of Ethnography* (Berkeley: University of California Press, 1986), p. 112. Quoted by Charles Forsdick in *Travel in Twentieth Century French and Francophone Culture: The Persistence of Diversity* (Oxford and New York: Oxford University Press, 2005), p. 69.
11. J. Michael Dash, *Edouard Glissant* (Cambridge: Cambridge University Press, 1995), p. 148.
12. Confiant, *Aimé Césaire*, p. 260.
13. Daniel Delas, *Littératures des Caraïbes de langue française* (Paris: Nathan, 1999), p. 20.
14. Confiant, *Aimé Césaire*, p. 87.
15. Raphaël Confiant, *Le Cahier de romances* (Paris: Gallimard, Folio, 2006 [2000]), pp. 214–15.
16. Chamoiseau, interview with Corcoran and Milne.
17. Ibid.
18. A. James Arnold, *Modernism and Negritude: The Poetry and Poetics of Aimé Césaire* (Cambridge, MA: Harvard University Press, 1981), p. 133.
19. Ibid.
20. Régis Antoine, *La Littérature franco-antillaise: Haïti, Guadeloupe et Martinique* (Paris: Karthala, 1992), pp. 207–8.
21. Homi K. Bhabha (ed.), *The Location of Culture* (London and New York: Routledge, 1994), p. 85.

22. Martin Munro, *Shaping and Reshaping the Caribbean: The Work of Aimé Césaire and René Depestre* (Leeds: MRHA/Money, 2000), p. 84.

23. Confiant, *Aimé Césaire*, p. 35.

24. Christopher L. Miller, *Nationalists and Nomads: Essays on Francophone Literature and Culture* (Chicago: Chicago University Press, 1998), p. 63. See also pp. 47–67.

25. Robert J. C. Young, *Postcolonialism: An Historical Introduction* (Oxford: Blackwell, 2001), p. 274.

26. Bhabha, *The Location of Culture*, pp. 41 and 42–3.

27. Ibid., p. 43.

28. René Depestre, 'Les aventures de la créolité' in Ralph Ludwig (ed.), *Ecrire la 'parole de nuit': la nouvelle littérature antillaise* (Paris: Gallimard, 1994), pp.159–70.

29. H. Adlai Murdoch, *Creole Identity in the French Caribbean Novel* (Gainsville: University of Florida Press), p. 198.

30. Chamoiseau, interview with Corcoran and Milne.

31. Celia M. Britton, *Edouard Glissant and Postcolonial Theory: Strategies of Language and Resistance* (Charlottesville and London: University Press of Virginia, 1999). p. 103 (Britton's italics).

32. Chamoiseau, interview with Corcoran and Milne.

33. Edouard Glissant, 'Le chaos-monde, l'oral et l'écrit' in Ludwig (ed.), *Ecrire la 'parole de nuit'*, p. 126.

34. Ibid., p. 128.

35. Dash, *Edouard Glissant*, p. 20.

36. Edouard Glissant, *Mahagony* (Paris: Seuil, 1987), p. 14.

37. Delas, *Littératures des Caraïbes de langue française*, p. 83.

38. Confiant, *Aimé Césaire*, p. 77.

39. Suk, *Postcolonial Paradoxes*, p. 18.

40. Lionnet, *Postcolonial Representations*, pp. 69–71.

41. Ibid., pp. 78–9.

42. Murdoch, *Creole Identity in the French Caribbean Novel*, p. 100.

43. Françoise Lionnet, *Autobiographical Voices: Race, Gender, Self-Portraiture* (Ithaca: Cornell University Press, 1989), p. 175.

44. 'Strategic essentialism' is a controversial notion proposed by Gayatri Spivak and developed in her work with the Indian-based Subaltern Studies group. The 'subalterns' in this context are first and foremost the oppressed, 'voiceless' women of the Indian subcontinent whose history has been silenced by the very fact of their marginalisation. The term 'subaltern' can readily be extended to other oppressed groups and these particular cases of gender-based oppression have consequently acquired a more general relevance.

45. Gayatri C. Spivak, 'La mise en scène du temps dans *Hérémakhonon*' in Madeleine Cottenet-Hage and Lydie Moudileno, *Maryse Condé: une nomade inconvenante* (Guadeloupe: Ibis Rouge, 2002). A section of the essay is reproduced in a slightly different version in *Death of a Discipline* (New York: Columbia University Press, 2003), pp. 16–19.

46. Lionnet, *Postcolonial Representations*, p. 81.
47. Quoted in Jack Corzani, Léon-François Hoffmann and Marie-Lyne Piccione, *Littératures francophones*, vol. 2, *Les Amériques: Haïti, Antilles-Guyane, Québec* (Paris: Belin, 1998), p. 28.
48. Delas, *Littératures des Caraïbes de langue française*, p. 91.

Conclusion

1. Harrison, *Postcolonial Criticism*, p. 109.
2. Quoted in Girardet, *L'Idée coloniale en France*, pp. 229–30.
3. Kwame Anthony Appiah, *In My Father's House: Africa in the Philosophy of Culture* (Oxford and New York: Oxford University Press, 1992), p. 155.

Bibliography

Primary texts

Alexis, Jacques Stephen, *Compère Général Soleil* (Paris: Gallimard, 1955).
  L'Espace d'un cillement (Paris: Gallimard, 1959).
  Romancero aux étoiles (Paris: Gallimard, 1960).
Ben Jelloun, Tahar, *La Réclusion solitaire* (Paris: Seuil, Points, 1981 [1976]).
  Moha le fou Moha le sage (Paris: Seuil, Points, 1980 [1978]).
  L'Enfant de sable (Paris: Seuil, Points, 1995 [1985]).
  La Nuit sacrée (Paris: Seuil, Points, 1995 [1987]).
  L'Ange aveugle (Paris: Seuil, Points, 1995 [1992]).
  Le Premier Amour est toujours le dernier (Paris: Seuil, Points, 1995).
  Les Raisins de la galère (Paris: Fayard, 1996).
  La Soudure fraternelle (Paris: Seuil, Points, 1996).
  Le Racisme expliqué à ma fille (Paris: Seuil, 1998).
  Eloge de l'amitié, ombre de la trahison (Paris: Seuil, Points, 2003).
  Amours sorcières (Paris: Seuil, Points, 2003).
Beti, Mongo, *Le Pauvre Christ de Bomba* (Paris: Présence Africaine, 1976 [1956])
  Mission Terminée (Paris: Corréa-Buchet-Chastel, 1957).
  Le Roi miraculé (Paris: Corréa-Buchet-Chastel, 1958).
Blais, Marie-Claire, *La Belle Bête* (Montreal: Pierre Tisseyre, 1968 [1959]).
  Une Saison dans la vie d'Emmanuel (Paris: Seuil, Points, 1996 [1965]).
Boto, Eza (alias Mongo Beti), *Ville cruelle* (Paris: Présence Africaine, 1971 [1954]).
Boudjedra, Rachid, *La Répudiation* (Paris: Denoël, Folio, 2003 [1969]).
  L'Insolation (Paris: Denoël, 1972).
  Topographie idéale pour une aggression caractérisée (Paris: Denoël, 1996 [1975]).
  L'Escargot entêté (Paris: Denoël, Folio, 2005 [1977]).
  FIS de la haine (Paris: Denoël, 1992).
  Timimoun (Paris: Denoël, Folio, 2001 [1994]).
  Lettres algériennes (Paris: Grasset et Fasquelle, Le Livre de Poche, 1997 [1995]).
Camara Laye, *L'Enfant noir* (Paris: Presses Pocket, 1976 [1953]).
  Le Maître de la parole: Kouma Lafôlô Kouma (Paris: Presses Pocket, 1984 [1978]).

Césaire, Aimé, *Cahier d'un retour au pays natal* (Paris: Présence Africaine, 1983 [1939]).
  Discours sur le colonialisme (Paris: Présence Africaine, 1973 [1955]).
  Et les chiens se taisaient (Paris: Présence Africaine, 1989 [1958]).
  La Tragédie du Roi Christophe (Paris: Présence Africaine, 1970 [1963]).
  Une tempête (Paris: Seuil, Points, 1997 [1969]).
Chamoiseau, Patrick, *Chronique des sept misères* (Paris: Gallimard, Folio, 1992 [1986]).
  Solibo magnifique (Paris: Gallimard, Folio, 1995 [1988]).
  Texaco (Paris: Gallimard, Folio, 1996 [1992]).
  Antan d'Enfance (Paris: Gallimard, Folio, 1996 [1990]).
  Chemin-d'école (Paris: Gallimard, Folio, 1996 [1994]).
  L'Esclave vieil homme et le molosse (Paris: Gallimard, Folio, 1997).
  Ecrire en pays dominé (Paris: Gallimard, Folio, 1997).
  Biblique des derniers gestes (Paris: Gallimard, Folio, 2002).
Chraïbi, Driss, *Le Passé simple* (Paris: Denoël, Folio, 2001 [1954]).
  Les Boucs (Paris: Denoël, Folio, 1999 [1955]).
  Succession ouverte (Paris: Denoël, Folio, 1999 [1962]).
  La Civilisation, ma mère! . . . (Paris: Denoël, Folio, 2003 [1972]).
  Une enquête au pays (Paris: Seuil, Points, 1982 [1981]).
  La Mère du printemps (L'Oum-er-Bia) (Paris: Seuil, Points, 1995 [1982]).
  Naissance à l'aube (Paris: Seuil, Points, 1999 [1986]).
  L'Inspecteur Ali (Paris: Denoël, Folio, 1993 [1991]).
  L'Inspecteur Ali à Trinity College (Paris: Denoël, 1996)
  L'Inspecteur Ali et la C.I.A. (Paris: Denoël, 1997).
  Le Monde à côté (Paris: Denoël, Folio, 2003 [2001]).
  L'Homme qui venait du passé (Paris: Denoël, 2004).
Condé, Maryse, *Hérémakhonon* (Paris: UGE, 1976).
  Ségou: les murailles de la terre (Paris: Laffont, Pocket, 1984).
  Ségou: la terre en miettes (Paris: Laffont, Pocket, 1985).
  Moi, Tituba sorcière . . . noire de Salem (Paris: Mercure de France, Folio, 1991 [1986]).
  La Vie scélérate (Paris: Seghers, 1987).
  Traversée de la mangrove (Paris: Mercure de France, Folio, 1992 [1989]).
  Les Derniers Rois mages (Paris: Mercure de France, Folio, 1995 [1992]).
  Le Cœur à rire et à pleurer: souvenirs de mon enfance (Paris: Laffont, Pocket, 1999).
  Histoire de la femme cannibale (Paris: Mercure de France, Folio, 2005 [2003]).
Confiant, Raphaël, *Le Nègre et l'amiral* (Paris: Grasset, Le Livre de Poche, 1993 [1988]).
  Eau de Café (Paris: Grasset, Le Livre de Poche, 2000 [1991]).
  Ravines du devant-jour (Paris: Gallimard, Folio, 1995 [1993]).
  L'Allée des soupirs (Paris: Grasset, 1994).
  Bassin des ouragans (Paris: Les Mille et Une Nuits, 1994).
  La Savane des pétrifications (Paris: Les Mille et Une Nuits, 1995).

La Vierge du grand retour (Paris: Grasset, Le Livre de Poche, 1998 [1996]).

La Baignoire de Joséphine (Paris: Les Mille et Une Nuits, 1997).

Le Meurtre du Samedi-Gloria (Paris: Mercure de France, Folio, 2001 [1997]).

L'Archet du colonel (Paris: Mercure de France, Folio, 2001 [1998]).

La Dernière Java de Mama Josépha (Paris: Les Mille et Une Nuits, 1999).

Le Cahier de romances (Paris: Gallimard, Folio, 2006 [2000]).

Nuée ardente (Paris: Mercure de France, Folio, 2004 [2002]).

Le Barbare enchanté (Paris: Ecriture, 2003).

La Panse du chacal (Paris: Mercure de France, 2004).

Adèle et la pacotilleuse (Paris: Mercure de France, 2005).

Cossery, Albert, *Les Hommes oubliés de Dieu* (Paris: Joëlle Losfeld, 2000 [1941]).

La Maison de la mort certaine (Paris: Joëlle Losfeld, 2000 [1944]).

Les Fainéants dans la vallée fertile (Paris: Joëlle Losfeld, 2000 [1948]).

Mendiants et orgueilleux (Paris: Joëlle Losfeld, 2000 [1955]).

La Violence et la dérision (Paris: Joëlle Losfeld, 2000 [1964]).

Un Complot de saltimbanques (Paris: Joëlle Losfeld, 2000 [1975]).

Une ambition dans le désert (Paris: Joëlle Losfeld, 2000 [1984]).

Les Couleurs de l'infamie (Paris: Joëlle Losfeld, 2000 [1999]).

Damas, Léon-Gontran, *Pigments névralgies* (Paris: Présence Africaine, 1972 [1937 and 1966])

Devi, Ananda, *Solstices* (Port-Louis: Patrick Mackay, 1976).

Le Poids des êtres (Rose-Hill: Les Editions de l'Océan Indien, 1987).

Rue la poudrière (Abidjan: Nouvelles Editions Africaines, 1988).

Le Voile de Drapaudi (Paris: L'Harmattan, 1993).

L'Arbre fouet (Paris: L'Harmattan, 1997).

Pagli (Paris: Gallimard, Continents noirs, 2001).

Soupir (Paris: Gallimard, Continents noirs, 2002).

La Vie de Joséphin le fou (Paris: Gallimard, Continents noirs, 2003).

Eve de ses décombres (Paris: Gallimard, 2006).

Dib, Mohammed, *La Grande Maison* (Paris: Seuil, Points, 1996 [1952]).

L'Incendie (Paris: Seuil, Points, 2001 [1954]).

Le Métier à tisser (Paris: Seuil, Points, 2001 [1957]).

Un Eté africain (Paris: Seuil, Points, 1998 [1959]).

Qui se souvient de la mer (Paris: Seuil, 1990 [1962]).

Cours sur la rive sauvage (Paris: Seuil, Points, 2005 [1964]).

La Danse du roi (Paris: Seuil, 1968).

Dieu en Barbarie (Paris: Seuil, 1970).

Le Maître de chasse (Paris: Seuil, 1973).

Habel (Paris: Seuil, 1977).

Les Terrasses d'Orsol (Paris: Minos La Différence, 2002 [1985]).

Le Sommeil d'Eve (Paris: Minos La Différence, 2003 [1989]).

Neiges de marbre (Paris: Sindbad, 1990).

Le Désert sans détour (Paris: Sindbad, 1992).

Djebar, Assia, *La Soif* (Paris: Julliard, 1957).

Les Alouettes naïves (Paris: Julliard, 1967).

Femmes d'Alger dans leur appartement (Paris: Antoine Fouque, 1997 [1980]).

L'Amour, la fantasia (Paris: Lattès, Le Livre de Poche, 2002 [1985]).

Ombre sultane (Paris: Lattès, 1987).

Loin de Médine (Paris: Albin Michel, Le Livre de Poche, 2001 [1991]).

Vaste est la prison (Paris: Albin Michel, Le Livre de Poche, 2003 [1995]).

Ces voix qui m'assiègent (Paris: Albin Michel, 1999).

La Femme sans sépulture (Paris: Albin Michel, Le Livre de Poche, 2004 [2002]).

Dongala, Emmanuel, *Johnny Chien Méchant* (Paris: Le Serpent à Plumes, 2002).

Un fusil dans la main, un poème dans la poche (Paris: Le Serpent à Plumes, 2003).

Ducharme, Réjean, *L'Avalée des avalés* (Paris: Gallimard, Folio, 2005 [1966]).

Le Nez qui voque (Paris: Gallimard, Folio, 1993 [1967]).

L'Océantume (Paris: Gallimard, Folio, 1999 [1968]).

L'Hiver de force (Paris: Gallimard, Folio, 1994 [1973]).

Les Enfantômes (Paris: Gallimard, Folio, 1996 [1976]).

Dévadé (Paris: Gallimard, Folio, 2001 [1990]).

Gros Mots (Paris: Gallimard, Folio, 2001 [1999]).

Etienne, Frank (Frankétienne), *L'Oiseau schizophone* (Port-au-Prince: Editions des Antilles, 1993).

Fanon, Frantz, *Peau noire masques blancs* (Paris: Seuil, Points, 1986 [1952]).

Les Damnés de la terre (Paris: Gallimard, Folio, 1991 [1961])

Pour la Révolution africaine (Paris: Maspero, 1969).

Feraoun, Mouloud, *Le Fils du pauvre* (Paris: Seuil, 1954 [1950]).

La Terre et le sang (Paris: Seuil, Points, 1976 [1953]).

Journal 1955–1962 (Paris: Seuil, 1962).

Jours de Kabylie (Paris: Seuil, Points, 2003 [1968]).

Lettres à ses amis (Paris: Seuil, 1969).

L'Anniversaire (Paris: Seuil, Points, 1989 [1972]).

Gauvin, Axel, *Du créole opprimé au créole libéré: défense de la langue réunionnaise* (Paris: L'Harmattan, 1977).

Faims d'enfance (Paris: Seuil, 1987).

L'Aimé (Paris: Seuil, Points, 1992 [1990]).

Cravate et fils (Paris: Seuil, 1996).

Train fou (Paris: Seuil, 2000).

Glissant, Edouard, *La Lézarde* (Paris: Seuil, Points, 2003 [1958]).

Le Quatrième Siècle (Paris: Gallimard, L'Imaginaire, 1990 [1964]).

Malemort (Paris: Gallimard, 1997 [1975]).

La Case du commandeur (Paris: Seuil, 1981).

Pays rêvé, pays réel, suivi de *Fastes et de Les Grands Chaos* (Paris: Gallimard, Poésie, 2000 [1985]).

Mahagony (Paris: Seuil, 1987).

Tout-monde (Paris: Gallimard, Folio, 1993).

Sartorius: le roman des Batoutos (Paris: Gallimard, 1999).

Godbout, Jacques, *L'Aquarium* (Paris: Seuil, 1962).

Le Couteau sur la table (Paris: Seuil, 1965).

Salut Galarneau! (Paris: Seuil, Points, 1982 [1967]).

D'Amour, P. Q. (Paris: Seuil, 1972).

Les Têtes à Papineau (Paris: Seuil, 1981).

Une histoire américaine (Paris: Seuil, Points, 1988 [1986]).

Guèvremont, Germaine, *Le Survenant* (Montreal: Fides, 1984 [1945]).

Hampaté Bâ, Amadou, *L'Etrange Destin de Wangrin* (Paris: UGE, 10/18, 1992 [1973]).

Kaïdara (Abidjan: Nouvelles Editions Africaines, 1985).

Njeddo Dewal: mère de la calamité (Abidjan: Nouvelles Editions Africaines, 1985).

Petit Bodiel (Abidjan: Nouvelles Editions Africaines, 1987).

La Poignée de poussière (Abidjan: Nouvelles Editions Africaines, 1987).

Amkoullel, l'enfant peul (Arles: Actes Sud, 1991).

Oui Mon Commandant! (Arles: Actes Sud, 1994).

Hébert, Anne, *Les Chambres de Bois* (Paris: Seuil, 1958).

Poèmes (Paris: Seuil, 1960).

Kamouraska (Paris: Seuil, 1970).

Les Fous de Bassan (Paris: Seuil, 1982).

Le Premier Jardin (Paris: Seuil, 1988).

Hémon, Louis, *Maria Chapdelaine* (Paris: Grasset, Le Livre de Poche, 1985 [1916]).

Kane, Cheikh Hamidou, *L'Aventure ambiguë* (Paris: UGE, 10/18, 1979 [1961]).

Ken Bugul, *Le Baobab fou* (Dakar: NEA, 1983).

Cendres et braises (Paris: L'Harmattan, 1994).

Riwan ou le chemin de sable (Paris: Présence Africaine, 1999).

La Folie et la mort (Paris: Présence Africaine, 2000).

De l'autre côté du regard (Paris: Le Serpent à Plumes, 2003).

Rue Félix-Faure (Paris: Le Serpent à Plumes, 2004).

Kourouma, Ahmadou, *Les Soleils des indépendances* (Paris: Seuil, Points, 1990 [1968]).

Monnè, outrages et défis (Paris: Seuil, 1990).

En attendant le vote des bêtes sauvages (Paris: Seuil, 1998).

Allah n'est pas obligé (Paris: Seuil, 2000).

Quand on refuse on dit non (Paris: Seuil, 2004).

Labou Tansi, Sony, *Conscience de tracteur* (Dakar/Yaoundè: NEA/CLE, 1979 [1973]).

La Parenthèse de sang suivi de *Je soussigné cardiaque* (Paris: Hatier, 1981).

La Vie et demie (Paris: Seuil, Points, 1988 [1979]).

L'Etat honteux (Paris: Seuil, 1981).

L'Anté-peuple (Paris: Seuil, 1983).

Les Sept Solitudes de Lorsa Lopez (Paris: Seuil, Points, 1994 [1985]).

Antoine m'a vendu son destin in *Equateur*, 1 (Paris, 1986).

Qui a mangé Madame d'Avoine Bergotha (Carnières-Morlanwelz: Lansman, 1995 [1989]).

Laleau, Léon, *Musique nègre* (Port-au-Prince: Imprimerie de l'Etat, 1931).
Lopes, Henri, *Tribaliques* (Yaoundé: CLE, 1971).
    La Nouvelle Romance (Yaoundé: CLE, 1976).
    Sans tam-tam (Yaoundé: CLE, 1977).
    Le Pleurer-rire (Paris: Présence Africaine, 1982).
    Le Chercheur d'Afriques (Paris: Seuil, 1990).
    Sur l'autre rive (Paris: Seuil, 1992).
    Le Lys et le flamboyant (Paris: Seuil, 1997).
    Dossier classé (Paris: Seuil, 2002).
Maalouf, Amin, *Les Croisades vues par les Arabes* (Paris: J'ai Lu, 1989 [1983]).
    Léon l'Africain (Paris: Lattès, Le Livre de Poche, 1988 [1986]).
    Samarcande (Paris: Lattès, 1988).
    Les Jardins de lumière (Paris: Lattès, Le Livre de Poche, 1992 [1991]).
    Le Premier Siècle après Bérénice (Paris: Grasset et Fasquelle, Le Livre de
        Poche, 2004 [1992]).
    Le Rocher de Tanios (Paris: Grasset et Fasquelle, Le Livre de Poche, 2004
        [1993]).
    Les Identités meurtrières (Paris: Grasset et Fasquelle, Le Livre de Poche, 2005
        [1998]).
    Origines (Paris: Grasset et Fasquelle, Le Livre de Poche, 2006 [2004]).
Mammeri, Mouloud, *La Colline oubliée* (Paris: Plon, 1952).
Memmi, Albert, *La Statue de sel* (Paris: Gallimard, Folio, 2004 [1953]).
    Agar (Paris: Gallimard, Folio, 1999 [1955]).
    Portrait du colonisé, précédé de *Portrait du colonisateur* (Paris: Gallimard,
        1995 [1957]).
    Portrait d'un Juif (Paris: Gallimard, 1962).
    L'Homme dominé (Paris: Gallimard, 1968).
    Le Scorpion ou la confession imaginaire (Paris: Gallimard, Folio, 2001 [1969]).
    Le Désert ou la vie et les aventures de Jubaïr Ouali El-Mammi (Paris:
        Gallimard, 1977).
    Le Pharaon (Paris: Julliard, 1988).
    Le Nomade immobile (Paris: Arléa, 2000).
Mimouni, Rachid, *Le Fleuve détourné* (Paris: Laffont, 1982).
    L'Honneur de la tribu (Paris: Laffont, 1989).
Monenembo, Thierno, *L'Aîné des orphelins* (Paris: Seuil, 2000).
    Peuls (Paris: Seuil, 2004).
Ndao, Cheikh Aliou, *Mbaam Dictateur* (Paris: Présence Africaine, 1997).
Oyono, Ferdinand, *Une vie de boy* (Paris: Presses Pocket, 1970 [1956]).
    Le Vieux Nègre et la médaille (Paris: Presses Pocket, 1979 [1956]).
Pépin, Ernest, *Au verso du silence* (Paris: L'Harmattan, 1984).
    Boucan de mots libres (Havana: Casa de las Americas, 1990).
    L'Homme-au-Bâton (Paris: Gallimard, 1992).
    Tambour-Babel (Paris: Gallimard, 1996).
    Le Tango de la haine (Paris: Gallimard, 1999).
Poulin, Jacques, *Volkswagen Blues* (Paris: Actes Sud/Leméac, Babel, 1998 [1984]).
Raharimanana, *Lucarne* (Paris: Le Serpent à Plumes, 1996).

Rêves sous le linceul (Paris: Le Serpent à Plumes, 1998).

Nour, 1947 (Paris: Le Serpent à Plumes, 2001).

Roumain, Jacques, *Gouverneurs de la Rosée* (Port-au-Prince: Imprimerie de l'Etat, 1944).

Roy, Gabrielle, *Bonheur d'occasion* (Montreal: Stanké, 1977 [1945]).

La Petite Poule d'eau (Montreal: Stanké, 1980 [1950]).

Alexandre Chenevert: caissier (Paris: Flammarion, 1954).

Rue Deschambault (Montreal: Stanké, 1985 [1955]).

Fragiles Lumières de la terre: ecrits divers 1942–1970 (Montreal: Stanké, 1982 [1978]).

Sassine, Williams, *Le Jeune Homme de sable* (Paris: Seuil, 1979).

Schwarz-Bart, Simone, *Pluie et vent sur Télumée Miracle* (Paris: Seuil, Points, 1972).

Ti Jean L'Horizon (Paris: Seuil, Points, 1972).

Sembene Ousmane, *Le Docker noir* (Paris: Présence Africaine, 1957).

Les Bouts de bois de Dieu (Paris: Présence Africaine, 1960).

Voltaïque (Paris: Présence Africaine, 1962).

Le Mandat (Paris: Présence Africaine, 1966).

Xala (Paris: Présence Africaine, 1973).

L'Harmattan (Paris: Présence Africaine, 1980).

Le Dernier de l'empire (Paris: L'Harmattan, 1981).

Guelwaar (Paris: Présence Africaine, 1996).

Senghor, Léopold-Sédar, *Anthologie de la nouvelle poésie nègre et malgache de langue française* (Paris: Presses Universitaires de France, Quadrige, 1985 [1948]).

Chants d'ombre (Paris: Seuil, 1945).

Sow Fall, Aminata, *L'Ex-père de la nation* (Paris: L'Harmattan, 1987).

Tadjo, Véronique, *L'Ombre d'Imana: voyages jusqu'au bout du Rwanda* (Arles: Actes Sud, 2000).

Torabully, Khal, *Cale d'étoiles, Coolitude* (Ile de la Réunion: Alizées, 1992).

Tremblay, Michel, *Théâtre I* (Montreal/Arles: Leméac/Actes Sud, 1991).

Les Belles-Sœurs (1968), in *Théâtre I.*

Waberi, Abdourahman A., *Moisson de crânes: textes pour le Rwanda* (Paris: Le Serpent à Plumes, 2000).

Rifts, Routes, Rails (Paris: Gallimard, Continents noirs, 2001).

Transit (Paris: Le Serpent à Plumes, 2003).

Yacine, Kateb, *Nedjma* (Paris: Seuil, Points, 2003 [1956]).

Le Cercle des représailles (Paris: Seuil, 1959).

Le Polygone étoilé (Paris: Seuil, Points, 2001 [1966]).

Secondary texts

A. B., *Trois écrivains noirs* (Paris: Présence Africaine, 1954).

Alim, Yacine, 'L'ami de ceux qui titubent', *El Watan*, 18 December 2004.

Amuta, Chidi, *The Theory of African Literature: Implications for Practical Criticism* (London: Zed Books, 1989).

Antoine, Régis, *La Littérature franco-antillaise: Haïti, Guadeloupe et Martinique* (Paris: Karthala, 1992).

Appiah, Kwame Anthony, *In My Father's House: Africa in the Philosophy of Culture* (Oxford and New York: Oxford University Press, 1992).

Arnold, A. James, *Modernism and Negritude: The Poetry and Poetics of Aimé Césaire* (Cambridge, MA: Harvard University Press, 1981).

Bekri, Tahar, 'De l'étoile secrète au printemps blessé', *Notre Librairie*, 108 (January–March 1992), pp. 91–4.

Bensmaïa, Reda, '*La Nouba des femmes du mont Chenoua*: introduction à l'œuvre fragmentale cinématographique' in Sada Niang (ed.), *Littérature et cinéma en Afrique francophone: Ousmane Sembène et Assia Djebar* (Paris: L'Harmattan, 1996), pp. 161–77.

Bernabé, Jean, Patrick Chamoiseau and Raphaël Confiant, *Eloge de la créolité* (Paris: Gallimard, 1993 [1989]).

Bhabha, Homi K. (ed.), *The Location of Culture* (London and New York: Routledge, 1994).

Boehmer, Elleke, *Colonial and Postcolonial Literature: Migrant Metaphors* (Oxford and New York: Oxford University Press, 1995).

Bonn, Charles and Farida Boualit (eds.), *Paysages littéraires algériens des années 90: témoigner d'une tragédie?* (Paris: L'Harmattan, 1999).

Boudjedra, Rachid, 'La fascination de la forme', *Le Matin*, 24 June 2003.

     'L'Ecriture est une jubilation', *La Nouvelle République*, 6 January 2005.

Bragard, Véronique, *International Journal of Francophone Studies*, 8. 2 (August 2005), pp. 219–33.

Britton, Celia M., *Edouard Glissant and Postcolonial Theory: Strategies of Language and Resistance* (Charlottesville and London: University Press of Virginia, 1999).

Cagnon, Maurice, *The French Novel of Quebec* (Boston: Twayne, 1986).

Camus, Albert, *Essais* (Paris: Gallimard, Pléiade, 1965).

Chamoiseau, Patrick and Raphaël Confiant, *Lettres Créoles: tracées antillaises et continentales de la littérature* (Paris: Gallimard, 1999).

Chaume, Delphine, 'Au bord de l'abîme', *Le Magazine Littéraire*, 451 (March 2006).

Confiant, Raphaël, *Aimé Césaire: une traversée paradoxale du siècle* (Paris: Ecriture, 2007 [1993]).

Corzani, Jack, Léon-François Hoffmann and Marie-Lyne Piccione (eds.), *Littératures francophones*, vol. 2: *Les Amériques: Haïti, Antilles-Guyane, Québec* (Paris: Belin, 1998).

Cottenet-Hage, Madeleine and Lydie Moudileno (eds.), *Maryse Condé: une nomade inconvenante* (Guadeloupe: Ibis Rouge, 2002).

Dash, J. Michael, *Edouard Glissant* (Cambridge: Cambridge University Press, 1995).

Déjeux, Jean, *La Littérature maghrébine de langue française* (Ottawa: Namaan, 1973).

Delas, Daniel, *Littératures des Caraïbes de langue française* (Paris: Nathan, 1999).

Depestre, René, 'Les aventures de la créolité' in Ralph Ludwig (ed.), *Ecrire la 'parole de nuit': la nouvelle littérature antillaise* (Paris: Gallimard, 1994), pp. 159–70.

Devi, Ananda, Interview, 'L'écriture est le monde, elle est le chemin et le but', www.indereunion.net/actu/ananda/intervad.htm, consulted 18 December 2006.

Djebar, Assia, 'Idiome de l'exil et langue de l'irréductibilité', www.remue.net/article.php3?id_article=683, consulted 9 March 2006.

Donadey, Anne, *Recasting Postcolonialism: Women Writing between Worlds*, Studies in African Literature (Portsmouth, NH: Heinemann, 2001).

Dunwoodie, Peter, *Writing French Algeria* (Oxford: Clarendon Press, 1998).

Forsdick, Charles, *Travel in Twentieth-Century French and Francophone Cultures: The Persistence of Diversity* (Oxford and New York: Oxford University Press, 2005).

Gauvin, Lise, *Langagement: l'écrivain et la langue au Québec* (Montreal: Boréal, 2000).

Girardet, Raoul, *L'Idée coloniale en France de 1871 à 1962* (Paris: Seuil, Pluriels, 1972).

Glissant, Edouard, *Le Discours Antillais* (Paris: Gallimard, Folio essais, 1997 [1981]).

　Poétique de la Relation (Paris: Gallimard, 1990).

　'Le chaos-monde, l'oral et l'écrit' in Ralph Ludwig (ed.), *Ecrire la 'parole de nuit': la nouvelle littérature antillaise* (Paris: Gallimard, 1994), pp. 111–29.

Godbout, Jacques, *Le Murmure Marchand 1978–1984* (Montreal: Boréal Express, 1984).

Goldmann, Lucien, *Structures mentales et création culturelle* (Paris: UGE, 10/18, 1970).

Hallward, Peter, *Absolutely Postcolonial: Writing between the Singular and the Specific* (Manchester and New York: Manchester University Press, 2001).

Harrison, Nicholas, *Postcolonial Criticism: History, Theory and the Work of Fiction* (Oxford: Polity, 2003).

Jack, Belinda, *Francophone Literatures: An Introductory Survey* (Oxford: Oxford University Press, 1996).

Kelly, Debra, *Autobiography and Independence: Selfhood and Creativity in North African Postcolonial Writing in French* (Liverpool: Liverpool University Press, 2005).

Khatibi, Abdelkébir, *Le Roman maghrébin: essai* (Paris: Maspero, 1968).

Kourouma, Ahmadou, *Je témoigne pour l'Afrique* (Grigny: Editions Paroles d'Aube, 1998).

Labou Tansi, Sony, 'Réinventer la logique à la mesure de notre temps', *Equateur*, 1 (1986), pp. 33–5.

　'Sony Labou Tansi face à douze mots', *Equateur*, 1 (1986), pp. 29–32.

Lionnet, Françoise, *Autobiographical Voices: Race, Gender, Self-Portraiture* (Ithaca: Cornell University Press, 1989).

Postcolonial Representations: Women, Literature, Identity (Ithaca and London: Cornell University Press, 1995).

Ludwig, Ralph (ed.), *Ecrire la 'parole de nuit': la nouvelle littérature antillaise* (Paris: Gallimard, 1994).

Magnier, Bernard, 'Ahmadou Kourouma', *Notre Librairie*, 87 (April 1987), pp. 11–15.

Marcotte, Gilles, *Le Roman à l'imparfait: la 'Révolution tranquille' du roman québecois* (Quebec: Hexagone, 1989 [1976]).

Martin-Grenel, Nicolas, *Rires noirs* (Paris: Sepia, 1991).

Memmi, Albert (ed.), *Anthologie des écrivains maghrébins d'expression française* (Paris: Présence Africaine, 1965).

Miller, Christopher L., *Nationalists and Nomads: Essays on Francophone African Literature and Culture* (Chicago: University of Chicago Press, 1998).

Mongo-Mboussa, Boniface, 'Ken Bugul ou la passion de la liberté' in *Désir d'Afrique* (Paris: Gallimard, Continents noirs, 2002), pp. 107–13.

Moore-Gilbert, Bart, *Postcolonial Theory: Contexts, Practices, Politics* (London: Verso, 1997).

Mouralis, Bernard, *Littérature et développement: esssai sur le statut, la fonction et la représentation de la littérature négro-africaine d'expression française* (Paris: Silex, 1984).

Munro, Martin, *Shaping and Reshaping the Caribbean: The Work of Aimé Césaire and René Depestre* (Leeds: MRHA/Maney, 2000).

Murdoch, H. Adlai, *Creole Identity in the French Caribbean Novel* (Gainesville: University Press of Florida, 2001).

Murphy, David, 'De-centring French studies: towards a postcolonial theory of Francophone cultures', *French Cultural Studies*, 13.2 (2002), pp. 165–85.

Ngandu Nkashama, Pius, 'L'autobiographie chez les femmes africaines', *Notre Librairie*, 117 (April–June 1994), pp. 129–37.

Niang, Sada (ed.), *Littérature et cinéma en Afrique francophone: Ousmane Sembène et Assia Djebar* (Paris: l'Harmattan, 1996).

Parker, Gabrielle, 'The Fifth Republic and the Francophone Project' in Kamal Salih (ed.), *French in and out of France: Language Policies, Intercultural Antagonisms and Dialogue* (Oxford and Bern: Lang, 2002), pp. 11–33.

Pratt, Marie-Louise, *Imperial Eyes: Travel Writing and Transculturation* (London and New York: Routledge, 1992).

Raharimanana, 'Sortir du bois', *Africultures*, 59 (18 May 2004).

'Le creuset des possibles', *Le Magazine Littéraire*, 451 (March 2006).

Saïd, Edward W., *Orientalism* (London: Vintage, 1998 [1978]).

Salih, Kamal (ed.), *French in and out of France: Language Policies, Intercultural Antagonisms and Dialogue* (Oxford and Bern: Lang, 2002).

Sartre, Jean-Paul, 'Orphée noir' in Léopold-Sédar Senghor, *Anthologie de la nouvelle poésie nègre et malgache de langue française* (Paris: Presses Universitaires de France, Quadrige, 1985 [1948]), pp. ix–xliv.

Shek, Ben-Zion, *French-Canadian and Québécois Novels* (Toronto: Oxford University Press, 1991).

Spivak, Gayatri Chakravorty, 'La mise en scène du temps dans *Hérémakhonon'* in Madeleine Cottenet-Hage and Lydie Moudileno, *Maryse Condé: une nomade inconvenante* (Guadeloupe: Ibis Rouge, 2002), pp. 73–85.

Death of a Discipline (New York: Columbia University Press, 2003).

Suk, Jeannie, *Postcolonial Paradoxes in French Caribbean Writing: Césaire, Glissant, Condé* (Oxford: Oxford University Press, 2001).

Tougas, Gérard, *La Littérature Canadienne-Française* (Paris: Presses Universitaires de France, 1960).

Young, Robert J. C., *White Mythologies: Writing History and the West* (London and New York: Routledge, 1990).

Postcolonialism: An Historical Introduction (Oxford: Blackwell, 2001).

Further reading

1. Works dealing with francophone literature from a postcolonial perspective, rather than dealing with it as an adjunct to French literature, are relatively scarce. Where they do exist they tend to avoid presenting the literature chronologically or in terms of 'literary history'. They tend rather to examine 'issues' or wider cultural themes, or adopt a regional approach (as this book does). Interesting texts include:

Bardolph, Jacqueline, *Etudes postcoloniales et littérature* (Paris: Champion, 2001).

Bessière, Jean and Jean-Marc Moura (eds.), *Littératures postcoloniales et représentations de l'ailleurs: Afrique, Caraïbe, Canada* (Paris: Champion, 1999).

Britton, Celia and Michael Syrotinski (eds.), 'Francophone texts and postcolonial theory', *Paragraph*, 24.3 (2001).

D'Hulst, Lieven and Jean-Marc Moura (eds.), *Les Etudes littéraires francophones: état des lieux*, UL3 Travaux et recherches (Lille: Université de Lille III, 2003).

Forsdick, Charles and David Murphy (eds.), *Francophone Postcolonial Studies: A Critical Introduction* (London: Arnold, 2003).

Miller, Christopher L., *Theories of Africans: Francophone Literature and Anthropology in Africa* (Chicago: University of Chicago Press, 1990).

Moura, Jean-Marc, *Littératures francophones et théorie postcoloniale* (Paris: Presses Universitaires de France, 1999).

Murdoch, H. Adlai and Anne Donadey (eds.), *Postcolonial Theory and Francophone Literary Studies* (Gainesville: University Press of Florida, 2005).

2. There are any number of works available on aspects of postcolonial theory and postcolonial criticism. In addition to the works cited in the bibliography the following texts and collections of articles/essays are particularly worth consulting:

Ashcroft, Bill, Gareth Griffiths and Helen Tiffin, *The Empire Writes Back: Theory and Practice in Post-colonial Literatures* (London: Routledge, 1989).
The Post-colonial Studies Reader (London and New York: Routledge, 1995).

Bhabha (ed.), Homi K., *Nation and Narration* (London and New York: Routledge, 1990).

Chambers, Iain and Lidia Curti (eds.), *The Postcolonial Question: Common Skies Divided Horizons* (London: Routledge, 1996).

Huggan, Graham, *The Postcolonial Exotic: Marketing the Margins* (London: Routledge, 2001).

Loomba, Ania, *Colonialism/Postcolonialism*, The New Critical Idiom (London: Routledge, 1998).

McLeod, John, *Beginning Postcolonialism* (Manchester: Manchester University Press, 2000).

Saïd, Edward W., *Culture and Imperialism* (Vintage: London, 1993).

Williams, Patrick and Laura Chrisman (eds.), *Colonial Discourse and Postcolonial Theory: A Reader* (New York: Columbia University Press, 1994).

Young, Robert J. C., *Postcolonialism: A Very Short Introduction* (Oxford: Oxford University Press, 2003).

Index